PENGUIN BOOKS

Incarnations

'An incisive work of popular history . . . undercutting, irreverent, and impish. It attempts to show, through prodigious but lightly worn scholarship, how complex and heterodox the Indian past was, and how it has been, and continues to be, constructed . . . Khilnani offers a fresh, cosmopolitan way of examining the Indian past. Everywhere he looks he sees rivers of influence and thought and ideas' Karan Mahajan, *New Yorker*

'*Incarnations* makes the mind fly across time, place and history. You may smile as, mentally, you walk alongside Khilnani up some flinty slope. You will keep thinking about what he said long after' Gillian Reynolds, *Daily Telegraph*

'Incisive and elegantly written . . . A work of distinction' John Keay, *The Times Literary Supplement*

'Like the best after-dinner speeches, Khilnani's incarnations leave you informed, entertained, amused and wanting to hear more, especially about some of the unsung makers of Indian history' Zareer Masani, *History Today*

'Though the prose is deceptively easy, you probably want to take your time as you savour the book . . . I know I will be placing a copy with each of my children so that they may know, in these anxiety-inducing times, what it truly means to be Indian' Aditya Sinha, *Mint* (India)

'Scholarly and playful' *Daily Telegraph*

'Inherently, and pleasingly subversive . . . an essential and timely read . . . An exceptionally liberating intellectual journey to take. Mr Khilnani's prose is light and fast-paced . . . [and his] ability to empathize with people long dead is also astonishing' Nilanjana S. Roy, *Business Standard, New Delhi*

'I enjoyed everything about this book' Charles Allen, *Literary Review*

'Beautifully written with both scholarship and an enviably light touch, thoughtfully constructed and enviably erudite in its wide-ranging references, and as much at ease discussing higher mathematics and philosophy as politics and art, *Incarnations* is a major work by one of India's most impressive minds' William Dalrymple, *Guardian*

'Welcome and refreshing . . . captures the vitality, diversity and uniqueness of India's civilization in an original and stimulating format' Andrew Robinson, *BBC History Magazine*

ABOUT THE AUTHOR

Sunil Khilnani is the author of *The Idea of India* (Penguin). He is currently Avantha Professor and Director of the India Institute at King's College, London.

SUNIL KHILNANI

Incarnations

A History of India in 50 Lives

PENGUIN BOOKS

PENGUIN BOOKS

UK | USA | Canada | Ireland | Australia
India | New Zealand | South Africa

Penguin Books is part of the Penguin Random House group of companies
whose addresses can be found at global.penguinrandomhouse.com

First published by Allen Lane 2016
This edition published in Penguin Books 2017
001

By arrangement with the BBC
The BBC Radio 4 logo is a registered trade mark of the British Broadcasting
Corporation and is used under licence
Radio 4 logo © Radio 4, 2011

Set in 9.25/12.5 pt Sabon LT Std
Typeset by Jouve (UK), Milton Keynes
Printed in Great Britain by Clays Ltd, St Ives plc

A CIP catalogue record for this book is available from the British Library

ISBN: 978-0-141-98143-7

www.greenpenguin.co.uk

Penguin Random House is committed to a
sustainable future for our business, our readers
and our planet. This book is made from Forest
Stewardship Council® certified paper.

For
Uma
Khemchand
Clinton

and for Katherine

*

Incarnators all

Contents

CONTENTS

Introduction

India's history is a curiously unpeopled place. As usually told, it has dynasties, epochs, religions and castes – but not many individuals. Beyond a few iconic names, most of the important historical figures recede into a haze, both for people outside India and for many Indians themselves. *Incarnations* is an experiment in dispelling some of the fog by telling India's story through fifty remarkable lives.

The essays in this book move headlong across 2,500 years of history, from the political and moral preoccupations of India's earliest historical personality, the Buddha, to the late twentieth-century capitalist imagination of the industrialist Dhirubhai Ambani. On the way, we meet kings, religious thinkers and freedom fighters, as well as poets, painters, mathematicians and radical social reformers.

Jawaharlal Nehru famously described this past as a palimpsest, where each successively dominant culture, religion or group left its traces, never quite effacing what came before it. It is a beautiful image, evocative of the country's deep civilizational stratigraphy, but I've come to think of it as too passive. To me, India's past is an arena of ferocious contest, its dead heroes continually springing back to life and dispatched to the frontlines of equally ferocious contemporary cultural and political battles. So this book is also concerned with the afterlives of historical figures: the often intriguing ways in which they are put to later use by government officials, entrepreneurs or tribal leaders across the Indian interior, or in physics labs, health clinics, hip-hop tracks and yoga studios across the East and West.

The subcontinent on which these stories unfold is the only place where each of the world's four great religions – Hinduism,

Buddhism, Christianity and Islam – has at different times ruled large areas. Through religious collisions and philosophical and ethical explorations, many of the individuals in this book were part of intense arguments that have been kept going for millennia: about what kind of life is worth living, what kind of society is worth having, which hierarchies are morally legitimate, what role religion has in the political and legal order and what kind of place India should be.

Such arguments have kept India in a permanent – and, on balance, productive – state of openness about what the country and its people are. A civilization able to produce a Mahavira, a Mirabai, a Malik Ambar, a Periyar, a Muhammad Iqbal and a Mohandas Gandhi is a place open to radical experiments with self-definition. It is particularly worth recalling that history and creative energy at a moment when some in India seek to transform the ferment of ideas over what India is and should be into a singular religious concoction.

Of course, much still remains unknown and disputed about Indian history, especially for the period before 1000 CE. About the lives of Indian women, apart from a few queens, the records are distressingly sparse right through to the twentieth century. Even now, much of India's history is endangered: some of who we were and what we've done sits in uncatalogued heaps, often in languages few still know. And yet in the past few decades we've made significant advances in our ability to make sense of the Indian past, through developments in archaeology, philosophy, mathematics, art history and literature. I draw on this important work as I try to track the fifty figures in this book: to see how they navigated the intellectual confluences and the practical constraints of their times, and made choices that changed, in small and large and sometimes unintended ways, the circumstances of the figures who succeeded them.

Many of the essays in *Incarnations* are driven by arguments, ranging from the nature of power to how to live a healthy life to the conditions of individual liberty. Here's one argument to start with: that India's non-fictional past is sufficiently complex, unexpected and rich in inspiring example that fictionalized heroes are a little redundant. By insisting that figures from India's past be preserved in memory as saints, above human consideration, we deny them not just their real natures, but their genuine achievements.

If you don't yet know the arresting stories behind some of the names I've mentioned (say, Malik Ambar, a gifted seventeenth-century Abyssinian slave turned Deccan warrior-king) or others you'll encounter in this book (such as Chidambaram Pillai, a dogged Tamil nationalist who took on the steamship might of the British Empire), that is perhaps not accidental. Who gets remembered, how history is told, and who gets to tell it are all matters of political dispute in India. Some historical icons are so staunchly defended against scrutiny that libraries whose collections have enabled scholars to write about those icons have been attacked. Books thought insufficiently reverent towards cherished figures are pulped and banned, their authors threatened, silenced, or worse.

As I chased down often-elusive lives in far-flung communities, in archives and in texts, I sometimes found an absurd gap between the superhero guises that some figures are forced to don today and the searching, self-critical natures that animated them in their own lifetimes. The impulse to make Indian historical lives exemplary and didactic goes back a long way – right back to the Buddha, at least. It's an ahistorical habit of mind mirrored by those who exalt India's culture as ineffable and spiritual – something that turns out to go back quite a long way, too.

British imperialists liked to suggest Indians were indifferent to their history (and inept at independent thinking to boot) because of their attachment to doll-like gods and caste rituals. Indians saw things differently, of course: the colonizers had pillaged the subcontinent's historical resources with the same voraciousness as they had plundered the teakwood and tea, unmooring their subjects from their traditions and pasts. Beginning in Bengal after the turn of the twentieth century, successive generations of nationalists struggled to gain control of their own history. And after Independence was won, in 1947, a host of long-suppressed claimants – regions, castes, religious communities – pushed for the primacy of their own favourite leaders within a new Indian pantheon. One of the most predictable acts of newly elected state or national governments was – and is – to rewrite history textbooks to their liking. The country's current ruling ideology aspires to define India as a Hindu nation, and to endow it with appropriately Hindu antecedents, with the inevitable simplifications that involves.

Despite such a tricky political climate, or maybe because of it, this seemed a crucial moment to explore the Indian past, in search of a little more complexity and nuance. It is often said of India that, given all its tensions, it's a miracle it holds together. To me, that's partly explicable, and some answers can be found in the intellectual and cultural capital embodied by the lives I've chosen for this book.

One striking feature of India's history (and one running theme of this book) is how many imaginative struggles have been waged against what remains a profoundly rigid society. Sometimes – as with the sixteenth-century ruler Krishnadevaraya, the poet Rabindranath Tagore and the painter Amrita Sher-Gil – the battle against conformity has been inward and psychological. Sometimes it has been outward, against the social order, frequently assuming the form of an assault on the hierarchies of caste. From the Buddha and Mahavira onwards to Phule, Periyar and Ambedkar, we see some of India's most original minds engaging with this system of social oppression, which has elicited condemnation for almost as long as it has existed, yet has time and again been able to absorb and even gain a degree of immunity from such critiques.

While I was working on this book, some other figures whose stories I'd grown up with became more affecting to me than the legends. Crouched alongside loom pits in a neighbourhood of Muslim weavers, I better understood the urge of the fifteenth-century poet Kabir to break free and smite the houses of the powerful. Listening to Indian policymakers, I grasped anew the devilish utility of Kautilya, the mysterious political thinker from around the turn of the Common Era, whose ideas about rulership might have offered Stalin a lesson or two. I sensed more clearly the Brahminic rage at Ashoka's Buddhist-inspired message when, at Sannati near the excavated Buddhist site of Kanaganahalli, I came across a stone tablet inscribed with his edicts. It had for centuries been turned face down, its centre smashed out and the stone appropriated as an altar in a Hindu temple. I gained fresh appreciation for the military intelligence of the seventeenth-century ruler Shivaji when surveying from one of his forts the arduous landscape he had conquered, and fresh respect, too, for how the twentieth-century diplomat Krishna Menon changed India's standing in the world despite personal anguish laid bare in intelligence files and private letters. And I encountered the uncanny modern cadences in the poetry of Basava, a twelfth-century social visionary.

Occasionally, as I travelled around for this project, I overheard kids cheerfully explaining to their friends what I was up to: 'He's telling the story of how India became number one.' Indeed, it's a habit of national histories to justify the present as the perfect and necessary outcome of what came before. But as I pursued the stories that make up this book, my own thinking sometimes veered in the opposite direction: I was moved by how many of these lives pose challenges to the Indian present and remind us of future possibilities that are at risk of being closed off.

Meanwhile, though, new possibilities have undeniably opened up. As recently as a few decades ago, what happened in India was often considered peripheral to what used to be called the first world. Those of us who wrote about the country had to make arguments for its relevance to, for instance, the larger story of democracy. Then, as India's presence in the global economy, and its culture and politics, became more visible, much of the writing about it was driven by perplexity: where was India going, what did it want?

Today, India, in both its positive and negative aspects, is far less peripheral to discussions about the world at large. Given that, I hope the ideas and arguments embodied by the fifty people in this book help complicate not just the stories Indians like to tell themselves, but also the stories the world tells about us – and about itself. India's most compelling minds have often been forced to exist in splendid isolation; I'd like to see them restored to their rightful place in the world – as figures engaged with other individuals and ideas across time and borders. In this way, I think readers might better grasp that many concepts the West sees as unique to itself actually have parallels, resonances and counter-arguments in other parts of the globe.

Attempting to tell in fifty lives the history of any nation – let alone one as vast and various as India – is an exercise designed to provoke. But the impossibility of being representative, or all-inclusive, has also given me freedom. I've chosen to leave out some familiar names, to allow space to bring in a few others who should be more widely known – a choice with which I think one of the figures I have excluded, Nehru, would have agreed.

In this happily partial exercise, one of my criteria for inclusion was the light old lives might shed on urgent issues of the present. So, nearly all of the lives in this book illuminate, in some way or another, pressing contemporary questions: about the position of women in society, about the nature of love and sexual choice, about cults of personal political power, about claims to water and land, about racial prejudice, about economic inequality and even about the mechanics of the universe. But I also hope that readers will argue strenuously about the fifty names I've chosen – to dispute those who have been left out and to make alternative selections.

For that's how I see *Incarnations*, in the end: as an open invitation to a different kind of conversation about India's past, and its future. And among my hopes is that, after finishing the last of these fifty portraits, a reader might share at least some of what I've come to feel strongly: that India's capacity to change itself, and to challenge its own dogmas (and sometimes those of the wider world), is not just a historical relic. It's a still-available capacity, one more necessary than ever.

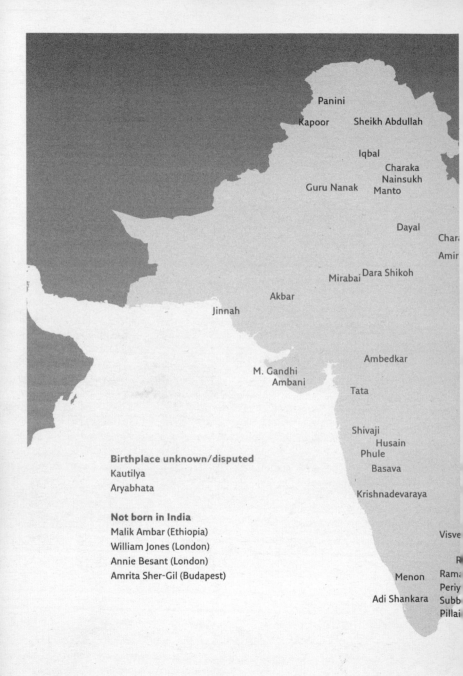

Panini

Kapoor   Sheikh Abdullah

          Iqbal
                    Charaka
                    Nainsukh
Guru Nanak   Manto

                    Dayal
                              Char:
                              Amir

          Mirabai Dara Shikoh

      Akbar

Jinnah

                    Ambedkar

      M. Gandhi
      Ambani
              Tata

              Shivaji
                    Husain
              Phule
              Basava

              Krishnadevaraya

Birthplace unknown/disputed
Kautilya
Aryabhata
                                        Visve

Not born in India   R
Malik Ambar (Ethiopia)   Rama
William Jones (London)   Periy
Annie Besant (London)   Menon   Subb
Amrita Sher-Gil (Budapest)   Pillai
                    Adi Shankara

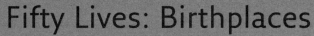

Fifty Lives: Birthplaces

an Singh

Khusrau   The Buddha
                 Mahavira

                 Ashoka
I. Gandhi   Lakshmi Bai
                 Kabir

         Birsa
         Rammohun Roy   Tagore
                         Ray
                 Vivekananda

         Bose

svaraya

ajaraja Chola
anujan
ar
ulakshmi

List of Illustrations

I
The Buddha

Waking India Up
5th century BCE

The sun has slipped behind the tarpaulin roofs of a Mumbai slum. Day labourers are streaming home from ten-hour shifts working on construction sites or tending the gardens of nearby private schools. In this particular web of slum lanes, many workers are Dalit, the untouchables of old – a status so low they were not even part of the caste order. Most months, their financial situation boils down to what people around here call 'earn and eat'. But for two years, some of these families set aside what little they could for bricks and mortar, and now they have a deep-blue room, five metres a side, that stands distinct from all the other hand-built homes in the slum.

A temple devoted to the Buddha: many slums in urban India have one. This particular place of worship is tucked behind a scrap shop. In the West, the Buddha is often seen as an extinguisher of his own personality, the original Impersonal Man. Indeed, after attaining his enlightenment, it is said that he referred to himself as *tathagata*, 'gone'. But he is far more surprising than that conventional image – or the one of a placid sage sitting in the lotus position, half smiling – lets on. Although many aspects of the Buddha's life remain elusive, he is perhaps the first individual personality that we can recognize in the subcontinent's history. In modern India, his legacy has helped hundreds of millions of low-caste citizens to become newly present – allowing them to emerge from the Hindu caste system's iron cage.

Fifteen-year-old Vijay watched his father lay bricks for the little blue temple. 'Buddha had no caste, so I have no caste,' he says. 'It's better this way.' His older brother Siddhartha chimes in: 'Buddha was for *equality*.'

Siddhartha is one of a dozen boys in the slum who were named after the Buddha – a man born Siddhartha Gautama near the foothills of Nepal's southern border with India, probably in the fifth century BCE. In his lifetime, the Buddha created a spiritual philosophy that has rightly been called one of the turning points in the history of civilization. Less known, but perhaps equally important, were his rational challenges to reigning beliefs about caste and religious authority. Some scholars see him as a social subversive, some as a wry critic of self-important merchants, priests and kings. To others, he was primarily a philosophical, and even political, experimentalist – one who explored new ways of organizing and conducting human life.

The religion that began with his experiments eventually spread throughout Asia, from the western edges of Afghanistan to Japan, gradually becoming what it is now: the fourth largest in the world. But in India it flourished for a millennium, and then all but disappeared, for reasons that are still mysterious. Only in the mid-twentieth century, as British colonial rule gave way to an independent India, was the Indian Buddha revived in the place of his birth – dusted off and reclaimed for his political utility as much as for his ethics. To several of the fathers of the modern nation, the Buddha provided a rational faith that could be weaponized against the hierarchies that still warp Indian society. And today, the Buddha continues to inspire people like Siddhartha and Vijay in their struggles to assert their own individualities.

Evidence for civilization on the Indian subcontinent dates back to at least 2500 BCE, when city settlements began to develop in the Indus Valley, in today's Pakistan. From these sites, archaeologists have excavated many objects, but the script of this civilization remains unintelligible to us – if it is a script at all. The composition of the earliest Vedas, the oldest sources of Hindu thought, seems to have begun roughly a millennium later. Beyond these hymns to the gods, though, we have no physical evidence of this world; and neither from the Indus Valley sites nor in the Vedas can we feel the pulse of any historical individuals. It's only a thousand or more years after the

Vedas were composed – with the arrival of the Buddha – that real personalities appear to us on the stage of Indian history.

Even before it began to be written down, the story of the Buddha was given permanence in painting and sculpture. In the oldest of the caves at Ajanta, in western India, are probably the earliest surviving representations of the Buddha's life – vivid frescoes, some of which date back to the first century BCE. 'There, in front of you, are the oldest Indian faces in existence,' the writer and historian William Dalrymple says. 'They inhabited a world incredibly different from ours. But you can look into the eyes of these people, of individuals, and their emotions are immediately recognizable.'

Although scholars still debate the Buddha's exact dates, with an elastic range for his death that stretches from roughly 500 to 400 BCE, it's clear he lived in an era of remarkable invention world-wide. Within the space of a couple of centuries, Confucius articulated his social philosophy in China, written versions of the Old Testament crystallized in Palestine, and Socrates conducted the dialogues that would lay many of the foundations of Western philosophy. On the Gangetic plains of northern India, iron tools, writing and coinage were producing and circulating new wealth. Trade contacts with Persia and western Asia were creating cosmopolitan cities, bustling with commerce and competing ideas about how to live a good life. Many of the forms of Hinduism familiar to Indians today – as well as many conflicting worldviews – also took shape in this period.

The Buddha's life played out in the midst of this flux. He grew up within sight of the high mountains of Nepal, on the northern edges of the Magadha region. Social life was largely regulated by the rituals contained in the Vedas. These practices, and the sacred verses describing them, were in turn fiercely controlled by the priestly castes that constituted the highest varna, or estate, of men – the Brahmins.

But across Magadha, communities were beginning to reject both Brahminic power and Vedic rituals, such as animal sacrifice. Some of these communities were chiefdoms dominated by men from the warrior and trading varnas. The Buddha himself was a member of the second-highest varna, the Kshatriyas, made up of warrior castes. He was 'a product of his own time', the Harvard scholar Charles

Hallisey says, but he was also 'an innovator, someone who creates something new in the world – and this tension is right at the centre of everything we think about who the Buddha was historically'.

There are almost as many versions of how the Buddha developed his radical moral vision as there are Buddhist traditions around the world today. Perhaps the most well known, depicted on the walls of the Ajanta caves, is an inward drama – the story of one man's religious, psychological and ethical experimentation. After a cosseted upbringing, Siddhartha Gautama was deeply shaken by his first encounters with human suffering. (Let's set aside how sheltered he must have been, to have grown up *not* encountering suffering.) Undone by his belated exposure to worldly pain, he resolved to escape it. Renouncing his wealthy family, he took up the life of a wandering ascetic. 'My body became extremely lean,' he later said. 'When I thought I would touch the skin of my stomach, I actually took hold of my spine.'

Over the course of six years, Siddhartha explored a number of the spiritual practices and philosophies swirling around northern India, but his attempts to find a release from suffering proved fruitless. Then, after abandoning these efforts, he was jolted, Proust-like, by a childhood memory of how, as his father worked nearby, Siddhartha had sat under the shade of a rose-apple tree in a state of pure joy, 'without sensual desires, without evil ideas'. How could he recover that state? Days passed in mental struggle, and then one spring night, while sitting under a Bodhi tree, he achieved it. And in that state, he believed he had grasped the causes of suffering, and its cure. He had now awakened, emerging from our worldly life of attachments, desires and pain as if from an interminable dream.

Around 500 kilometres south of Ajanta, in the rice paddy and cotton fields of northern Karnataka, is another major Buddhist site, Kanaganahalli, where the remains of a large domed reliquary shrine, or stupa, dating from roughly the first century BCE, were uncovered just twenty years ago. In the centuries after the Buddha's life, many ordinary, non-literate Indians would have learned of him through Jatakas, popular morality tales about his imagined previous lives, which were often depicted on sculptural friezes that decorated stupas like the one at Kanaganahalli. There is something particularly captivating about these sculptures, perhaps because the soft, grey limestone gave the carvers a freer hand to imbue the friezes with a sense of liveliness and humour. But we also see the Buddha represented here just by symbols: an empty seat that expresses the extinction of his self, the Bodhi tree where he reached enlightenment, and the *cakka* or *cakra*, the great wheel, which has come to represent his teaching.

After waking into his new state of consciousness, the Buddha decided to share his liberating insights. He began to advocate a path he called the middle way, which avoided both asceticism and worldly indulgence. His teachings became the *dhamma*, which roughly means 'law'; it was a set of principles to be followed, but also a teaching about the principle or essence of suffering and experience. The term was originally a Brahmin one, the Sanskrit *dharma*, which prescribed a different law for each caste – laws that encompassed every dimension of life, from marriage to work to meals. The Buddha took this established term and bent it to his own purpose; his dhamma was a single ethical vision embracing all living beings. 'Identify oneself with all,' he taught – regard every creature in the universe with compassion.

The Buddha's solution to suffering lay in the individual mind. But he was also sketching a new form of society. His relative egalitarianism is clear even from the language he used to teach his followers. Brahmins fiercely protected the Sanskrit in which the Vedas were expressed, and the lower orders were forbidden from learning this 'language of the gods'. Instead of Sanskrit, the Buddha used the local dialect of the people. He also dispensed with the idea of a deity, and with a priestly caste meant to direct social life according to scripture. As his following grew, he founded an order of monks, the *sangha*, which adopted broadly collectivist principles, taking important decisions through discussion in council and sharing much of what little property they were permitted to have. Low-caste members were allowed the same religious education that was open to other followers – another practice barred within Brahminic society. After some resistance – it seems the Buddha was not entirely immune from patriarchal attitudes – he allowed women to be admitted to the order as nuns. The Buddha also rejected doctrines of predestination, by which birth supposedly determined people's roles in society. He was a moral meritocrat, and to an extent a social one too.

Following the Buddha's death, his teachings spread first by word of mouth, and then by imperial enthusiasm. In the third century BCE, India's greatest empire-builder, **Ashoka (5)**, embraced the Buddha's teachings and accelerated their transmission throughout India, inscribing messages inspired by them on pillars and rock faces across the subcontinent. Judging from the archaeological evidence alone, India for much of the next thousand years seems to have been at least as much Buddhist as it was Hindu.

By the seventh century CE, things had visibly changed. Xuanzang, a Chinese Buddhist pilgrim visiting the way-stations of the Buddha's life in northern India, found a dwindling community of monks and roughly a thousand monasteries 'deserted and in ruins. They are filled with wild shrubs, and solitary to the last degree.' How did this come to pass? In short, we don't know. As Xuanzang travelled, he recorded stories of attacks on Buddhist holy sites, including the top-pling of the original Bodhi tree where the Buddha had found enlightenment. Later Tibetan and other Buddhist chronicles also mention Hindu hostilities against the faith. What's clearer, histori-cally, is that Buddhism eventually came under assault from Muslim marauders – for instance, in the devastating twelfth-century sack of Nalanda, a great centre of Buddhist learning, which forever destroyed a major storehouse of human knowledge.

But it's possible that Hinduism also adapted over the centuries in ways that allowed it to win back followers. Around the start of the Common Era, there were efforts to formalize the great Hindu epics, the Mahabharata and the Ramayana, and legal treatises such as the Manusmriti or the Laws of Manu. Some scholars see in these works attempts to incorporate Buddhist ideas in order to neutralize and rebut Buddhism – effecting a kind of Brahminic counter-reformation. After all, Hinduism has never been a fixed doctrine moored to a single sacred text: it remained multiple and in some respects labile, a fact that allowed it to absorb criticism and challenges.

Once, in Japan, I travelled to the ancient capital of Nara to see its Buddhist temples and shrines. Built of massive timber beams, they've been protected, even burnished, by the wrap of Japanese civilization. So I was startled to come across images and statues bearing names I knew: Indian names for some of the Buddha's many incarnations. Discovering them in shrines used continuously for around twelve centuries, I was moved anew by the difficulty of the Buddha's course through the history of the land where he was born. The Sanskrit roots of the word 'Buddha' mean 'someone who has woken up'. In India, Buddhism seemed to sleep for centuries. It was only the anguished choice of one of modern India's founding figures that summoned the Buddha back to life.

On 14 October 1956, Dr Bhimrao Ramji **Ambedkar** (41), the leader of a political movement to gain rights and dignity for the country's Dalits, stood on a stage in the city of Nagpur and formally converted to Buddhism. Before him, in the crowd, were some 400,000 or more of his followers. Though Ambedkar had been an architect of the new Indian Constitution, he doubted that lower-caste citizens would be able to thrive in what remained, despite his active struggle, a caste-dominated polity. After taking his own oaths, he turned to administer a set of conversion vows to the individuals in the massive crowd:

> I renounce the Hindu religion which has obstructed the evolution of my former humanity and considered humans unequal and inferior . . . I regard all human beings as equals . . . From this time forward I vow that I will behave according to the Buddha's teachings.

Ambedkar was chiselling his own Buddha: near enough a social revolutionary, or an ancient Indian Rousseau. Like other founders of modern India, he was recycling historical figures who could be endowed with new life in order to solve the problems of Indian society – a little like the scrap-shop workers just behind the Mumbai slum temple, sifting through their bags for something of continuing value.

2
Mahavira

Soldier of Non-violence
5th century BCE

Mohandas Gandhi, the Mahatma, was fond of the parable of the blind men and the elephant. One blind man, grabbing the elephant's tail, said that an elephant was like a rope. Another, holding its trunk, countered that it was like a snake. A third, touching one of its legs, protested that it was really like a tree. Those touching its ears or sides made still other claims. All were 'right from their respective points of view', Gandhi wrote in the mid-1920s, 'and wrong from the point of view of one another, and right and wrong from the point of view of the man who knew the elephant'.

For Gandhi, the parable illustrated 'the doctrine of the many-sidedness of reality'. 'It is this doctrine that has taught me to judge a Mussalman from his own standpoint and a Christian from his,' he continued. 'I used to resent the ignorance of my opponents. Today I can love them because I am gifted with the eye to see myself as others see me and vice versa . . . My *anekantavada* is the result of the twin doctrine of *Satya* and *Ahimsa*.'

Anekantavada, satya and ahimsa: many-sidedness, truth and non-violence. These principles were particularly urgent for Gandhi in the 1920s, as relations between Hindus and Muslims slid into rioting and bloodshed. Though Gandhi would give these virtues his own characteristic twist, they were rooted deep in Indian thought, in a critique of Vedic Hinduism that coalesced in the Gangetic river basin some 2,500 years ago. That critique eventually became Jainism, one of the four great religions born in India (along with Hinduism, Buddhism and Sikhism). The man who systematized the Jain worldview, in the fifth century BCE, is known by the honorific Mahavira, which

8

means 'the great hero'. Ahimsa, rigorous attachment to the truth, and the doctrine of anekantavada were central to Mahavira's teaching, and he would later be canonized by Gandhi (along with the Buddha and Tolstoy) as a 'soldier' of non-violence.

Mahavira, according to Jain tradition, was the last in a line of twenty-four superhuman figures known as *tirthankaras*, or 'ford-makers': beings who had crossed over from the mundane world of human suffering and violence into the realm of spiritual liberation, and could help others do the same. In our human history, he was the descendant of a Kshatriya martial clan – like the Buddha, his contemporary in fifth-century Magadha. Also like the Buddha, he became one of the most compelling of a range of early Indian religious philosophers generally referred to as Shramanas, or 'seekers' – renouncers who turned their backs on domestic life and explored various paths to individual spiritual liberation, while rejecting the priestly role of the Brahmin caste.

Mahavira's teachings shared many important features with the Buddha's; in particular, they both opposed beliefs at the core of the Vedas, the earliest Hindu texts, about the role of caste in spiritual life, the supremacy of the gods, and the indispensable nobility of ritual sacrifice. These sacrifices often required animal slaughter and supposedly generated a potent creative force that sustained both individual life and the cosmos.

The rejection of sacrificial rituals was especially significant for Mahavira and his followers. 'All forms of existence, according to Jainism, are embodied souls – the Jain term is *jiva*, which means life force,' explains Paul Dundas, a professor at the University of Edinburgh and scholar of Jainism. For Jains, this life force is manifest not just in humans, animals and plants; it is also present as unseen souls moving through earth, air, fire and water. 'So we are surrounded by life, and the correct stance towards this is to govern oneself,' Dundas says, 'to discipline one's behaviour so that we can minimize the destruction of life, whether witting or unwitting.'

This, in essence, is the Jain doctrine of ahimsa – a direct inversion of Vedic beliefs about the sustaining powers of animal sacrifice.

Mahavira's teachings required not only that one abstain from violent acts (except in extraordinary circumstances), but also, more importantly, that one adopt a fundamental stance of benign intention towards the world. Some have tried to connect this stance directly to anekantavada, as Gandhi did, claiming that the spirit of non-violence informed an attitude of intellectual humility and religious tolerance that is manifest in the works of several important early Jain thinkers.

You can see the Jain attitude towards living creatures at a two-storey hospital on the premises of the seventeenth-century Digambar Jain temple in Delhi's old city. The hospital is not for humans, but for birds. In its 400 cages, cooled by ceiling fans, fluttering convalescents are fed compound medicine and liquid protein and then released into the air, or into the arms of little boys, who race home with their healed roosters.

Strict Jain vegetarianism prohibits the eating not just of animals or eggs, but also of root vegetables, in part because pulling them from the ground disturbs the lives of other plants and little creatures. Today, in the Chowpatty area of South Mumbai, which is home to many Jain laypeople, these dietary guidelines are adhered to even in the popular new Starbucks.

The stereotypical image of the Jain renunciant is a monk (or possibly nun) dutifully sweeping the ground gently before him with a small broom, so that he doesn't tread on any living creatures, with his mouth covered to prevent the accidental swallowing of any small bugs. But Mahavira also took his inversion of Vedic Hinduism one step further, transforming the *tapas*, or heat, of the Brahminic sacrificial fire into the *tapas*, or austerity, of a severe personal discipline. For the Jains, salvation might indeed be the sum of sacrifices: not of living beings, but of one's self.

Most of what we know about the life of Mahavira derives from two Jain hagiographies: the proselytizing *Kalpa Sutra*, written centuries after Mahavira, and the earlier *Acharanga Sutra*, which supposedly contains his own words. (There are also tantalizing references to Mahavira in some relatively early Buddhist texts.) He was born

Vardhaman, the son of a clan leader, in Kundagrama, a kingdom in today's Bihar – though his exact place of birth remains a subject of contentious village rivalries in the state's pilgrim tourist trade. In the *Kalpa Sutra*, his anti-Brahminism predates even his birth: in the nick of time, Mahavira's embryo was transplanted from the womb of a Brahmin woman into a woman from the Kshatriya caste. He was also apparently a very early adopter of non-violence: the *Kalpa Sutra* reports that he kept calm and still in his mother's womb, so as not to discomfit her, though he quivered from time to time to reassure her he was alive.

The Acharanga Sutra paints a strikingly austere picture of Mahavira's life. Much in his story echoes the biography we have inherited for the Buddha, though with differences that seem calibrated to depict Mahavira as the more benign, rigorous and therefore righteous of the two. Brahminic male ideals of maintaining a household were not for Mahavira. In some Jain accounts, he was married with a child before he left to become a celibate; in others, he was celibate for life. But the traditions agree that he abandoned a comfortable (and probably aristocratic) home to wander naked and alone through the wilderness. In at least one version of the Mahavira story, his renunciation was more sensitively plotted than the Buddha's, who supposedly fled in the middle of the night, abandoning his wife and son. Mahavira is said to have waited, better mannered, until after his elderly parents had died so as not to upset them.

Mahavira's path towards enlightenment began with a famously violent, flamboyant act. For him (and subsequently for his disciples), it was not enough to shave his head as the Buddhists did. 'After fasting two and a half days without drinking water,' the *Kalpa Sutra* says, Mahavira 'put on a divine robe, and, quite alone, nobody else being present, he tore out his hair ... and entered the state of houselessness.'

He was thirty years old, roughly the same age as the Buddha was at his renunciation; but his period of mendicant wandering lasted twelve years, twice as long as the Buddha's phase of spiritual experimentation. During these years, Mahavira engaged in deep reflective meditation and harsh physical penances, eating next to nothing and suffering the violent contempt of those who couldn't fathom his actions. He finally found enlightenment at the age of forty-two, in a characteristically self-punishing way. 'The Buddha is always depicted as sitting underneath the Tree of Enlightenment,' Dundas says. In contrast, 'a very old description of Mahavira's enlightenment has him sitting near this tree, but under the heat of a blazing sun, squatting on his heels in a rather uncomfortable position, and maintaining this position for two and a half days until he attained enlightenment.'

If Mahavira's austerity represented a direct challenge to Brahminism, and stood as a reproach to the softer 'middle path' of the Buddha, it was nevertheless a clear extension of the martial mores of Mahavira's warrior caste – though directed to a very different end. As Dundas puts it, 'The notion of vigour, of heroism, very much informs the Jain ascetic ideal. I think in a modern world, many of us view asceticism in rather more negative terms. But fasting, forms of physical torture or pain which certain types of religious people have always inflicted on themselves – in India this was regarded in a highly positive way, as almost a form of warrior activity.' As it would later be for **Gandhi** (38), the endurance of physical and psychological hardship was seen as necessary to becoming a non-violent actor.

This conquering spirit extended itself into the intellectual realm as well. The disputes reflected in the biographies of the Buddha and Mahavira were set within a broader context of intellectual competition between rival philosophers and teachers. Alongside the Kalpa and Acharanga Sutras, one of the earliest Jain texts contains the doctrines of sects with whom the Jains actively disagreed. These may have included materialists, who denied the existence of a spiritual realm and therefore the possibility of salvation, and fatalists, who denied that human beings could exert any influence whatsoever on their paths to spiritual liberation.

Mahavira and subsequent Jains attacked these views, basing their own claims to pre-eminence on the rigorous requirements of Jain religious practice, and on their analysis of reality. These, in turn, were supposedly the fruits of revelation. According to Jainism,

Mahavira's enlightenment – and the enlightenments of the other ford-makers – constituted a state of omniscience. We might say that he became like the man who knew the elephant for what it was, and could help transmit that knowledge to his followers.

But such a thoroughgoing philosophical victory contained a paradox within it. The Jain analysis of reality was largely founded on anekantavada, the doctrine of many-sidedness, with its inherent critique of the limitations of human understanding. On what basis, then, could Mahavira and his philosophy claim to speak from a position of omniscience? This was also a problem for later commentators who wished to link anekantavada directly to ahimsa. While the early Jains may have been socially tolerant, they maintained a faith in their own intellectual and religious certitude. And, ultimately, anekantavada was not a doctrine of relativism: the blind men were, in the end, arguing over the same elephant. As Dundas has written, 'Jainism's consistent historical stance with regard to itself is that ... it is at the most profound level different from and superior to other paths.'

Today, we can see Mahavira's brand of extreme asceticism and spiritual confidence embodied in the beautiful sculptural forms of the Jain tradition, which represent the ford-makers and other mythical Jains. With spare, powerful physiques and lustrous skin – a lustre, it is said, that comes with the renunciation of many foods – these sculptures stand in an ethereal nakedness, which was once described by the German Indologist Heinrich Zimmer as 'a strange but perfect aloofness, a nudity of chilling majesty'. So still are they in their rejection of earthly life that they often have climbing vines carved around their thighs.

The most remarkable of these monoliths is the statue of Bahubali or Gommata, who, according to one Jain sect, was the first person other than a ford-maker to achieve liberation. Erected at the end of the tenth century, in a period when Buddhism and Buddhist sites in India seem to have been under attack, it still looms above the plains of southern Karnataka. At seventeen metres high and eight metres wide, it's one of the biggest statues of the human form anywhere in the world.

Despite Jainism's intellectual aggression, and its hostility to the power of the Brahmin caste, over the course of its history the religion seems to have engendered little retaliatory violence. Perhaps ahimsa made the Jains seem innocuous, or perhaps the Jains themselves recognized that a religion whose monastic and lay members were drawn largely from the middle and lower castes could not afford to antagonize its neighbours and trading partners. At the same time, the austerity that protected the religion may also have limited its appeal, and prevented it from spreading, as Buddhism did, outside of India. Remaining small in scale, perhaps it was never seen as a threat.

The faith also saw internal schisms. One issue that continues to divide the Jain community is whether women, too, can advance on the path to enlightenment. The strictest of the leading Jain traditions contends that women can't be ordained ascetics, since their bodies produce eggs that are killed during menstruation. In addition, it argues that only those who abandon all possessions, clothes included, and live 'sky clad' – the lovely Jain phrase for nakedness – can wander towards grace.

It was difficult in Mahavira's time to be a hard-core Jain practitioner, and it is difficult in modern India too. Attributed to him are five uncompromising ethical rules that continue to guide Jains in their struggle towards salvation: the renunciation of killing, of speaking untruths, of sexual pleasure, of greed, and of all attachments to living beings and non-living things. Of course, not all five million or so current followers of Jainism can strictly adhere to these principles. There is a large lay community, especially among the trading castes, that, while observing strict vegetarianism, continues to do business, procreate and support the small number of Jain monks and, in some sects, nuns.

So why did Gandhi, as he advocated his views on religious tolerance and non-violence amidst the turmoil of pre-independence India, reach for this ancient, renunciatory tradition? It has been argued that his understanding of non-violence was shaped more by the example of Christ, and specifically by Tolstoy's ideas, than by Jainism. But perhaps the political message of Gandhi's non-violence, which extended beyond the Jain conception, at the same time demanded a specifically Indian expression. Gandhi was not only pursuing religious amity – he was fighting for freedom from the British, for a sovereign India for Indians. And, for Gandhi, Indian self-rule had to begin with rule over the self – something he believed his soldiers of non-violence had achieved. 'Only they saw deeper and truer in their profession, and found the secret of a true, happy, honourable and godly life,' Gandhi wrote of them. 'Let us be joint sharers with these teachers and this land of ours will once more be the abode of gods.'

3
Panini

Catching the Ocean in a Cow's Hoofprint
4th century BCE

At the end of the last century, Bangalore became synonymous with Indian software. And in this century, it's not entirely outlandish to think that Indians may become synonymous with American start-ups. Already, according to Google's Eric Schmidt, around 40 per cent of start-ups in California's Silicon Valley are run by people from Indian backgrounds.

One reason for this predominance is that Indians have the highest incomes of any group of American immigrants, and can secure elite, high-tech US educations. Similarly rigorous educations can be acquired in India at places like the Indian Institutes of Technology, modelled on MIT and established by India's first prime minister, Jawaharlal Nehru. But perhaps there is another, subtler reason for the rise of Indians in IT – one that takes us back 2,500 years, to the original nerd.

His name was Panini, and he created, in what amounts to a mere forty pages, the most complete linguistic system in history. This masterwork, known as the *Ashtadhyayi*, or *Eight Chapters*, helped to make Sanskrit the lingua franca of the Asian world for more than a thousand years. 'It's one of the most astonishing intellectual achievements of the human mind, and a very beautiful system,' Paul Kiparsky, Professor of Linguistics at Stanford University, says. 'It's intensely pleasurable to explore – and one reason to be preoccupied with it is that there's so much more to find out.'

Panini was born into the Brahmin varna, the highest of the Hindu orders – and the only one whose members were permitted to use the

Sanskrit language. It's believed he lived around the fourth century BCE, in the subcontinent's northwest – in a town called Salatura, near today's Peshawar, close to Pakistan's border with Afghanistan. The outlines of Panini's life are misty, but the imprint of his mind when reading the *Ashtadhyayi* is unmistakable. It's quite clearly the work of a single individual, an ancient obsessive fascinated with deconstructing things in order to understand how they work.

What Panini took apart and held up to the light of his mind was Sanskrit, the language of the Vedas. Transmitted by memorized recitation, the sounds and rhythms of these sacred hymns and incantations, and the language itself, were believed to reflect eternal truths about the universe. To analyse and understand this language – the task of Brahminic scholars, or pandits, such as Panini – was nothing less than to grasp the nature of the cosmos. 'Precisely understanding human action, which includes language, is a source of religious merit,' Kiparsky explains. 'Just as in yoga, the idea is that we breathe mindful of the breath itself, and that is a way towards salvation – so, if we speak mindful of the structure of the system underlying speech, that also brings us closer to salvation.'

'Sanskrit' means 'perfectly made'. It is a language of extraordinary precision. In English, for example, the role that nouns play in a sentence – subject, direct object, indirect object and so forth – can usually be gleaned only from the context. But Sanskrit uses eight different suffixes to embed these meanings into the form of the words themselves. You can tell from a single Sanskrit noun, even in isolation, its syntactical function: that is, whether it is the possessor of some object or quality, the instrument with which some action was performed, the location where a process unfolded, and more. Other features of the language can be equally expressive of such subtleties.

Panini set out to capture in exacting detail how this sacred language worked. To do this, he needed what linguists call a metalanguage – a way of talking about the features and structure of Sanskrit that wasn't entirely present in Sanskrit itself. When you encounter terms like 'noun' and 'indirect object' in English, you're encountering bits of a metalanguage invented so we can better discuss the language. Panini's metalanguage, however, had to be concise enough to be committed to memory and passed on orally. Describing Sanskrit in ordinary terms would have been unwieldy, so he developed a shorthand or code that he used to express its grammatical structure and other features.

To create his coded metalanguage, Panini borrowed the building blocks of Sanskrit. He split the spiritually charged language up into its constituent sounds, and assigned to each a coded linguistic meaning. In Panini's system, various features of Sanskrit – noun cases, classes of sounds, and so on – are represented by abbreviations, often single syllables or letters. Panini then combined these abbreviations into verse-like strings, or sutras, which set out the rules of Sanskrit in a highly compressed form. Take this sutra, for example, which consists entirely of code 'words': *iko yan. aci*. Decoded and translated into English, it means '*i, u, r.* and *l.* are replaced by *y, v, r* and *l* respectively when followed by a vowel'. Though one recent English translation ran to over 1,300 pages, the 4,000 sutras that Panini created to describe Sanskrit's phonology, morphology and syntax can be recited in around two and a half hours.

Concision was only one of Panini's goals. He wanted his account of Sanskrit to be exhaustive as well. This ambition was far greater than it might at first seem: Panini didn't want his system just to describe all the features of Sanskrit, he wanted it to be capable of generating a virtually infinite number of well-formed words and grammatically correct sentences. Any Sanskrit utterance from the Vedas, or any possible Sanskrit sentence created elsewhere in the world, should be derivable using Panini's system.

This aim led Panini to his most important innovation. The sutras of the *Ashtadhyayi* were expressed as a set of procedures for transforming linguistic inputs (for example, the equivalent of the English 'be') into various well-formed Sanskrit outputs (such as 'they are' and 'they have been', instead of 'they been' and 'they have are'). He structured these rules so that they would interact in highly complex ways – like the steps of a tough algorithm, or the lines of a computer programme. The outputs that were produced by some rules could become the inputs of other rules, and could combine with other outputs to become the inputs of still further rules – and so on. Through combinations of a finite number of general rules and specific exceptions, the system could transform basic linguistic inputs (many of which were listed in appendices to the *Ashtadhyayi*) into a limitless number of grammatical words and sentences – some of which may not even be part of actual usage.

In modern linguistics, Panini's system is what's known as a 'generative grammar'. The term was only coined in the late 1950s, when contemporary research into language finally caught up with what Panini and his subsequent pandit commentators had been doing for 2,500 years. (There is a story to be written tracing the direct links between Panini's work and the emergence of modern linguistics: three founders of the field – Ferdinand de Saussure, Leonard Bloomfield and Zellig Harris – were all scholars of Sanskrit.)

Paul Kiparsky was part of the first-generation students of the Western version of this type of linguistics. 'When I started studying generative grammar with Noam Chomsky and Morris Halle back in 1962, we were trying to write precise and comprehensive descriptions of languages,' he says. 'Our main interest was in the question of what all languages have in common and how it's possible to acquire a language. In order to study that question, we tried to construct explicit and comprehensive grammars. I was quite amazed to find that Panini already had one that was beautifully constructed. It's a kind of miracle that this was achieved on the basis of one language.' So awesome was Panini's ability to articulate and compress the rules of Sanskrit that it was said he had managed to capture the ocean in a cow's hoofprint.

The Sanskrit word used to describe Panini's work is *vyakarana*. Often translated as 'grammar', its meaning is broader – something closer to 'language analysis'. Among pandits, vyakarana was one of the six 'auxiliary sciences' or 'limbs' of the Veda – learning not found within the Vedas, but essential in order to comprehend them. These ancillary disciplines were the mother lodes of Sanskrit knowledge, the basis of all other understanding. Among them, vyakarana was pre-eminent; it was known as the *sastranam sastram*, the 'science of sciences'.

Indeed, many scholars have seen vyakarana as the paradigm for other major fields of inquiry in ancient India, such as astronomy and philosophy. The Dutch linguist and philosopher Frits Staal, for one, often compared the derivational qualities of Panini's grammar to the deductive principles of Euclid's geometry, and argued that Panini had played as foundational a role in creating standards for inquiry and knowledge in India as Euclid had in the Hellenistic world, and later in the West. At the very least, many if not all of the classical Indian thinkers who subsequently worked in Sanskrit would have studied the language's grammar 'and therefore undergone the influence of Panini'.

Though the extent of the epistemological influence of Panini's grammar remains uncertain, its broader cultural impact was undeniable. In large part because Sanskrit was considered the timeless language of the divine, it also had extraordinary currency in the historical world of men. Perhaps paradoxically, no one seems to have done more to enable the extension of this currency than Panini.

In his own time, Sanskrit was monopolized by Brahmins like him, and confined to a relatively small area of India's northwest (though he himself recognized, and designed the *Ashtadhyayi* so that it could cope with, regional variations and non-Vedic uses of Sanskrit). But the language's privileged status made it desirable to other social orders and religious traditions, and Sanskrit gradually took wing. It became a language in which great works of literature were composed and, as it spread in the centuries after Panini, Sanskrit helped give India a cultural and social cohesion that no political power would be able to establish until at least the twentieth century. It also did something else: it made India an exporter of cultural capital. From the start of the Common Era and for well over a millennium thereafter, Sanskrit bound together a huge civilizational territory, continental in scale.

Sheldon Pollock, Professor of Sanskrit at Columbia University, has called this the 'Sanskrit cosmopolis'. At its peak, a quarter of the world's population lived within it. Sanskrit became, he says, 'the sign, across this vast space, for a kind of style of polity and civility and beauty – across an entire world, from Afghanistan to Java. And it lasted for a thousand years, because it was cool, it was beautiful. It was a sign of participating in a big world – you're not just a little local person; you have people in Cambodia quoting you and you're living in Delhi.'

For Sanskrit recitations on the Indochinese peninsula to feature the work of northern Indian poets, regional variation had to be kept to an absolute minimum. Cambodian princes wrote a Sanskrit no different from poets in Tamil Nadu and Gujarat. Panini's grammar played a role in securing that coherent intelligibility, setting standards to which later users of classical Sanskrit strove to adhere. As literacy spread through the subcontinent, his oral codification of Sanskrit was eventually written down. Ultimately, this made it harder to restrict access to the classical Sanskrit that Panini in large part helped create. In this way, the revered vyakarana of the Brahmin Panini became a pathway for the expansion of Sanskrit to new groups, both within and beyond the Hindu varna system. From its origins as the language of power, Sanskrit became the language in which people could create and participate in a shared literary imagination – which sometimes questioned power itself.

It's not that Panini and his system somehow 'froze' Sanskrit, stultifying the language even as it made it more broadly accessible. As Pollock points out, despite the normative influence that the *Ashtadhyayi* exerted, Sanskrit continued to evolve, just as it had in Panini's day. That the language eventually declined had most likely to do with global and local politics, especially the rise of Persian, which was spread, often by the sword, by central Asian Muslim empires that conquered northern India at the start of the thirteenth century.

Today, you can hear Sanskrit intoned in temple and family rituals and practised in classrooms, but it's no longer a language of intellectual inquiry or debate. Governments can proclaim 'Sanskrit weeks' and millions of students are made to endure Sanskrit classes each year in Indian schools, but most learn absolutely nothing. In 2014, some ministers in Prime Minister Narendra Modi's Hindunationalist government, revivalist in their hopes, even took their Cabinet oaths in the language. But it's all a bit of a sham.

With the decline of Sanskrit learning came a decline in popular interest in Panini, though the novelist Vikram Chandra recently did his part to reverse the trend. A former computer programmer, he wrote a book about software and Sanskrit called *Geek Sublime: The Beauty of Code, the Code of Beauty* – in its way, an ode to the great grammarian.

To Chandra, the lack of appreciation for Panini reflects a 'kind of post-colonial amnesia', a condition that endures despite the many realms in which Panini's influence can still be felt. 'He plays a very important role in the growth of modern linguistics,' Chandra says, 'and in a very strange way he's connected to the world that we live in today, because all the programming languages that we use to change our landscape are in some sense dependent on some of his insights and ideas.'

While there are resonances between Panini's work and the way computer programmers operate, any direct inheritance from his grammar to computer code is fanciful. But there may in fact be a more oblique connection between the decline of Sanskrit scholarship and the success of Indians in the world of information technology. Sheldon Pollock puts it this way:

> Did the best minds go into Western science? Did the best minds go into business? Did the best minds go into politics? Did the best minds start writing code? If you look at the backgrounds of a lot of the kids in Bangalore – they've told me, 'Oh, you are a Sanskrit-ist. My great-grandfather was a wonderful Sanskritist.' So, long traditions of literacy, particularly in Sanskrit, have produced the kind of brilliance that has allowed India to emerge as one of the great IT capitals of the world. I don't think that it's accidental that India makes software and China makes hardware. Software requires a certain kind of literacy, and I think this was in part a Sanskritic literacy.

Sanskrit's decline represents a serious break in contact with India's classical traditions – and with it, a loss of the multiplicity of voices, often dissenting and inventive, that those traditions contained. For Sanskrit became something more than just the prerogative of the

Brahmins. From its origins as the language of power, it became the language in which people sought to disrupt power, and to explore the literary imagination. Unlike other global languages – Latin, Arabic or English – Sanskrit spread not through conquest or colonization, but because it served a purpose. It's consoling to imagine it has a new purpose, helping to build a new cosmopolis, the global world of IT.

4
Kautilya

The Ring of Power
1st century CE

A little over a hundred years ago, in southern India's princely state of Mysore, a humble librarian chanced upon a monumental discovery. Rudrapatnam Shamashastry worked at the Mysore Government Oriental Library, a cream-coloured jumble of classical Greek pillars and faux-Hindu architectural motifs, built in 1887 to commemorate Queen Victoria's Golden Jubilee. Shamashastry's job was to look after the library's ancient manuscripts, many of which were fragmentary and crumbling. One day, shortly before 1905, a nameless 'Brahmin from Tanjore' arrived at the library and handed him a manuscript made out of dried palm leaves. Although Shamashastry had never seen anything like it, he quickly realized its significance. Here was a Sanskrit text that may have lain unread for almost a thousand years – and that would revolutionize our sense of the Indian past.

Written on those palm leaves was the two-millennia-old *Arthashastra*, a massive, detailed treatise on statecraft and the art of government. The opening folios enumerated the contents of the work, ranging from chapters on the 'Establishment of Clandestine Operatives' and 'Pacifying a Territory Gained' to the 'Surveillance of People with Secret Income' and 'Investigation through Interrogation and Torture'. Eerily contemporary, this is the only complete text on non-religious matters to reach us from the classical or early period of Indian history. Its discovery summarily exploded a Western cliché: that Indians were primarily ethereal, spiritual thinkers. Here was a strategic work focused on worldly ends, advocating ruthless means to achieve and maintain power.

Shamashastry started to publish bits of the *Arthashastra* in English translation in 1905. The reaction in India and beyond was electric. He released more sections of the text, rather like a Victorian serial novel, as the audience grew. Soon the mysterious treatise was not just providing historians with an unprecedented wealth of detail about early India; it proved to be a timely gift for those seeking freedom from colonial rule.

The publication of the first translations coincided with an event that led many in Asia and India to believe that their star was now ascendant, while the West's was in decline: 1905 was the year of the naval battle at Tsushima, in which the Japanese dealt Russia a shock defeat. It was the first modern victory of an Asian nation over a Western power, and it encouraged Indians to think of themselves as part of a common Asian world. (On hearing news of the Japanese victory led by Admiral Togo, a fifteen-year-old Jawaharlal Nehru, then on his way to boarding school at Harrow, sent a one-line postcard to his cousin: 'Three Cheers for Togo'.) The ancient manuscript would help Indian nationalists imagine a realpolitik for an aspiring India of the twentieth century. Here was a self-help manual for a start-up nation.

After the Indian uprising of 1857, when violence across northern and central India seriously threatened colonial rule (see **23 Lakshmi Bai, Rani of Jhansi**), there had been a hardening of British attitudes towards the country. 'The narrative shifted,' says Shivshankar Menon, a former National Security Adviser to the Indian prime minister, and one of the country's most distinguished diplomats. 'Many of the subsequent histories written by outsiders were about how there was no domestic tradition of history, which is false; that there was no domestic tradition of statecraft, which is also false. This is why the discovery of the *Arthashastra*, rightly or wrongly, was so useful to the nationalists to help build a consciousness, a sense of India's own past and what India could do.'

At the Mysore library, now known as the Oriental Research Institute, the *Arthashastra* is presented like a sumptuous dish, or a holy icon, on a plate bedecked with fresh flowers. Their scent mixes with the smell of citronella oil, which the library uses to preserve its store of palm-leaf manuscripts. The pages are held together by a single length of string, and filled with the beautifully precise letters of the 1,500-year-old Grantha script. They almost look as if they have been printed, but the words have all been meticulously inscribed by hand.

This manuscript would have been produced more than a thousand years after the *Arthashastra* was first composed. The original author is thought to have been a man known variously as Kautilya or Chanakya. Some have argued that he was the minister of the great king Chandragupta, who, in the fourth century BCE, laid the foundations of the Mauryan Empire, India's first and for a long time its largest imperium (see **5 Ashoka**). Although the manuscript would be forgotten, Kautilya or Chanakya became the subject of stories and legends throughout Indian history.

As far back as the Gupta Empire, in the fifth century CE, we find a dramatization of the life of Chanakya or Kautilya – both names are used, along with a third one, Vishnugupta – set in the Mauryan court. The Sanskrit play *Mudrarakshasa* or 'The Ring of Power', by Vishakhadatta, sought to embellish the imperial ambitions of the Guptas by linking their reign back to the era of the Mauryas, some 700 years previously. It is an early example of the kind of appropriation of past lives that recurs across Indian history, as Indians search for glorious precursors to embody their own aspirations. In the fifth century CE play, Kautilya comes into possession of a signet ring belonging to the minister of a rival king, and uses it to impersonate and intrigue so that his own king ascends to the imperial throne.

In another popular story, Kautilya overhears a mother telling off her hungry, impatient child for burning his hand by sticking it in the middle of a bowl of hot gruel. Eat from the edges of the bowl, the mother says. It's cooler there. From this, Kautilya develops an innovative theory of conquest: don't attack an opponent's capital – move in, stealthily, from the periphery. As a result of such stories, Kautilya is often presented as the Bismarckian mind behind the great Mauryan emperor Chandragupta's conquests. Sadly, recent scholarship says the dates of the two men don't align. But if Kautilya the man remains veiled, the *Arthashastra* itself stands out within the Indian tradition – and beyond. The conception of power it embodies includes military might, but goes well beyond it, encompassing the use of wit and intellect, as well as guile, cunning and deceit. 'An arrow unleashed by an archer may kill a single man or not kill anyone,' the author writes. 'But a strategy unleashed by a wise man kills even those still in the womb.'

If we lay the *Arthashastra* alongside other accounts of power and politics from its broad historical era – the works of, say, Plato or Aristotle, with their focus on moral virtue – we can see how unique its perspective is. Many compare it to the treatise that disrupted western ethical and religious beliefs in the sixteenth century, Niccolò Machiavelli's *The Prince*. But Max Weber, the German social theorist, thought such a comparison anodyne. To him, the *Arthashastra*'s radicalism made *The Prince* look 'harmless'.

Kautilya's work suggests he inhabited a world unlike the clan-led oligarchic society into which the Buddha and Mahavira were born. His world was one of kings in perpetual conflict. 'Kautilya for the most part is a political strategist,' says Patrick Olivelle, Professor Emeritus at the University of Texas at Austin, and the most recent translator of the *Arthashastra*. 'He is serving a king and trying to enhance that king's power. And for "king" he uses a very technical term in Sanskrit, *vijigishu*, which means a person who is yearning, desiring, to conquer. So conquest, expanding one's power, is at the heart of the Kautilyan strategy.' Kautilya specifies no particular territory or space to be subjugated – it is potentially and rightfully the entire earth.

The grandiosity of these imperial ambitions embody a high degree of fantasy, but the world Kautilya imagined – of circles, or mandalas, of competing influence and interests, in which one's enemy's enemy was one's friend – is a familiar one. 'This man was thinking about the same problems that we think about,' Shivshankar Menon says. 'And he was thinking about it in a situation where there were many states, which is very much like the situation we're in today – a multi-polar world.' According to Menon, this was a vision of politics that would only coalesce in the West after the Peace of Westphalia in 1648, which brought an end to the Thirty Years War by establishing a system of sovereign states in Europe.

A ruthless, if strategic, expansionary policy was only part of Kautilya's vision for the state. However much his ideal king might dream of exercising power without restraint, he was always enmeshed in dependencies – the concentric circles of enemies, and the allies needed to subdue them. Above all, the king – drawn from the Kshatriya or warrior varna – could never gain authority simply by amassing power. He was caught in a dilemma facing all rulers in India: how to combine his power with the authority only the Brahmin priestly order could claim. Some have called this India's 'inner conflict of tradition'. To acquire legitimacy, a ruler has to show his disinterest in worldly power for its own sake and to manifest a renunciatory streak – but never so much as to hobble his pursuit of power. The never-ending struggle to achieve that balance continues to challenge India's rulers today.

In part to address this dilemma, Kautilya urged his king to adopt a benign aspect. 'Power is sought after for itself – that's one side of it,' Olivelle says. 'But the Indian concept of kingship has a different angle also. The king is viewed as a father, as the person who is actually looking after the interests of his subjects, who are called *prajaa*, which also means children. So in a sense Kautilya weaves into his narrative these two somewhat opposite and irreconcilable goals of political power.'

In the balancing act between liberty, security and prosperity, the *Arthashastra* places its weight behind the latter two. To fulfil his functions, a king requires wealth and the means to maintain a well-ordered state. These concerns are very much at the centre of the *Arthashastra*, whose title means something like the 'Treatise on Success'. Four main sources of wealth were central to the empire that Kautilya imagined: resources acquired through imperial expansion; revenues from royal monopolies; trade with other kingdoms; and taxes collected from private enterprise, especially agriculture. Indeed, Kautilya was no early advocate of the free market. Olivelle characterizes his prescriptions as 'a mixed economy', not unlike the one practised by post-Independence India – or the British East India Company. At the same time, 'a lot of private enterprise was allowed

and encouraged', Olivelle says, particularly through the relief of taxation, the creation of infrastructure and the maintenance of security.

The government Kautilya described was a vast bureaucracy
designed to regulate both economic and social life. And the watchers
had, above all, to be watched; Kautilya mentions forty forms of
embezzlement and, in a memorable image, captures the endemic,
often invisible corruption that is present even in India today: 'Just as
it is impossible to know when fish, moving about in water, are drinking water, so it is impossible to know when officers appointed to
carry out tasks are embezzling money.'

The sovereign's tools of control included not only officialdom, but
propaganda, coercion, domestic espionage and violence. Among
other things, Kautilya offers extensive guidance on how a ruler
should win over his own people by 'seduction': the king should perform illusory acts to give him the aura of miraculous powers, and
should make liberal use of manipulation. He should also cultivate an
army of spies, and Kautilya devotes a whole section of his treatise to
'Secret Conduct'. Quite often these agents were 'monks' – men with
'shaven heads or matted hair' – and even nuns. They flitted among
the populace collecting information and, if necessary, seeding uncertainty, mistrust and fear, thus reinforcing the need for a powerful,
paternal king.

Kautilya seems to have taken particular pleasure in the details of
punishment. Wherever *lèse-majesté* was exposed, strict royal action
was needed. Here, for instance, is his catalogue of the 'eighteen-fold
torture' to be meted out to real reprobates:

> Nine strokes with a cane, twelve whip-lashes, two thigh-encirclings,
> twenty strokes with a nakta malastick, thirty-two slaps, two scor-
> pion bindings, and two hangings-up, needle in the hand, burning
> one joint of a finger of one who has drunk gruel, heating in the sun
> for one day for one who has drunk fat, and a bed of balbaja points
> on a winter night.

Beatings, exposure to extreme temperatures, suspension torture –
not so different from what's in the 2014 US Senate Select Committee on
Intelligence report on the CIA's 'enhanced interrogation techniques'.

Indeed, Kautilya's conception of the state is disturbingly familiar today: like an iceberg, one part towers above us, a beacon of majestic power, while another part hides in the deep – a state of secrecy, duplicity, manipulation and constant surveillance.

But this sort of power proves, in the end, to be a trap. A ruler cannot trust his own officials. Kautilya warns, 'Even if it is possible to know the path of birds as they are flying in the air, it is never possible to know the path of officials as they move with concealed designs.' He must ever be wary of his retinue. As Patrick Olivelle puts it:

> The subject of the king's food becomes important because poisoning the king is one of the easiest ways to get rid of him. There are all these people, including his family, who are the greatest threat to him personally, who are vying to get rid of him. It becomes a real treadmill: he does not know where a threat may come from – and it can come from anywhere.

If this sounds like the kind of paranoia worthy of Saddam Hussein or Colonel Gaddafi, there's another piece of Kautilyan practice that they both followed: reduce the risk of assassination by employing a double. The author of the *Arthashastra* was a man who clearly understood the risks of power and captured the paradoxical instabilities of those who rule: their minds are eternally filled with the fear of losing what they have acquired.

Kautilya's treatise eventually proved too radical in at least one respect: it showed no deference to Brahminic conceptions of dharma, to religious ethics and moral duties. You might call it a profoundly disenchanted work. As Olivelle has argued, the text must have been modified a few centuries after it was composed in order, in part, to bring the decidedly secular *Arthashastra* 'more into line with the mainstream of Brahminical social ideology'.

In this century, in a subcontinent where kings no longer reign, the *Arthashastra* has been repurposed. It's become a how-to guide for ambitious entrepreneurs seeking to amass wealth in an increasingly competitive and globalizing country, much in the same way that Sun Tzu's *Art of War* has become a manual for the world's aspiring business leaders. It's also become a touchstone for foreign policy wonks in the nationalist slipstream, struggling to devise a distinctively Indian view of international relations and India's place in the world. And in the Pakistani military, Kautilya gets assigned to young officers to give them insights into the supposed deviousness of the Indian mind.

Some other suggested reading for Pakistani military schools might be a 1937 essay published in Calcutta's *Modern Review*. It attacked a young politician then still on the rise in India's freedom movement – Jawaharlal Nehru – for his authoritarian, anti-democratic tendencies and his will to dominate. Its author was Chanakya, the variant of Kautilya – clearly a pseudonym. The real author was in fact Nehru himself, who only a decade later would become democratic India's first elected leader, and who did much to establish India as a democracy, serving for many years in Parliament House. But his article implied that inside every democrat is a Chanakyan, totalitarian temptation – that Kautilya is the Mr Hyde lurking in every democratic Dr Jekyll.

5
Ashoka

Power as Persuasion
304–232 BCE

Every time someone mails a letter or hands over a currency note in India, every time an Indian bureaucrat stamps a document with an official seal, they are handling a symbol that dates back over 2,000 years: four lions sculpted in stone, one facing in each direction. The man who created this potent and enduring icon is a towering, mysterious figure in India's history, a king from the third century BCE whose ideas – above all, that a ruler must accept the diversity of his subjects' beliefs – were long forgotten, but returned to inspire the modern-day Indian state.

We know him today by the name Ashoka, and to look at he was unprepossessing – a bit of a lens-breaker, as they say in Bollywood: short, fat and famously afflicted by bad skin. Yet he was a lucky man too, known in his lifetime as *devanampiya*, 'beloved of the gods'. He transformed what was still a nascent sect – Buddhism – into a world religion, transmitting its ethical vision across the subcontinent and the rest of Asia. And, most unusually for a royal – in any country at the time or since – he spread his ideas not through violence, but through moral force and persuasion.

Emperor Ashoka reigned for nearly forty years, during an era when persuasion was not the usual modus operandi. He came to power around 268 BCE, when the Romans were fighting Carthage in the first of the Punic Wars, Persia was engulfed in a civil war, and in China the first Qin emperor was building his Great Wall. Most of the world's other empires were trapped in warfare and isolationism. Ashoka's message was off-chord: it was about the need to reduce suffering and to pursue peace, openness and tolerance. It was a message he took to his people through dozens of edicts, carved in stone and scattered the length and breadth of the subcontinent and beyond. Many of the edicts were on craggy rocks in remote corners like Erragudi in today's Andhra Pradesh; some were etched in polished pillars and erected at strategic locations. And beside many of these pillars were Ashoka's lions, gazing down from on high.

Ashoka came from India's first great empire, the Mauryan dynasty. He was the grandson of Chandragupta, who created the empire by force and who may have learned his lessons in realpolitik from the *Arthashastra* (some believe **Kautilya** (4) was Chandragupta's minister, though that's unlikely). The Mauryan martial style of imperial conquest was continued by Ashoka's father Bindusara, and Ashoka himself further extended the empire across the subcontinent – encompassing pretty much all of it except for the southern tip. It wasn't until the British Raj that so much of India was incorporated under a single ruler again.

Empires are won by arms, but they are sustained by communications. Like their Roman contemporaries, the Mauryans built extensive roads. The most important of these was the Uttarapatha or northern route, the Mauryan Royal Highway which began in Taxila, in the northwest plains of today's Pakistan. It swung down some 2,000 kilometres to Pataliputra, the Mauryan capital, whose traces are now buried beneath the heaving city of Patna in the eastern Indian state of Bihar. The highway drew a physical connection between the very different groups under Mauryan rule, from master-slave societies to caste-based farming communities to forest-dwellers; from speakers of Greek and Aramaic to those who used Prakrit and other Indian languages. The route was later remade by the Mughals, and then by the British, as the Grand Trunk Road, or GTR, now India's smoky National Highway One.

Where Ashoka stood out, even among the Mauryans, was in his mastery of communications. 'Wherever there are stone pillars or stone slabs,' he declared, in what is now known as the Seventh Pillar Edict, his words were to be engraved so that they 'may long endure . . . as long as my sons and great-grandsons reign and as long as the sun and the moon shine.' Like his lion capital, they *have* endured, speaking to us across more than two millennia. The Seventh Edict appears on a pillar that today stands in the ruins of Delhi's Feroz Shah Kotla, but fragments of the same edict have also been unearthed as far west as Kandahar. We know of thirty-three edict texts altogether, and it seems likely each was inscribed at hundreds of sites throughout the empire. One has been found as far south as Karnataka.

As the Canadian scholar Harold Innis (the teacher of Marshall McLuhan) once argued, empires come in two forms. Some embed themselves in time: they favour heavy materials like stone and clay in which to record their communications, and this allows them to aspire to permanence, but requires that they rule in a more decentralized fashion. Other empires embed themselves in space: they tend to use lighter, more ephemeral materials, like papyrus, paper and palm leaf, that can be easily disseminated. This achieves a more centralized, but often less lasting, control. Ashoka was decidedly in the first camp.

The edicts were mainly chiselled in Prakrit (in a script known as Brahmi), the language spoken in the core area of Ashoka's empire, though several have been found in Greek and Aramaic scripts. Most of the edicts speak of Ashoka in the third person, but in some inscriptions an enigmatic 'I' surfaces, giving us a glimpse of his sensibility. He commanded his vast empire, he wanted his people to know, by hard work and a listening ear:

> ... I have made the following arrangement: the reporters may appear before me for reporting the affairs of the people at any time and place, whether I am engaged in eating or am in the harem or in the bed-chamber or on a promenade or in a carriage or on the march.

One rock inscription, discovered a few decades ago on the wall of a rock shelter at Panguraria, in central India, is unexpectedly intimate, at least in one version: 'The king, who is called Priyadarsin ["lovely to behold"] once came to this place on a pleasure tour while he was still a prince, living together with his unwedded consort.' Not all scholars would accept that translation, but here, in words that cut through clouds of legend and centuries of religious and later nationalist consecration, one might detect the pulse of the young prince.

To reconstruct Ashoka's life, we can glean clues from the rock inscriptions and from archaeological finds, and sift religious stories, especially Buddhist ones. Both the legends and Ashoka's own words describe a life split in two, much like the life of the man who became his ethical master. The first part was spent in pursuit of worldly pleasure and power, and in the exercise of brutality. The dispensing of moral instruction and benefaction came later.

The legends say his father, the Emperor Bindusara, took a dislike to the young Ashoka and sent him first to distant Taxila. The city had been part of Achaemenid Persia's sphere of influence – a cosmopolitan crossroads, far from the centre of Mauryan power, where Ashoka was required to put down a rebellion. He was then sent as viceroy to the city of Ujjain, in central India. On his way there he fell in love with the daughter of a local merchant (the consort mentioned in that intimate wall graffiti). 'Pleasure tours' seem to have become a pastime, earning him the name Kamashoka, 'pleasure-seeking Ashoka'.

Bindusara had chosen Ashoka's elder brother Susima to succeed him. But, at their father's death, Ashoka rebelled. He killed Susima – and, according to some legends, ninety-eight other brothers, the sons of Bindusara by various wives (more realistic is the story that has him killing off a mere six). What's clear is that it was a bloody, protracted struggle for the throne. Only after four years did Ashoka feel secure enough to crown himself. He was thirty-four years of age, hardly young; but he celebrated his accession by marrying another princess. Though his pleasure harem was large, some women found him repulsive. It is said he had them burned alive. 'Candashoka' he was sometimes called: rage-filled Ashoka.

Brutal intemperance also marked his first campaign of imperial conquest, in 261/260 BCE, a war against the Kalingas, who ruled what is now Orissa state. 'One hundred and fifty thousand persons were carried away captive,' Ashoka had inscribed on a rock edict. 'One hundred thousand were slain, and many times that number died.' This victory took the Mauryan Empire eastward to the shores of the Bay of Bengal, and established Ashoka's sway for the next three decades. But the conquest was so bloody that it seems to have triggered something in Ashoka. He declared his remorse, and his life took a sharp swerve towards the embrace of ideas that were still comparatively fresh in India: the teachings of the Buddha.

In Buddhist traditions across Asia, Ashoka is a revered figure – a world conqueror who became a world renouncer, a paragon for Buddhist rulers and regimes today. The stories of his conversion come from Buddhist legends, produced many centuries after his death, so a proselytizing agenda is inevitable. In pre-conversion days he seemed like the vilest reprobate, the better to show how Buddhism transformed him! It's Shakespeare's Prince Hal trick, but a good deal more gruesome.

There are legends about Ashoka in most major Asian languages – Sanskrit and Pali, but also Chinese, Japanese, Burmese, Tibetan, Thai and Sinhala. Many of them tell of his furthering the faith by building 84,000 stupas to house the Buddha's relics and to mark the eighty-four tenets of his teaching. So fervent was Ashoka's devotion that he gradually bankrupted the treasury, giving away everything to the Buddhist sangha, down to his last mango. Ashoka, once the lord of India, or Jambudvipa, the land of cherry plums, ended up as lord of half a cherry plum. Such exemplary devotion led to the conquest of Buddhism over Asia.

Legends aside, in India Ashoka used the faith to create an exceptional doctrine of rule – one that may have stemmed from regret over his youthful aggression, but was also a shrewd response to the empire he controlled. The Mauryan world was a hub with many connections. Ashoka's grandfather, Chandragupta, had links with classical Greece, and it is said that as a young man Chandragupta met Alexander the Great. Chandragupta is thought to have followed the teachings of the Buddha's contemporary **Mahavira** (2), and to have become an adherent of the Jain faith, ending his life according to Jain teachings by slow, regulated starvation. Ashoka's father, Bindusara, wrote to King Antiochus I, ruler of a now forgotten empire in modern-day Turkey, asking for sweet wine, figs and a Sophist philosopher.

These interconnections brought change to the Mauryan economy; the increase of wealth and urbanization that characterized the Buddha's period accelerated, along with demands from lower orders for a greater share in society's privileges. Ashoka was governing a far more varied society than any previous Indian ruler. To maintain a grip over the vast spread and variety of his realm – a task for which force would never be adequate – he needed a unifying worldview. What he created was his own extraordinary version of dhamma – infusing this concept, which the Buddha had borrowed and reinterpreted from Brahminic usage, with many of his own ideas.

Ashoka's dhamma was for both the sovereign and his society – a moral code of action by which he sought to rule, as well as one he exhorted his subjects to follow. It focused on worldly deeds and was designed to dampen social conflicts. It spoke for tolerance, and against zealotry and violence. It described a ruler's duty to interest himself in the health and happiness of his people. It even committed him to planting banyan trees and mango groves along the roads, to provide water and resting places for travellers. And, although Ashoka was a follower of the Buddha, under his own dhamma he pledged to protect all his subjects, whatever their religious beliefs. It was a remarkable early statement of the distinction between the private faith of a leader and the responsibilities of public office.

While the Mauryan world was radically different from our own, the ideas Ashoka advocated are as arrestingly familiar as Kautilya's – though in happily different ways. He spoke of the need for moderation and impartiality, urging his subjects to leave behind 'tendencies like jealousy, anger, cruelty, haste, stubbornness, laziness, and fatigue ... The principle of all this is to avoid inconsistency and haste in the exercise of your functions.' Impartiality, consistency, deliberation – all solid liberal constitutional values, and it is remarkable to find a ruler who could connect them into an integrated vision so early in recorded history. Equally striking was Ashoka's articulation of the notion of moral progress – implicit in Buddhism, but which we tend

to think of as a modern idea. As he stated in Rock Edict IV: 'Promulgation of dhamma has increased that which did not exist over
many centuries: abstention from killing, kindness to creatures,
respect to relatives, respect for Brahmins and Shramanas, and obedience to mother, father and elders. This dhamma conduct has
increased in diverse ways, and will increase more thanks to King
Piyadassi, beloved of the gods.'

But perhaps Ashoka's most resonant statement is Rock Edict XII.
It is a call for religious tolerance and civility in public life – or, as he
puts it, 'restraint in speech':

> ... that is, not praising one's own religion or condemning the reli-
> gion of others without good cause ... Whoever praises his own
> religion, due to excessive devotion, and condemns others with the
> thought 'Let me glorify my own religion' only harms his own reli-
> gion. Therefore, contact between religions is good. One should
> listen to and respect the doctrines professed by others. Beloved-of-
> the-gods, King Piyadassi, desires that all should be well learned in
> the good doctrines of other religions.

'Restraint of speech' is a brilliant, if also potentially illiberal, formulation. It isn't the sort of inclusive political philosophy that a ruler
could practise alone. To make sure his empire embraced dhamma,
Ashoka addressed his people directly, going on *dhammayatas* or
'dhamma tours', during which he preached and held discussions.
And it was in a surprisingly frank, gently cajoling voice, without the
kingly bombast one might expect, that he ordered his scribes and
stonemasons to chisel into great stones and pillars across the length
and breadth of India, creating landscapes that resolved themselves
into words and sentences. While most of the inscriptions are now
lost to us, new ones are still being discovered – most recently at
Ratanpurwa in Bihar, in 2009.

In modern times, the idea of a country dominated by messages
emanating from a single brain may evoke Orwell's Ministry of Truth
or North Korea's ubiquitous billboards and tinny loudspeakers.
Indeed, the rock edicts were not all tending towards the toasty liberal. One forbade unofficial gatherings – perhaps because those

meetings could be used to criticize the king's heterodox ideas. Ashoka also created a special class of officials, *dhamma-mahamatas* or 'dhamma superintendents', who were instructed to spread the word across the population – a creepy echo of Kautilya's roving armies of spies and mischief-makers. Yet Ashoka's edicts said that true conquest was the conquest by piety and virtue, and that these ideas could not be enjoined by force:

> Beloved-of-the-gods, King Piyadassi, speaks thus: This progress among the people through dhamma has been done by two means, by dhamma regulations and by persuasion. Of these, dhamma regulation is of little effect, while persuasion has much more effect. The dhamma regulations I have given are that various animals must be protected . . . But it is by persuasion that progress among the people through dhamma has had a greater effect in respect of harmlessness to living beings and the non-killing of living beings.

Ashoka did not always live up to his pronouncements, especially in his later years, when he seems to have become more religiously devout, even zealous. He ordered dissident monks to be expelled from Buddhist monasteries, he acknowledged the persistence of war, and he was aggressive in his treatment of forest-dwellers who were challenging his rule. He became, in some of the later Buddhist portrayals which praise his fervour, a 'monster of piety'.

Ashoka died in 232 BCE. In the following decades, the Mauryan Empire went into decline. Eventually, Ashoka himself was largely forgotten in, or effaced from, the Indian imagination. The Prakrit language and Brahmi script fell into disuse, and no one knew how to read his edicts. For centuries, he seems to have lived on mainly in Buddhist texts outside India – though some scholars now believe that, like the Buddha's, his challenge to Brahminical orthodoxy and his advocacy of ideas such as ahimsa (the protection of all living beings) provoked active rebuttals. Works like the Hindu epic the Mahabharata, in which his name appears, might be seen as a response to Ashoka's particular brand of dhamma as much as to Buddhist ideas.

It was British gentleman scholars, the now-mocked Orientalists, who rediscovered Ashoka in the eighteenth and nineteenth centuries. **William Jones (21)** started the work, but it was his successor James Prinsep who deciphered the Brahmi script, becoming the first man in many centuries to comprehend the edicts. In the words of his fellow Ashokan explorer Alexander Cunningham, he lifted 'the thick crust of oblivion' that had settled over the Mauryan world.

After the British rediscovered him, Ashoka went on to become an inspiration to India's nationalists. He was plucked out of the legends portraying him as a Buddhist ruler and incarnated in a new national myth as a historical Indian king who, with his unifying political will, stood above any single religion and embodied universal principles of justice and non-violence. Here was an Indian ruler who could symbolize the ambitious agenda of cultural and religious pluralism that both Gandhi and Nehru believed necessary for India. Nehru's vision for the new nation did not expunge religion from public life, but recognized its value as a realm of vital individual choice and expression, which therefore required equal space for all faiths. It looked a lot like Ashoka's version of religious restraint.

Speaking in the Constituent Assembly in July 1947, just days before India was due to gain independence and as religious killings spread across the country, Nehru moved a resolution to adopt a design for a national flag, which had at its centre another Ashokan symbol – the chakra, or wheel, part of the lion capital. 'I am exceedingly happy,' Nehru said, that 'we have associated with this Flag of ours not only this emblem but in a sense the name of Ashoka, one of the most magnificent names not only in India's history but in world history. It is well that at this moment of strife, conflict and intolerance, our minds should go back towards what India stood for in the ancient days.'

It's not clear whether the ideas of the ancient Mauryan can in fact offer a resource for India's continuing struggles to create a tolerant, secular state. Still, as Ashoka knew, symbols do matter. His four lions have become the currency – literally and metaphorically – of every Indian life. And his message, of moderation and restraint, remains in equal parts an admonition and an inspiration to Indians today.

6
Charaka

On Not Violating Good Judgement
c.2nd century CE

Next to a cacophonous building site, where Indian labourers and engineers are working alongside international consultants to build a new station for Delhi's world-class metro, stands one of the grimy glass-and-concrete office blocks ubiquitous in urban India. But up its staircase, past the workspaces of outsourcers and traders and accountants, you'll find an unexpected concern: a dial-in health clinic whose care is based on the thinking of a man who lived roughly 2,000 years ago.

Though what is practised here at the Jiva Institute, in Delhi's industrial suburb of Faridabad, has a faddish following in the West, it's part of an Indian tradition as old as the Buddha. Its leading figure was a man known as Charaka, who is sometimes pridefully referred to in India as 'the father of medicine'. We know little about his personal story, but we still have his celebrated manual on the ancient medical system known as ayurveda. *Veda* translates as 'knowledge' and *ayus* means 'long life' or 'vitality', and Charaka's treatise is as much a guide to how to live as it is about how to get better.

Ayurveda is the best known of the three major South Asian medical traditions, along with siddha and unani. Charaka is thought to have set out its basic principles sometime in the centuries around the start of the Common Era. In the early twentieth century, the tradition became professionalized, and now it is part of government policy, with ayurveda and other old medical practices assigned a ministry of their own. Today, ayurveda is often blended into a potpourri of beliefs about individualized cure and personal attention, and at a time when access to affordable, reliable Western medicine remains beyond the means of most Indians, it serves as a popular – if sometimes desperate – alternative.

The Jiva Institute's interior is built with materials you might find in a rather beautiful village home: it has neem-wood counters, cubicles fashioned from bamboo cane, sinuously curving earthen walls. But its technology is very much of the twenty-first century. Its raft of teleconsultants dispense ayurveda's ancient wisdom to India's young and wired through a state-of-the-art call centre. A Muslim woman has just rung in, explaining how long she's had a pain in her stomach. Another doctor's assistant listens attentively to the symptoms of Ajay from Bihar. The Institute claims it averages 2,000 calls a day, on conditions from acne to cancer. The staff listens, consults Charaka and his successors, and prescribes.

The clinic's main reference for ayurvedic knowledge is also our only source for Charaka's biography: the *Charaka Samhita*, or 'Compendium of Charaka'. The version that's come down to us was composed sometime between the third and fifth century of the Common Era – a century or more after his lifetime. The text mentions Himalayan place names, and plants and foods found in the hills, so we can be pretty sure that he lived in north India. A Chinese source of the fifth century claims that Charaka was the physician to a Kushan king named Kanishka, whose mountainous realm, in the second century of the Common Era, stretched from Bactria to today's Bihar. But it's uncertain whether the name Charaka refers to one man, or to the members of a school of thought – perhaps even to a clan or community of practitioners. Indeed, the *Charaka Samhita* encompasses multiple voices and a range of subjects, presenting the alternative views of more than one physician. Like **Aryabhata** (7), its author (or one of them) claims he received his knowledge from the gods – though that's not much help in fixing his identity.

The *Charaka Samhita* is an 'encyclopedic work', says Dominik Wujastyk, a professor of Ancient Indian Studies, who has been part of a research team at the University of Vienna working on a definitive edition. The treatise, he says, covers 'all aspects of life':

epidemics, heredity, the reasons why we live as long as we live, how lives can be made longer or shorter, from earthy topics like how you should immediately go to the toilet if you feel like it and not hold on, to sublime ones such as the nature of wisdom and why the abrogation or violation of wisdom causes all diseases, how to build and supply and run a hospital, and many, many other topics. So it covers everything: what time you should get up in the morning, what you should eat, the kind of people you should associate with, how to live a virtuous life.

The *Charaka Samhita* is written in Sanskrit, and like other texts from early Indian history, it was composed in a poetic style so that it could be chanted, memorized and passed down across the generations.

Charaka's model of the body and its functions was in many ways radically different from one we would recognize today, and his concepts don't translate easily into modern terminology. There's no circulating blood, for instance, no beating heart. Ayurveda's operating principles are based instead on a conception of the body's basic humours – *vatta*, *pitta* and *kapha* (wind, bile and phlegm) – and on the belief that if these elements are displaced from their proper bodily locations, illness follows.

Like other traditional medical systems, ayurveda sees the human body as part of a vast natural, even cosmic, system of causality. But within that system, individuals play an important role as moral actors shaping their own lives and trying to help sustain the order of the universe. The karmic effects of one's actions on the next life have consequences for well-being in this life as well. Disturbances of the humours and other afflictions are often caused by our disregard of basic principles of well-being – what Charaka calls 'violations of good judgement':

> The way to stop external diseases from happening is explained as follows: give up violations of judgement; calm the senses; be mindful; be aware of time, place and yourself; adopt a good lifestyle. To the extent that he wishes for his own good, the wise man will do all this in good time.

Dr Partap Chauhan, the director of the Jiva Institute and one of its founders, began his practice in a garage some twenty years ago. He showed me an old, battered, and obviously very loved edition of the text – his ayurveda 'Bible', he said with a wink. 'Yeah, I like this,' Dr Chauhan said, turning a page and reciting in Sanskrit: 'It's a definition of ayurveda that focuses on ... what is beneficial to life, what is non-beneficial to life, what is a happy life, and what is an unhappy life. It also mentions longevity and how to live a long life. So it actually describes the fundamental principles of being happy and healthy.' Lately, Dr Chauhan's business on the back of Charaka has been very good. Phone consultations at Jiva are free, but consultants invariably recommend to callers some of 'over 500 classical and more than 70 proprietary authentic healthcare and beauty products' that Jiva sells.

Ideas about good conduct proposed in treatises such as the *Charaka Samhita* do 'not represent a completely unique ayurvedic point of view', Dagmar Wujastyk, an Indologist at the University of Vienna (and Dominik Wujastyk's wife), has written. Rather, they share a great deal with the general worldview conveyed in other Sanskrit Brahminical literature. But the *Charaka Samhita* diverges from that worldview in its more dialectic spirit. Charaka commends debate as the central method to advance knowledge about life and health. He sets out precise rules for 'parleys of specialists', and much of his treatise is in the form of questions and answers between a teacher and a disciple.

Dialogue is also the method used by ayurvedic practitioners, or *vaidyas*, who probe their patients with questions to get at the root of an ailment, rather than sending them off for diagnostic tests. At the Jiva telemedicine centre, the consultants listen to each caller in great detail, noting their symptoms and developing an extensive medical history. That said, medieval vaidyas appear to have been as harried as many modern-day doctors, and ayurvedic clinics in India today are often crowded, unrelaxed places, the vaidyas rushing through their consultations.

The advice to be found in the *Charaka Samhita* can also be pretty blunt and generic. The Jiva teleconsultants receive regular call-ins about fertility issues – especially the question of how to produce a male heir. It's an Indian obsession that has kept the life-chances of girls far lower than those of boys, and has led to an abnormal, distressing ratio of males to females in the population. A feminist fertility counsellor, Charaka is not. As one scholar summarizes his advice:

> To produce a son the parents are to copulate on even days after the onset of menstruation . . . The woman is cautioned not to lie prone or on either side lest the phlegm obstruct the passage of semen to the womb or the semen and blood be burned by bile. A woman's over-eating, excessive hunger or thirst, fear, disrespect, depression, anger, desire for sexual congress with another man, or ardent passion will render her unable to conceive or else her offspring will be lacking in qualities.

Some ayurvedic practices have been submitted to randomized controlled trials, with mixed results. But many Indians still see ayurveda as a valuable supplement to Western medicine. Dr Sankaran Valiathan is one of them. He's a distinguished heart surgeon and former president of the Indian National Science Academy, and also author of a book on Charaka. He's a man, in other words, equally familiar with the Western and ayurvedic medical traditions. 'Ayurveda is personalized medicine,' he says:

> One of the fundamental concepts is what is called *prakriti*. At the time of conception, everyone's prakriti is determined and it doesn't change. This consists of a series of physical traits, mental traits, behavioural traits. These determine whether a man belongs to vatta prakriti, pitta prakriti, or kapha prakriti – the three primary constitutional types. In Ayurveda it is so important because you have to determine this in every patient who comes to you, because that determines the predisposition to diseases. Second, it determines the course of the disease. In certain people, they get tuberculosis and it's a very rapid course, a violent course; in others it will keep on lingering for weeks and months. Most importantly, prakriti determines response to treatment. So the same treatment will not have identical effects on different constitutions.

Although the concept of prakriti enables practitioners to identify treatments for their patients that are non-generic, it's not exactly individually customized. As Dominik Wujastyk says, it's quite a fine-grained diagnostic tool – but it shouldn't be confused with New Age ideas of 'treating the whole man, and not just the symptoms'.

Texts like the *Charaka Samhita* continued to be studied, and their ideas followed, by traditional practitioners right through the medieval period and into the nineteenth century. The emergence of ayurveda as a field of modern professional practice, however, dates back to the late nineteenth century, when Indian scholars started to publish print editions of the *Charaka Samhita*. This caught the attention of Western scholars, and resulted in an eruption of Charakamania in medical and Indological circles in the West during the 1890s.

That interest filtered back to a Western-educated and increasingly nationalist Indian elite, which was searching for aspects of their own history and tradition by which to counter British dominance. Mohandas **Gandhi** (38), though not himself an advocate of ayurveda – he favoured naturopathy – saw the readoption of Indian medical principles as a way to recover autonomy, or *swaraj*. Of all his books, the bestseller remains *A Guide to Health*, a self-help book based on his own principles of health, fasting and dieting. This was practical advice, but it also had a political dimension; in *Hind Swaraj*, Gandhi's coruscating text on Indian self-rule, he attacked Western medicine and doctors for undermining our self-control:

> Doctors have almost unhinged us . . . I have indigestion, I go to a doctor, he gives me medicine, I am cured. I overeat again, I take his pills again. Had I not taken the pills in the first instance, I would have suffered the punishment deserved by me and I would not have overeaten again. The doctor intervened and helped me to indulge myself . . .

Indian pride in, and claims about, its ancient medicine sometimes spill over the top. Inaugurating a private hospital in Mumbai, filled with state-of-the-art Western technology (and named after the wife of the country's most successful industrialist, **Dhirubai Ambani** (50), Prime Minister Narendra Modi cited the example of the god Ganesh as a pioneering instance of plastic surgery. Ganesh's elephant head, Modi claimed, was medically grafted onto a human body. At the same time, the country faces a host of public health challenges that remain unresolved: it has an extraordinarily high rate of premature deaths from preventable illnesses, a major lack of qualified doctors and nurses, a weak health safety net that forces more than sixty million people into poverty every year, and a meagre public health budget.

Ironically, the stress and ill-health created by increasing wealth, rapid urbanization and aggressive competition for jobs at all levels of the economy have helped ayurveda flourish in contemporary India. The software engineer has to minimize physical uncertainties in order to keep working twelve-hour days – uncertainties that can be severe given the country's poor public health. In this often isolating environment, ayurveda can seem like a motherly presence, watching over your eating habits, cajoling and reassuring you.

So perhaps it's no surprise that ayurveda has adapted to mass media. Dr Chauhan now has a television show in addition to his call-in centre – with the telephone number of the clinic flashing on the screen. When the show airs, the Jiva Institute receives a surge of incoming calls. And those who lack the privacy to ring from work or home about their complaints (including those of work–life balance, naturally) can turn to the Institute for an online consultation instead.

Ayurveda may not be capable of miracles, nor can it hope to solve India's public health crisis. But as medical care becomes more and more like an assembly line in fiscally strapped health systems around the world, as doctors read genetic codes for predispositions instead of looking at the patient on the table, the idea of staying away from the medical industrial complex – annoying for the rich, expensive for the middle class, and devastating for the poor – can be compelling. People turn to ayurveda because it seems to promise them more recognition as individuals. Perhaps it does – but only in the quite specific sense of placing on each one of us a greater responsibility for our health, enjoining us to live as Charaka teaches: with a little more judgement.

7
Aryabhata

The Boat of Intellect
476–c.550 CE

In 1975, India launched its first satellite into space – a moment of great pride for a nation determined to stake its claim as a global power. Here was evidence that a country long seen in the West as backward belonged to the modern age. But the bundle of technological wizardry India sent into orbit had a name that evoked an older claim to scientific genius: that of the mathematician Aryabhata.

In the West, this name may not rank with those of Euclid or Ptolemy, but it should. At the end of the fifth century, Aryabhata, a young man, produced the first systematic compilation of mathematical and astronomical knowledge known to Indian history. 'By the grace of Brahma,' he claimed, 'the precious sunken jewel of true knowledge has been rescued by me, by means of the boat of my own intellect, from the ocean which consists of true and false knowledge.'

He salvaged some significant findings. He worked out a very close approximation of the value of pi; perfected the 'rule of three', which is still used to calculate ratios; and, using trigonometry, expounded a scientific explanation for solar and lunar eclipses. He also put forward – a millennium before Copernicus and Galileo – the argument that the earth rotates on its axis. Though some of his ideas were not accepted in his own day, they provided a springboard for the subsequent evolution of Indian classical astronomy.

Aryabhata's reputation is based on a single treatise, the *Aryabhatiya*. Composed in Sanskrit sutras (aphoristic rules expressed in verse), it is the only work of his that has survived. It contains a medley of scientific riddles, big ideas and mathematical results – many ingenious, some woefully wrong. Taken together, these insights and

48

errors represent perhaps our most important window into the way that early Indian science conceived of its relationship to the world.

The *Aryabhatiya* also holds out the tantalizing promise that we are merely at the threshold of our understanding of early Indian scientific thought. The treatise is among the fraction – just a tenth or less – of the trove of many thousands of fragile Indian scientific manuscripts that have so far been published and closely studied. According to the acclaimed eleventh-century central Asian astronomer al-Biruni, classical Indian mathematics was like 'a mixture of pearls and dung'. It's possible that there are many more pearls to be discovered – though perhaps few may be as impressive as those produced by Aryabhata.

The *Aryabhatiya* reveals frustratingly little about its author, though Aryabhata does tell us when he was born – in the form of a brain-teaser. 'When sixty times sixty years and three quarters of the yuga had elapsed,' he says, 'twenty three years had passed since my birth.' The answer, if you know your yugas – a Hindu time unit lasting between twelve and forty-eight centuries – is 476 CE.

This playfulness is characteristic of the twenty-three-year-old's work. 'There's a lot in the *Aryabhatiya* which is fun and ingenious,' Professor Kim Plofker, a historian of Sanskrit mathematics at Union College in New York state, says. 'Aryabhata is one of the early Indian scientists that I think it would have been most interesting to work with personally, if you were the calibre of student who understood what he was getting at, because he's clearly a very creative and audacious and innovative mind.'

Aryabhata most likely taught at Kusumapura, a scholarly centre close to present-day Patna on the banks of the river Ganga in northeast India. He lived towards the end of the Gupta dynasty, a supposed 'golden age' of artistic creation and intellectual discovery much celebrated in Indian nationalist history.

The sciences flourished too, and Aryabhata was certainly a product of this moment. As Plofker puts it, 'The type of computation Aryabhata was doing – applying trigonometry and other sophisticated mathematics to astronomical calculations – had been done for at least several centuries before him.' While many of the insights attributed to Aryabhata are his own, she adds, 'they are not confined to innovations of his own. Like every mathematician, astronomer, or scientist that we know of, he stood on the shoulders of giants.'

Some of Aryabhata's own ideas would prove too awkward for his fellow astronomers to accept. Though he didn't put forward a helio-centric model of the universe, his idea of a rotating earth was sufficiently radical that it embarrassed his followers. They shared with early Western astronomers a belief that the sky was the moving element. What's more, it wasn't easy to reconcile Aryabhata's theory with the cosmology found in Vedic and post-Vedic Sanskrit texts. So, in later editions of his work, his disciples did him what they thought was the favour of editing out or correcting what they believed to be his mistakes.

Knowledge of the paths and alignments of the planetary spheres has long played a central role in how people in India order their lives – when to get married, when to start a business, and so on – and it still does today. Despite the radicalism of some of Aryabhata's cos-mology, his techniques to predict planetary movements proved useful for very conventional tasks, such as calculating the correct time to hold religious rituals, and for trying to divine future prospects – uses of astronomical knowledge that remain popular.

The idea that the planets have some influence over terrestrial events is an Aristotelian one. Ptolemy had a whole treatise on astrol-ogy, the *Tetrabiblos*, and it is clear that Hellenistic influences brought such ideas to India. They took deep root and gave mathematicians like Aryabhata a very practical social utility. In Aryabhata's time, mathematicians did their calculations on boards covered with dust, and their work was known, unglamorously, as *dhulikarman* – 'dust work'.

Like other early Indian scientific disciplines, the principles under-lying dhulikarman calculations were part of an oral tradition, and the sutras of a tract like the *Aryabhatiya* were meant to be memo-rized. As a further mnemonic aid, Aryabhata created his own alphabetic system in which letters took the place of numbers, creat-ing unpronounceable 'words'. Their purpose was to represent very large integers in a few syllables, thereby making them much easier to remember than long strings of digits.

It is a method reminiscent of **Panini**'s invention of code to express his rules (3). According to Christopher Minkowski, Boden Professor of Sanskrit at Oxford, Aryabhata was 'unique in the concision with which he expresses his texts'. This capacity to distil technical principles and data into crystalline phrasing was something much prized by certain Indian intellectual traditions. Aryabhata, Minkowski says, 'is able to present, in just a very limited number of verses, all sorts of mathematical ideas. So in thirty-two verses he deals with the decimal place value system, squares, cubes, square roots, cube roots, triangles – all of that and more. In thirty-two verses, it's a lot of mathematics, but there is a great deal of art in the way that he expresses himself in Sanskrit.'

It's revealing to compare Aryabhata with Isaac Newton, who also expressed some of his discoveries in natural language. He chose quite simple Latin to do this (not much like the complex Sanskrit used by Indian mathematicians). But Newton also formulated his laws in the form of equations – notations that developed into a universal symbolic language, in a way that mathematics in the Sanskrit tradition never did.

In the Western tradition, mathematics sits at the very top of the pyramid of human knowledge. It's the paradigmatic science, the one by which reality can be abstracted into fundamental truths. But this wasn't so in India, where mathematical reasoning was just one among several forms of knowledge, and certainly not superior to the understanding of language – as Panini had established. Unlike Euclid, Aryabhata and his tradition didn't give much importance to establishing axioms and deducing proofs.

In fact, like grammar, early Indian mathematics seems to have been concerned primarily with the way things worked in real life. Take, for example, the notion of a sphere. For Aryabhata and his successors, a sphere was like an iron ball: it had to have flat surfaces, 'for only thus can it be stable on level ground', as the Indologist Johannes Bronkhorst has put it. 'Classical Indian geometry,' he added, 'like grammar, describes objects that exist in the material world, not abstractions.' In other words, mathematical calculations were taken as true if they corresponded well to the real world, whether or not they could be proven in some abstract way. The results mattered more than the methods used to get to them. This means that it's often difficult to follow Aryabhata's reasoning, even as one is impressed by his conclusion. As Kim Plofker says, 'Euclid is more like modern mathematics because the modern mathematics we do nowadays is still essentially Greek: it's axioms, proposition, proof, structure. The *Aryabhatiya* is not playing the same intellectual game, so to speak. It's got its own set of rules for the mathematics that it's doing and what it's creating.'

Aryabhata's ideas, translated into Arabic, were influential to later generations of Islamic astronomers and mathematicians. And in India, several schools of astronomers and mathematicians – the latter mainly located in the southern state of Kerala – developed his insights. But, because he wasn't working within the framework of his Western counterparts, his ideas didn't feed directly into the global stream of scientific discovery (in the way that, say, Newton's did). Despite the significance of the *Aryabhatiya*, for a long time its author remained in relative obscurity, even in the subcontinent.

It was only when science and technology began to flourish in modern India that his reputation got a relaunch. Indian scientists, trained in Western techniques, nevertheless wanted their own national lineage. According to Professor U. R. Rao, a senior scientist at the Indian Space Research Organisation, who oversaw that first satellite project, the mission helped restore Aryabhata's reputation. 'There was a great realization of our own past,' Rao says. 'It was a forgotten chapter of our history, and that was changed completely.'

The launch of the Aryabhata satellite was only a partial success, however. After five days in space, it stopped transmitting. But it was India's first step in a space programme that has already put an Indian spacecraft in orbit around Mars, at a lesser cost than some Hollywood science fiction movies. And it helped to bring popular attention to India's long neglected heritage of scientific thinking – including, of course, the thinking of Aryabhata.

Today, his reputation is even a little overblown. Some people claim he invented zero, identified gravity a thousand years before Newton, and more. None of this is true, but gaining a more historically accurate appreciation of the achievements of early Indian mathematics and science is just beginning. Only in recent decades have we begun to study seriously the wealth of India's ancient treatises. When it comes to the ocean of Sanskrit science, the boat of our historical knowledge has only just set forth.

8
Adi Shankara

A God without Qualities
8th century CE

Dawn in the south Indian pilgrimage town of Sringeri, in Karnataka. It's a brief moment of stillness and cool. Walking sleepily in the half-light, I'm startled by something coiled on a veranda – a snake, which, from the looks of it, is drowsy too. But as my eyes adjust to the rising light, I look again and laugh: it's not a snake – merely a coiled rope, left behind by a man who's been fixing the tiled roof.

This bit of self-deception – mistaking a rope for a snake – is an occasional false alarm in Indian life. It's also among the most well-known, even hackneyed, examples cited in Indian philosophical thought. Its purpose is to show that, although the sensory world is out there, our imaginations sometimes intervene between us and reality. Our minds, in other words, are tricksters. At the same time, what we perceive – the snake superimposed on the rope – has real power. As another famous example from Indian philosophy runs, even someone who only *thinks* he has been bitten by a snake can die from shock.

Mistakings pervade Hindu philosophy, which is full of metaphors of concealment and obscuration. Many serve as examples of *maya*, the reality that substantially and unarguably presents itself to us but whose true nature remains elusive because of the limitations of our consciousness. Push aside this slippery, illusory world and something pure and constant is revealed: god, the divine, or the universal spirit – *Brahman*.

Although the varieties of Hinduism defy doctrinal unity, maya and Brahman are essential parts of a philosophical vision that many people now identify with the religion. In large part, we owe this vision to Adi Shankara, a religious thinker – perhaps the nearest that Hinduism might have to a theologian – who, roughly twelve hundred years ago, transformed Hindu beliefs and practices, established temples and schools across the subcontinent, and in many ways laid the foundations of modern Hinduism, which is now the third largest religion in the world.

In Europe, the eighth century was the era of Charlemagne's bloody expansion of Christendom, through campaigns against the Saxons, Saracens, Moors and Slavs, and of his ascension to Rome's Christian imperium. Shankara's roughly contemporaneous efforts to establish a monastic order and assert his religious vision in India were vastly different: his was an intellectual struggle, prosecuted through debates across the subcontinent. At the heart of Shankara's interpretation of Hinduism is an idea that remains as powerful as it is paradoxical – *nirguna Brahman*, a god without qualities.

The narrow roads to Sringeri wind up through the Sahyadri Hills, past miles of laboriously tended coffee plantations, stands of palm and splays of bamboo. Here, in this remote temple town, Shankara is said to have founded his first Hindu monastery, or *mutth* – one of four he would establish, along with various temples, at the cardinal points of the subcontinent: at Badrinath, in the Himalayan foothills of the north; at Puri, on the Bay of Bengal in the east; at Dwarka, where the Gulf of Kutch opens into the Arabian Sea, in what is now the western state of Gujarat; and here at Sringeri, in the south.

Shankara, or Shankaracharya as he was also known, supposedly began travelling across India at a young age. As with so many of these ancient figures, there's uncertainty and dispute about his early life. It's generally reckoned that he was born in the eighth century, in the Malabar region of southern India, now in the state of Kerala. Some religious biographies, written in verse several hundred years after Shankara's death, claim that the deity Shiva appeared to Shankara's parents in a dream and gave them the choice of producing a son who was 'all-knowing and virtuous but short-lived', or one who would live long but 'without any special virtue or greatness'. They opted for the former, and named their precocious child

Shankara, another name for Shiva. As promised, the boy turned out to be a prodigy, but was just thirty-two when he died.

It was said that Shankara only had to hear something once to remember it, and that he had mastered the four Vedas, the oldest Hindu scriptures, by the age of eight. Around the same time, or possibly even earlier, Shankara declared his desire to become a *sannyasi*, an ascetic, wandering monk. This announcement scandalized his by then widowed mother. In the traditional lifecycle of a Hindu male, *sannyas* – renunciation of the world – is the fourth and final stage. A boy first has to grow to be a student and then an adult householder, and then later withdraw into hermetic retirement. Only after that can he take the final step and become a religious wanderer.

But Shankara prevailed and, by the age of sixteen – with half his life already spent as an ascetic – he was producing sophisticated scriptural commentaries and articulating a radical new version of what eventually became known as Hinduism. He remained devoted to his mother, though. After she died, Shankara returned home intending to perform the death rites, but his community refused to let him. Only a householder could do the rites, they said – not a sannyasi. It was a painful snub, and perhaps the pivotal incident that turned Shankara against high Brahminical rituals and towards what he considered the undervalued inner wisdom of post-Vedic texts.

In celebratory biographies like the *Shankara-Vijayas*, or the 'Conquests of Shankara', the earliest of which date from around the fourteenth century, Shankara is portrayed as more than just a wandering religious figure. He is miraculous in physique as well as deeds: a face like the full moon, a broad chest, arms so long they reached his knees, and fingernails the colour of blood. But what really awed people was his capacity for intellectual jousting and dialectic victories over scholarly rivals. The most dramatic was over the venerable pandit Mandana Misra, an old-style believer in ritual recitation of *mantras* and *japas*. These were sounds, conveying no meaning as such, but considered purifying because they were believed to have been handed down from the gods.

Shankara was directed to meet Mandana by a dying sage: he was told to look for a big house, surrounded by walls and with a tall locked gate, where parrots could be heard chanting Vedic mantras. He triggered yogic powers to leap into the courtyard and, after exchanging insults with Mandana by way of introduction, the two decided to debate the validity of their beliefs. Mandana's wife was chosen as umpire. She placed two fresh garlands around their necks, declaring that whichever one faded first would indicate the loser.

The disputations went on for eighteen days. Finally, Mandana's flowers wilted and he conceded defeat. His wife took up the challenge and thought she had found a subject for debate that would surely flummox the celibate Shankara: the art of love. But Shankara asked for a month to investigate. Using his yogic powers once more, he entered the body of a king, proved a quick student at gathering the necessary knowledge, and returned to claim victory.

Shankara turned now to spreading his message across the country, arguing down rivals one by one. According to one of the *Shankara-Vijayas*, he continued his 'merciless refutation of all hostile creeds and philosophies: the teachings of the Tathagata [the Buddha] became lifeless, the school of Kumarila became silent, the Naiyayika philosophy became weak and paralysed, and the Kapila's system also followed suit'.

In Shankara's day, there existed a range of religious sects devoted to various gods – sects that followed distinct practices, from animal sacrifice and fire rituals to Tantric sex and magic. These beliefs, along with Buddhism and a range of other philosophical schools, sustained a world of debate and controversy, and challenged the Brahminic tradition.

Shankara aimed to bring some order to this profusion of belief and practice, both orthodox and heterodox. By his time, Sanskrit texts of the Vedas existed alongside oral versions, and the canon had expanded to include a collection of 200 broadly philosophical works known as the Upanishads. Also known as the Vedanta (literally, 'after Vedas' or 'at the Vedas' end'), the Upanishads ventured answers to questions posed in the Vedas: where did we come from, why are we here, where do we go? Shankara seized on these writings and turned them, through his commentaries, into a powerful new doctrine.

According to Jonardon Ganeri, Professor of Philosophy at New York University, 'Shankara's ambition as a thinker was to provide a unified, coherent reading of the great plurality and diversity of the Hindu scriptures.' Ultimately, Ganeri says, this project was a moral one: 'I think of Shankara as a theologian, interpreting canonical religious texts as providing the foundation around which a moral vision is organized.'

For Shankara, the focus of this vision was the *jnana*, or knowledge, contained in the Vedas and Vedanta, that revealed the essential unity of the cosmos. 'Shankara thought there was just one real entity, Brahman, the fundamental grounding principle of the universe,' Ganeri says. 'Everything else – all the apparent distinctions and differences in the world, including differences between different individual selves – is illusory.' Perhaps most radically, Shankara held that the distinction between self (*atman*) and the divine (Brahman), which appears so evident in the sensory world of maya, was also a misapprehension. This was the core of the monist doctrine that Shankara systematized. It is now known as Advaita Vedanta – that is, 'non-dualist' Vedanta – because it does not recognize two substances in the universe, but only one.

As a result of this tenet, Vedic Hinduism had to be newly formulated, and turned away from popular forms of worship, which, according to Shankara, misunderstood the individual spirit's path to liberation. Obsession with rituals had to be replaced by asceticism, celibacy, the giving up of family life, and an intellectual rigour that could help others grasp the truth that the seeking person divined. Instead of mantras, Shankara prescribed meditative reflection, through which each individual could pierce the veil of maya and come to recognize the identity between his or her own essence and the universal spirit. Once we grasp that oneness with the eternal, Shankara said, we attain *moksha*, or release from the cycle of life and death.

Shankara explicated this moral vision in volume after volume – some estimate the number at 400 – of subtle commentaries on the Upanishadic texts. In other modes, Shankara could be direct, for instance in his popular call to devotion, *Bhajagovindam*. But in his efforts to capture the ineffable oneness of the universe, he produced a beautiful, if at times confounding, literature:

> I am neither earth nor water nor fire nor air nor sense-organ nor the aggregate of all these; for all these are transient, variable by nature . . . I am neither above nor below, neither inside nor outside, neither middle nor across, neither the east nor west; for I am indivisible, one by nature, and all pervading like space.

Though the term 'Hindu', denoting those who lived in the subcontinent, beyond the Indus river, was known to the Greek historian Herodotus in the fifth century BCE, 'Hinduism' only entered the historical record around Shankara's time. It was a name used by Arabs who were attempting to describe the different religious strands that they encountered in India. Indeed, some scholars see in Shankara a response to the first incursions into the subcontinent of that great proselytizing monotheistic religion, Islam, in the mid-seventh century (and many later monistic Hindu sects became proselytizing themselves, emulating what they opposed). But Shankara's monism was crucially different from monotheism: unlike the jealous, paternal God of the Abrahamic faiths, or the superhuman personal gods of the Vedic pantheon, his Brahman was without positive attributes – an essential substance rather than a divine agent.

Arguably more important than any response Shankara may have been making to Islam was the way he took on Buddhism, then by no means at the end of its Indian decline. Throughout the subcontinent, he engaged in verbal combat with Buddhist philosophers, who taught, as the Buddha had, such doctrines as the momentariness of all things, and the denial of the existence of a deity. At the same time, however, he learned a trick or two from them and also adopted in his mutths organizational aspects of the Buddhist sangha. Some later critics spoke of Shankara's 'hidden Buddhism'. Others denounced his theory of monism by quipping that Shankara was simply too dim to count beyond one. But perhaps his ability to adopt important features of Buddhist practice, such as the monastic order, into Hindu tradition was one small part of what forced Buddhism in the subcontinent into its long dormancy.

Unlike Buddhism at its inception, and during its Dalit renewal in the middle of the twentieth century, Hindu monistic doctrines, of which Shankara's became the most prominent, sometimes slid towards intolerance. Shankara himself maintained that only Brahmins could renounce the world (and thus achieve moksha). Moreover, as Wendy Doniger, Professor of the History of Religions at the University of Chicago, has argued, the belief that the lived world is 'ultimately unreal generally siphons off the impulse to take action against social injustices, against poverty and cruelty'.

Even commentators sympathetic to Shankara detected troubling contradictions in his account of liberation. In particular, the lack of distinction between atman and Brahman led to a sort of paradox of inquiry: if we are one with the undifferentiated, quality-less essence of the universe, how can we possibly reflect on that universe in order to discover what we truly are? Furthermore, if the Vedas, Vedanta and Shankara's own thought are all part of the illusory world of maya, how can we hope to find in them the truth of the unity of being?

According to Jonardon Ganeri, Shankara's most startling idea (one shared by Hindu philosophers in other, connected schools) was that 'the way out of colossal error' – out of maya – was 'to embed within the illusion the catalyst of its own destruction'. In other words, Shankara turned on its head the example of the imagined but no less fatal snake bite: even (the right set of) illusory beliefs and practices can help lever one into an awareness of the truth.

By mid-morning, Sringeri fills with pilgrims and tourists who swarm the mutth and temples. It's a sight repeated on most days at the four corners of the country. Shankara's monasteries continue to thrive and, along with a fifth established at Kanchi, have become some of the most important Hindu religious sites in modern India. Each one is headed by a Shankaracharya, who adopts Shankara's name as an official title.

In his lifetime, Shankara's teachings gained him many devoted followers, but it's the afterlife of his teachings that makes his doctrine far more popular today than it ever was in the eighth century.

His pruned-down version of Hinduism caught the interest of the broad-minded Mughal emperor **Akbar** (16) in the sixteenth century, and later found a ready ear among India's nineteenth-century colonial masters. Wendy Doniger explains:

> One branch of Hinduism, which includes the Shankara tradition, the philosophical tradition, was very attractive to the British when they came to India and established the Raj. They liked the fact that there was a philosophical tradition; they could come to terms with it. The rest of Hinduism, which is to say most of Hinduism – with the gods with many arms and goddesses that drink warm blood – the British didn't really like that part of Hinduism.

In addition, Christian missionaries, who were often the forerunners of the colonial administrators and factory men of the Raj, sought to undermine the various forms of Hinduism they encountered. 'They wanted to find points of weakness, and polytheism was one of the principal targets,' Jonardon Ganeri says. 'They accused Hinduism of not being a well-organized, coherent religion precisely because of its polytheism.'

Many educated Indians, working closely with British overlords in the vast machinery of the subcontinental empire, came to adopt these prejudices – and the Christian model of religion, if not its content, seeped into the culture at large. Elite Hindus grew ashamed of the lack of systematization and scriptural authority in their religion, yet, according to Doniger, they did not abandon Hinduism altogether: 'They became proud of the philosophy of Shankara.'

In this way, the absorption of British prejudices had the contradictory effect of consolidating Hinduism, albeit in a very particular form. At the end of the nineteenth century and into the twentieth, Hindu revivalists and Indian nationalists embraced Shankara's philosophy as a muscular indigenous religion. Thinkers such as Swami **Vivekananda** (28) invoked Shankara's ideas and argued for the creation of schools to promote Advaita Vedanta and foster national pride.

Despite the powerful afterlife of Shankara's doctrine, even today his version of the religion is by no means one that all Hindus would recognize. Doniger has compared Hinduism to a Venn diagram without a centre: clusters of overlapping practices and beliefs, with no single feature shared by all of the religion's many manifestations. 'Shankara's there, everybody knows about him,' Doniger says. 'Some people use him as their own guide to thinking about the meaning of life, and those people say that's what Hinduism really is. But that's really not true: it's what some of Hinduism is.'

On a hill leading up to the Sringeri mutth is a clutch of market stalls selling trinkets, images of Shankara and other religious paraphernalia – the kind of thing I imagine that Shankara himself would not have had much time for: idols within a world of illusion. And, at the top of the path that leads to the monastery, you can hear monks reciting mantras, apparently oblivious to Shankara's rejection of such practices.

But it's that constant capacity to allow beliefs, however abstract, to be observed and practised in different ways that keeps Hinduism invigorated. Shankara's thought, Ganeri says, 'performed an admirable function by providing a Hindu analogue of European ways of thinking, but it was just the opposite from what I think is the essence of Hinduism – its great diversity and polycentricity and plurality'.

That plurality clearly survives. The present-day Shankaracharyas may be the nearest thing Hinduism has to a Pope or papacy, but Hinduism itself remains much as it was in the eighth century, when the Arabs first tried to label it: multiple in form, bubbling with internal arguments, accepting of different types of belief. There is no single, defining text or interpreter. What we have are mesmerizing questions, puzzles, early morning doubts about the nature of our perceptions, the limits of self, and the relationship between that self and the wider flow of time.

9
Rajaraja Chola

Cosmos, Temple and Territory
10th century CE

Most south Indian cities have a temple at their heart. The one in Tamil Nadu's Thanjavur, or Tanjore, is a thousand years old. Locals call this stone building Periya Koyil, 'the big temple'; the scholar David Shulman has termed it a 'rhapsody to size'. A decade in the making, it was crowned by a gilded finial that stretched its super-structure to sixty-six metres high – making it for centuries the tallest temple in India. It was the signal architectural achievement of the Chola dynasty, which from the late ninth century to the late thir-teenth sustained one of India's most sophisticated cultures. The ruler who ordered its construction was born with the name Arulmolivar-man; but ascending the Chola throne in 985, he became simply Rajaraja – the king of kings. His temple, which stood at the centre of a loosely assembled empire whose influence extended from the Mal-dives to Indonesia and the South China Sea, was a symbol of his power, his munificence and his proximity to the divine.

'He builds a temple which he modestly names after himself, the Rajarajeshwara temple, and it is really the most magnificent temple of the early eleventh century anywhere in India,' says George Michell, an expert on Indian architectural history. 'It stands to this day as a testimony to the financial resources, the architectural magnificence and the artistic skills that Rajaraja could command to build this great monument.' There were important south Indian temples before this, Michell adds, 'but suddenly, with Rajaraja, everything gets three or four times larger'.

Nineteenth-century British colonialists found the height quite useful: they mounted a theodolite on the temple's shimmering spire as part of their quest to survey the Indian landscape. But it must have seemed unearthly to the medieval peasants of the Kaveri river belt who watched the structure rise, block by granite block, over their rice paddies – a great pyramid of tiered stone to evoke the Himalayan abodes of the gods.

I have always wondered if the building of this grand temple was a sign of how uneasy Rajaraja was about his power. He had acquired the throne at a shaky moment in Chola history, and much was shifting and tenuous in his world. The Cholas were one of several south Indian dynasties; about a century before Rajaraja's birth, these other kingdoms had almost fought themselves into exhaustion, and the Cholas had begun to assert themselves. But when Rajaraja came to power, his kingdom was still recovering from a significant defeat at the hands of rival Kannada rulers. In addition, the realm he governed comprised many networks of local kings and village strongmen; merchant groups, traders and port controllers; Brahmins; and the masses tending the paddy – along with a cacophony of local cults of worship connected with different deities and caste groups. Rajaraja had to bring this diverse society under his command without the benefit of a standing army or the sort of octopus-like bureaucracy **Kautilya (4)** had prescribed.

But he succeeded. His genius lay in cultivating a command over the imagination of his subjects – and he did this by creating an inclusive religious and imperial ideology centred on the temple at Thanjavur, which celebrated Rajaraja both as a conqueror and as a devotee of unbounded generosity. The shrine combined his worship of the god Shiva with elements drawn from Vedic Hinduism, southern devotional traditions and popular cults, and served as a metaphor for the unification of south Indian society under his rule.

'Building a temple is a major legitimating device,' says Professor R. Champakalakshmi, a scholar of the Chola political system. 'Unless you build a temple, you cannot claim to be a sovereign, you cannot claim to have sovereign rights over the territory you wish to control.' But Rajaraja's temple went even further:

> It was the symbol of royal and political power, and he tries to combine in this temple all kinds of art – sculpture, painting, music,

dance, everything – into one, making it culturally the most significant of all the south Indian temples. But the importance also has something to do with the expression of the territorial control over a very large area, which is now called Tamil Nadu but was then divided into smaller subcultural regions. All these were integrated into a single whole – and that is what this temple represents.

In short, according to Champakalakshmi, Rajaraja created 'an equivalence' between 'cosmos, temple and territory'.

A narrow, high-ceilinged corridor skirts the temple's dark inner sanctum, and around one corner you'll find one of the richest examples of wall painting in Hindu art. It's part of a cycle of murals – a form usually associated, in early Indian history, with Buddhism – that was painted over at some point during the sixteenth or seventeenth century. The murals were rediscovered in 1931 by a Madras professor wielding a Baby Petromax lantern.

In the dim light, you can just make out a large portrait of Lord Shiva. He's smiling impassively as his dancing feet trample Apasmara, an epileptic dwarf who personifies ignorance in Hindu mythology. To Shiva's right, under a canopy, stands a muscular, bearded man, lightly dressed and with no adornments, his black hair pulled up in a bun. He's leaning forward in a stance of worship, palms outward, offering flowers to his lord. According to George Michell, this is the earliest identifiable portrait of any king in Indian painting – Rajaraja himself, installed beside the temple's deity. This is a temple to him as much as to any god.

Some people argue that, over the centuries, south India has sustained a more pure, Vedic Hinduism, because, unlike the north, it wasn't set upon by central Asian and Islamic invaders. But nowhere in the country will you find religion set in amber – not even in this sombrely beautiful place. Throughout the temple there are images of Shiva – often as Nataraja, the creator and destroyer – carved into the walls. Rajaraja and his Brahmin priests practised an eclectic Shaivism, drawing on *bhakti* forms of *puja*, or worship of images of the deity, by offering flowers, clothing, food and precious things – practices whose purpose and pay-off were different from those of Vedic sacrificial rituals.

At the centre of the temple is a massive lingam, a phallic monolith nearly four metres tall that represents Shiva. According to Champakalakshmi, it's a symbol derived from the Puranic tradition of Hinduism – in many ways an earthier, if not necessarily a more demotic, strain. There are Vedic gods here too – the *Dikpalakas*, or 'guardians of the directions' – but they are posted outside the main sanctuary.

Drawing on various religious streams, but expressing a distinct hierarchy, the temple iconography echoes the structure of Chola society. 'Rajaraja had to bring together these people who are of different ethnic groups, different tribal groups, who worship different deities,' Champakalakshmi says. 'The temple is an instrument of integration, and not only for various religious rituals and deities, together building up a pantheon. It also brings all these ethnic and other groups into the Brahminical order of society.' As part of this cultural assimilation – which surely included elements of coercion as well – Rajaraja took those of his subjects who had previously been outside the varna system and incorporated them into the fourth – the Shudra or servant – estate.

He also invested in the creation of exquisite portable icons of Shiva and the other gods, statues that remain some of the greatest products of Indian sculptural art. At its consecration, he arranged a gift of sixty such figures to the temple. They were solid and cast largely from bronze, often over half a metre tall, and some of the metal that went into them is likely to have come from across the seas. Perhaps the most famous depict Shiva as he is in the mural near the temple's sanctum sanctorum: as Nataraja, encircled by flames, serenely dancing the cosmos into destruction and renewal.

We see these Chola bronzes today as ethereal figures, frozen in movements that are at once dynamic and perfectly poised, emanating a sensuous elegance. But in Chola times, they were adorned with the finest muslin and silk, jewels and flowers, and carried by priestly assistants at the head of raucous parades. Drums were beaten, conch shells were blown, and many coconuts were cracked.

In the Chola temples, *darshan* – worship through the act of seeing, or being in the presence of, the deity – was strictly out of bounds to the lower castes. In fact, they were only allowed into the temple compound to sweep and service it. As for women, while the inscriptions tell us of some who donated gold and jewels, only queens and *devadasis*, ritual temple dancers, could enter. So the festive outdoor processions of the bronze gods were among the few occasions at which peasants could 'receive' darshan, a spiritually charged glimpse of their gods. In the lives of the very poor, these were dancing, chanting, ecstatic events – and Rajaraja got the credit for them.

In the mural near the temple's centre, three queens stand to Rajaraja's side, and a little behind him. They are small women made more substantial by their heavily jewelled cuffs and belts. It's no accident that the skin of each woman varies in shade: the queens are each of different ethnic origin. The mural testifies, with more subtlety than usual for the Chola emperor, to the breadth of the dominion he achieved.

'King of Jewels, Incomparable Chola, Great Saviour, Jewel of the Solar Dynasty, Lion among Kings' – these were Rajaraja's titles, which he had engraved in stone and on hundreds of copperplates. Religious institutions anywhere you go reflect secular and historical truths, in addition to transcendental ones, and Rajaraja understood that well. The walls of his temple are covered in thousands upon thousands of verses, in the Tamil language and script; many are testaments to his generosity and devotional renunciation. The temple had other donors too, and one can also see records of their gifts all over these walls. But it was Rajaraja who gave the most – more than 200 kilograms of gold by the end of his reign, along with copious amounts of silver and jewels. These contributions, and those he made to Indian architecture and art, were financed in part by trade and taxation, and in part by plunder.

Historians of India often focus on India's westward connections – the overland 'silk road' to central Asia and beyond, and later colonial and commercial ties with Europe. Often missed are the adventuresome seaborne links Chola rulers forged between south India and

South East Asia and China. Trading-minded Tamil sailors had mastered the currents and monsoon winds. They raced their pearls and spices, as well as their textiles (a major industry in Tamil Nadu today), across the Bay of Bengal, which was then known as the Chola Lake or Chola Sea. The traders would return laden with camphor, metals and Chinese porcelain – fragments of which archaeologists continue to find along the shores of south-eastern India. Ships moving goods between the Arab world and China would also harbour at Nagapattinam, a port south of today's Chennai – stops that gave Rajaraja and his successors the chance to impose lucrative taxes on the precious cargo.

In addition, Rajaraja pulled off something no Indian ruler before him seems to have done: commandeering timber trading boats, he launched maritime expeditions, bringing far-flung wealth back home to the Coromandel Coast. Then, as now, the China trade was a prize, and the Cholas competed for it fiercely with the Buddhist rulers of Srivijaya in Sumatra, whose port was a rival transit point. This wasn't always commercial competition. Rajaraja also sent expeditions to northern Sri Lanka to ransack Buddhist temples. According to the *Culavamsa*, a twelfth-century chronicle from the island, the capital at Anuradhapura, a great religious centre that housed relics of the Buddha, was 'utterly destroyed'. 'Like blood sucking yakkhas,' the text goes on, the Cholas 'took all the treasures of Lanka for themselves.'

Rajaraja was also hoovering up wealth from mainland India. He assembled mercenaries – archers, spearmen and swordsmen – and troops of elephants to plunder treasure from neighbouring southern kingdoms. Though it's likely to have been a face-saving exaggeration by the defeated, an inscription found in one of these conquered realms speaks of 900,000 pillaging Chola troops.

Closer to home, his beneficence was underwritten by the riches of a territory that stretched inland from the Coromandel Coast to the Kaveri basin. 'Even though it's in a sort of tropical zone, it's a rather dryish part of the world, but with this great river flowing through it,' George Michell says. 'With irrigation, the region was able to yield huge amounts of produce – and the Cholas were able to command the management of water. The population was extremely dense, as it continues to be today, and there was a lot of wealth from the land.' (Control of the Kaveri continues too to be of critical importance; Tamil Nadu has been in a dispute with its western neighbour, Karnataka, over how to distribute the river's waters since at least the nineteenth century.) Temple inscriptions show that Rajaraja used temple functionaries to organize revenue-collection, accumulating the proceeds within the sacred building.

In fact, from what we can tell about his administration, the temple was his throne as well as his storehouse and shrine. Although Tanjore has a palace, it dates from a much later period, when Maratha Nayak kings ruled; Rajaraja ran his kingdom from within the godly precinct. 'The temple received land grants from the king, and from the higher levels of chiefs and officers,' Champakalakshmi says. 'And it becomes the landlord who redistributes these resources to people who serve the temple in various ways – from the priestly group right down to the sweepers, the lowest group of workers, all of whom have a place in temple society.' Thus, economically and socially, as much as religiously, Rajaraja's monument became a microcosm, an ideal image, of the sort of empire he was fashioning.

Some see the period of Rajaraja's reign, which ended with his death in 1014, as initiating an era when the centre of gravity of Indian history moved southwards. Certainly, his legacy – the Thanjavur temple, the Chola bronzes, his pioneering maritime expeditions – remains unsurpassed in some respects. Taller temples were eventually built, and there have been many other patrons of Indian art, but perhaps few other Indian kings worked quite as hard as Rajaraja to capture the imaginations of those over whom they ruled.

A thousand years after Rajaraja, wielding such power is still a south Indian art. Even today in this region, boon-dispensing leaders have their own devotional cults, and people will tell you that the politics of Tamil Nadu remain different from those in the rest of the country. For a start, people here are sometimes willing to die for their leaders. When the state's chief minister, Jayalalithaa, was imprisoned in 2014 on charges of corruption and had to resign her

position, newspapers reported the deaths of more than 150 people –
many of shock, but around forty by their own hand. On her first
birthday out of power, another supporter nailed himself to a cross in
ritual crucifixion. Nowhere else in India do politicians inspire such
cultish passion. When Mumbai's Bal Thackeray, revered by many of
his fellow Maharashtrians, died in 2012, authorities geared up for a
wave of public violence and sympathy deaths. Nothing happened.

Jayalalithaa has since been acquitted on appeal. Whether or not
she was venal, she successfully cultivated an image of magnanimous
bounty: distributing to her people televisions, motorbikes and school
fees for girls. They call her *Amma*, Mother – and to many, her qualities make her divine. One poster put up after her conviction asked,
'Can a mortal punish God?'

It takes me back to those paintings of Rajaraja near the inner
sanctum of his temple, which show him worshipping, but also making himself an object of worship. Did he invent this cult of the leader
in the Tamil lands, or had he tapped into a current that was already,
quietly, coursing through them?

10

Basava

A Voice in the Air
12th century CE

> Make of my body the beam of a lute
> of my head the sounding gourd
> of my nerves the strings
> of my fingers the plucking rods.
>
> Clutch me close
> and play your thirty-two songs
> O lord of the meeting rivers!

These sensuous lines to the god Shiva were left to us by the twelfth-century poet Basava, a religious guru of revolutionary ideas who preached the immorality of caste and the intrinsic value of people who happened to be born poor. His deceptively simple verses were written in Kannada – a Dravidian language of the south, spoken by some fifty million Indians today – but we can read many of them now in the beautiful translations of the twentieth-century poet and scholar A. K. Ramanujan.

Over the centuries, Basava's words have inspired many other Indian poets, writers and dramatists – and some very British poets, too, including Ted Hughes. Hughes found in Ramanujan's translations of Basava a voice so uncannily natural that it reminded the famously immodest Hughes of himself. He said he heard in Basava the sort of poetry he wrote when young and relatively unstudied – a style that moved like 'a voice in the air'.

Today, Basava himself is a bit like a voice in the air. As scholars dispute the dates and details of his life, his followers speak of him in reverent fables; to them he is known more respectfully as Basavana, elder brother, or even Basaveswara, Lord Basava. His verses, though, are what explain him best. They have a directness that reveals an independent thinker, social reformer and religious teacher who sometimes struggled to resist worldly temptations. Each of his poems evokes his passionate devotion to Shiva – lord of the meeting rivers, as Basava called him – and leaves classical formality behind.

> I don't know anything like time-beats and metre
> Nor the arithmetic of strings and drums:
> I don't know the count of iamb and dactyl
>
> My lord of the meeting rivers,
> As nothing will hurt you
> I'll sing as I love.

'I'll sing as I love': no high language, just an open invitation to all – including the unlettered. This informal, almost spoken quality, joined to unconventional or even anti-conventional politics, is why the twelfth-century guru speaks so powerfully to many writers in India today. Girish Karnad, a leading playwright, is one of them:

> The marvellous thing about Basava and his followers was that they rejected any kind of permanent structures. They wanted to be continually moving, they wanted to be continually changing, they wanted to continually respond to life. They seem modern because, for a start, the idioms are entirely living and colloquial. They're not trying to impress anyone with their scholarship or their knowledge. They are just talking. And, because these poets are talking to people, they seem as they would have seemed to the people of that period. That's what makes them modern.

Basava's early life, as told in legend, is a characteristically Indian story of a spiritual search. Like the Buddha or Mahavira, the hero renounces his high birth, leaves home and wanders, before finding enlightenment. He was born in the early 1100s, in today's Karnataka. We're told that his parents, high-caste Brahmins, died young. He was raised by his extended family and trained in the Sanskrit tradition, but something pushed him to question their orthodox beliefs. He left home around the age of sixteen with an emphatic gesture. According to at least one version of the story, he didn't just cut ties with his family; he literally cut the sacred thread Brahmins wear to represent their 'twice-born' status.

At Kudalasangama, one of the great rivers of the south, the Krishna, receives a smaller tributary, the Malaprabha. From bank to bank, the confluence is about a mile wide. Basava spent several years here in spiritual retreat. 'Lord of the meeting rivers': the phrase became a regular refrain in his verses because it was at this river juncture, or *sangam*, that he discovered his personal god.

But Basava's spiritualism had a worldly edge. He eventually moved to the city of Kalyana and became, of all things, an accountant. Marrying strategically, he rose to the rank of chief treasurer to the local king. But as with Wallace Stevens, insurance executive, or T. S. Eliot, bank clerk, or Philip Larkin, librarian, the day job belied the fullness of the life.

In the West, poetry is sometimes seen as an indulgence. But in India it's been an essential medium of thought – partly because, for much of the subcontinent's history, few had pen and paper or the opportunity to know their uses. Instead, Indians had to think in rhythm and metre so that thought became memorable, able to carry mathematics, philosophy, political and religious ideas through time and space. And across Indian history, poetic verse has been a central medium of intellectual expression. It also became a means of political assertion and social critique.

Basava's ideas and his spiritual devotion, as well as the difficulty of achieving it, are expressed in his *vachanas*, a rhythmic form of poetic prose which developed in the Kannada language and which Basava perfected.

> Like a monkey on a tree
> it leaps from branch to branch
> how can I believe or trust

this burning thing, this heart?
It will not let me go
to my father,
my lord of the meeting rivers.

Kalyana became the centre of the vachana movement and Basava its leader. The poets of this tradition, who came mostly from the lower castes and included a number of women, were known as *vachana-karas*, 'makers of utterances' – an appropriately artisanal description. The vachana poets embraced the local language, Kannada, not the customary literary language, Sanskrit. In the adamantine Sanskrit tradition of religious texts in which Basava was raised, the emphasis is on *sruti* – what is heard or received from the priest or pandit. But vachana signifies what is said – a direct address, immediate and unrefracted. 'If one speaks,' Basava wrote, 'it should be like a dagger of "crystal".'

You are a blacksmith if you heat the iron,
A washerman if you wash clothes
A weaver if you lay the warp
A Brahmin if you read the Vedas.
False, utterly false, are the stories of divine birth.
The higher type of man is the man
Who knows himself.

At Kalyana, Basava's double life multiplied: in addition to being a treasurer and poet, he also emerged as the chief teacher of the proselytizing community of Virashaivas ('militants of Shiva'). The movement's origins are obscure, and its philosophy sometimes esoteric, but it clearly had a disruptive practical force. All over Kudalasangama and some parts of Karnataka there are romantic images, icons and drawings of Basava: an open, ardent face, with a moustache befitting a poetic revolutionary, and three horizontal tilak markings on his forehead that declare him a follower of Shiva.

Basava and the Virashaivas considered all members of their community equal. They mocked religious authority and social order, finding an alternative source of power in individual devotion, open to all. Strikingly, given that this was the twelfth century, women got the same treatment as men – at least in theory. Each kind, each caste and each individual was considered deserving of dignity and respect.

> The crookedness of the serpent
> is straight enough for the snake-hole.
>
> The crookedness of the river
> is straight enough for the sea.
>
> And the crookedness of our Lord's men
> is straight enough for our Lord!

The object of Basava's ridicule was not just high Brahminism, but also the skittishness of folk beliefs. Those who saw gods in their pots, combs, bowstrings and cups would be mocked.

To some post-colonial critics, A. K. Ramanujan, whose modern translations, in the volume *Speaking of Siva*, brought Basava and other vachana poets back to life in the English language, gave an overly modern interpretation of their work – portraying them almost as individual dissenters in the Protestant mould. It's a caution worth considering. Yet in many translations Basava's verses speak of struggle and self-doubt, and of his anti-establishment devotional community, which believed in direct service to God, not to political or priestly power. In this, some see Virashaivism as a strand of the bhakti tradition, one of India's most powerful religious forms of popular social reform and change (see **12 Kabir and 15 Mirabai**).

Bhakti was a periodically resurgent tradition that motivated a deep devotion. Like the vachana poets, the bhakti saints and their followers rejected the idea that God could only be accessed through the Sanskrit-uttering Brahmins. Instead, they spoke proudly in India's common, everyday languages. (The name bhakti comes from the word *bhaj*, which means to share, and bhakti worship often took congregational forms quite different from orthodox rituals.)

Bhakti could be a hard path. Even as Basava cajoled people into finding their own personal relationships with God, he was candid about the psychological anguish it caused. When a twelfth-century follower chose to estrange him or herself so arrantly from social convention, there was usually no going back.

> Don't you take on
> This thing called bhakti
> Like a saw
> It cuts when it goes
> And it cuts again
> When it comes.

The flow of the Krishna river has now been altered by the Almatti dam, completed in 2005, which submerged many of the fields around Kudalasangama. But the engineers managed to save Basava's *samadhi*, his last resting place – and even give it an added mystery. At the bottom of a deep spiral stairwell, about forty metres below the sangam where the two rivers join, is a canopied memorial, where people come to pray and make offerings to Basava.

Today, the memory of Basava and his teachings is maintained by a substantial religious community called the Lingayats. To what might have been Basava's consternation, they function as a caste group, with their own internal hierarchy. There are some seven or eight million followers, concentrated in northern Karnataka. The name Lingayat comes from the lingam – in this case, a small polished stone or phallic object symbolizing Shiva – which members of the community wear in a pouch around their necks. Though a religious minority, they are a force in Karnataka's electoral politics.

Near the end of Basava's life, his radicalism proved his personal undoing. In challenging the social and political order, he took a step too far and sanctioned an inter-caste marriage. The marriage was to join two children from his community of followers: a boy, born an outcaste, and a girl, born a Brahmin. The orders from his offended king were brutal. Members of the wedding party had their eyes gouged out. Their bodies were trampled by elephants in the streets. Rioting ensued, as Basava's outraged followers ignored their guru's pleas not to turn violent. Before long, the king was murdered, the Virashaiva community was scattered, and a broken Basava fled the city. His death came shortly after.

The episode is the subject of a play, *Taledanda*, by Girish Karnad. He explains:

> I wrote the play in 1990 when there were caste riots going on in north India, and it seemed absolutely relevant, because many of the issues are issues that are still alive today. You see, the whole idea of egalitarianism, of caste, everyone being together was beautiful in theory. Everyone loved it. But what happened is that they made the mistake of putting it into practice, and a Brahmin girl was married to a lower-caste boy from the cobbler community. Now if it was the other way round, it's OK – Brahmins are allowed to marry women from lower castes. But this was unthinkable, and there was a tremendous reaction against this wedding. The whole movement came to an end overnight just like that, because of that one wedding. It's a very fascinating episode, because it could happen today. It's still very raw. That's what makes Basava's vachanas so relevant.

In some of his vachanas, Basava noted how arbitrary the gods could be at the end of a man's life. No number of rituals or generous deeds could guarantee favour, because the gods would do as they damned well pleased. Still, he mused about his inability to curry last-minute favour with Shiva in the royal way – by furiously building temples, as a rajaraja, or 'king of kings', might do.

Does Basava sound worried, though? It's as if he's known the answer all along – that in exceptional cases, like this one, words outlast the great constructions of kings.

> The rich
> Will make temples for Shiva.
> What shall I,
> A poor man, do?
>
> My legs are pillars,
> The body the shrine

INCARNATIONS

The head a cupola
Of gold

Listen, O lord of the meeting rivers,
Things standing shall fall,
But the moving ever shall stay.

11
Amir Khusrau

The Parrot of India
1253–1325

Night's just falling over a green and tranquil stretch of south Delhi – one of those enclaves where serried ranks of Audis and BMWs stand ready behind driveway gates. You'd never guess, pausing outside the five-star Oberoi Hotel, that you're a short walk from the still-beating heart of a medieval city.

Across a busy flyover, through a maze of thrumming byways, you'll find hawkers selling prayer caps and shawls, rose petals and kebabs. As the lane narrows, the crowd grows conspicuously poorer, with many people begging for alms. At a canopied gully that feels like a tunnel, the pace of footsteps starts to quicken, and suddenly a green archway appears. It opens into a courtyard of carved pillars and filigreed screens. Hidden at the centre of this old labyrinth, this irruption of history, is a tomb: the *dargah* of the thirteenth-century poet Amir Khusrau.

Khusrau called himself *Tuti-yi-Hind*, 'The Parrot of India'. The title hints at his ability to flit between roles and voices during his long life. By turns warrior, court poet and passionate Sufi devotee, he was above all a quick-witted literary survivor. His sensitivity to the tastes of all manner of patrons and audiences, added to his faith in Sufism, have helped his words endure for 700 years.

He was a poet of profound ambiguity. The Mughal emperor Jahangir, who ruled a vast dominion from Delhi three centuries after Khusrau's death, was said to joke about a court singer who, asked to explain one of Khusrau's lyrics, perished from the exertion. In those lyrics, layered with meanings, perspectives suddenly shift, much as they do in the imperial metropolis that was his home:

There is a prosperous and populous city
Where fragments of moon gleam at every turn.
Each fragment holds a shard of my shattered heart.

A man of many names, he was known also as Amir Khusrau Dihlavi – one who belongs to Delhi. He was the first to bring the city into the literary imagination – and to give it one. Khusrau's Delhi was compared by one of his contemporaries, the historian Ziya al-Din Barani, to Baghdad and Cairo, Constantinople and Jerusalem. As it would become again after the Partition of 1947, it was in large part a refugee city: a beneficiary in its day of an influx of émigrés from west and central Asia, fleeing the Mongol conquests. Scholars, religious thinkers, artisans and poets settled there in such numbers that it came to be known as the Qubbat al-Islam, the Dome of Islam. And Delhi had riches too – plundered bounty that fed the Persianate tastes of the successive Afghan and Turkic Sultans who sat atop a north Indian culture strongly, though by no means unequivocally, Hindu.

In this culturally layered and mobile society, Khusrau was a marvel of linguistic and social dexterity. So artfully did his verses, composed in Persian and in the local language of Hindavi (the precursor to modern-day Urdu), seem to integrate the traditions of Sufi Islam and Hindu India that, in the twentieth century, the founding fathers of the modern Indian state made him a mascot of cultural harmony. But his style wasn't about reconciling differences between Hindu and Muslim cultures; rather, it spoke *across* beliefs and traditions.

There's a cinematic quality to the story of Amir Khusrau's life: it is outsized, over-dramatized even, but it nevertheless captures something about the often violent flux of his time. From his writing, we know his father was driven from his home in the Turkic regions of central Asia by Mongol invasions and brought to India, possibly as a slave; he later became a devout soldier in the ranks of a Delhi sultan. Khusrau's mother, born a Hindu, had converted to Islam. A decade or so after the marriage, her husband died in battle and Khusrau, their precocious second son, now eight, was sent to Delhi to live with his prosperous grandfather.

There, the story goes, he met a man from the same region as his father, who would eventually change his life: Nizam al-Din Auliya, one the great saints of India's Sufi tradition. Nile Green, Professor of History at the University of California, Los Angeles, explains: 'According to tradition, Amir Khusrau meets Nizam al-Din Auliya when he's a child, and even as a kind of child protégé, if you like, a kind of medieval Persianate Mozart. He's said to have improvised for Nizam al-Din the verse:

> *Tu an shahi ke bar aiwan-e-qasrat*
> *Kabutar gar nashinad baz gardad*

> You are the great king that,
> if a pigeon should sit on the roof of his palace,
> it will become a hawk.

This fabled meeting would help secure Khusrau's place in Indian history – but not before he had lived through religious war, imprisonment, innumerable wine-induced hangovers and unparalleled celebrity as a poet in the royal courts.

Although Khusrau started composing verse when very young, like most poets, then and now, he had to make a living. So he followed his father's example and became a fighter for Muslim rule. He was just five years old when the Mongols sacked Baghdad, the centre of the Abbasid Caliphate, which at one point ruled from north India to Algiers. As a young man, Khusrau took part in several campaigns against the Mongols and for the expansion of Islam, before he was captured – a traumatic experience that he later tried to put into words.

The Muslim martyrs dyed the desert with their blood, while the Muslim captives had their necks tied together like so many flowers into garlands. I was also taken prisoner, and from fear that they would shed my blood, not a drop of blood remained in my veins . . . My tongue was parched and dry from excessive thirst and my stomach seemed to have collapsed for want of food. They left me nude like a leafless tree in winter or a flower that has been much lacerated by thorns.

Eventually Khusrau escaped, returning to Delhi and transforming himself from a soldier into a poet. He used family connections to enter the *shahi majlis* or royal gatherings where, in the company of musicians and young boys, poets extemporized, competing with each other in a sort of medieval poetry slam. Nile Green describes the milieu:

> The king and his closest companions are gathering round, no doubt drinking a great deal of wine – wine is one of the key subjects of the poetry that Amir Khusrau and other Persian poets of the period write about. And while they're sitting there getting drunk and listening to music, Amir Khusrau or other *nadim*, other drinking companions, would simply improvise on a theme that the sultan or another patron would throw out. 'Improvise me a poem on the mole on the cheek of this beautiful boy sitting here!' Immediately, they'd have to improvise in that way. If it was a good line, a good *bait*, a good couplet, then perhaps the king would throw the poet a gold coin or two. And indeed Amir Khusrau gets his first pen name, Sultani, precisely after the name of one of these gold coins.

The Persian poetry of the court revelled in multiple registers, winking between worldly passion and spiritual ecstasy. Khusrau fast became an adept, weaving subtle innuendos into his popular songs. There is plenty of homoeroticism in his verse, which endears him to modern social progressives, and certainly pleased those sultans with a taste for young boys, though the more puritanical might choose to hear it as innocent praise of the city:

> O Delhi and its artless idols,
> Who wear turbans and crooked beards,
> They drink the blood of lovers openly,
> Although they drink wine secretly.
> They do not obey commands because
> They are made wilful by their extreme beauty.
> Muslims have become sun-worshippers
> Due to these saucy and innocent Hindus.
> These pure Hindu boys

Have caused me to go to ruin and to drink.
Ensnared in their curly tresses
Khusrau is like a dog with a collar.

Khusrau's playfulness flowed from his use of a rhetorical device he claimed to have invented, *iham*, meaning 'of the imagination'. For Khusrau, the poet must unveil the multiple meanings of words, so as to stimulate the audience's imagination. Equally, though, the audience must bring to the poem enough subtlety of intelligence to uncover the poet's intended meaning.

Khusrau was entertaining royals at a particularly turbulent period in the history of Delhi; in his adulthood, five sultans would rise and fall. As he sycophantically celebrated the virtues of patron after patron, he was invited to join ever-larger courts. The last one he served was centred at Tughlaqabad, a once grand fortified city, now a hauntingly desolate place surrounded by modern-day Delhi's relentless sprawl. These were courts rife with feuds, betrayals and murder – not the best environments for writerly contemplation. Still, somehow, he continued to be inventive in his work, writing poems and verse in every genre he knew.

Soon he became the most admired court poet of his time. But his words suggest a creeping exhaustion, the medieval equivalent of burnout. He wrote of being enslaved at his patron's feet, of drinking his ruler's dregs. The Parrot of India was rich, much admired – and seemingly depressed.

Composing panegyric kills the heart,
Even if the poetry is fresh and elegant.

Though Amir Khusrau is buried at the Delhi dargah, the larger shrine complex is dedicated not to him but to the man entombed beside him: Nizam al-Din Auliya, the Sufi master Khusrau first met in his grandfather's house. Sufism flourished in India during the era in which Khusrau lived. It offered mystical unity with God, with different Sufi masters teaching their own paths, or *tariqa*, to that end. The mystic states and secrets of Sufism could not be learned from books, however – only through the close bond between spiritual teacher and devotee.

When Khusrau was aged around fifty, he turned to Nizam al-Din for spiritual strength. The mystic had a compound – a sort of parallel court – in Ghiyaspur, a village on the edges of Delhi. Among his many devotees were other artists and intellectuals who sought refuge from palace politics. There, under Nizam al-Din's protection, Khusrau finally found a stable home.

Nile Green believes the tenuousness of life at court may have broken Khusrau. 'He was working in that extremely tense environment, with a couple of quite psychotic sultans, very bloodthirsty figures,' Green says. 'I can't help but think that it was the stress of that environment that drove Amir Khusrau – not as a poet, but as an ordinary human being trying to do his job in court – to the solace and the comfort and the sympathy of the Sufi environment.'

Increasingly, Khusrau seemed to consider himself a *Turk-e Hindi*, an Indian Turk. When accused by a contemporary of stylistic blemishes in his verse, Khusrau struck back with pride and irritation:

> I am an Indian Turk, I reply in Hindavi;
> I have no Egyptian candy with which to speak to an Arab.

It was a signal that the ethnic origins he shared with his master were becoming more important to him. His work expressed what would come to be seen as the ideal of Sufi devotion: a merging of identity between master and follower. In some of his best-known lyrics, there's also a sense of rich friendship with Nizam al-Din – an equal relationship of the sort that would have been unimaginable with the sultans:

> I have become you, you have become me.
> I have become life, you have become body.
> From now on, let no one say that
> I am other and you are another.

Even more than Khusrau's Sufi devotional poems or Persian verses, his popular songs – *qawwalis* and lyric *ghazals* he composed in

Hindavi – have sustained his fame over the centuries. Through many generations, Khusrau's songs were transmitted orally; by the time they were written down in the eighteenth and nineteenth centuries, a huge body of songs, poems and verses had been attributed to him. In the decades after India's independence, many of them – rearranged – became staples of Indian cinema. Although a fair number might not actually have been composed by Khusrau, they were nevertheless absorbed into his legend.

Javed Akhtar, a poet and master songwriter of contemporary Indian cinema, emphasizes how embedded Khusrau – 'an intellectual giant with a multifaceted personality' – has become in the Indian imagination. 'This concept of Sufi poetry, this concept of an amalgamation of dialects and a language called Urdu, it has all started from Khusrau,' he says. 'And we've internalized what he started so much that we are not even conscious that we are doing it.'

Partly as a result of the fluent combination in his lyrics of Persian tropes and imagery, and metaphors drawn from the Indian landscape, Khusrau became an embodiment of the nation's unofficial motto, 'unity in diversity'. When Gandhi listened to Hindu and Muslim musicians playing and singing Khusrau together, he would ask, 'When shall we see the same fraternal union in other affairs of our life?'

Today in India, Khusrau's Persian is read by only a handful of scholars. In Iran and Afghanistan, where he might find many more readers, the Parrot of India is seen as too Indian a writer to be part of the literary canon. His is the fate of those whose linguistic universe, or cosmopolis, has been chopped up by the boundaries of national identity. Across north India, however, millions of people still turn for comfort to the melancholic beauty of Khusrau's Hindavi songs, and his tomb, in the city he loved, is very much a living shrine.

Like Khusrau's poetry, Delhi, too, remains ambiguous in its cultural mixing – not a melting pot, but home to hundreds of different communities, living adjacent to one another, often with benign indifference. As with Khusrau himself, a certain vision – often brittle – of a cosmopolitan, tolerant nation has been projected onto the city. But Delhi is also a hard place, marked by gross inequalities, spasms of communal violence and the peremptoriness of political power – a city that requires you to speak in different voices to different people, and that might, as Khusrau said, break your heart.

Every Thursday, in the dargah's enclosure, musicians in shimmering turquoise kurtas, their fingers bejewelled with bling, perform qawwalis attributed to Khusrau in rapturous, resonant voices for worshippers and visitors of all backgrounds. But beyond the dargah, and the medieval warren in which it sits, north India's present-day politics can be a good deal less accommodating of religious diversity. As elections approach, tensions between religious communities get exploited by major political parties. Newspapers tell of riots over the desecration of a mosque, of a church destroyed, of forced conversions in neighbouring states.

The world of cultural amalgamation and mixing that some think Khusrau inspired can seem illusory, even unnecessary, to many people in power today. It is a troubling thought – one that makes me reach back for Khusrau's artful straddling of awkward differences. His faith in the civility of this city rings in my head, and has me hoping that he's right:

> If a Khurasani, Greek, or Arab comes here
> he will not face any problems,
> for the people will treat him kindly, as their own,
> making him feel happy and at ease.

12
Kabir

'Hey, you!'
c.1440–c.1518

The Jaipur Literature Festival, held every winter in the capital of Rajasthan, is the world's largest free literary festival, and perhaps the most freewheeling. In 2015, a quarter of a million people came to hear some 300 writers speak. At a time when free expression in India is under pressure from many directions – heavy-handed governments, thin-skinned communities of caste and religion, offendables of all sorts – the podiums and shamiana tents of the Jaipur festival have become pop-up shops for thinkers with contrarian positions.

To judge by how often he's invoked, the festival's guiding spirit is the fifteenth-century poet Kabir – a man who is also venerated across northern India as a saint, almost a god. It's a rare being who manages to be claimed by conservative religious sects and the liberal literati both. But the broad-spectrum adulation might have made him uneasy: Kabir was an aggressive critic of institutions and orthodoxies in pretty much any form, a debunker of humbug in an unadorned poetic style. There is no other voice from the Indian past quite like his:

> Strutting about,
> A smirk on your face,
> Have you forgotten
> The ten months spent
> In a foetal crouch?
>
> Cremation turns you to ashes,
> Burial into a feast
> For an army of worms.

Your athlete's body's only clay,
A leaky pot,
A jug with nine holes.

As bees store up honey,
You gathered wealth.
But after you're dead,
This is what's said,
'Take away the corpse.
It stinks.'

Death undermining mortal follies and pretension: one of Kabir's favourite themes. These are his verses in translation by the poet Arvind Krishna Mehrotra. Like many of Kabir's poems, they are directed straight at you. 'Kabir challenges us,' says Linda Hess, a professor at Stanford University and a Kabir scholar. 'He says, "Hey, you! Listen!" Hey, you saint or you truth-seeker or you idiot or you brother or you mother or you priest, you mullah. Sometimes he challenges our foolishness, our blindness, our ignorance, our hypocrisy, our pretentiousness – all those kinds of things. And when we first encounter it we think he's talking about those other idiots and it's not about us. But of course he is talking about us.'

Benares, or Varanasi, is India's holiest city. Built on the western banks of the Ganga as the sacred river curves northwards through the eastern part of Uttar Pradesh, it's one of those places that seem to hold the whole world. In its streets and lanes you'll find relentless commerce and the pursuit of pleasure and perfection, from the finest betel leaf to the most refined classical music. Deep learning and deep poverty intermingle. Death is ever present in cremation rituals and, over loudspeakers or in concentrated silence, the living are everywhere at prayer. Hindus call Benares Kashi, the City of Light. It is said to be the god Shiva's favourite spot, and the great Kashi Vishwanath temple here is consecrated to him.

Among the city's thousands of shrines, dedicated to many different gods and saints, is the Kabir Chaura and mutth. This monastic compound in the heart of the city is built around what is said to be the hut where Kabir lived, the platform where he preached, and his samadhi, a shrine to his mortal remains. On display in one of the rooms is a pair of wooden sandals he supposedly wore.

Like the location of this shrine to Kabir, most stories about the poet's life are based on guesswork – or total *bakwaas*, as a modern-day Kabir might say. By some accounts, he was rescued from the abjection of being born low-caste by a Brahmin whom he had tricked into becoming his guru by tripping him on the ghats that lead down to the river Ganga as the Brahmin went for his morning bath. After Kabir's death, other stories say, his body was transformed into flowers – ensuring he was neither cremated by Hindus nor buried by Muslims, each of whom claimed him as their own. The only things we know for sure about Kabir, however, are that he was alive in the fifteenth century, composed poetry, came from a caste of Muslim weavers, and lived in Benares. And that's it.

So, instead of taking the Kabir pilgrimage tour organized by the monastery's disciples, you might visit Bazardiha, a poor, low-lying neighbourhood towards the western flank of the city that floods during the rainy season. The area is populated mostly by Sunni Muslims, who identify themselves by caste, a common practice for communities of different faiths across India. This is Kabir's lineage – low-caste Ansari, or Julaha, weavers.

'A weaver's son / Possessed of a weaver's / Patience,' Kabir once sang of himself. If those lines almost romanticize the labour, we should remember that, historically, even the name of Kabir's caste, Julaha, was a slur – basically, shorthand for poverty and ignorance. In Bazardiha, sitting in cramped rooms among men without enough work, you start to hear Kabir's insistent, urgent tone emerge. Patient weaver's son? Hardly. His is one of the most impatient, acerbic, fed-up voices in the Indian cultural canon. With Kabir, 'there's no beating about the bush,' Arvind Krishna Mehrotra says. 'He's always haranguing you, catching you by the collar, constantly drawing your attention to certain things – and he wants you to look at them in *his* way. So there is a great element of the didactic in him – telling you as directly as he can in a language that you will understand.'

*

You can only follow me if you are prepared to burn your house, Kabir said in another poem. For 'house' we might easily read 'bridges': he was an equal-opportunity offender, sparing no one with his scathing tongue. Religious men were particularly mocked – the Hindu pandits and Muslim (or, as they were still referred to back then, 'Turk') mullahs who said that only they could, for a fee, show low-caste individuals the way to God:

> If you say you're a Brahmin
> Born of a mother who's a Brahmin,
> Was there a special canal
> Through which you were born?
>
> And if you say you're a Turk
> And your mother's a Turk,
> Why weren't you circumcised
> Before birth?

As Mehrotra puts it, 'There's no aspect of religion that Kabir leaves untouched, whether it's a sacred thread or a place of pilgrimage or a holy book or praying so many times a day.'

Though born Muslim, today Kabir is one of the most famous sants, or saints, of the broadly Hindu movement known as bhakti, which often used poetry and song – composed not in Sanskrit, but in local spoken languages – to upend social orthodoxies. The rise of bhakti devotion in north India paralleled the spread of the Sufi movement in Islam; both embraced the idea of a personal relationship with God. Priests or mullahs didn't matter; precise ritual didn't matter; caste didn't matter. Sincere avowals of faith, no matter how rough-hewn or coarsely spoken, still had the power to reach the ears of God.

> I'm Rama's slave
> And Rama brought me to
> The slave mart where Rama
> Is the one who buys and sells.
>
> He puts me up for sale,
> But you can't buy what's Rama's.

He keeps me off the block.
Well then I can't be sold.

My body's dead
My memory's blank.
My master's name, says Kabir,
Is all I know.

Woven into bhakti as individual worship were also strands of social protest and even rebellion, and much of what Kabir composed was experienced collectively, by congregations of followers. Most Indians know Kabir's words – or words that are ascribed to him – through his songs, which have been performed in every possible style, from the incandescent renditions of another independent spirit, the classical vocalist Kumar Gandharva, to the qawwalis of Fareed Ayaz Qawwal, to the smooth Sufi gospel style of Sonam Kalra. The aspect of performance was always central to bhakti and could help to instil psychological fortitude in people who had been excluded from other forms of power. For the oppressed in India, as for the slaves of nineteenth-century America, collective singing could be both consolation and a musical assertion of strength in numbers.

After studying performances of Kabir's work, Linda Hess believes that the spirit of his poetry is more in song than in texts. Kabir, she notes, made fun of people who were too dependent on books. There is a studied intention in his choice of everyday, simple words, and there's craft in the rhythmic arrangements he gave them, lifting phrases from ordinary speech into song.

Like many other early Indian poets, Kabir probably could not read or write. He had to find other means to keep his poetry alive. The metrical word beats of his verses, called *padas*, made them easily memorizable, which allowed them to be handed from singer to singer, and from community to community – easily memorizable, but also open to improvisation and collective revision. Every singer can bring his own dialect, her own language to what was supposedly first Kabir's. Different communities add different nuances; lines are dropped and added, tone is varied. But even as the verses undergo changes in performance, they keep a family resemblance, as blues or jazz performances do.

Kabir's verses have travelled across India from Benares westwards to Rajasthan, and east to Bengal. They've also travelled across the world, translated by major poets. Rabindranath **Tagore** (32), Ezra Pound, Czesław Miłosz and Robert Bly have all produced their own versions of Kabir's verse – though Arvind Krishna Mehrotra's translations are by some way the most audacious. 'The same poem has existed in three different manuscript traditions, in three different ways,' Mehrotra says. 'That frees the translator from sticking too closely to the original, because at the end of day there *is* no original.' One of Mehrotra's boldest translations echoes Kabir's perennial theme:

> 'Me shogun.'
> 'Me bigwig.'
> 'Me the chief's son.
> I make the rules here.'
>
> It's a load of crap.
> Laughing, skipping,
> Tumbling, they're all
> Headed for Deathville.
>
> In the blink
> Of an eye, says Kabir,
> The king will be
> Separated from his kingdom.

In Benares, the weaving community that Kabir came from has been foundering for decades – a decline unrelieved by the growth of India's national economy. The artisan tradition was first undercut by power looms, then cheap Chinese yarns. What's left of it today is being further crippled by innovations like WhatsApp: traders flash the sari designs of Benares weavers to print shops in Surat, which mass-produce saris at a quarter of the price of hand-woven pieces.

Kabir himself has suffered a similar appropriation. Benares's Kabir temple and mutth are run by higher-caste Hindus, who have made him one of their own. On the tended grounds of the chaura, you can see life-size plaster statues, burnished in copper-coloured paint, of the poet leading a band of his singing followers, preaching and enacting various scenes from the story of his life. This is Kabir as religious figurehead. His devotees have even assembled his words into a holy book, the *Bijak*.

It's one of the ways radical lives get assimilated. The powerful make a house pet out of the people who mock and excoriate them. But upper-caste Hindus aren't the only ones who try to pocket Kabir's memory. Leftists and progressives see him as a radical social critic or messenger of inter-faith harmony; lower-caste activists have adopted him as an anti-caste evangelist; and still others hear in him the voice of a benign humanist. Mehrotra captures the paradox well: 'Every now and then someone comes up and tells you exactly how it is. And what Indians tend to do is – they absorb him into the pantheon. Which is exactly what has happened to Kabir. He said as bluntly as he could things about Hindus, Muslims, the caste system – none of it has made any difference to anyone. It's not that he changed the world.'

The eastern banks of the Ganga river, opposite the ghats of Kashi, are largely deserted. It's a swathe of sand, some neglected land, and a few fields. The area is known as Katesar, but locals sometimes speak of it as Magahar, a metaphorical reference to the actual town of that name, some 200 kilometres away. It's considered a place of ill-luck. In the *Bijak*, it's said that if you die there, you come back as a donkey – exactly the opposite of what happens if you die on the other side of the bank.

Kabir quite possibly came to these desolate shores when his poetic dissidence got him exiled. Or perhaps he exiled himself here. But then of course, I'm probably making this story up, just as so many others have been made up about Kabir. Still, I imagine him coming here, gazing across the slow-flowing water and thinking about the absurdity of life in the busy world of the city.

> I've squandered my whole life
> in Shiva's city:
> Now that it's time to die,
> I've risen and come to Magahar.

Kashi, Magahar: for a thoughtful man,
they're one and the same.
My devotion's depleted:
how will it land me on the other shore?

Today in India, dissenting views are often exiled – forced out of the public sphere by state interference and by religious and social groups within civil society. Claiming offence, these groups make threats to the public order, pressuring courts and authorities to invoke colonial-era restrictions on free speech. Books and documentary films are frequently banned. Publishers are intimidated into censoring their authors. Celebrity voices such as Salman Rushdie's have been silenced – even, famously, at liberal havens like the Jaipur festival. Meanwhile, other writers and thinkers, less well known, are being muffled all over the country. So now perhaps it's as important as ever to reject reverent incarnations of Kabir and recognize the edgier social critic and sceptic – the one whose verses are rightly woven into the long, rich, often-endangered tradition of dissent in Indian life.

13
Guru Nanak

The Discipline of Deeds
1469–1539

Indian religions love their wandering heroes. There's the Buddha, who wandered for six years; Mahavira, who doubled that; and the many saints and yogis of Hinduism who meander homeless all across the Indian past. The fifteenth-century founder of the Sikh religion, Guru Nanak, also took to the road – for some twenty-three years. He made it as far afield as Mecca and Medina, as well as to the mythic mountain Sumeru, meeting emperors and carpenters, sages and thugs along the way – or so say the *Janam Sakhis*, a collection of hagiographical stories about his life.

But there's a crucial difference between Nanak and the Buddha or Mahavira, who renounced their families and communities to find spiritual truth. After Nanak achieved enlightenment, he returned to the fertile fields of his homeland, the Punjab, and made room in his religious life for members of his previous, unenlightened domesticity. For him, devotion did not require asceticism, renunciation or an attachment to holy men and their institutions, but what scholars of the Sikh religion have called a 'disciplined worldliness'.

The writer and diplomat Navtej Sarna recounts a well-known story that captures something of Nanak's philosophy and personality:

He's supposed to have met a large number of very wise *siddhas*, the old spiritual sages who have gone away and have been meditating in the Himalayas for years and years. And they ask him, 'Child, what is the situation down in the world?' So he said, 'What can there be? If all the wise men have come here, what do you expect to be happening there?' So, from this you can see that his belief was that this

95

world is a real world, and you have to seek salvation within it. There is no other world to seek salvation in. That is cowardliness – renunciation of this world. You have to seek salvation through your living.

Nanak insisted that religious beliefs are not just to be felt in this world, but should change it. As a result, his life and afterlife, through the religion he founded, have often challenged India's other communities of faith, including at times that most modern one – the nation.

Nanak was known during his lifetime as Baba Nanak (the title of Guru came later). He was born in 1469 into a relatively well-to-do family. His father was possibly an accountant, and his education may have included Persian (the signifier of a superior education at the time), taught to him by a Muslim tutor. He later wrote hundreds of beautiful hymns and poems in his own language, Punjabi, drawing on Persian and Arabic words – verses that often combine poetry, spiritual striving and agricultural labour into hard-working metaphors:

> As a team of oxen we are driven
> By the ploughman, our teacher.
> By the furrows made are thus writ
> Our actions – on the earth, our paper.
> The sweat of labour is as beads
> Falling by the ploughman as seeds sown.
> We reap according to our measure.
> Some for ourselves to keep, some to others give.
> O Nanak, this is the way to truly live.

The Punjab lands that inspired much of his verse were not the isolated, parochial village communities of popular imagination. Invaders, commercial riches and ideas were continuously passing through: from India's northwest towards the Gangetic plains, a steady flow of culture and conquest. During Nanak's lifetime, the central Asian warlord Babur, a descendant of Timur, or Tamerlane, swept across the Punjab, captured Delhi from the Lodhi dynasty in 1526, and declared himself the first of the Mughal rulers of India.

A mix of religious sects and teachers also swirled through the Punjab, inspiring new experiments in belief and practice. Sufi Islam flourished in cities like Lahore and Multan, though most people remained followers of various forms of Hinduism. Besides Shiva worship, there were sects of yogis known as Naths, who drew on Tantric traditions. Bhakti movements associated with sants such as Kabir were also popular.

In some legends, Kabir was an influence on, or even a teacher of, Nanak. That wasn't actually the case, but the two certainly shared a terse disdain for religious authorities of all stripes. As one of Nanak's verses put it:

> The Qazi tells untruths and eats filth,
> The Brahmin kills and takes a holy bath,
> The blind yogi knows not the true way,
> All three make for mankind's ruin.

Even the way Nanak dressed had a religiously polemical edge. According to Navtej Sarna, he wore the long, loose shirt of a Muslim dervish, but in the ochre colour of a Hindu sannyasi; around his waist he tied a white cloth belt, like a fakir; around his neck hung a bone necklace. Unlike many other Indian religious figures who went barefoot, he wore sandals, each a different kind and colour. He topped the outfit off with a Sufi Qalandar cap partially covered by a flat, short turban. It was a sartorial farrago that seems to have been styled to bewilder, perhaps even provoke.

Philosophically, however, Nanak was no bricoleur. In one of his most famous sayings, he proclaimed, 'Na ko Hindu hai na ko Mussalman' – there is neither Hindu nor Muslim. That could be heard as a pulling down of barriers between the faiths, even a message of reconciliation, and it has become common to interpret Nanak's teachings as aimed at a synthesis of the two major religions of the subcontinent. That's not so: he was turning his back on both, in order to create something new. As he expressed it in another well-known aphorism, 'Neither the Veda nor the Kateb [the book of the Qur'an] know the mystery.'

Nanak, like Kabir, believed in a universal God that was *nirankar*, without form. This formless divinity could nevertheless be discovered, almost like an inner voice, operating within us all. One of Nanak's most powerful verses points towards this presence. 'There is but one God, true is His Name,' begins the Mul Mantra of Nanak's *Japji* – verses to be recited, without music, at daybreak.

> The Creator, fearless, without rancour,
> Timeless, unborn, self-existent
> By God's grace he is known
> Meditate on Him
> He was true
> In the beginning, in the primal time . . .

But where Kabir remained at heart a rebel and a critic, and where both Sufism and many of the bhakti movements of his time centred on personal devotion and salvation, Nanak brought into being a belief system that required of its followers not just worship but social action, and the creation of a community of belief and works.

Indians can be notoriously fussy about food – what's in it, who cooked it, who served it. The concern is rooted in the caste system, with its fearful taboos about purity and pollution, and its humiliating rules about who can and can't prepare food and who is allowed to eat together. Despite decades of reform efforts, in rural and urban India today there remain upper-caste people who will break a cup if a Dalit has touched it. Eating a meal cooked by a Dalit or someone from a different religion? Unthinkable still for many Indians.

The Sikh *langar*, a communal kitchen and collective meal, blows apart these rules. Food cooked in a Sikh temple, or gurudwara, is served by volunteers to anyone who comes. Everyone eats together, seated on the floor. It's an equalizing act, an effacing of caste and other boundaries. While many hungry people go to the langars in Delhi's gurudwaras, or in Birmingham, or the two in Queens, New York, because the food is good and free, there's a decidedly political dimension: a small protest against old ways of thinking that are diminishing but by no means dead.

This everyday act of radicalism was introduced by Nanak. In his fifties, when he had finished wandering, he established a village at Kartarpur, in the Punjab, on the banks of the Ravi river, and lived there for the last two decades of his life with his wife and two sons. The members of this community, or *panth*, became his first followers or 'learners' – the original meaning of 'Sikh'. The Guru taught his disciples to practise an intense personal devotion to the formless, ever-present God, as well as to pursue an active life in the world. And he cemented the bonds of the community by having everyone, regardless of caste or gender or status, eat together on the floor.

Navtej Sarna explains the significance of the langar:

> If one God created this whole creation then how could he have created men differently – men and women for that matter? And if you're sitting on the floor and eating off leaves it brings this message through even more clearly. When you take it back five-hundred-odd years, you can see what a major achievement this must have been. Society was not only marked by the rich and the poor, but it was also very straight-laced between the castes and sub-castes.

Nanak also knew how to use food in an incendiary way. It's said in the *Janam Sakhis* that he challenged the vegetarianism of certain Hindus by deliberately cooking the meat of a deer on an auspicious day. 'Those who abjure meat,' he wrote in one of his verses,

> and sit holding their noses,
> Eat men at night;
> They make a show of hypocrisy for others
> But have no true knowledge of God.

The inclusion from the very beginning of women within the panth created a significant legacy. It is said that Nanak's first follower was his elder sister, Nanaki, with whom he was close. Sikh families were encouraged to educate their girls, and in later centuries women were allowed to read from the scriptures during public worship. It is no surprise that today many Sikh women are confident professionals with distinguished careers in public service. They've perhaps benefited from the relative equality which their religion encouraged for centuries.

If the real and metaphorical dimensions of agrarian society and manual labour, and the cycle of the seasons, remained a hallmark of Nanak's verse, they also shaped his religious vision. 'Liberation in Sikhism is to be obtained by living the life of a householder – through marriage, through work,' the writer and journalist Hartosh Singh Bal says. In one story from the hagiographic tradition which captures this ethos, Nanak goes to a rich merchant's house to dine, but when he looks at the man's hands, he notices they don't have calluses. 'So he says, "This is not a house where I can eat".'

Kirat karni, or working with your hands, remains one of the three basic tenets of Sikhism. The others are *naam japna*, or meditation on the names of the Supreme Being, as embodied by the verses of Nanak and his successors, which were collected in a holy book called the *Adi Granth*; and *wand chhakna*, or sharing some of your earnings through charitable giving. Bal says, 'If anybody is to distil the message of Sikhism as it is known to most people in ordinary belief, these are its three senses.'

Sikh identity did not emerge fully formed from Nanak's mind, however. Like most religions, the Sikhism we know today evolved by a long and gradual process. But because Sikhism is one of the newest of the major world religions, with a rich trail of documentation, we can gain a relatively clear view of its evolution.

Nanak was succeeded by nine other gurus who, over 200 years, helped to build and consolidate the Sikh faith. Over that time, the religion's differences from Islam and various strains of Hinduism sharpened, and confrontations with Muslim rulers and then Hindus grew more frequent.

The last of the gurus in the line Nanak founded was Gobind Singh, who, shortly before his death in 1708, abolished the role of Guru. After his sons were killed in the fight against the Mughals and their ruling agents, he wished to foreclose later struggles for succession within his own religion. In the place of a human hierarchy, he set a book, the *Guru Granth Sahib*, a remarkable work assembled by an earlier guru, which, in addition to the words of the gurus compiled in the *Adi Granth*, also contains verses by Kabir and other sants, as well as Sufi texts. From then on, this has been the religion's supreme guide.

But Gobind Singh's more radical innovation was to create the Khalsa, a brotherhood of initiates. His father had been executed at Delhi's Chandni Chowk by the Mughal emperor Aurangzeb for his refusal to give up his faith. Embattled against the Mughals and their regional military chiefs – many of them Hindu rajas – Gobind Singh saw a need for Sikhs to organize better to defend themselves, and henceforth, the traditions of martial action and martyrdom became important within Sikhism. In 1705 Gobind Singh composed a letter to Aurangzeb, the *Zafarnama*, which contains these lines, resonant across the history of the Sikhs:

> When all has been tried, yet
> Justice is not in sight,
> It is then right to pick up the sword,
> It is then right to fight.

The Khalsa would be that band of men dedicated to defending the religion. Membership was marked by five outward symbols, called 'the five Ks', that are still embraced – and worn – by many Sikhs today: the *kesh*, or long hair; the *kangha*, a small wooden comb; the *kirpan*, a curved dagger; the *kara*, a metal bracelet; and the *kacchaa*, a pair of loose breeches. According to Hartosh Singh Bal, these five, along with an unspoken sixth, form three pairs symbolizing power and restraint. 'Guru Gobind Singh says you have to think of these in terms of polar opposites,' Bal says.

> Hair in the Indian tradition – unshorn hair, loose hair – is a sign of spiritual power. The comb is a polar opposite – that is, spiritual power must be under a certain discipline. The kirpan is a sign of physical power, and the kara is a symbol of restraint on this. And the fifth symbol obviously goes with the unsaid idea of sexual power, tantric power, with the kacchaa as a symbol of restraint. So these three great forces of power in the Indian tradition must be harnessed in Sikhism, but they must be harnessed with a sense of restraint and control.

To other Indians, perhaps the most problematic dimension of Sikh identity has been the claim that Sikhs constitute their own *quam*, a term broadly meaning 'nation' which is often translated as 'people who stand together'. The urge among some Sikhs to establish the panth as a nation conceived in more modern terms goes back to the 1940s; it was, in part, a reaction to the demand for the creation of Pakistan as a homeland for the subcontinent's Muslims. The Partition of the subcontinent was in many ways most brutally felt in the Punjab, a region slit and torn by end-of-empire map-making. It created a large Sikh refugee population – many of whom fled for safety to Delhi – and the bright embers of a demand for a separate Sikh homeland, Khalistan.

In the 1980s, those embers were stoked into ferocious violence by radical young Sikh preachers, a supportive diaspora, and the subversion of democratic politics in the Punjab by India's leadership in New Delhi. In 1984, Prime Minister **Indira Gandhi (46)** ordered an assault on the Golden Temple at Amritsar, the site of the most important Sikh symbols of spiritual and temporal authority, which had become a fortified redoubt of Sikh militancy. Five months later, she was gunned down by her own Sikh bodyguards. Days of anti-Sikh massacres in the capital followed, in which more than 3,000 Sikhs are estimated to have been killed. The perpetrators of these massacres were never tried or convicted under the Indian justice system, and it took several years more of military repression before the Sikh secessionists were defeated. So deep was Sikh disaffection that it seemed hard to imagine their reintegration. And yet, barely twenty years later, India had a Sikh prime minister, Manmohan Singh. This isn't to suggest an easy story of acceptance and reconciliation. Martyrdom is a current that runs deep in the Sikh tradition, as does a powerful sense of justice. But there's also that recognition of needing to return from the mountain realm of sages and purist visions: to live down here, in the world.

14
Krishnadevaraya

'Kingship is Strange'
reigned 1509–1529

Imagine an imperial court in south India at the beginning of the sixteenth century. The king sits at the centre, flanked by women 'with eyes like blue sapphires', who are cooling the air with yak-tail fans. Seated in front of him, scholars discuss the fine points of Paninian grammar, atomistic philosophy and metaphysics. Warriors hold swords darkly glowing in the afternoon light, which filters across the hall, refracting through the jewelled crowns of defeated rivals, as it comes to rest on the king himself.

This king ruled over the largest empire ever in south India, and the description of his court comes from his favourite poet, the great Telugu writer Allasani Peddana. The king's capital, built at Hampi in the central Deccan, was called Vijayanagara, the 'City of Victory'.

His name was Krishnadevaraya, and he had a talent for turning conflict into order. Like quite a few triumphant Hindu kings of the precolonial era, he often gets recruited into Indian history's platoon of resisters to Muslim domination – in his case, against the sultanates of the Deccan whose borders edged the Vijayanagara empire. But Krishnadevaraya was a successful warrior ruling in a brutal age – a fact that lent itself to an unsentimental, tactical and highly flexible approach to politics, reminiscent of **Kautilya**'s (4).

Krishnadevaraya was also living at a moment when the literary imagination of south India was being revolutionized. 'The whole system underwent a kind of civilizational shift,' says David Shulman, Professor at the Hebrew University in Jerusalem and a scholar of south Indian literature. 'And one of the elements of that shift was the emergence of a new notion of the individual.' For Krishnadevaraya, this meant that, in addition to conquering and ruling, he embraced poetry, a form in which he could consider himself not just as a monarch, but as a human being too.

In his verse, he at times expressed disinterest in – even disdain for – the power that enabled him to rule. His attitude was a way to address the perennial conundrum of Hindu kingship: how to convert power into authority. The Hindu map of society drew boundaries between different social orders: power, wealth and status could never be consolidated in one group or person. Kings and warriors might have power. Wealth belonged to merchants and traders. Brahmins, of course, had status. A king might try to acquire authority by associating himself with those who had status – he could seek out Brahmins to support him – but neither king nor Brahmin could get too close to one another, for fear of blurring their own distinct characters. Another way, perhaps more risky for an ambitious king, was to appear not to be that interested in power at all – to renounce it, or at least to seem to.

> Oh! What is this glorious empire?
> What are these pleasures?
> Why these emotions?
>
> I've enjoyed this life without ever considering the path to freedom,
> but have I really lived?

Those are Krishnadevaraya's words – the words of an epicurean intellectual as well as a self-doubting king. 'One hears in the poetry of Krishnadevaraya sceptical tones, earthy, romantic, passionate tones,' Shulman says. 'When you read his work you have the sense that you are listening to an authentic, very subjective, unusual, creative and original voice.'

Krishnadevaraya was in his early twenties when he gained the Vijayanagara throne, in 1509. At the time, the empire was in the doldrums – weakened by famines and riven by internal family jealousies. He quickly turned around its fortunes, winning new lands and, as was the custom, endowing temples to thank the gods for his acquisitions. He expanded his capital, set in the rocky outcrops of Hampi, into a prospering city. When the writer V. S. Naipaul visited its ruins in the 1970s, his pulse quickened at what he saw as evidence of a purely Hindu bastion, resisting the Muslim tide engulfing India. In fact Vijayanagara was a heterogeneous place, absorbing a variety of religions. 'In this city', said a Portuguese visitor who thought it grander than Rome, 'you will find men belonging to every nation and people.'

That diversity was reflected in the city's mix of cultural and architectural styles. Architectural historian George Michell, who has studied and worked at Vijayanagara for four decades, was startled when he first saw some of the buildings Krishnadevaraya had put up in his capital. 'The whole thing is built in what we call a sultanate style,' Michell says about the imposing row of stables where the king's elephants were kept. The architects and builders seemed to have had knowledge, and perhaps experience, of the styles of rival sultan kings of the Deccan. 'So the question to ask,' says Michell, 'is, what the hell is this sultanate-type architecture of the so-called enemy doing in the middle of a royal centre of a Hindu imperial city?'

The answer, contends Michell, is that Krishnadevaraya's was 'a city and culture set up to be, in a way, what we would call cosmopolitan – that is, embracing all the known cultures and architectural techniques and styles of the period. That's what imperial culture is. It embraces everything.' The Vijayanagara kings were Hindu in their religious worship, and Krishnadevaraya was himself a devout worshipper of Vishnu. But in their secular activities – in fighting wars and administering their empire, in their courtly manners and even in their dress styles – they were influenced by the Islamic culture and standards of taste which they encountered in neighbouring and sometimes rival Muslim-ruled kingdoms, and also through their trading links with the Arab and central Asian world.

Krishnadevaraya, too, was shaped by these elements, but his driving concern was how to extend his own sway. He broke with the older Vijayanagara ruling style, which was based on sharing spoils with, and delegating regional authority to, kinsmen. Instead, he recruited warriors and administrators who didn't share clan or caste identities with the kingdom's hereditary elite. Some of these men were self-made and maverick, but he also brought in Brahmins. Krishnadevaraya promoted all of them to rule over his imperial conquests, and so secured their loyalty – a strategy that allowed him to mobilize large armies, as well as to enjoy the prestige that came of having the support of the priestly caste. By the middle of his reign, he had expanded his territory roughly 1,000 kilometres northeast, into today's Orissa.

Krishnadevaraya projected himself as the unifying centre of this spreading realm. His subjects spoke all the languages of south India. They worshipped Shiva and Vishnu. Many were Muslims. And some of those subjects were themselves kings. So among the titles used to describe Krishnadevaraya was *Hindurayasuratrana*, the 'Sultan over Hindu Kings'. In temple inscriptions we also find him described as *Yavanarajya-sthapanacharya*, 'The lord who established the kingdom of the Muslims'. By coining such curious, hybrid titles he was proclaiming himself a ruler who protected and advanced the interests of all under his command, whatever their religion or language; he was transforming himself from a king into an emperor. As Shulman puts it, 'He embodies this sort of integrative moment where a single major player, the Vijayanagaram king, could control nearly all of India's southern peninsula ... I think that's why he's remembered today as the last of the great universal south Indian kings.'

Emperors must command armies; but after conquest comes rule. To keep the throne, they must win allegiance and belief. **Ashoka** (5) had his dhamma and his rock edicts. **Rajaraja** (9) had his sky-scraping temple and his personality cult. Krishnadevaraya went for poetry.

Poems were regularly read in the great hall he had built, called 'Conquest of the World', which looks out on the boulder piles and rice paddies of Hampi. It was later said that Krishnadevaraya gathered around him in the hall eight great poets of the south Indian languages, including the greatest of them all, Allasani Peddana. Peddana, who described the scene with its blue-eyed women, philosophers and warriors, tells us of his king's true passion:

Seated enthroned in the hall known as 'Conquest of the World',
in the company of learned people,
he was struck by the joy of poetry, so he turned to me
and gently said:
'They say that out of the seven kinds of children a person may have,
the only one that lasts is a poem.
Make a poem for me, Peddanaraya . . . '

The work Peddana wrote for his king, the *Manucaritramu*, was perhaps the finest to come out of the Vijayanagara court. It tells the
story of the birth of Manu (the mysterious progeny of a divine cour-
tesan's unrequited passion for a Brahmin) and his development into
a human personality. According to Shulman, it's a narrative poem
about 'what it means to be a human being and how you can produce
a human being – what happens in terms of the inner workings of the
mind and the mind–body complex in order to make a real human
being come alive'.

When you read Peddana, and even Krishnadevaraya, you sense
that there's something explosive about Telugu literature of the sixteenth century. It mixes roguishness and decorum, divinity and
eroticism, a will to power and vertiginous self-doubt. Most strikingly, though, there's the upsurge of an interior voice, the creation of
a new, psychologically real sensibility. 'Books like you had never
seen before in India' began appearing in the language, Shulman says.
'The great breakthrough to a new kind of textual world happened in
Telugu.'

Telugu was not Krishnadevaraya's mother tongue, but as he
reached for a medium through which he could command the belief of
his manifold subjects, the language presented itself as a divinely
inspired choice. Like the architecture of his city, Krishnadevaraya's
own poetry had to reflect his complex ruling ideology – to show the
king as a universal imperial monarch, and at the same time worthy of
ruling as a Hindu over a caste-based society that believed that status,
power and wealth ought to be separated between the social orders.
Telugu was spoken by a large number of his subjects, including many
of his warrior chiefs, and its literary flowering was investing it with a

new status. To write in Telugu was to write in a language regarded with immense respect and pleasure among elites, but also the wider populace, and knowing Telugu poetry was a recognized sign of cultivation. Perhaps Krishnadevaraya was also attracted by the possibilities for inward reflection opened up by Telugu narrative poetry such as Peddana's. With this language and its literary forms, he could step back a little from the vainglory that went with being kingly. He could present himself as a spiritually aware individual bent not on usurping status and wealth from the other orders, but serving them.

Krishnadevaraya claims that the god Vishnu himself commanded that he compose a poem in Telugu:

If you ask 'Why Telugu?'
It is because this is Telugu country and I am a Telugu king.
Telugu is one of a kind.
After speaking with all the kings that serve you, didn't you realize –
Amongst all the regional languages, Telugu is the best.

That line, 'Telugu is the best', would some 450 years later become a rallying cry in the demand for the creation of independent India's first linguistic state, Andhra Pradesh.

Krishnadevaraya moulded the language into his long poem the *Amuktamalyada* ('The Woman who Gives a Garland Already Worn'), about kingship and the worldly pleasures that go with it, but also about the renunciatory urges and self-doubts of its author. The *Amuktamalyada* is full of hard-boiled advice about how to raise money to fight wars, how to control ambitious Brahmins, and how to put down rebellious forest- and hill-folk.

If a neighbouring kingdom is headed for ruin,
help him along.
If he manages to recover, become his friend.
If he's your enemy, it's the king beyond
who can help against him.
When they fight, your borders are safe.

This practical wisdom was shaped by the tradition known as *niti*: reflections and prescriptions on rulership and statecraft which looked back to Kautilya's *Arthashastra* – a tradition Krishnadevaraya would certainly have been aware of.

But then the *Amuktamalyada* starts to get much more interesting, as it moves away from the usual kingly self-presentation, the customary display of wisdom, cunning and ruthlessness. We begin to hear doubts and questionings, the stirrings of a subjective voice. Scholars of Indian history and culture have generally viewed the arrival of colonial ideas as enabling the emergence of a modern Indian sensibility. In Shulman's provocative assessment, Krishnadevaraya might be seen as part of an 'early, authentic, indigenous modernism' taking shape in India, characterized by 'a sense of introspection, of an individual who has many complex voices, new images of what love is all about, different configurations of the relations between men and women, new ideas of the state' and much more.

In the *Amuktamalyada*, Krishnadevaraya dramatizes debates about the nature of kingship, about who is the best king, about whether it is better to rule or to renounce. He's having a debate with himself. He's turning around in his mind the contradictions and ambivalences of royal life – the inner conflict of tradition:

> The king is non-violent, though he kills.
> Chaste, though he has women.
> Truthful, though he lies.
> Ever fasting, though he eats well.
> A hero, though he uses trickery.
> Rich, though he gives away.
> Kingship is rather strange.

15
Mirabai

I Go the Other Way
1498–1557

Across north India, the brief season of spring weather erupts with the festival of Holi – a no-holds-barred celebration in the villages and city streets. Water sprays everywhere, children throw coloured powder at each other, and soggy T-shirts and kurtas abound. It's a holiday some girls experience as an equalizing moment, a rare chance to play freely with boys. Other girls, though, view Holi warily – as a celebration that gives cover to sexual harassers. It's a charged moment in the gender politics of Indian life, and in many communities the soundtrack to that experience is 'Rang Barse', as performed by the Bollywood legend Amitabh Bachchan in a film from the 1980s.

The lines of this famous song are suggestive, as are many Bollywood lyrics: they tell of a beautiful woman, damp and colour-stained from playing Holi, besotted with a man who is not her husband. Men deceived in love – it's a familiar trope in Hindi music. The only atypical thing about this song is the strong-willed woman it celebrates: she's over 500 years old. The film lyricist based it on a centuries-old song about Mirabai, a mystic poet of spiritual love and longing, who lived during the sixteenth century and is today one of India's most revered female saints.

She was born Mira, into an elite and conservative warrior caste, the Rajputs of Rajasthan (the 'bai', a term of respect, came later). A flouter of conventions whose family tried to suppress her ecstatic religious longings, she broke with them and their Rajput social codes. She took to the road, singing and mixing freely with people of all types. She later became a heroine of the bhakti tradition (see **10 Basava and 12 Kabir**), which encouraged devotion to one's personal god, without the intermediaries of priests, rituals or temples. In bhakti, all you need is a simple offering of your love – a flower, a fruit, a song. In her lifetime, Mira composed perhaps a hundred songs called *bhajans*, which were passed down through the centuries by oral tradition, as with **Khusrau** (11) and Kabir. And, like their bodies of work, Mira's expanded as her legend grew.

According to Wendy Doniger, Professor at the University of Chicago, there were few important women in early Indian religious history. 'Women originally were not allowed to learn Sanskrit, were not supposed to speak Sanskrit. They're quoted a lot in religious texts written by men, but a real woman's voice is hard to find. Not impossible – there are women from time to time. But Mirabai is the first loud and clear woman's voice.'

Few women since have engaged the popular Indian imagination like Mirabai. Even Mahatma Gandhi was a fan: her songs filled him with 'rare joy'. 'Mira sang because she could not help singing. Her songs well forth straight from her heart.' He celebrated his last birthday, in October 1947, listening to one of her songs, sung to him by the south Indian Carnatic singer M. S. **Subbulakshmi** (45).

Subbulakshmi helped spread Mirabai's fame through a remarkable screen performance, in *Meera*, directed by an American, Ellis R. Dungan. At the November 1947 premiere of the Hindi version of the film, Nehru and the Mountbattens were in the audience. 'She became Mira herself,' Dungan said of Subbulakshmi's mesmeric incarnation of the medieval princess, which set off a revival of the cult of Mira in the newly independent nation.

> How will the night pass?
> How long have I been standing
> Gazing down the road?
> The pain of absence keeps me awake
> night and day.

The one Mira is yearning for, here and in all her bhajans, is her god, Krishna. And when her songs are performed in some rural villages, Mira is a simple paragon of religious devotion. But her historical uses have been expansive. In her afterlives, she's both an enemy of caste hierarchy and a rebellious feminist icon. You can understand why: the central challenge of her life – how to overcome rigid social expectations in order to pursue one's own, freely chosen values – is a struggle women all over India are engaged in today.

> Some praise me, some blame me. I go the other way.
> On the narrow path I found God's people.
> For what should I turn back?

As with all legends, there's a dense thicket of hagiography surrounding Mirabai. But her royal Rajput ancestry is historically clear. In the Rajasthan dry lands, where warring factions were ever vying for dominance, her grandfather founded a little kingdom. Mira grew up, most likely an only child, in the fief – perhaps twelve villages – controlled by her father.

As the story goes, Mira's religious fervour surfaced early and provided some family amusement. When she was four or five, a wandering ascetic came to the family home. Mira wheedled from him a doll-like icon of Krishna, the mischievous boy-god also called Girdhar. She became so attached to the icon that her mother teased her, saying Krishna would be her bridegroom. It turned out to be a prophetic jest.

Mira's mother died when she was small, and the girl's religious worship grew still more intense – excessive, even. Sensual and physically uninhibited in her rapture, she broke the strict purdah rules imposed on Rajput women, and proved ungovernable in her spiritual energy. As rumours of wanton and unstable behaviour chased her, her family arranged her marriage. She was given to a *rana*, a Rajput prince. In the Rajput tradition – as with many other traditions across the world in medieval times – daughters were married off to seal political alliances or quell potential wars. But Mira's marriage failed to bring about peace even in her own household.

Soon, though, her husband was dead – perhaps poisoned – and her father died too. Mira found herself under the thumb of her conservative in-laws, who were swarming her like bees, she sang. She had insulted them by not throwing herself on her husband's funeral pyre – committing sati in accordance with some Rajput traditions. They responded, according to the songs, by trying to kill her with a venomous snake. She managed to pacify it, and wore it as a necklace.

> How can anyone touch me?
> I will not descend
> From the back of an elephant
> To ride upon an ass.

Social scientist Parita Mukta has studied the history and legacies of Mirabai, and the tradition of *vair*, or vendetta, among the Rajputs:

> I think the very fact that Mira survived says so much about her. The workings of Rajput society are based around vair and hatred, where women are exchanged as part of a process of subjugating lesser chiefs or lesser Rajput lords. And Mira stood up against it. She absolutely did not want to participate in the politics of hatred, the politics of revenge, or the politics of subjugation.

'Your slanders are sweet to me,' Mira sang defiantly of her community's attacks. The supposed privileges of her birthright felt to her like chains. So she broke them, seeking her freedom by mixing with very different kinds of people – with itinerant thinkers, and with people from ostracized castes, the leather workers and the weavers. It's said that she took up with a teacher and poet, Ravidas or Raidas, who was an untouchable.

Singing her songs of devotion to Krishna, she wandered through Rajasthan and into northern India, her hair unbraided, her eyes unrimmed with kohl. Ankle bells and *karthals*, or castanets, were her chosen adornments. As she moved from village to village, her following grew, and soon she was leading a popular push against social boundaries.

The era of Muslim rule across parts of India had loosened the grip of Hindu orthodoxy, leading to the rise of movements that questioned the hierarchies of caste. The egalitarian spirit of bhakti that arose in southern India had slowly spread north, reaching Rajasthan around the fifteenth century. The paradox of bhakti travelled too.

While each individual might find her own link with God, devotion was stronger when people gathered together to sing. As Parita Mukta observes, after watching many village performances of Mira's songs, collective singing is 'a regenerative power, a power which nourishes the spirit, which nourishes one's whole being actually, and which nourishes a community to search for a better alternative'.

> On your lips there is a flute
> And a garland of jasmine adorns your chest.
> Mirabai says, the Lord is a giver of joy to the pious
> And the protector of the poor.

In independent India, where protecting the poor and so-called backward classes and castes is a constitutional concern, Mira's embrace of the lower castes has kept her memory alive in some villages and city slums, where contemporary performances of her songs are sometimes tuneful protests against the privileges of the elite. The humiliations of being at the lower end of the social order often get brought out sharply in such performances – and the religious devotion rings out too. But Mira's rejection of traditional family life and of curbs on women gets elided, even today. The need for girls and young women to subjugate their personal hopes and desires to the aspirations of their families is still seen as essential to Indian social cohesion. Postcards and comic books often show Mira singing or dancing seductively – your typical pin-up girl saint. The subversive and sometimes bitter transgressor of gender conventions – the Mirabai that Indian feminists embrace – figures little in popular culture.

Still, it would be a mistake to construe Mirabai and the bhakti tradition as nearly modern in their egalitarian impulses. Several aspects of the historical tradition were suppressed in the nationalist appropriation of bhakti, because they failed to set salutary examples for contemporary India. Allison Busch, a scholar of Hindi literature at Columbia University, notes the advice mentioned by another bhakti poet, Tulsidas: that women, like drums, are suitable for beating. In some of the older stories, Mira herself beats her low-caste servants when they try to force her to get married.

Gender, caste and class don't always align as comfortably in historical works as modern sensibilities might like. Lives get sifted, and reassembled, in light of contemporary desires. As Wendy Doniger puts it, 'The stories about who she was and what she did, they're pure hagiography – and Bollywood is welcome to it as far as I see. Now, you can't say they're wrong. But obviously she serves different purposes for different generations.'

It's an observation borne out when I ask schoolchildren in Rajasthan to tell me who Mirabai was:

> 'Mirabai was a freedom fighter.'
> 'Err . . . she was Krishna's lover?'
> 'She's written poetries and songs.'
> 'Mirabai? I don't know. I don't study history.'

So which Mirabai to choose? We can return to where we began, with Holi. How you experience it depends on who you are – or maybe on how much power you have. Is Mira a passionate religious inspiration? An emblem of caste blindness and inter-caste friendship? A potent symbol of feminism and self-transformation – a one-woman protest movement as much as a saint? History can't quite decide. So, perhaps fittingly, given Mira's own independent-mindedness, the choice is ultimately our own.

> Approve of me or disapprove of me:
> I take the path that human
> beings have taken for centuries.

16
Akbar

The World and the Bridge
1542–1605

Around forty kilometres west of India's most iconic building, the Taj Mahal, stands an abandoned city, one like no other in the world. Built just over 400 years ago, out of the red sandstone of the surrounding plains, Fatehpur Sikri sprawls, severe and elegant, across the semi-arid landscape. An English merchant, visiting the city in 1585, at the end of its brief flourishing, described it as more crowded than his home town, London.

Sikri's battlements, palaces and shrines proclaim imperial grandeur. But its airy pavilions and halls have little in common with the heavy monumentalism of Versailles or the Habsburg seats of power. Parts of the city have the feeling of a tent encampment, except that animal skins and wood frames have been replaced by stone and marble, carved with great skill by local craftsmen. Walking through this now desolate cityscape in the dry heat, you might feel, at certain turns, as if you were in one of M. C. Escher's drawings, reworked with the stark surrealism of Giorgio de Chirico. It's like touring the physical manifestation of a mind – the expansive, syncretic mind of its creator: Akbar, the greatest of the Mughal emperors.

Akbar started building at Sikri in 1571, to mark the birth of his first son, Jahangir. He originally envisioned it as a religious compound for his spiritual mentor, Shaikh Salim Chishti, who had foretold Jahangir's arrival. Shaikh Salim was the leader of a mystical yet orthodox Sufi sect, and Akbar built him a mosque whose floor he sometimes swept himself, in a show of devotion. Soon, around the mosque, a city began to take shape. It became one in a shifting series of Akbar's capitals, which also included Agra and Lahore.

It was from Sikri that Akbar, a master strategist of war and religious opportunity, launched the expansion of the Mughal Empire and amassed its fabled wealth. He trebled the size of his dominion, so that it covered a great stretch of the Indian subcontinent, from the Bay of Bengal to the Arabian Sea, and southwards to the Deccan. Only Ashoka's empire almost 2,000 years before, and the British Raj several centuries later, surpassed it.

Today, tour guides will confidently tell you what took place in each of Sikri's many spaces, pointing to music rooms, a treasury, a queen's bedroom, and the like. But despite much academic labour, the purposes and symbolism of many of the buildings still remain obscure. We're left with the mystery of the structures themselves: filigreed colonnades and tiered halls, waterways and parapets, studded towers and archways, and a throne room whose full significance still baffles scholars.

One hall we do know about is the Ibadat Khana, or House of Worship. Akbar was certain of his right to conquer by force, and did so freely. In matters of faith, however, he was something of an experimentalist, willing to entertain challenges and argument. The Ibadat Khana was a hall where he gathered divines and philosophers to debate the principles of belief. In the *Akbarnama*, or Book of Akbar, a magnificently illustrated contemporary chronicle of his reign, we find miniature paintings that show the emperor seated in this hall with men of different religions and sects, listening to their disputations.

In this openness, Akbar stands out in the history of Islamic kingship. As a result, he has become an icon for modern secularists and liberals – their favourite wielder of imperious power. Along with **Ashoka** (5) and poets like **Kabir** (12) and **Khusrau** (11), Akbar is incorporated into a lineage of Indians who advocate tolerance and diversity. His reign is often used as a rebuttal to Hindu nationalist arguments that Muslim rule in India was an unremittingly dark age for Hindus, and as a reminder to conservative Muslims of Islam's capacity for enlightened accommodation.

Akbar's religious explorations were indeed significant, and ushered in some imperial policies that we might think of today as socially liberal. But they were first motivated by pragmatic considerations, and then increasingly by a desire to create a new vision of kingship to legitimate his power. Liberal ideals such as religious freedom or equal treatment were at best afterthoughts, if thoughts at all. What he adopted instead was a new imperial ideology, with himself at its centre.

Jalal al-Din Muhammad Akbar was born far from the comfort and splendour of any imperial palace or intellectual sanctuary, on the sands of the Sindh desert, in the subcontinent's northwest. In his early years, he moved about with his father Humayun, the second Mughal emperor, who had lost control of his kingdom and was in exile. The itinerant Akbar never learned to read; he seems to have been dyslexic. But he developed a phenomenal memory, and those who underestimated the boy's shrewdness did so at their peril.

With Persian help, his father eventually recaptured his one-time capital, Delhi, from the Pashtun Sur dynasty that had usurped him – only to meet his death by a fall in his library a few months later. Barely a teenager, Akbar was crowned the new ruler in 1556 – the beginning of a reign that would last forty-nine years. He immediately faced challenges, and dealt with them decisively. First, he broke with his manipulative foster-mother and his regent. As for his foster-mother's over-ambitious son, Akbar ordered him flung from the harem terrace. When the man didn't die, it is said, Akbar had him hauled back up and pitched him off the terrace himself to finish the job. Such acts, made iconic through miniature paintings and popular retellings, endowed the emperor with an aura of steely dominance. A Jesuit priest who later came to tutor Akbar's sons observed, 'His expression is tranquil, serene and open, full also of dignity ... and when he is angry, of awful majesty.'

The priest, Antonio Monserrate, was fascinated by Akbar's ability to compensate for his illiteracy. In addition to developing an obsession for record-keeping on every aspect of his reign, Akbar surrounded himself with scholastic teachers of philosophy, history, theology and religion, sharpening his judgement on others' whetstones. 'He can give his opinion on any question so shrewdly and keenly, that no one who did not know that he is illiterate would suppose him to be anything but very learned and erudite,' Monser-rate noted. Akbar also had a commanding physical presence, as his son Jahangir, the future emperor, recalled:

> his eyes and eyebrows were black, and his complexion dark rather than fair; he was lion-bodied, with a broad chest, and his hands and arms long. On the left side of his nose he had a fleshy mole, very agreeable in appearance, of the size of half a pea ... His august voice was very loud, and in speaking and explaining had a peculiar richness. In his actions and movements he was not like the people of the world.

To secure his rule, Akbar had to weaken the influence of the clerical authorities and of independently powerful Sufi sheikhs. So, in the early years of his reign, he was particularly zealous in demonstrating the authenticity of his faith. He sponsored pilgrims on Hajj to Mecca, and made his own 300-kilometre pilgrimage, on foot, from Sikri to Ajmer, the holiest shrine of the Chishti sect.

As importantly, he had to control the Muslim nobility, an unruly mix of Afghans, Uzbeks, Persians and local fighters, and to subordi-nate Hindu warriors who might challenge his power. Towards the latter, he could be unsparing. The young emperor described some of his early battles as jihad – fighting against the infidels. The most destructive encounter was at the siege of Chittorgarh Fort, in what is now the western state of Rajasthan, in 1568. The Rajput Hindu defenders chose mass suicide when the fort was breached, but Akbar went on with his armies to slaughter, some say, more than 25,000 locals. The Rajput kings had not seen ruthlessness of this kind before. Most recognized they could not defeat the man who had unleashed it.

In 1572, Akbar captured Gujarat, crushing a force of 15,000 with a field army one-fifth of that size, many of them mounted on camels. To commemorate the victory, he erected the Buland Darwaza, or Gate of Magnificence. Placed at the southwest edge of Sikri, it became the ceremonial entrance to the city. Forty metres high, thirty-five metres wide, built from blocks of red and buff sandstone, and decorated with black and white marble, it's not a structure to argue with. But chiselled across its colossal profile are two delicate calligraphic inscriptions. The first, unsurprisingly, proclaims Akbar's achievements and victories. The second, though, is striking: written in Persian are the words 'Jesus, Son of Mary, says, "The world is a bridge; pass over it, but build no house upon it."'

In this and other unexpected remnants scattered across Sikri are the traces of Akbar's own open-mindedness, at least when off the battlefield. It was a stance unusual for a ruler of his time. Though he was for much of his life fervent and public in his practice of Islam, from early on Akbar grasped the diversity of belief and culture across the lands he ruled.

Akbar's army, which grew six-fold over the course of twenty-five years, was a reflection of this diversity – and the practical uses to which Akbar put it. His forces eventually included commanders and warriors with different ethnic backgrounds, whom he organized by strict ranks. Titles weren't inherited. They had to be won and kept by service. But his most successful military innovation was social: the incorporation of Rajput Hindu warriors into Mughal military service.

In return for Mughal support, the granting of land, and respect for their Rajput martial codes of honour and vengeance, many Rajput kings and princes pledged allegiance to the Mughal throne. Their incorporation into the Mughal order rested on the concept of *svamidharma*, 'service to the overlord'. They recognized Akbar as in effect a Muslim Rajput. His offer of an open hand was not exactly one they could refuse (they had also seen him wield an iron fist). The alliance was sealed and sustained across generations by the inter-marriage of Mughal elites with Rajput women. Akbar himself led the way by marrying a Jodhpur princess, Jodha Bai, who became Jahangir's mother. Through such marriages into the Mughal order, Rajput warrior clans and their princes became pillars of imperial rule for the next two centuries.

In another shrewd act of political equipoise, Akbar adopted Persian as the new language of imperial authority. Persian was more culturally supple than either Sanskrit or Arabic (each of which was

associated with a distinct religion), and therefore more acceptable to
locals. There's a parallel with the way English later acquired a certain neutrality in relation to the multiplicity of India's regional
languages. Akbar had Persian works read aloud to him, including
the *Masnavi* of the great Persian Sufi Jalal al-Din Rumi, which he
listened to every night. It contains lines such as these:

> Thou hast come to unite
> not to separate.
> The people of Hind worship in the idiom of Hindi.
> The people of Sindh do so in their own.

Akbar was ruling in a period of eclectic belief across the subcontinent. In Europe, the Inquisition was underway, intent on purging
the heresies of rival Christian beliefs. Religious intolerance was the
natural condition in other parts of the world, too. But in large parts
of northern India, the messages spread by bhakti devotees like **Kabir**
(**12**) and **Mirabai** (**15**), by religious leaders like **Guru Nanak** (**13**), and
by Sufi saints, were blending elements from multiple religious traditions to create new types of devotion.

While at Sikri, Akbar began his own explorations of this rich
religious landscape by what we might call the comparative method.
In the Ibadat Khana, he assembled learned religious men to expound
their beliefs and philosophies. Initially the gatherings were restricted
to Islamic theologians, but Akbar was apparently bored by their
tenuous logic, and by affirmations that seemed merely rote. He
brought in Jains, Hindus, Zoroastrians and Christians to sharpen
the debate.

His religious sparring sessions made his policies less doctrinal. But
necessity also shaped his ruling style. His expanding realm contained
mainly non-Muslim subjects. Mass conversion was impracticable
and, in any event, Akbar showed no interest in it. But he went further.
Breaking with injunctions of Islamic rule, he also set aside sharia
law. Hindus who had been forcibly converted to Islam were allowed
to convert back, and individuals who might otherwise have been
regarded as heretics were instead allowed to defend their beliefs.

More materially, in 1579, Akbar abolished the *jizya*, a graduated property tax on non-Muslims, a policy that endured for a century, until his great-grandson, the Mughal emperor Aurangzeb, reversed it. Ending jizya lifted a real burden on the poor, and promised, at least symbolically, a greater equality between the followers of different faiths. That same year, Akbar declared himself the supreme arbiter of religious affairs within his realm, thus wresting power from the clerics and investing himself as Khalifa, or Caliph, of the entire Muslim world, in a direct challenge to the Ottoman Sultan.

Despite the religious accommodations of his reign, Akbar's attitude to religion, and to differing beliefs, wasn't a type of protoliberalism. Our understanding of him has tended to rely on Mughal and Persian chronicles and on contemporary European sources. How interlocutors in this supposed cultural dialogue – for instance, his elite Hindu subjects – may have seen things has only recently become a subject of study, and what the mass of Akbar's Hindu subjects thought remains largely unexplored. Strikingly, none of the Hindu courtly literature engages with Akbar's religious policy, and it shows no interest in Akbar's debates in the Ibadat Khana. What it reveals, instead, are sixteenth-century power equations, which sought to make use of religious divisions, instead of trying to overcome them.

Still, Akbar's spiritual questing shouldn't be reduced to politics; there were also other forces driving it. Some think it was the result of a personal crisis brought on by a kind of melancholia, or that he was subject to trances that may have been a mild form of epilepsy. While psychology or physiology may have been a factor, his rule also coincided with a charged moment in the history of Islam, as the religion approached its first millennium in 1591. This historical pivot probably lay behind Akbar's interest in investigating other religious ideas. The approach of the Islamic millennium gave rise to prophecies of every imaginable type, from the coming of the Mahdi, the Islamic redeemer, to changes in dynastic order and in the nature of religion itself.

To prepare for the event, in 1585 Akbar commissioned a mixed group of Sunni and Shia scholars, as well as some who believed in the Mahdi, to produce for him a 'Millennial History', the *Ta'rikh-i-alfi*.

Consisting of thousands of folio pages, many of them given over to the banal recounting of dates and events, the work gave a central importance to the idea of dialogue. Competition between rival voices and traditions would make possible the discovery of higher truths, which could be used to define and control the era that was about to begin. And it was only the emperor himself, Akbar, who could adjudicate these debates and identify their new insights. His ability to reach such insights supposedly lay in his possession of *insaaf*, the intellectual capacity for fairness or impartial arbitration. As the Preface of the *Ta'rikh-i-alfi* put it:

> With the help of reason (*aql*) he has lifted insaaf to glory from its usual abject state . . . The gates of the safe house of his insaaf are open to the practitioners of all religions. By his just command, wolves are herding sheep. Thanks to his insaaf, infidels are caring for Muslims . . . He is a friend of meaning and an enemy of chatter. He cares about what is spoken, regardless of who speaks it.

As the day of the millennium approached, and after it had passed, Akbar came to think of himself not merely as a political sovereign, but as the possessor, if not of divine attributes, then of *karamat*, extraordinary powers to perform supernatural acts.

The architect of this arcane new ideology was Abu'l Fazl, one of the brightest and most loyal of the intellectual stars in Akbar's court. Abu'l Fazl oversaw the production of the *Akbarnama*, which is a dazzling exhibition of the art of storytelling, refined flattery and the symbolic projection of power. Steeped in Timurid ideas of kingship and mysticism, it portrays Akbar as the fount of all light, illuminating the world:

> Knowest thou at all who is this world-girdling luminary and radiant spirit? Or whose august advent has bestowed this grace? 'Tis he who, by virtue of his enlightenment and truth, is the world-protecting sovereign of our age – to wit, that Lord of the hosts of sciences, theatre of God's power, station of infinite bounties, unique of the eternal temple, . . . bezel of God's signet-ring, . . . origin of the canons of world-government, author of universal conquest . . . sublime concentration of humanity, heir apparent of the sun . . .

By the 1580s, Akbar had turned away from public prayer and orthodox Islamic practices. He began to worship the sun, and introduced
fire rituals into his court. He was inventing his own system of religious belief: Din-i Ilahi, or Divine Faith. Abu'l Fazl described Din-i
Ilahi as having 'the great advantage of not losing what is good in any
one religion, while gaining whatever is better in another' – a combination of elements designed to secure Akbar's claim to be the
universal sovereign.

For reasons unknown, Akbar abandoned Fatehpur Sikri and the Ibadat Khana and its multi-confessional debates twenty years before he
died. He had occupied the city for less than two decades. One theory
is that supplying water to the city, perched so high on a stony ridge,
became a problem. A more likely reason for its abandonment was
Akbar's changing religious priorities. In particular, he had ceased to
worship at Sufi shrines and at mosques.

An index of the vast wealth Akbar had accumulated is that he
could build a city like this and then forsake it without suffering
major economic loss. He moved his capital to the stronger fortifica-
tions of nearby Agra, and his empire continued to grow. The massive
treasury he accumulated allowed his descendants (especially Jahangir and Shah Jahan, who built the Taj Mahal) to become the Medicis
of India: exalted patrons of art and architecture and connoisseurs of
utmost taste.

Akbar continues to be a historical anchor for Indian liberals, who
are particularly drawn to his inquisitive intellectual style in matters
of faith, and who overlook the idiosyncratic religious dimensions of
his imperial vision. But even if there's more hope than history in the
view that he was some kind of secular precursor, he still stands out
in the global context of his times – questioning, doubting and reinventing faith in an age when many rulers stayed steadfast in their
beliefs.

17
Malik Ambar

The Dark-fated One
1548–1626

Years ago, I managed to get tickets to the first cricket Test Match to
be played in the city of Ahmedabad in Gujarat. Opposing the Indian
team was a West Indian eleven which included the peerless Viv Rich-
ards. The excitement as the crowds streamed to the new test ground
was manic, joyful, but I left the match remembering neither the score
nor individual performances. The reactions of the Ahmedabad spec-
tators, though, I won't forget. As the West Indians took to the field,
loud monkey whoops filled the air, and bananas came raining down
from the stands. The pelted players – probably the greatest West
Indian team in history – stood there in their flannels, stunned.

Indians' particular contempt for people of African descent – a
racism shared even by Mahatma Gandhi, as evident in his South
African years – doesn't get talked about much, which is surely one
reason little has changed in the thirty-odd years since I watched that
troubling match. It's telling that a word still widely used in Hindi to
refer to black Africans is *habshi* – shorthand in common usage for a
dark-skinned slave.

The word habshi, derived from Arabic and Persian terms for an
Abyssinian, has a long history in India, one that's not often remem-
bered in the contemporary nation, or beyond. The standard image of
sixteenth- and seventeenth-century slavery is of ships moving west
from Africa, their shackled human cargo destined to feed the New
World's demand for mass labour on cotton and tobacco plantations.
But the slave economy was a genuinely global one, stretching from
Africa to East Asia. Slaves were also sent eastwards across the Indian

Ocean, to bolster the public and private militias of the Deccan Plateau of southern India.

One of these slaves, whose story is rarely told, rose to become a power broker, even a kingmaker, in the Deccan. A persistent tormentor and nemesis of the vast Mughal Empire to the north, he helped set the contours of power in the subcontinent in the century before the dawn of the colonial era. His name was Malik Ambar.

In an early, unsettling seventeenth-century miniature painting of Malik Ambar, his severed head is impaled on a spear. A short distance away, a Mughal archer, balanced on a globe and dressed in a wine-coloured robe, jewelled belt and white slippers, takes careful aim at the African's face. To Richard Eaton, Professor at the University of Arizona and a scholar of Deccan history, 'It's a remarkable painting filled with symbolism. Around Malik Ambar you have owls – live owls and dead owls – associating him with darkness and rebellion.'

Malik Ambar was born in the mid-1500s. His given name was Chapu. He was probably a pagan, and he was sold into slavery – possibly by his own impoverished parents – very young. The interests that conspired to send the boy born Chapu to India were rooted in trade, a story that also has cotton at its heart. The flow of slaves 'was driven largely by the demand for Indian textiles on the part of the Ethiopian kingdom', Richard Eaton explains, 'so on one side – the western, African side – you have demand for Indian textiles. And on the eastern side you have an equal demand for military slavery.'

The trade in African slave warriors flourished in places riven by political instability, places with enmities between, and within, clans – places, in other words, much like the sixteenth-century Deccan. The Deccan Plateau covers much of central southern India, and with its western ports and rich hinterlands, it was a global crossroads. With the flow of incomers came native resentments. But the habshis were detached both from their own families and from the tangled knots of local alliances and feuds. That estrangement made them valuable tools to their masters. Recognizing that they would never return home to Africa, they had little choice but to throw in their lot with their owners.

Malik Ambar's own journey from Abyssinia to the Deccan was a meandering one. When first enslaved, he'd been sent to Baghdad, where he was converted to Islam and renamed. He was manifestly clever, and his first owner taught him finance and administration, in Arabic – a practice of education not uncommon in the warrior-slave trade. African slaves were valued not just for their strength but also for their leadership abilities, strategic intelligence and cultural flexibility.

When his first master died, Malik Ambar was sold again, perhaps repeatedly. At some point during his west Asian sojourn, he picked up Iranian irrigation techniques. We actually have a contemporary Dutch record of one transaction in which Malik Ambar was sold for an impressive price of 80 guilders, a twisted tribute to his exceptional capabilities. Then, perhaps late in his teens, he ended up with many compatriots in an Arab dhow, ploughing southeast across the Arabian Sea towards the Konkan coast, in today's Maharashtra. He had acquired by now a cultural education to rival that of his future owners.

Malik Ambar's new Indian master was Chengiz Khan, *peshwa* or chief minister of the Deccan's fading Nizam Shahi sultanate. Chengiz was known to give his habshis room for advancement – for he was himself a habshi and former slave. Malik Ambar made it his business to watch Chengiz closely as he managed his role as peshwa. Eventually, the slave who already had financial management and engineering skills began absorbing political strategy from his master, who would prove to be his last.

Malik Ambar's story complicates our assumptions about slavery, particularly the view that all slaves were cut off from the avenues of social mobility enjoyed by free men. The reason he would, over time, be able to mimic his master and rise from slave to kingmaker had to do not just with his own abilities, but also with the military slavery system that dated back to the Arab world of the tenth century. When not on the battlefield, these elite slaves were often appointed to trusted roles within the household: bodyguards, valets and guardians of the harem. They were educated and nurtured by their masters, treated almost like sons – in exchange for their total loyalty, of course. And when their masters died, they were often freed.

Some of these educated, capable freed slaves became freelancers and mercenaries, and a few manoeuvred themselves into positions of genuine power, as Malik Ambar's own master had done. When Chengiz Khan died in 1575, Malik Ambar was still in his mid-twenties. He was smart, ambitious, charismatic, highly skilled – and now free.

As a mercenary serving a series of local commanders, Malik Ambar spent the next two decades building a band of loyal soldiers of his own – many of them, ironically, Ethiopian habshis engaged by him on the usual slave-terms. Having seen what Chengiz Khan achieved, he wanted to go further, and succeeded in part by lucky timing. By 1595, he had built a large army at a crucial moment in Deccan history. The Sultan he was employed by needed him desperately, for the Mughal Empire, expanding by the day under **Akbar**'s strategic brilliance (**16**), was knocking on the door.

Akbar's forces had been edging steadily southward, seeking to capture Maratha territory and subdue the rulers of the Deccan. They laid siege to the fortified city of Ahmednagar, the politically fractious capital of the Nizam Shahi sultanate. But in a daring night-time manoeuvre, Malik Ambar and his troops managed to break out of the city and escape through the enemy lines. While the city fell, many of the cavalrymen of the defeated ruler joined Malik Ambar. He could now command a mixed group of around 7,000 crack fighters. For the next three decades, successive Mughal emperors would send their forces to try to control the Deccan countryside. Against Malik Ambar, they would fail.

As Richard Eaton observes, 'Malik Ambar was one of several African commanders who were able to attract other Africans and other Indians, Marathas, to their sides and wage guerrilla warfare. It seems to have been his ability in mastering guerrilla warfare that propelled his career. And this happened rather rapidly.'

The terrain Malik Ambar mastered was hilly, forested and full of deep ravines – 'nasty turf', in modern US military parlance, not lending itself to 'Clear, Hold, Build'. But Malik Ambar had surveyed many of these lands as an administrator, while also absorbing the combat techniques of the indigenous Marathas. Recall those owls, dead and alive, scattered about that gruesome painting of Malik Ambar's impaled head? Maybe they symbolized not just his supposedly dark soul, but his ability to attack under cover of darkness. Thanks to his knowledge of the contours of the area, he could cut off the supply lines of his enemy. He built his forces to some 50,000, and from time to time his swift-moving light cavalry surprised the Mughals in the ravines and hacked them down.

In 1610 Malik Ambar captured the citadel at Daulatabad. Set high on a hill, heavily fortified, it was one of the trophies for Deccan military campaigners. Briefly, it served as his capital. In the palace here, he consolidated his power by sometimes grim political stratagems. Earlier, in a shrewd move, he had married off his daughter to the local Sultan. From her, he came to know that the Sultan's senior wife, of Persian origin, had insulted him as being a mere slave – the pretext he needed to poison both her and the Sultan. He then installed on the throne the dead Sultan's five-year-old son – and proceeded to rule, not just as peshwa but also effectively as regent.

A Dutch merchant, Pieter van den Broecke, travelled across the Deccan in the late 1610s and left a description of Malik Ambar in his prime: a 'cruel Roman face, of tall and strong build, with white glassy eyes, which are very misplaced on him'. Still, van den Broecke noted, Malik Ambar was 'loved and respected by everyone and keeps good government'. Thanks to the ruler's uncompromising punishments for highway robbers, 'one may travel through his country with gold'. Drunken soldiers in the ranks had molten lead poured down their throats.

It's from such sources, and those of his enemies, that we get our sense of Malik Ambar. Regrettably, despite his wide education and expertise, he left none of his own writings. So there are no personal insights, and no clarity on his private life.

We're more certain about the afterlife of his guerrilla tactics, known as *bargi-giri*, which were adopted and refined by the Maratha leader **Shivaji (19)**. That connection with Shivaji is an interesting one: Shivaji is the defining hero of his region, the Hindu warrior who defied the Mughals. And in the Indian nationalist story too, Shivaji was the great resister against the Muslim invaders. Yet with Malik Ambar we have evidence of someone even earlier who took on the Mughals – and whom they could not defeat. He's not a Hindu. He's not a native defending some ancient motherland. He's an Ethiopian opportunist and power-entrepreneur. One of the main resisters to Mughal expansion into the south turns out to have been an Ethiopian slave. He doesn't fit neatly into any of the standard narrative silos of Indian history – Hindu, Muslim or European.

Even more than the later exploits of Shivaji, Malik Ambar's military strategy unsettled the Mughals. As the seventeenth century began, Emperor Jahangir inherited the goal of his father Akbar: crushing the Ethiopian parvenu. His preoccupation with Malik Ambar bordered on neurosis. Like other Mughal emperors before and after, Jahangir insisted on being portrayed as a source of light, bringing peace and illumination to his people. Frustrated by Malik Ambar, he cast his rival as the polar opposite, his dark skin equated with a dark and cunning heart. Jahangir's memoirs call him 'Ambar of dark fate', 'the ill-starred Ambar', 'the rebel Ambar', 'the black-fated one' and, simply, 'that disastrous man'.

Which brings us back to the painting of Malik Ambar's severed head on a spear, shot through by the archer in red robe and white slippers. The archer is Jahangir himself. The emperor commissioned the gifted artist Abu'l Hasan to paint it in 1615, exactly twenty years after the Mughal pursuit of Malik Ambar's head had begun. But in fact Jahangir never defeated Ambar in battle, and certainly never got to release arrows into his disembodied head. As Richard Eaton notes, 'The painting is conveying his fantasy of accomplishing in art what he simply was not able to do on the battlefield.'

Malik Ambar's career marked the zenith of the habshi story in India: his realm extended from the island fortress of Janjira, on the Konkan coast, deep into the Deccan hinterland. With the fall of the Deccani sultanates, successor powers stopped using military slavery, and the African diaspora of India either intermarried or retreated to relatively remote parts of Gujarat, Maharashtra and Karnataka – though Malik Ambar's fortified port at Janjira remained controlled by habshis right down to 1948. Neither the Portuguese nor the British, nor even the redoubtable Shivaji, could make it their own.

The neglect of Malik Ambar's story, and of the African historical contribution and experience in India more generally, is rooted in a racial prejudice that shows little sign of abating. Recently in urban India it's become fashionable to hire young Indians of African descent as bouncers at nightclubs and bars. (Employers instruct these modern strongmen to speak only English, in order to maintain the illusion of their exotic origins.) But most of the 100,000 or so descendants of former slaves now live in isolated communities in western India: places where they're routinely denied the very means of upward mobility – a good education and recognition of merit – that turned a remarkable slave into an unvanquished power some five centuries ago.

18

Dara Shikoh

The Meeting-place of the Two Oceans
1615–1659

On 8 September 1659, huge crowds gathered in Delhi to watch a Mughal prince parade through the streets. Cavalrymen, accompanied by lines of soldiers, rode beside him. The prince, named Dara Shikoh, was perched in a howdah on the back of an elephant, heading for the Red Fort. But this was no coronation, or victorious homecoming after battle – it was an elaborate public humiliation. A French adventurer at the Mughal court was at the scene:

> This was not one of the majestic elephants of Pegu or Ceylon, which Dara had been in the habit of mounting, pompously caparisoned . . . Dara was now seen seated on a miserable and wornout animal, covered with filth; he no longer wore the necklace of large pearls which distinguish the princes of Hindoustan . . . and his sorry turban was wrapt round with a Kashmir shawl or scarf, resembling that worn by the meanest of the people.

Dara Shikoh, the eldest son of Emperor Shah Jahan, had been his father's chosen heir to the Mughals' vast empire. As Shah Jahan sent his younger sons to govern far-flung provinces, he kept Dara close to home, giving him an annual allowance of some twenty million rupees, a sum far in excess of what other senior figures in the Mughal court received. Not surprisingly, some at court called the favourite son Baba Dara ('infant Dara') – a Mughal daddy's boy. So what twist of fate brought this prince, descended from the emperor Akbar, to humiliation on the Delhi streets?

What drives Dara's story is his inquiring mind – his great strength, which became his downfall. He spent his princely stipend exploring religious ideas and philosophy, and commissioning splendid albums of calligraphy and miniature paintings. His interests stretched across cultures and traditions, and he surrounded himself with Sufi mystics, yogis, fakirs and holy men from a variety of faiths. With their help, he devoted much of his life to translating the world's major scriptures into Persian. Most significantly, he immersed himself in Sanskrit works, and beginning in 1656 he assembled a group of Brahmin pandits to translate the Upanishads, the philosophical bases of Vedantic Hinduism (see **8 Shankara**).

But Dara Shikoh's story ran in parallel with another: that of his religiously conservative brother, Aurangzeb. 'The relationship between the two men was poisonous – and poisonous from a very early age,' says Munis Faruqui, a historian at the University of California, Berkeley. 'It's the larger context that forces these brothers to ultimately see one another as competitors, and to see one another as potential killers.' The story of Dara and Aurangzeb has the elements of Shakespearean drama: the aesthete dreamer and his brother, the zealot soldier, thrown against each other in a war of succession. Aurangzeb imprisoned their ailing father and staged his own coronation at Delhi's Red Fort, only three months before Dara's debasing procession. He would go on to rule for nearly fifty years.

Dara's defeat is popularly conceived as a switch point of Indian history, which supplies liberals with a favourite parlour-game counterfactual. What if Aurangzeb had been paraded through Delhi on that bedraggled elephant and Dara had become emperor instead? Looking back at the subcontinent's religiously divided, conflict-ridden twentieth-century history, wishful thinkers hold that Dara's heterodox approach might have kept the Mughal Empire from dissipating, as it ultimately did following his brother's death in 1707. Had Dara's type of cultural inquisitiveness endured, India might have experienced an intellectual renaissance. This in turn might have enabled the country to meet the West on equal terms, sparing it the century and a half of colonial subjection that ended, in 1947, with a bloody religious partition.

However you play the 'what if?' game, the historical record of Dara Shikoh offers a beguiling resource for liberals seeking historical examples to parry religious extremists – one that also sheds light on possibilities for cross-cultural understanding. The Persian translations that Dara commissioned and guided gave Europeans their first knowledge of Sanskrit philosophical texts like the Upanishads. But Dara wasn't particularly interested in fostering dialogue across religious divides; rather, he was in pursuit of mystical unities. We, relativists by default, think of translation as giving us access to unfamiliar knowledge and experience, as a window on differences, a way to savour diversity. Dara, though, saw his reading of the Upanishads and works from other traditions as affirming the truth he already knew.

In a seventeenth-century ink drawing, a trim young Dara Shikoh holds a falcon as he stands before his father, the emperor best known for commemorating his dead wife by building the Taj Mahal. The sketch is on fine Japanese paper, the artist Dutch – Rembrandt, in fact. He was fascinated by Mughal miniatures, and this was one of at least twenty-five studies he made of a batch of Mughal paintings that entered Holland's art market at mid-century. In the drawing, Shah Jahan's head is surrounded by an almost explosive imperial halo – one that seems to cast a dark, billowing shadow behind Dara's dainty feet. A foreboding detail, if only in retrospect.

Rembrandt's sketch is a small reminder of the seventeenth century's global currents, in which Dara was carried too. As a young man, the devotion of his father freed him to be intellectually audacious. His passionate inquiries into religion and philosophy took him far from the Persianate culture of the Mughal court. He and his scholarly assistants embarked on translations of religious texts including the Old and New Testaments. Around 1654, he composed a major work of his own, *Majma'al-bahrayn* (The Meeting-place of the Two Oceans), which embodied his growing interest in discovering esoteric and mystical knowledge, available only to a visionary few. Dara prefaced his work by describing how, after his studies of Sufi doctrines, he wanted to understand philosophical truth as expressed in Indian thought:

> Since [this book] is the meeting-place of the realities and gnostic truths of two groups that know God, it is known as The

Meeting-place of the Two Oceans . . . I have written this investigation in accordance with my own mystical unveiling and experience, for the sake of my own family, and I have nothing to do with the common people of either community.

In other words, Dara's interest was in esotericism, not in bridging everyday religious differences between Islam and Hinduism. Delving deep into the Upanishads, he oversaw the translation of around fifty of them in a volume entitled *Sirr-i Akbar* – 'The Greatest Mystery'. 'Nobody at that time who wasn't the heir apparent could have pulled it off,' says Jonardon Ganeri, Professor of Philosophy at New York University. 'Dara had the backing, the resources, and the personal commitment to learn Sanskrit. I don't know of any other Mughal who learned Sanskrit to the extent he did.'

How far he got in learning Sanskrit is debatable. In his search for affinities between religions, Dara seized on a famous passage in the Qur'an that speaks of a hidden book and became convinced that it was a reference to the Upanishads which Hindu pandits had kept from the Muslims. But the pandits in his employ were seeking confluences too, Ganeri says. 'They were clever: they selected the passages from the Upanishads that would have appealed to him – the ones that were more monotheistic.'

Dara's commissioned translations, though, were accurate, and he had reason to admire his Persian renderings – 'in a clear style, an exact and literal translation', he said. Later scholars broadly agreed. Although he wasn't forcing meaning into the translations themselves, he believed that his study of the Upanishads was uncovering the deepest truths about his own religion, Islam – knowledge so special and so arcane that he imagined it would carry him unchallenged to the throne.

'People often tend to hive off his intellectual activities from his political activities but I suspect from the time that he was a young man he knew that he was going to have to fight for the Mughal throne,' says Munis Faruqui. 'And this was a treadmill that one could not step off. One had to participate in this fratricidal struggle. And if he was going to remain at the Mughal court, I suspect that a very important part of his larger political calculations was this possibility of presenting himself as a Perfect Man – someone who would have access to certain kinds of divine secrets that no mere mortal would have.'

If that was the plan, it sorely backfired. Dynastic succession in the Mughal Empire was always a messy business; every son of a ruling emperor could stake a claim to the throne, but none could assume it was theirs. Dara's bold intellectual project, coupled with his father's indulgence, gave him an arrogant air and alienated the very courtiers whose support he would need when his father eventually ceded the throne. Some today might see Dara's openness to different religions as a sign of a man ahead of his time. His contemporaries saw him as a man enamoured of himself, and out of his depth.

François Bernier, the observant French physician who would later describe Dara's abjection in the Delhi streets, noted how the prince's self-regard left him politically isolated:

> Over-confident in his opinion of himself, considering himself competent in all things and having no need of advisers. He despised those who gave him counsel. Thus it was that his dearest friends never ventured to inform him of the most essential things . . . He assumed that fortune would invariably favour him, and imagined that everybody loved him . . .

'Maybe he was a dreamer,' Jonardon Ganeri says, laughing. 'As all philosophers, he spent time thinking about ideas and not thinking about governance. He might have been better off thinking more about government and less about religious unity.'

> The fear of seeing the Muhammadan religion oppressed in Hindustan if my brother Dara Shikoh ascended the throne, that of beholding the ruin of the kingdom, which I looked on as inevitable if my father's reign had continued, by reason of his bad government: these are the only causes why I have always opposed myself strongly and without self-seeking to the attempts of everyone to supplant me.

Here was Aurangzeb, having taken over the empire, setting down his justification for posterity. The spectre of cultural and religious

dissolution combined with the threat of poor governance: its argu-
mentation is not unlike the election manifestos (or dog-whistle
politics) of many right-wing parties today. Then, as now, it was an
appeal that worked – and one that Aurangzeb seemed entirely qualified to make. While Dara had spent his years of princely privilege
seeking elective affinities between religions, his brother focused on
building his military strength, expanding his political influence and
making ready to seize the throne. Munis Faruqui describes Aurangzeb's princely preparations:

> He's serving all around the empire. He's in central India, he has two
> long stints in the Deccan, he's in Gujarat, he's in Multan, he's part
> of the invasion of northern Afghanistan, he has two Kandahar
> campaigns – he's all over the place. Inasmuch as our memory of
> Aurangzeb is of a zealot, it is largely derived from his years as an
> emperor as opposed to his years as a prince. But his [princely career]
> is when he really forges a personality as a general, administrator,
> and leader of men. He's seen as one who cares deeply for the men
> who work under him.

Aurangzeb thought Dara was unsuited to rule because of his slight
record in military campaigns, and because his dabbling in other
religions veered dangerously towards apostasy. Aurangzeb's latter
concern was shared by other nobles, who wanted the Mughal state
to move to a stricter interpretation of the Muslim law of sharia.
Faruqui says, 'If you look at Aurangzeb's interactions with the
Mughal nobles or people working at the Mughal court, you see
him working extremely hard to build friendships, to cultivate loyalties among these groups. It's not surprising that when the war of
succession happens many of these individuals throw their weight
behind him.'

In autumn 1657, Shah Jahan fell seriously ill. Though he would
eventually recover, his incapacity precipitated the military struggle
for the throne. Its climax took place on the plain of Samugarh near
the banks of the River Yamuna, roughly sixteen kilometres east of
Agra, in May 1658.

Dara had come from Agra to Samugarh by elephant, with a

large army marching behind him. But some of the most influential nobles, whose religion he had arguably transgressed and who were sceptical of his leadership abilities, refused to send their troops to his aid. Many of his soldiers were conscripted butchers, barbers and blacksmiths – a ragtag bunch largely unseasoned in battle. Dara's anaemic showings in previous campaigns could not have helped the poor men's morale. Though fewer in number, Aurangzeb's troops were hardened veterans; many of them had fought with him on his successful campaigns in the Deccan. When the two armies met, the battle was predictably brief.

By some accounts, Aurangzeb came close to being killed by one of his brother's Rajput soldiers, but quickly recovered as Dara hesitated over strategy. When a rocket struck Dara's howdah – an easy target – the prince dismounted his elephant so quickly that his troops read his haste as fear, and panicked. In three hours, Dara lost 10,000 men. His surviving conscripts deserted him, returning to Agra to plunder his palace. The prince became a fugitive, fleeing west towards Sindh, his fine silks replaced by a thin tunic and cheap shoes. The endgame was his betrayal by a Baluch chieftain called Malik Jiwan, who promised him protection but then delivered him to his brother.

And that's how Dara Shikoh found himself moving through Delhi in tatters on a wretched, undersized elephant. At a show trial in Aurangzeb's court, the gathered clerics and noblemen called nearly unanimously for his execution. On 9 September 1659, he was stabbed to death by a posse of slaves. His head was hacked off, according to some accounts, and presented to Aurangzeb; his body, unwashed and in the rags he'd been paraded in, was buried without ceremony somewhere in the grounds of his great-great-grandfather Humayun's tomb compound, eight kilometres south of the Red Fort.

In old Delhi, away from the picnickers and tourists who nowadays visit Humayun's tomb, are the ruins of a seventeenth-century build-ing. Over the years, this plot has been the residence of a Punjabi noble, a British knight, and several municipal schools; today, the ruins are encircled by the campus of a government-run university. But behind a British classical façade with Roman pillars you can still find the outlines of a row of Mughal cusped arches. Fashioned from red sandstone, they've since been bricked in and white-washed. This is what remains of the library built by Dara's father for his adored, book-loving son. The marooned library is a fitting place in which to reconsider the great 'what if?' – the alternative history that might have been had Dara ascended his father's throne.

The idea that Dara Shikoh would have been an enlightened philosopher-king is tantalizing, but based on a misreading of his project. A man who believes he has grasped the deepest religious truths may prove to be a saint, a fool, or – if his belief coincides with absolute power – a tyrant. Had Dara become emperor, his evident arrogance and his absent political skills suggest that his reign may have led the Mughal Empire to an early, chaotic collapse. But his intellectual legacy stands out even without overblown counterfactuals.

By Mughal standards, Dara, who became known as the 'ill-fated one', was a failure – one of many princes who fell by the wayside in endless battles for dynastic succession. But after his death, his translations of the Upanishads and other Sanskrit works became a vital link not just between Islam and Hinduism, but between India and the West – introducing, for instance, the nineteenth-century German philosopher Arthur Schopenhauer to Sanskrit philosophy (in which he found, he would say, the greatest consolation of his life) and helping to spread its influence into Western thought.

So here's another 'what if?' What if Dara had never done that work? He might have been a more successful prince, even become emperor. But our minds would be narrower places today.

19
Shivaji

Dreaming Big
1627–1680

The warrior king Shivaji may have died over 300 years ago, but he's still here to greet every arrival to India's financial centre, Mumbai. Fly into the city, and you land at the Chhatrapati Shivaji International Airport. Come by train, and you alight at Chhatrapati Shivaji Terminus, the Victoria Terminus of old. Come by boat, and soon the major landmark may no longer be the triumphal Gateway of India, built to commemorate George V's 1911 visit. In the next few years, a statue of Shivaji, twice as big as the Statue of Liberty, is scheduled to be built on a rock four kilometres offshore.

Mumbai, the capital of Maharashtra, is a city of migrants and mixing. It also has a fierce brand of native patriotism, which has often, in recent decades, turned violent. Competition for jobs is the great struggle in this and every other megacity of the twenty-first century. Among the most popular political parties here is the Shiv Sena, which claims to stand for the interests of the local Hindu Marathas. Its name means 'Shivaji's Army'. The party's cadres, often lower- and middle-class 'sons of the soil', believe that too much of Mumbai's wealth, and too many of its jobs, have been claimed by outsiders: north and south Indian migrants, the city's cosmopolitan elites and Muslims. The cadres see themselves as the true successors of Shivaji, the presiding hero of Mumbai and its state.

At a gym just opposite the local Shiv Sena office in the Mumbai suburb of Andheri East, young men spend much of the day bench-pressing and squatting and curling. It's a low-tech place, with basic equipment – no fancy digital trackers here. 'This gym is basically for helping the poor and middle class, because it's quite cheap,' says a young Maharashtrian named Alok. 'It also helps you reduce weight quite a lot.'

The young men are Shivaji enthusiasts, and as they exercise you can almost imagine them as soldiers limbering up for battle. But their main concern, when we get talking, is work, not war. They want to move up from their jobs as security guards or gardeners – no easy task in this job-starved town. Some dream even bigger. 'I want to give work to Indians,' says Alok. 'I'll create my own business, better infrastructure, schools. So for that I need, basically, cash – money to create . . . '

With nerve, skill and wit, Shivaji defended his homeland and defied the Mughal Empire, becoming a potent symbol of Hindu resistance. When Alok and his friends think of him, it's mainly as a defender of Hindu pride: the figure portrayed in statues, sword in hand, astride a springing horse. But there's another aspect of his life, less known, that might speak to Mumbai's youth: Shivaji was self-made. From relatively provincial, if not entirely humble, beginnings, he plotted, sweated and traded up to glory. It's a story the gardeners and security guards would like to make their own.

Much of Maharashtra sits atop the western Deccan Plateau, in sometimes rugged, unforgiving terrain. Earlier generations of inhabitants had to be ingenious to survive. But standing amidst the ruins of one of its many hilltop forts, looking out across a spectacular landscape, you understand better their deep attachment to this land.

Xuanzang, the Chinese Buddhist pilgrim who travelled across India 1,000 years before Shivaji lived, described the Maratha people as 'proud-spirited and warlike, grateful for favours and revengeful for wrongs, self-sacrificing towards suppliants in distress and sanguinary to death with any who treated them insultingly'. Other early accounts portray Maratha societies as self-reliant and relatively egalitarian. Given the terrain, the rich were not very rich, and the poor, unable to till much from the soil, often joined militias. That gave them a living and a step up the social ladder.

These were Shivaji's people. He was born in 1627 to Shahaji Bhonsle, a lower-caste Maratha fighter in the service of the Adil

Shah, who ruled one of the major Muslim sultanates of the Deccan. Shahaji soon became an absentee father, moving south and starting a second family there. Shivaji was raised by his mother, Jijabai, whose devotion to him would become part of his myth.

Shivaji's only brother died young, and Shivaji was still an adolescent when his distant father assigned him the administrative charge of a small domain around Pune, which was under the nominal control of the Adil Shah. But the teenager was too ambitious to be satisfied by administration: he began to build his own forces instead, leading them out to capture nearby forts and lay claim to the surrounding districts. It was a bold gambit. As James Laine, Professor of Religious Studies at Macalester College in Minnesota, puts it: 'This teenage boy's first political military gesture is mounting a campaign against forts that are the property of the Adil Shah, so he's resisting his father's employer.'

Laine wonders if Shivaji's mother encouraged his rebelliousness. By the sixteenth century, bhakti devotional practices in the Deccan had softened some of the rigidities of caste, and some people even married across caste boundaries. Jijabai was a Yadava, a relatively higher caste than her Maratha Kunbi husband, and one that claimed descent from the god Krishna. Shivaji grew up absorbing her tales of ancestral glory, and perhaps her desire that her son recover the social position she had forsaken by marrying down. It's said that the devout Jijabai foretold that her son would one day be crowned Chhatrapati, or lord of the umbrellas (a title with imperial resonances) – a prophecy she would just barely live to see come true.

It was an ascent like a lot of ascents in the mountainous western Deccan: possible only with planning, care and effort. In a region full of enmities, Shivaji worked with anyone who could be useful to him, capturing territory along the way. One of his early annexations was a domain under the control of another Maratha Hindu chieftain – a detail worth noting, since today parties like the Shiv Sena idealize Shivaji for antagonizing Muslims, not fellow Marathas. But Shivaji cultivated allies as needed and cut deals when expedient, in a world where friends and enemies were not defined by religion alone. 'The political situation and military situation was complicated, and it's very important to realize that this would not have been a battle between a Muslim force and an indigenous Hindu force,' Laine says. 'The Hindu kings would have had Muslim soldiers; the Muslim kings would have had Hindu soldiers; they would have had allies across those boundaries.'

Seeing Shivaji in these terms – as a real historical person, with less than superhuman motivations, and fighting for something other than a pure religious ideology – can be a risky business. In 2004, after Laine's book about Shivaji was published in India, a hundred enraged Marathas ransacked the Bhandarkar Oriental Research Institute in Pune, whose archivists had helped Laine conduct research among its invaluable collection of rare books and manuscripts. But it wasn't only Maratha hardliners who attacked the book. The state government also had it banned (the ban was later overturned by the Indian Supreme Court).

The chauvinist ideal of Shivaji does not come from his own writings. He left no personal letters or diaries; like many warriors of his era and region, he was probably illiterate. But the glorification of his efforts began to take shape in his own lifetime, not least when he commissioned an epic Sanskrit poem about his feats for his coronation as Chhatrapati in 1674. A rich seam of Maratha literary sources, beginning with late seventeenth-century ballads and later comprising chronicles known as *bakhars*, reinforced the image of Shivaji as a heroic figure. Many of those accounts feature a story that is regularly enacted by schoolchildren across Maharashtra today. In 1659, Afzal Khan, a particularly vicious anti-Hindu warlord, was dispatched from the court of the Adil Shah to subdue the restless young Maratha. Shivaji was summoned to a meeting at which he was expected to declare his fealty to the Sultan, as his father had done. Antennae ever alert, he arrived secretly armed, with steel 'tiger claws' hidden in his hands. As Khan – who had his own dagger at the ready – moved in to feign greetings, Shivaji pounced, clawing Khan apart. In the mayhem that ensued, Khan's head was chopped off.

Shivaji's rise – or, as others prefer to see it, his defence of his Hindu homeland against Muslim invasion – now accelerated. Before long, he was in open revolt against the Mughal emperor Aurangzeb, and had humiliated one of Aurangzeb's most senior commanders. Then, in 1664, he captured and sacked the wealthy Gujarati city of Surat, which was the Mughal Empire's most vital commercial port and its departure point for the Hajj. (He returned in 1670 to plunder it, his treasury in need of replenishment.) In the earliest of the narratives praising Shivaji, a bakhar in the Marathi language dating from 1694, Aurangzeb is driven mad by Shivaji's constant nose-thumbing. 'What is the solution? . . . What will I do to crush this pest?' Aurangzeb is made to groan as he stomps his feet.

The big showdown between the Mughal emperor and the Maratha upstart occurred not on the battlefield, but at Aurangzeb's Agra court, in 1666. The previous year, one of Aurangzeb's generals had dealt a partial defeat to Shivaji's forces, and the Mughals now hoped to incorporate him into their empire. They thought they could buy him off in the way the emperor **Akbar (16)** had done two generations before with the troublesome Rajputs.

Shivaji saw advantages to the idea, so he journeyed to Agra in hopes of striking a deal. Once there, however, he was slighted and mistreated by Aurangzeb, who placed him under house arrest. Shivaji outwitted his captor, slipping away, the stories say, in a basket of sweets. (More likely, he slipped his guards some silver coin.) He then headed back to his hill forts – not to hide, but to announce himself as a new power.

Aurangzeb never forgot this humiliation. In his will he recorded: 'Negligence for a single moment becomes the cause of disgrace for long years. The escape of the wretch Shiva took place through carelessness, and I have to labour hard [against the Marathas] to the end of my life [as a result of it].' François Bernier, Aurangzeb's French physician, observed on his departure from India in 1667 that Shivaji was mocking the Mughal Empire, 'exercising all the powers of an independent sovereign'.

At the beginning of June 1674, roughly 11,000 people climbed – or were borne – up a steep hill to Raigad Fort, Shivaji's home base. They had come to witness his grand coronation. The event was four months in the planning, and reports from Dutch and British East

India Company officers described the intense preparations. Sacred water and earth had been hauled up to the fort from as far away as the river Ganga; large halls were built; and Shivaji sourced diamonds, pearls and jewellery from around the world. One Maharashtrian translator reported to a British official, 'Sevagee is making a throne very magnificent on which he spends much gold and jewels.' An English trading officer described the throne's design: 'on each side of the throne there hung (according to the Moores manner) on heads of guilded lances many emblems of Government and dominion, as on the right hand were two great fishes heads of gould with very large teeth; on the left hand severall horses tailes, a paire of gould scales on a very rich lance head poized equally, an emblem of justice.'

Shivaji's meticulously choreographed ceremony gives us an insight into how he wished to be seen by the world. A Maratha Kunbi like Shivaji, though he may have amassed considerable power, was not entitled to rule, according to the Hindu caste order. So preceding the ceremony were religious wheelings and dealings. Shivaji brought in around 1,000 Brahmins, including the renowned scholar and pandit Gaga Bhatt from the holy city of Benares. A fortnight before the coronation, in a sacred thread ceremony, Shivaji was initiated into the Kshatriya caste and raised to the Rajput warrior clan of Sisodias. Such genealogical sleights were not uncommon, and many Maratha tillers-turned-fighters, drawn from the Kunbi and other lower castes, would later claim descent from the higher-caste Rajput warriors of Rajasthan.

The price Shivaji had to pay for acquiring this caste legitimacy (a bit like a papal indulgence) had been vigorously negotiated by the presiding Brahmins: he was required to gift them a fifteen-kilogramme gold idol of Vishnu and to distribute other expensive commodities, measured out in his body weight, as well as 'many elephants, horses and money'.

The coronation, or *abhisheka*, finally took place under the Chhatradharan, the royal umbrella. The origins of the abhisheka lay in Vedic ritual; it was an intricate procedure involving several baths and changes of vestments. No ruler had performed the abhisheka ceremony for at least two centuries. Even Hindu rulers and courts drew on Persian styles and symbols associated with the Mughals. Shivaji dressed in the Persian style, and his coronation ceremonies included some Mughal emblems, but he was now announcing himself as a *Hindu* kingly power who would rule over Hindu society from within.

The coronation rituals were designed to mirror the orthodox Hindu social order that Shivaji claimed to defend. Here, for instance, is what happened during one of the several purification rituals: Brahmins poured ghee from a golden pot on his east side; Kshatriyas poured milk from a silver pot on his south side; Vaishyas poured curds from a copper pot at the west; and Shudras poured water from an earthen pot to his north.

Despite its clear Brahminic symbolism, Shivaji's spectacular coronation has become controversial among some Marathas. For many from the lower castes, to accept that Brahmins led the ceremonies is to cede control over Shivaji's memory to the upper castes. But Shivaji's deal with the Brahmins can also be read another way. He was declaring that, even though a Maratha Kunbi – a 'peasant boy' was how his enemy Afzal Khan taunted him – might rank below a Brahmin, he could still pay for them to anoint him as ruler and buy their acquiescence. In that light, he wasn't so much affirming the power of the Brahmins as tainting and weakening their supposedly inviolable authority – even as he was acquiring some of it for himself.

By the time of his death in 1680, Shivaji commanded a realm of some 130,000 square kilometres (around 4 per cent of the subcontinent), collecting revenues equal to more than a fifth of what Aurangzeb drew. He had graduated from adolescent rebel to commander of the most important rival to the Mughal Empire until the expansion of British rule a century later.

In the nineteenth and twentieth centuries, some Indians likened Shivaji to the Italian Garibaldi, a fighter for national independence. Others saw him as a saintly figure in the bhakti tradition, fighting for the downtrodden and a more egalitarian order. For Hindus well beyond Maharashtra he remains an important champion, and, in Maharashtra, there's still no figure from history more beloved.

Shivaji, the Hindu avenger, though, might in coming decades seem less appealing than Shivaji, the maker of his own career. Today, senior managers bring their employees to his forts and battlegrounds on corporate bonding excursions, hoping that his ambition and spirit might lift individual performances – and company profits. 'Shivaji Maharaj is our idol,' a company CEO leading his employees around Raigad Fort tells me. 'He's our god. He's a right networker, to select the right people, to fight, to develop the right people. So we bring people here to understand how he created history in the world. So we bring people here to create history in their lives.'

20
Nainsukh

Owner Transfixed by Goose
1710–1784

There's a game you start to play after looking at hundreds of Indian miniature paintings – call it Mughal miniature bingo. Is there an imperious prince with a very straight back? Check. Pavilions? Check. Musicians? Gathered courtiers? Glorious gardens? Check, check, check. Most of these paintings, exquisite as they are technically, were controlled – even calculated – images. You start to feel this is rote work, and to sense the subservience of the artist to those who commissioned it.

In the Mughal era, many paintings were essentially press releases for royalty. So it's bracing to turn to portraits of Balwant Singh, a minor royal – pretty much a nobody in eighteenth-century India's princely hierarchy – who has become one of the more intriguing subjects in Indian art. We know about him today only because of his intimate, profoundly creative relationship with a painter from Guler named Nainsukh.

Guler, a small kingdom in the Himalayan foothills, was one of the homes of the well-established Pahari school of miniature painting. Nainsukh, though, was different from his predecessors – in the extraordinary precision of his lines, the bold use of blank space in his compositions, the emotional poise of his portraits. But what I love about Nainsukh's work is that everyday concerns of his time aren't banished from the frame.

In London's Victoria & Albert Museum, which holds around a dozen of Nainsukh's works, there's a striking painting of Balwant Singh being entertained by a group of musicians and players. As the prince smokes a hookah, one performer mimics him, pretending to drag from a long paper scroll. Come closer, though, and look at the lead singer with a magnifying glass. This thin man in a neat white and orange turban has tiny scars on his face – marks from smallpox, one of the leading causes of death in the eighteenth century.

It's often said that life in India is so chaotic, so overloaded with sensory stimuli, that Indians stop seeing what's all around them. Nainsukh, however, saw plenty – the domestic, the natural, the found comedy of courtly life. In Balwant Singh, he had a patron confident enough in his own self-image to allow Nainsukh to escape the stiff formalities often found in the miniature genre, and to express a more original vision. His technical skill, his clarity of sight, is focused on the quirks, and thus the humanity, of the individual – whether king, lowly musician, or himself.

The painter Howard Hodgkin is a connoisseur of Indian art and a collector of Nainsukh's work. 'He's a truly great artist,' Hodgkin says. 'He's not the first, of course, because many of the Mughal painters had an identity and were written about, but I would have said even so he was probably the first great *modern* artist of India.'

Nainsukh was born in 1710, into a family of highly skilled paint-ers. His father and brother schooled him in the Pahari tradition of the hill areas of northern India, which was characterized by simpli-fied landscapes or interiors, flat monochromatic backgrounds and, in the foreground, stylized, often static, portraiture. But Nainsukh learned his art in a period of stylistic transition, as elements of Mughal painting began to percolate through the Pahari artistic world. A greater interest in naturalistic details developed, along-side more subtle colour palettes, and a growing refinement of line. This gave Nainsukh scope to stretch the inherited boundaries of his art.

A self-portrait by Nainsukh at around twenty years old shows a lean face with a faint moustache, a shaven head adorned by a single tuft of hair under a sharply angled turban, and prominent front teeth. Truth was clearly more important than vanity. His left hand supports a *takhti*, or wooden drawing board. In his right hand, a brush is poised above blank paper. He is just at the moment of beginning to draw, and his expression is intent, as if he's fixing an image in his mind.

Around the time he created this portrait, Nainsukh met Balwant Singh at Jasrota, the citadel of a minor hill kingdom in today's Himachal Pradesh. Nainsukh had left his home in Guler in search of a patron, and had initially worked for Balwant's father, who was a princely relative of the Jasrota maharaja.

Nainsukh's first portraits of his new patron date from the early 1740s, when Balwant Singh was around seventeen. One of the earliest of these paintings was rediscovered a little over a decade ago, in a private collection in Lahore. It shows Balwant as a beard-less adolescent, in an elegant embroidered Mughal-style *jama*, or gown, sitting on a terrace furnished with bolsters. He has a hookah in hand, and a sword beside him. It's one of the most formal and conventional portraits Nainsukh ever painted. Yet he manages to break the stiffness by giving us what he saw rather than what was expected. Even as Singh is shown in a classical pose, his left hand – quite poorly drawn – is, unconventionally, turned backwards at the wrist.

Soon, Nainsukh was starting to experiment more boldly. He played with scale, giving depth to the background with a single horizontal line. Restraining his use of colour, he celebrated white and blank expanses of paper. Many of his paintings display a great compositional confidence, and equally striking is the sense of ease, even equality, in his portrayals of his patron. Nainsukh shows Singh obediently having his beard trimmed by a barber; huddled ill and depressed under a bulky quilt; and writing a letter bare-chested in his tent, while his attendant, fly whisk in hand, has dozed off in the hot afternoon.

Portraits like these were rare for the times, given the hierarchical relations between patron and court painter. There's an almost Instagram-like familiarity. B. N. Goswamy is one of India's leading art historians, and an authority on Nainsukh. 'He attached himself to this prince, who was not even a member of the main ruling family – probably was a pretender to the throne,' Goswamy says. 'But Nainsukh stayed with him. Twenty years or more he stayed

with him. I mean, he was like a shadow – or maybe Balwant Singh
was a shadow of Nainsukh.'

In one of Howard Hodgkin's favourite paintings, Balwant Singh,
wearing pink slippers and holding a sword, stares transfixed at his
pet goose. It's a humorous and moving play on convention. 'Of
course in the centre of it, it's all highly formalized,' Hodgkin says.
The goose, too, is 'completely transfixed by the look he gets from his
owner,' he says, laughing. 'As far as I can tell, this is almost unique
in the history of Indian painting. Balwant Singh was clearly a man of
real sensitivity. Well, they both were.'

Goswamy thinks that the two men must have had a regular dialogue about Nainsukh's work, but that Singh did not command him
to paint this or that scene. As a result, Goswamy says, Nainsukh
recorded things few court painters in Indian history could. 'No other
patron that I know of in the Indian context would have allowed it.'

Both Nainsukh and Balwant Singh shared a deep interest in music
and dance, and some of Nainsukh's most vivid paintings are of court
performances. In one of his greatest works, to my eye, music, patron
and artist all come together. It's a painting of Singh sitting on his
takht, or throne. In one hand, as was his custom, is a hookah. In the
other is a painting. It's been handed to him by Nainsukh, who stands
behind his patron, leaning forward, hands folded, all buck-teeth. He
seems to be waiting on the prince's verdict.

On the other side of the painting, looking on at artist and patron,
is a group of musicians and retainers. Each face is distinct; their
expressions, features and skin colours hint at a range of histories,
untold stories. These were people Nainsukh would quite probably
have hung out with. 'Watch the fingers of the man who's playing on
the drum and the one who's playing on the Jew's harp – it's astonishing,' Goswamy says. 'My guess is that after some time Nainsukh's
attention started shifting to the minor characters – the musicians, the
dancers, the retainers. Very penetrating and sympathetic studies – it
is the humanity in Nainsukh's work which is so extraordinarily
engaging.'

*

It's habitual to speak of Indian painting in terms of traditions, not individual talent or personality (in a way that T. S. Eliot, who wrote that art was an escape from personality, might have appreciated). But with Nainsukh, we encounter work that seems not just 'of his time', but also simply his own. Instead of the static brightness of the earlier Pahari style, we find intimacy and warmth, mystery and sly humour – individuality. What we don't find is sentimentality. Emotion is understated in Nainsukh. Only a flash of vulnerability or mockery ever gets shown. In his hands, that flash is enough. As Goswamy puts it, 'There's a kind of trilling quality about Nainsukh's work – a lightness of touch, wit and the ability to keep on paying homage to tradition, the classical, and then break free.'

In the last two decades of his life, Nainsukh returned to more conventional subjects: Ragamala paintings depicting musical moods, and scenes from the religious stories and epics – Krishna and the gopis, his cow-herd girl devotees, all in the brighter colours of the more traditional Pahari style. For once in Indian history, the explanation is simple: Balwant Singh died in 1763 and Nainsukh had to find a new patron. At Basholi, another hill kingdom, he found a prince with a more conventional sensibility.

If these late paintings are staid compared with what came before, Nainsukh's brilliance still surfaces occasionally. In one of his final masterpieces, it's night time. Villagers gather around a fire, smoking hookahs and chillums, some seen in silhouette and others illuminated by flame. A child, up past bedtime, nestles in the arms of one of the elders. A woman looks on from a doorway. Bright sparks fly up from the fire to the branches of a tree and mingle with the stars beyond. 'The way Nainsukh studies the reflections, shadows – it's not a night scene,' Goswamy says. 'It's his way of telling you: this is how night *falls*. Subtlety – subtlety is the essence.'

21

William Jones

Enlightenment Mughal
1746–1794

On 25 September 1783, a frigate named the *Crocodile* sailed up
the Hooghly river in Bengal and docked at Calcutta's Chandpal
Ghat. On board was a thirty-six-year-old Welsh scholar and barrister, bearing essentials for what he expected to be a six-year stint
in India. These included two large sheep and an intrepid young
wife whom he had married just four days before embarking from
England. Awaiting him in Calcutta was an East India Company
judgeship with a salary far greater than he had ever known. His
hope was to incorporate Hindu and Muslim laws into his own rul-
ings, so that the British could govern Indians according to Indians'
own 'manners and sentiments'. During the leisurely journey from
England, he put to paper an exhaustive list of topics he needed
to study:

> The Laws of the Hindus and Mohammedans; The History of the
> Ancient World; . . . Modern Politics and Geography of Hindustan;
> Best Mode of Governing Bengal; Arithmetic and Geometry and the
> mixed Sciences of the Asiatics; Medicine, Chemistry, Surgery, and
> Anatomy of the Indians; . . . The Poetry, Rhetoric, and the Morality
> of Asia; Music of the Eastern Nations . . .

The list went on. Ambitious as it was, this plan would eventually be
dwarfed by what he achieved in his eleven years in India. Sir William
Jones was to become the greatest Orientalist of his time. Two hundred years later, Edward Said and his epigones would turn that
word – 'Orientalist' – into a slur, but Jones produced a revolution
in knowledge about language and history. 'A far-seeing man,' the

German Romanticist Goethe would say of Jones, 'he seeks to connect the unknown to the known.'

Jones brought to Calcutta something more useful than sheep: an uncanny mastery of languages. Eventually, he would learn twenty-eight languages – or, as friends ribbed him, every language but his native Welsh. When he turned this prodigious skill to ancient Sanskrit texts, the effects were profound. He would go on to change not just the way the world sees India, but how Indians see their own history and culture.

In his lifetime, Jones garnered almost as many nicknames as he gleaned languages: Harmonious Jones, Persian Jones, Asiatic Jones, Oriental Jones. The son of an accomplished Anglesey mathematician, his genius was recognized early. A star at Harrow, he learned Greek and Latin as you might expect, but also French, Italian and Hebrew. A love of the *Arabian Nights* and Persian poetry in translation inspired him to cajole a native speaker at Oxford to teach him the language. Jones later remarked, 'From my earliest years, I was charmed with the poetry of the Greeks; nothing, I then thought, could be more sublime . . .; but when I had tasted the poetry of the Arabs and Persians—'

After Oxford, Jones wrote *A Grammar of the Persian Language*, and translated Confucius and Mandarin poetry to great acclaim. But these were not the sort of works to earn him much, so in 1774 he turned to legal practice. Nine years later, his ability to understand the languages, laws and customs of other cultures brought him an offer to become one of four judges on the Bengal Presidency's newly established Supreme Court in Calcutta – the first Supreme Court in the world.

Politically, Jones wasn't the safest choice for the job. He had ardently supported the American independence movement, wrote political tracts of a republican stripe, and was radical in many of his leanings. He was also that shifty unpredictable animal, a poet. But he reassured his patrons that his interests in India wouldn't extend to political rights, and that he would 'certainly not preach' democracy to the Indians, 'who must and will be governed by absolute power'.

Jones believed the authority of that absolute power must never-theless be established on the basis of India's ancient laws – not London's diktats. But presiding in the new court, he grew impatient, and not a little suspicious, at having to depend on Brahmin pandits for translations of Sanskrit ethics and legal codes, and of oaths in particular. (This topic greatly exercised the British: since Indians would not swear on the Bible, but instead offered a variety of other oaths, the veracity of their legal testimony was always suspect in British eyes.) Better, Jones thought, to learn the infernal language himself.

Few pandits were willing to teach a caste outsider, fearing ritual pollution and, perhaps not incidentally, a loss of their monopoly on the language. Instead, Jones found a scholar named Ramlochan, whom he hired for the then princely sum of 100 rupees a month. Ramlochan was a *vaidya*, from the caste of medical practitioners, and though not a Brahmin, he still feared that proximity to the eccentric white man would lead to loss of his caste status. So, in accordance with ritual strictures, a 'pure' room was constructed for their lessons, and its white marble flooring was cleansed every day with Ganga water.

Within months, Jones was industriously translating Sanskrit hymns to Hindu gods, then moving on to study the great epics, the Mahabharata and Ramayana (all while preparing to work on a Digest of Hindu and Muslim laws, the fulcrum of his day job). He soon gained access to a wealth of literary creativity that had remained unknown in the West. As the writer and historian William Dalrymple puts it:

Jones quickly discovers that he's stepped into an intellectual gold-mine. He discovers that Sanskrit is a language which is not only as old as Latin and Greek, he discovers what no European has realized to this point – that there is still surviving a vast body of Indian clas-sical literature which we know today is about one thousand times as large as the surviving classical literature of Greek and Latin com-bined. And he discovers that there are these great plays which are the equals of Shakespeare, that there are these epics which are the equal of Homer, and he can't believe his luck. He also can't believe that no one else has taken any interest in this stuff.

Jones's passion for Persian was now eclipsed by the majesty and depth of this new language. From his study of Sanskrit epics and plays, he began to glean historical clues about the opaque chronology of the Indian past. He found that he could match figures from Indian history to those mentioned in ancient Greek texts, whose dates were known. The Greek texts about Alexander the Great's Indian campaign, for instance, mentioned the name of an Indian king, Sandracottos, who ruled from the city of Palibothra. Jones, in his Sanskrit reading, had stumbled across the name of Chandragupta, and he realized this was the king the Greeks had been talking about. He managed to identify the Mauryan emperor, Ashoka's grandfather, whose capital had been Pataliputra – and was now able to date Chandragupta's reign to the fourth century BCE (see 5 **Ashoka**). Amidst the quicksand of Indian historical dates, Jones had broken through to chronological bedrock.

There would be other breakthroughs too. Jones's biggest realization emerged during his early months of Sanskrit study. He made an argument – still embraced by modern philologists – that utterly startled the reading public of the West:

> The *Sanscrit* language, whatever be its antiquity, is of a wonderful structure; more perfect than the *Greek*, more copious than the *Latin*, and more exquisitely refined than either, yet bearing to both of them a stronger affinity, both in the roots of verbs and the forms of grammar, than could possibly have been produced by accident; so strong indeed, that no philologer could examine them all three, without believing them to have sprung from some common source . . .

This insight – that Sanskrit and the European classical languages were all branches of a single, lost linguistic river – helped to challenge prejudice and reconnect the world. Jones was arguing that Sanskrit was a 'beautiful sister' of Greek and Latin. 'Imagine the effect of that upon Britain, upon people some of whom looked down on Indians' idolatrous practices and thought they were fit only to be servants,' Jones's biographer, Professor Michael Franklin of Swansea University, says. 'It was a disconcerting idea that Sanskrit is a more beautiful, a more refined language. To use the epithet "refined" of Indians – this was revolutionary.'

On 15 January 1784, Jones gathered thirty British residents of Calcutta in the grand jury room of the Supreme Court. As he put it, they were men of business, but he formed them into an amateur's club aiming at the highest level of academic study of the East.

The Asiatic Society of Bengal would be modelled on London's Royal Society. Jones's optimism and ambition rang out clearly in his first presentation to the Society, entitled 'A Discourse on the Institution of a Society for enquiring into the History, Civil and Natural, the Antiquities, Arts, Sciences and Literature of Asia'. In it, he declared, 'If now it be asked, what are the intended objects of our inquiries within these spacious limits, we answer, MAN and NATURE; whatever is performed by the one, or produced by the other.' The post of president of the Society was offered to Warren Hastings, India's first governor general and a great promoter and patron of scholarship on India. He declined, citing a want of leisure, so Jones was elected in his place.

Despite the practical money-making interests of its members, it's striking how fixed the focus of Jones's band of amateur scholars was on studies of the ancient and courtly languages, Sanskrit and Persian. The languages and life of the streets around them were not of interest. Jones had also wanted to induct learned Indians as members, to participate and aid in the society's explorations of ancient history, epigraphy, linguistics, astronomy, music, physiology and archaeology – but he was overruled (Indians weren't allowed to enter for another half century). The members, Jones not excepted, tended to be more appreciative of India's textual past than its human present.

The discoveries born of this interest would nevertheless have a lasting impact on India and the West. Many of the members of the Society produced works that contributed significantly to Western knowledge about the subcontinent. 'Jones is a catalyst,' William Dalrymple says. 'He uses his authority, his charisma to set all these other characters alight.' But no one's contribution outshone Jones's. Opening his 'First Discourse' he had said, 'Gentlemen, when I was at sea last August on my voyage to this country which I had long and ardently desired to visit, I found one evening on inspecting the observations of the day that India lay before us and Persia on our left. Whilst a breeze from Arabia blew nearly on our stern . . .' It was this sense of being in the midst of currents of different civilizations – Persian, Sanskrit, Arabic – that led him to the research to which he devoted the remaining years of his life.

Perhaps nothing excited the West more about the potential riches of Indian civilization than Jones's translation of Kalidasa's *Shakuntala*, one of the masterpieces of ancient Sanskrit literature, which he published in 1789. The original was 'so much like Shakespeare', Jones wrote, 'that I should have thought our great dramatick poet had studied Kalidasa'. In one scene, the Emperor of India first catches sight of the heroine, Shakuntala, 'so lovely a girl, who ravishes his soul', and gazes on her from behind a tree. In his translation Jones tried to maintain a balance between the sensuous and the restrained, but was not always comfortable with the easy eroticism of Kalidasa's verse:

> Her charms cannot be hidden, even though a robe of intertwisted fibres be thrown over her shoulders and conceal a part of her bosom, like a veil of yellow leaves enfolding a radiant flower. The water lily, though dark moss may settle on its head, is nevertheless beautiful; and the moon with dewy beams is rendered yet brighter by its black spots. The bark itself acquires elegance from the features of a girl with antelope's eyes and rather augments, than diminishes, my ardour. Many are the rough stalks which support the water lily; but many and exquisite are the blossoms which hang on them.

Jones's *Shakuntala* became a European sensation, setting off a bout of Indomania among tight-laced academicians. The German poet and philosopher Friedrich von Schlegel, for one, was enraptured. He wrote of the translated work, 'all is animated with a deep and lovely tenderness of feeling; an air of sweetness and beauty is diffused over the whole'.

From his letters home, it is gloriously clear that Jones's studies in India brought him joy. 'I never was unhappy in England; it was not in my nature to be so; but I never was so happy till I settled in India,' he wrote. But he was also frequently ill; a friend visiting from London once described him as a 'perfect skeleton'.

Still, he carried on with his work, allowing no concessions in his schedule. When he was not in court, his day looked like this:

> Morning . . . . One letter.
> Ten chapters of the Bible.
> Sanscrit Grammar.
> Hindu Law, &c.
> Afternoon . . . . Indian Geography.
> Evening . . . . Roman History.
> Chess. Ariosto.

In 1794, he finally published his translation of a Sanskrit compilation of Hindu law, *Institutes of Hindu Law: Or the Ordinances of Manu*, which he had first come across in 1785. This body of legal thought (which legend dates to roughly 10,000 years ago, but which most scholars believe was formalized within a few hundred years before or after the start of the Common Era) was held in high esteem by many Hindus, but it also served to enshrine the Brahminic conception of Hindu society, and ignored the vast diversity of local legal customs. Jones used it to develop principles of jurisprudence for all Hindus, while Muslims and other communities received their own laws.

For better or worse, Jones's translation would become the foundation for much of subsequent Indian jurisprudence. But the project, and India, had left him spent. His wife, finally finding the climate too much, had sailed back to England in 1793. The following April, as he was preparing to join her, Jones died from inflammation of the liver. After a decade in Calcutta, he left behind a huge list of future works to translate, plus an unfinished geography and history of

India. And his wife, the daughter of a radical bishop, proved herself far from the customary scholar's wife, thanked in acknowledgements for her patient suffering. It was Anna Maria Jones who, within less than two years of receiving the shipment of her dead husband's papers and manuscripts, turned them into a six-volume edition of his works.

Despite the scale of Jones's achievement, the wonder of Sanskrit and ancient Indian literature wore off pretty quickly in the West. By the early nineteenth century, the shield of Burkean conservatism, which offered to protect cultures and traditions, had been replaced by the reformist stick of Benthamite utilitarianism, intent on correcting cultural habits in the light of reason and utility. India, with its irrational laws and customs (sati, or widow immolation, being a prime example) was a perfect schooling ground. The British in India came to see plays like *Shakuntala* as examples of 'the greatest immorality and impurity', and, in 1835, Lord Macaulay, decreeing the educational curriculum for Indians, removed Sanskrit and Persian literature in favour of the moral uplift of Milton and Pope. As he put it then, in a line that has since become infamous, 'a single shelf of a good European library was worth the whole native literature of India and Arabia'.

But in some respects Jones's impact persists. Scholarship and power often go together; though Jones was devoted to literature and language, his labours also helped lay the groundwork for British rule in India, and helped, too, to give that dominion a legitimacy that sustained it for the next century and a half. Even as ruling ideologies changed, the British broadly maintained solicitude for Indian customs and laws. That legacy continues, not without controversy, in India today. The country still has multiple codes of civil law, specific to different religious communities – which some see as an anomaly in a country that claims to be a secular liberal republic.

In his search to understand India, Jones had also turned to the Brahmins. The pandits were often his interpreters and guides, and he saw Brahminism as the 'true' Hinduism. In this way, the studies of Jones and his fellow scholars seeded the ground for the later cultivation of a golden-hued nostalgia about the ancient Vedic past – which became in turn a source for the Hindu revivalism that nourishes the modern-day ideology of Hindutva.

You can't blame an industrious eighteenth-century scholar-judge for this – just as you can hardly blame him for those who would later take his idea of a common Indo-European language and pervert it into a genocidal origin myth about an ancient Aryan race. It's only slightly more plausible to write off Jones as an Orientalist in Edward Said's negative meaning: a man who celebrated the exoticism of the East as a way to deny it political legitimacy. Said was right – this did indeed happen on a huge scale. But there is also a long history of intellectual amateurs who laboured more for enthusiasm than profit. (Many of these amateurs were invisible to the East India Company, not shills for it.) William Jones was an Orientalist in this more positive sense: a man who arrived in India and studied its culture with humility, and then sought to awaken the West to its riches. The irony is that he also awakened the East.

22

Rammohun Roy

'Humanity in General'
1772–1833

In Bristol's wooded Arnos Vale cemetery there is an unusual memorial. Above neat rows of granite crosses and Victorian marble obelisks towers a pavilion some thirty feet high, built in an Indian style – twelve pillars, made of Bath stone, supporting a canopy topped by a four-sided dome of the sort typical in Bengal. Similar *chhatri* dot the Indian landscape, commemorating the dead, but one doesn't often see them in Britain. It's a fitting monument for a man who stood out not only in India, but also in the larger history of his age. 'Beneath this stone,' reads the epitaph,

> rest the remains of Raja Rammohun Roy Bahadoor, a conscientious and steadfast believer in the unity of the Godhead, he consecrated his life with entire devotion to the worship of the Divine Spirit alone, to great natural talents, he united thorough mastery of many languages and early distinguished himself as one of the greatest scholars of his day. His unwearied labours to promote the social, moral and physical condition of the people of India, his earnest endeavours to suppress idolatry, and the rite of suttee and his constant zealous advocacy of whatever tended to advance the glory of God and the welfare of man live in the grateful remembrance of his countrymen.

By the time of his death in Bristol in 1833, the Bengali scholar Rammohun Roy had become a worldwide intellectual celebrity. An English contemporary called him a 'lion of the season', and he was sufficiently dashing that a lock of his luxuriant hair has been preserved at the Bristol Museum. 'He was a man of charisma and he was

a man of determination,' Carla Contractor, a historian who has documented the three years Roy spent in Britain, says:

> He was six feet tall, a towering figure, and he made sure he dressed
> in flowing muslin robes, but with spats and European shoes. He
> wowed people, and they half-expected to be overwhelmed by this
> man. Whichever party he was invited to go to, he went. And he
> made sure that he spoke to the people that he wanted to. He was a
> networker of the first order.

Roy was part of an international set of late eighteenth- and early
nineteenth-century radicals and reformers who attacked established
religion and ruling despots, including the East India Company. He
corresponded with Thomas Paine, author of the *Rights of Man*, and
with the philosopher Jeremy Bentham, who wanted him to sit in the
Westminster House of Commons. In Spain, liberals dedicated the
country's 1812 Constitution to him. In America, the young Ralph
Waldo Emerson read him avidly. Roy celebrated Latin American
revolutions and dined with the king of France. 'Rammohun was the
first Indian to have a significant view of the outside world, not just
meaning the Mughal world or the Hindu world, but meaning the
European world,' the late Sir Christopher Bayly, Cambridge professor and a leading historian of India, told me. 'He also had some sense
that India was part of a world community.'

What gained Roy renown in the West, above all, was his advocacy
to improve the status of women in India, and to abolish the practice
of sati (or 'suttee', as it was then known), the Hindu rite in which
widows would immolate themselves on their husband's funeral
pyres. In his own country, however, Roy's contribution took on a
larger significance. He planted in India a universalist flag, urging his
compatriots to judge their society and its customs by international
standards, at the very moment when these standards were emerging
in the Enlightenment West.

Roy was born in the 1770s, to a Brahmin family in up-country Bengal. His early life was both privileged and unsettled. His father,
Ramakanta, was a *zamindar*, one of the rentier landlords who soon

benefited from the Permanent Settlement of landed property in Bengal, concluded in 1793, which the British devised in order to create a loyal class of wealthy Indians. Ramakanta had three wives, polygamy being standard practice in his Kulin Brahmin sub-caste. Although he and Roy's elder brother would eventually fail in business and be jailed as debtors, there was money enough for Roy to receive a solid education in Persian, Arabic and Sanskrit.

Roy's earliest known manuscript, in Persian, displays an attraction to rationalist arguments and a strong distaste for religious superstition and unquestioning faith. This was perhaps a reaction to the elaborate worship rituals observed by his mother, Tarini Devi – a 'peculiar delirium of pieties' which extended to requiring her son to recite sacred verses before even drinking a glass of water. (To say mother and son had difficulties is an understatement: Roy would eventually humiliate her, legally and socially, during a court battle over property, and she ended her years in retreat, sweeping temple floors.)

In his twenties, Roy went to work for the East India Company, where he started a profitable sideline lending its officers money. He also leveraged property he had inherited to acquire more. By 1814, at the age of forty-two, he finally had the financial wealth to devote himself fully to deeper passions – scholarship, and religious and social reform. For this new chapter in his life, Roy acquired a palatial Georgian mansion in Calcutta, where liberal impulses and ideas – about rationalism, reform and progress – were circulating. The city had publishing houses and major newspapers, and India's first free public library was soon to open there. Roy's home became a weekly meeting-place for freethinkers seeking to reform press censorship and other illiberal aspects of British rule. They were also looking to reform Hindu ritualism. 'I have never ceased,' he wrote of some of the more superstitious and inhumane Hindu customs, such as sati, 'to contemplate these practices with the strongest feelings of regret, and to view in them the moral debasement of a race who, I cannot help thinking, are capable of better things; whose susceptibility, patience, and mildness of character render them worthy of a better destiny.'

Roy is the first clear case of what would become the natural condition of many later Indian intellectuals. It can be described as an unhappy restlessness between two thoughts: could India be changed for the better using its own historical and intellectual resources? Or must Indians turn to Western and foreign values and ideas to achieve such change, thereby running the risk of undermining their own Indian identity?

Roy tried to resolve this dilemma by imagining a golden age in India's past, and thus a standard by which to criticize and change the fallen present. 'He never used the word reformer,' Christopher Bayly said, 'because his idea was that the ancient religion of India, Advaita Vedanta – the last books of the Vedas – was itself a form of religion which had been corrupted, from monotheism to polytheism, over 300 or 400 years. And his idea was to restore that ancient religion of India.'

Roy's public profile grew quickly, first in India and then in Europe. From 1815 onwards he published many volumes and translations, appropriating Vedantic writings and drawing extensively on the works and commentaries of **Shankara** (8), in order to vindicate his own views and establish himself among a European audience as the authoritative interpreter of Hindu thought and belief. Roy was effecting a crucial shift in the self-conception of the Indian public intellectual: from being a commentator on religious beliefs and texts to becoming an advocate for changing religiously sanctioned social practices.

Over the years, Roy's personal life was tumultuous – three wives, many more affairs, estranged children. But his self-belief was so strong that he eventually decided to start a new religious sect – elite in its membership and puritanical in its tendencies – which came to be known as the Brahmo Samaj. According to Bayly, the Samaj 'was a kind of organization of equals – they were mostly high caste, they were mostly educated – which sought to purge Hinduism of idolatry'.

Though it may have been largely an upper-caste, upper-class club, the Brahmo Samaj preached a religious ethics that combined something of the individuality of bhakti worship with a new vision of Indian society as a whole. 'He argued that it was important to stress that everybody – not just the high caste, not just the renouncers, not just the Brahmins, but the whole of Indian society – could achieve some knowledge of God through good practice, and also good practice in society,' Bayly added. 'It was very much the beginnings of a social turn in Indian society, and a way of breaking down its divisions.'

For Roy, the regeneration of India lay in the social domain, and changing its customs required reform of religious practices such as the worship of idols. Roy came to be known as a 'Hindu Unitarian', and the Indian writer Nirad Chaudhuri, himself a Brahmo, later described him as the instigator of a Hindu Protestant reformation. The influence of this reformation would be felt directly by many important twentieth-century Indians, particularly Bengalis, including the religious reformer **Vivekananda** (28), the poet and thinker Rabindranath **Tagore** (32) and the film-maker **Satyajit Ray** (47).

The Nobel prize-winning economist Amartya Sen also has family connections to the Brahmo Samaj. He sees as characteristic of Roy a certain restriction of vision in the issues that exercised him, matched by an admirable if abstracted human sympathy. 'He concentrated on those things which agitated him most,' Sen says. 'Given his class background, he was mainly concerned with upper-class problems – but he was very sympathetic to humanity in general. He had strong religious views – monotheistic, Unitarian – and he wanted to see the Hindu religion itself having that base at some time.' It was Roy's commitment to universalist principles, directly applied to the social world of his experience, that guided his evolving critique. Sen adds, 'He was initially not very critical of the British. But gradually, as time evolved, he changed that position. He was very much a progressive, upper-class reformer of his time. And he did some splendid things.'

In 1828, Fanny Parkes, a Welsh writer married to a clerk in the East India Company, described the funeral rites of a married Hindu man, which her husband had witnessed:

> After having bathed in the river, the widow lighted a brand, walked round the pile, set it on fire, and then mounted cheerfully: the flame

caught and blazed up instantly; she sat down, placing the head of the corpse on her lap, and repeated several times the usual form, 'Ram, Ram, suttee; Ram, Ram, suttee;' . . . 'God, God, I am chaste.'

As the wind drove the fierce fire upon her, she shook her arms and limbs as if in agony; at length she started up and approached the side to escape. An Hindoo, one of the police who had been placed near the pile to see she had fair play, and should not be burned by force, raised his sword to strike her, and the poor wretch shrank back into the flames.

Like other human acts that leave no survivors to articulate their meaning, sati is open to varying interpretations: is it the noblest form of self-sacrifice – or heinous, expedient murder, removing from families the responsibility to care for widows? Roy found it appalling – it is said that he once witnessed a relative forced to perform the rite – and many of his reform efforts leading up to the creation of the Brahmo Samaj centred on its abolition. In 1816, he visited the Baptist missionaries at Serampore, who regarded the rite as a form of human sacrifice. 'Forbid it, British Power! Forbid it, British humanity!' one of the missionaries urged the following year. By 1818, Roy had published his first tract on sati. His second tract, dedicated to the Marchioness of Hastings, came in 1820. It would make his name outside of India.

Until the nineteenth century, British officials had largely tolerated sati, unwilling to intervene in their subjects' religious customs. But Roy's campaign converged with the birth of an international concern with human rights. In the early decades of the nineteenth century, movements to abolish slavery and capital punishment, to promote the rights of women, and to articulate and uphold humanitarian values became the first global moral crusades.

Sati fitted into this larger discourse, though it was probably not the most pernicious social ill inflicted on Indian women. In most parts of the country, it was exceptionally rare and, if anything, on the decline. But sati had seen an upsurge in Bengal during Roy's lifetime; in 1823, there were approaching 600 recorded cases. The ritual was rooted in Hindu custom (instances can be found in the

Mahabharata), and Hindu practice certainly permitted it, if not actually prescribing it. To Amartya Sen, Roy's focus on sati accorded with Roy's generally patrician attitude to reform:

> The barbarity of it horrified him, so I don't think you have to ask why was Roy interested in it. He had good reason to be. But his natural sympathy was in the direction of preventing nastiness as opposed to social change. He's often taken to be a great social reformer, but there, I think, much more credit needs to go to people like Ishwar Chandra Vidyasagar, who was concerned with the remarriage of Hindus, preventing polygamy – these are subjects on which Rammohun had sympathy but didn't do very much.

Roy was not in favour of government interference in religious matters. Rather, he hoped Indians would abolish the practice of sati themselves. Among his main appeals to his fellow Indians was that it had no justification in Hindu law or scripture. And in order to remove any economic grounds for the practice, he also called for property rights to be given to women, which would help ensure their security after their husbands' deaths.

The campaign against sati was useful to Roy, enabling him to promote himself as a native moral conscience in tune with international norms. But he was not the only one for whom it was a boon, and reform ultimately came not from within India, but with a government ban, in 1829. The ruling marked a major shift in how the British saw their place in the country. Henceforth, part of their justification for ruling over Indians was the need to civilize them and educate them away from barbaric practices. Sati was a ready way of foregrounding the primitive bloodthirstiness of the Hindus, and of justifying the corrective despotism that the British now saw themselves as dispensing to India's benefit.

In the summer of 1833, while visiting Bristol, Rammohun Roy contracted meningitis and died suddenly. He had originally come to Britain in 1830 to lobby against a counter-petition by conservative Bengalis to overturn the ban on sati. 'He found himself arriving in England at just the moment to catch what was going on about

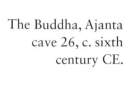
The Buddha, Ajanta cave 26, c. sixth century CE.

The seventeen-meter-tall statue of Bahubali, or Gommata, c. 983 CE, at Sravanabelagola, Karnataka.

Ashokan lions at the Great Stupa at Sanchi, Madhya Pradesh, photographed by Deen Dayal in the 1880s. The image has been rotated 90 degrees.

A colossal statue of Basava at Basavakalyan, Karnataka, constructed in 2012.

A courtly scene, frontispiece
to a collection of poetry
by Amir Khusrau Dhilavi.
Safavid school, Iran, 1609.

An eighteenth-century miniature showing Guru Nanak
with his companions Bhai Mardana and Bhai Bala.

Krishnadevaraya, as shown in a popular commercial print, twentieth century.

A contemporary poster showing the popular image of Mirabai.

The interior of the Diwan-i-Khas, or Hall of Public Audience, Fatehpur Sikri.

Jahangir Shooting Malik Ambar, painting by Abu'l Hasan, c. 1615.

Rembrandt van Rijn, *Shah Jahan and Dara Shikoh*, c. 1654–1656.

Nainsukh, *Self-Portrait*, 1730.

John Linnell after Joshua
Reynolds, *Sir William Jones*,
c. 1827.

Detail from Johann Zoffany, *Sacrifice of a Hindoo Woman
on the Funeral Pyre of Her Husband*, c. 1780.

Lakshmi Bai, Rani of
Jhansi, as shown in a
popular oleograph print,
c. 1930.

Deen Dayal's portrait of the Sixth Nizam of Hyderabad, The
Royal Champion Crackshot, displaying his hunting trophies,
1894.

Birsa Munda in manacles after his arrest, c. 1895.

Portrait of Jamsetji Tata by Deen Dayal, 1898.

The cover of a mid-twentieth-century matchbox, sold to accompany Vivekananda Beedies.

women's rights,' Carla Contractor says. 'And because he had fought for women's rights, particularly against concremation as he called it, he had a very warm reception.' When he died, an obituary in *The Times* of London concluded, 'A more remarkable man has not distinguished modern times and advance of opinion.'

Today, some Indians take a more critical view of Roy, seeing him as the ultimate colonized mind, in thrall to British ideas and expert at flattering his colonial masters. But others see in his life the early glimmerings of Indian nationalism. He came to believe that the ancient Indians had governed themselves democratically – a rejoinder to the British insistence that Indians were culturally habituated to despotic rule, and unaccustomed to democratic ideas. Roy's claim might have been as dubious as the British one, but it served as a lifeline, however imaginary, to Indian nationalists a century later.

Though Roy eagerly pursued fame and recognition, at home and in the West, one of his lasting legacies was to chide educated Indians into questioning their own habits in the light of universal values. Ever since, Indians have been part of a global argument about the nature of justice, rights and freedom – even as they've struggled to preserve their own traditions and systems of knowledge. Roy also showed how, in dreaming up a past better than the fallen present, Indians might aspire to a fairer future.

23
Lakshmi Bai, Rani of Jhansi

Bad-ass Queen
1828–1858

Even the terms used to describe the famous Indian uprising against the British in 1857 are political positions. Was it a mutiny, or India's First War of Independence? Rebellion or uprising? A nationalist movement or a string of local protests?

The violence began in Meerut, in present-day Uttar Pradesh, and the proximate cause was the British acquisition of Enfield rifles. To load these new weapons, Bengal sepoys – the security forces for the Raj – had to use their teeth to tear open paper cartridges produced, in accordance with a British design, at the Dumdum Arsenal, on the outskirts of Calcutta. A rumour had spread that the cartridges were greased with tallow and lard. Biting down on them was therefore an affront to Hindus and Muslims alike.

The first to be appalled was a Brahmin worker at the arsenal, which still today produces ordnance for the Indian military. His disgust quickly spread among the sepoys, and many refused to load the rifles. When they were punished, long-suppressed grievances erupted. In May 1857, some of the roughly 2,000 sepoys based in the Meerut cantonment turned on their officers, killing them and their families before moving to the town to massacre English residents there. They then marched on Delhi, where their numbers swelled. Over the course of a year, the rebellion spread across northern and central India. The violence was ferocious, producing long-remembered cruelties on both sides.

British colonialism had changed fundamentally in the decades since liberal polymaths like William Jones had tried to understand India and extract value from it, without interfering overmuch in local religious practice. An evangelical revival in early nineteenth-century Britain had sent missionaries to India to provide behaviour improvements and spiritual rescues – sometimes by means of forced conversions. Economic exploitation grew more brazen: from new taxes to the insatiable East India Company land grabs, which were dispossessing a chunk of the Indian aristocracy and others less visible. Mingling with such religious and economic affronts were many local grievances, which propelled lower-status people into the rebellion. 'An accumulation of adequate causes,' Benjamin Disraeli rightly noted in Parliament as the uprising began. The greased cartridges were a metaphorical match, lit and tossed, into a landscape ready to burn.

In India, the uprising produced many heroes – but only one celebrated heroine: Lakshmi Bai, the Rani, or Queen, of Jhansi, a mid-sized kingdom in the Bundelkhand region, around 400 kilometres south of Delhi. General Hugh Rose, the British officer determined to capture her and take control of her territory, famously said, 'The Indian Mutiny has produced but one man, and that man was a woman.'

In the Indian nationalist story, the Rani was transformed from a woman into a mythic being. At the height of the rebellion, General Rose's forces laid siege to her fort and thought they had her cornered. But in the dead of night, she mounted her horse, her young son holding on tight behind her, and made a do-or-die bid for freedom. She leapt from the ramparts and vanished into the darkness.

It's one hell of an image, engrained now in India's popular and political culture, and even celebrated in the West. Lakshmi Bai today is remembered in film and poster art as a rebel leader, a warrior queen. A few years ago, *Time* magazine listed her, along with Michelle Obama, as one of history's 'Top 10 Bad-Ass Wives'. Looking down from the battlements of Fort Jhansi, at the place where a big metal sign marks the spot of the legendary jump, you might feel a bit of vertigo. It is a sheer plunge of about fifteen metres – hard to imagine anyone human surviving it.

'She is a figure of belief in some ways,' says Harleen Singh, a professor at Brandeis University who has written a book about Lakshmi Bai. 'She allows the Indian imagination to think of a past that is a little bit out of reach, that is always in some ways jumping over the precipice, out of control, and signifies that kind of rebellious strong spirit.' There's also an important sense in which many Indian women might feel they share something with Lakshmi Bai's story. 'Young women today take umbrage at the fact that her fighting against the British is thought of as her acting like a man,' Singh continues. 'We're fighting every day in our lives, on the street, in living, in our households, in many different ways. And we don't fight like men. We fight like women because we have to fight for our rights as women.'

On a typical day for the Rani, weightlifting, wrestling and steeple-chase came before breakfast. Intelligent and simply dressed, she was a business-like ruler, occasionally punishing criminals herself – with a stick. We know this and other details about her from a fascinating account (only recently translated in full) by a Maharashtrian priest and mendicant, Vishnu Bhatt, who stayed at Jhansi in the 1850s. But little in the queen's life before 1857 augured her role as the British Empire's chief nineteenth-century villainess – 'This Jezebel Ranee', in the words of one member of General Rose's campaign.

Lakshmi Bai was born in 1828. Her original name was Mana-karnika, and she was also known as Manu. Her mother died when she was young, and it seems she was raised mainly in the company of boys, picking up horsemanship as part of her upbringing. At puberty she was married to a man with a much higher social position: Gangadhar Rao, the recently widowed Maharaja of Jhansi. A cultured, bookish man (who was given to cross-dressing, according to Vishnu Bhatt), he was well into his forties, childless, and looking for an heir.

The young queen, with her newly given name of Lakshmi Bai, was installed in the ornate, art-filled Jhansi palace, where servants laboured to fill the air with the scent of flowers. The Maharaja was less interested in his young wife than in other pursuits, so it is said the queen passed the time teaching horsemanship and swordsman-ship to her female servants; by some accounts, she created a well-drilled women's military unit. (In the 1940s, a women's regiment raised by Subhas Chandra Bose for his Indian National Army would be named the Rani of Jhansi Regiment: see **37 Bose**.)

Vishnu Bhatt put this all down to the region's arid climate, which made the men of the Bundelkhand 'somewhat weak of body and mind', and the women confident and strong. When Lakshmi Bai held court, 'she sometimes appeared in male clothing: pyjamas, a waist-coat and headgear with a starched, fan-like top,' he wrote. 'Around her waist, she tied a scarf with gold embroidery and hung from it a sword in a scabbard. She was a tall, fair woman – dressed thus, she looked like the avatar of a warrior goddess.'

In 1851, after nine years as a somewhat eccentric royal consort, she was celebrated throughout Jhansi for doing the more conventional thing: producing a son. The celebrations would be tragically short-lived. The child died when he was just three months old. Crucially, the Maharaja was also dying. Under the Doctrine of Lapse, a typically British form of colonial legal brigandage – thievery, sanctified by conversion into a Doctrine – the Raj gave itself the right to annex any territory under British influence if its ruler happened to die without an heir.

Desperate to preserve his family's dominion, the Maharaja adopted his cousin's son, Damodar Rao, and left instructions that Lakshmi Bai would govern Jhansi after he was gone. But when he died in 1853, the British annexed Jhansi anyway and hoped to pension off the Rani. She refused the annuity of 60,000 rupees they offered her, and petitioned Lord Dalhousie, the East India Company's Governor General, for redress. 'Does it entitle them to seize the Government and territory of Jhansi?' Lakshmi Bai wrote to Dalhousie in an official 'memorial' or petition. 'Does it entitle them to seize your memorialist's treasury – to pension off your memorialist on a pittance of the Treasures of the State, payable only during the period of your memorialist's life, and to deprive your memorialist's ward, or the heirs of the late Rajah, of their entire inheritance, except the petty reversion of his personal estate?'

The British were unmoved and stationed a garrison in Lakshmi Bai's kingdom to oversee the running of her state. For a time, she seemed an unimportant problem – until June 1857 when, after several weeks, the rebel sepoys reached Jhansi.

*

Fearful of the spreading unrest, sixty British officials had taken refuge with their families in the fort. As their food supplies dwindled, they were offered safe passage by the rebels on the condition that they lay down their arms. The British complied, but as the families filed out of the fort, they were corralled. The men were beheaded; the women and children hacked to pieces. The dismembered bodies were left to rot on the red earth for days, until eventually buried by British forces. (Later, the British erected a monument, which today stands a little forlornly behind locked gates, down a lane filled with small workshops repairing tyres and automotive parts.)

Though Lakshmi Bai denied any involvement, the British held her responsible for the massacre. We still don't know the truth. Nonetheless, British forces were soon advancing on Jhansi. There is evidence that Lakshmi Bai used her considerable diplomatic skills to try to stay out of the fighting, but she was now part of the uprising whether she liked it or not. Cornered, she exhorted her people to fight. 'We fight for independence,' she is supposed to have said. 'In the words of Lord Krishna we will, if we are victorious, enjoy the fruits of victory; if defeated and killed on the field of battle, we shall surely earn eternal glory and salvation.'

The British bombarded the fort, and were answered by heavy return fire, some of it from a massive thirty-inch cannon mounted on the ramparts, where the queen was said to stand, sword in hand, urging her fighters on. In his memoir, the visiting priest Bhatt wrote of eleven nights of harrowing fighting, including British projectiles that burst in a hail of pellets and nails. Fires swept through parts of the fort, setting off a powerful explosion in the armoury and destroying the temple. The British also had the advantage of telescopes, which allowed them to locate and blow up the water supply.

By the time the British finally breached the walls, the queen, whom they'd also stalked by telescope, had vanished. Just before they arrived, she had made her famous horseback leap – or, if we are to take the word of Bhatt, who was hiding in the fort at the time, her midnight escape down a back staircase. Indian martial traditions typically stress either victory or giving up one's life ('Do or Die', in Gandhi's later slogan). But there is a third option they allow, too, and it's built into the architecture of many Indian forts: it's known as the '*dharm-darvar*' or 'dharma-door', a small doorway or side gate through which a fort's defenders might discreetly and safely depart.

In the ruined fort, the queen left behind at least 3,000 dead Indians; the British had achieved retribution, at a ratio of fifty to one. From Gwalior, roughly a ten-hour ride south of Jhansi, General Rose would soon report the death of another. In Lakshmi Bai's final charge, she came galloping at the British dressed in red, like a male soldier, and brandishing her sword. According to Rose, her recovered corpse wore gold anklets and a necklace of pearls.

The death of the Rani of Jhansi was one of the final knells of the larger rebellion, though there continued to be reprisals by the British – a rash of retaliatory violence the Indians called the Devil's wind.

Lakshmi Bai's mythification began shortly thereafter. In this rare case, India and the West were on the same side. Characters based on her began appearing in popular British novels – women who were invariably seductive and potentially deadly. There were also Indian songs featuring versions of Lakshmi Bai – and novels, and eventually television series and Bollywood films. Even political leaders like **Indira Gandhi** (46) and Sonia Gandhi would both be portrayed, sometimes a little satirically, as Lakshmi Bai, atop her steed, mid-leap.

Lakshmi Bai's moat at Jhansi is now a field of scrub grass. Just beyond it is a little diorama of the battle. At its centre is the most iconic image of the queen: on her springing charger, with her sword held high – a bit like **Shivaji** (19), except she holds her reins between her teeth.

Lakshmi Bai was the most famous female figure of the uprising of 1857. But in fact she was not the only woman to have picked up arms against the British that year. Primary sources give us enigmatic glimpses of others: the so-called Maid of Delhi, who fought in the uniform of a man; the Lucknow woman firing her gun from a Pipal tree during the battle of Sikandar Bagh, hitting six British officers before being blasted right out of the branches. But because of Lakshmi Bai's social position and a fascination with her unusual story on both the British and Indian national sides, the sources for her life are relatively richer than those we have for many other women in Indian history – despite the fact that, in 1858, the British ran off with the boxes containing her administration's records.

Even as Indian society often subjugates its female citizens, a belief in feminine power and force is lodged deep in the popular psyche. Lakshmi Bai's famous image evokes powerful Hindu goddesses like Kali and Durga. What's troubling is that women who manage to excel in a largely male-dominated society are seldom construed as human, as examples capable of emulation. Instead, they're ascribed extra-human powers. Supposedly, this celebrates them, but in fact it denies the reality and thus the relevance of their experience.

Of the few women who figure in the Indian historical pantheon, most are royal or upper caste. Deified, even these few remain elusive. Harleen Singh, in her research on Lakshmi Bai, was tantalized by the idea of the queen's records, which were never recovered. 'It's a great wish of mine,' she says, 'a romantic desire you might say, that one day that box might be found – that one day we would have her own voice telling us her story rather than trying to reconstruct her life and her story from all these different sources that purport to tell us the Rani's story, when we know so little about her.'

I can imagine many such boxes, which together might contain the greatest lost treasure of Indian history: the voices of its women.

24

Jyotirao Phule

The Open Well
1827–1890

I've often fancied that behind every revolution lurks a gardener. Sixty years after flower-sellers took part in the storming of the Bastille in 1789, a young Indian man from a gardening caste – Jyotirao Phule, whose surname means 'flower' – began his own lifelong assault on a social order far older and even more rank-conscious than the French *ancien régime*. His intent was to uproot the Brahminical order, and with it the caste system, which blocked access to education, jobs and a sense of self-worth for people of his background.

Phule was born around 1827, and lived on the outskirts of the city of Poona (now Pune), once the headquarters of the Maratha states that **Shivaji (19)** had helped establish. His grandfather had been a *mali*, or gardener, in a royal compound, and his father farmed vegetables and flowers. Though as members of the mali caste the family was from the lowest, Shudra, order, they supplied the city's elite, moving between the homes of the upper castes and the fields and villages. That, I think, gave them a special insight into the advantages of privilege and the distribution of opportunity in their society. Phule grasped early on that Brahmins had reserved education for themselves, exploiting the ignorance of the lower castes and outcastes while mopping up the benefits of status.

In time, this young man's frustration would become a critique, and then an agenda for change. He set up first a chain of schools for outcastes (today's Dalits) and girls, and then a home for widows and orphans. His effort soon became a full-out polemical war against the Brahmins. Phule's nineteenth-century experiments in schooling the unprivileged helped show what a more democratic access to education might look like, and his systemic analysis of the psychological politics of being poor, as well as his attention to the consequences of exploitation for individual lives, have a cutting timeliness in contemporary India.

Phule is often clubbed together, misleadingly, with other Indian nationalists. 'He's really an anti-nationalist,' contends the scholar and social scientist Gail Omvedt. 'He's warning his people to be wary of instructions that they should put aside all grumblings about the hierarchies and distinctions in the country and become united.' Education, and not any idea of nation or territory, 'was his swadeshi', or patriotism, Omvedt says.

Phule's anti-Brahminism and democratic ideas about education had more in common with Christian missionary pedagogy, from which he had benefited directly. The irony of his story is that, if it were not for the usurping East India Company and the new order it established, one of the nineteenth century's great radical humanists – in any country – might have been just another unknown vegetable supplier. Stories such as Phule's complicate the idea of imperialism, according to novelist and activist Arundhati Roy. 'The British drained the wealth of a continent, impoverished it, and entrenched old values,' she says, 'but they also opened doors for Phule, **Ambedkar (41)** and others to enter the discourse and change it.'

Pune today is one of India's ten richest cities, a hub of education, manufacturing, IT and luxury-car assembly lines. Parts of it feel like the corridors of steel and glass found in any of the world's major business districts. It is easy to forget that the city is also the historical centre of several important, if mutually antagonistic, schools of Indian thought.

As the seat of Maratha power, Pune was once second only to Delhi on the subcontinent's political map. In the decades after the British gained control of the city, in 1818, it became fertile ground for Indian liberalism. Reform-minded intellectuals, many of them from the highest Chitpavan Brahmin caste, drew on their exposure to Western ideas to develop arguments for Indian constitutional government, the rule of law and individual rights – arguments that would later influence **Gandhi** (38), **Jinnah** (39) and Nehru. Meanwhile, more conservative Chitpavans advocated a militant effort to preserve Hindu values against perceived Christian and Muslim encroachment. Looking back at Pune's vigorous nineteenth-century intellectual history, we can now make out a third important strain of social and philosophical argument: the thought of the lower-caste Phule.

Phule's story is often told as a classic narrative of an individual bootstrapping himself out of poverty (school textbooks sometimes describe him as a child who worked the fields to survive). In truth, his father's respectability as a vegetable vendor and owner of fertile land gave Phule the social confidence and educational head-start that he would later use to launch a movement.

During the early colonial period, before rebellion and the hardening of British rule, Protestant missionaries were opening schools in many parts of the country. Not all of the educators were Bible-beating dogmatists, interested only in notching up conversions. In an era when many poor, lower-caste teenagers went to work after a brief and perfunctory primary education (if that), Phule was meeting the Enlightenment, alongside high-caste and Muslim students, in a Scottish missionary school. In addition to Christian tracts, he was taught about the lives of Martin Luther, George Washington and the Maratha warrior-king Shivaji. But the writings that most stirred Phule were those of Thomas Paine, the revolutionary critic of the clergy and of irrational authority, and author of the *Rights of Man*.

Phule acquired the missionaries' distaste for superstition and idolatry and would soon outdo them in his loathing of a Hindu system whose power was organized around mass deference towards the priestly castes. But in Phule's own telling, his transforming moment came at a classmate's wedding. You can almost picture him, a rugged and handsome youth in his late teens, amidst the wedding procession that escorted the bridegroom to the ceremony. The groom, one of his Brahmin schoolfriends, had invited him – innocently, so the story goes. But when orthodox elders noticed his presence, they commanded him to leave. A mere Shudra mali, he was contaminating the Brahmin ritual.

That this expulsion came as a deep shock to Phule suggests how sheltered he had been thus far from the daily discriminations and aggression to which ordinary low-caste and outcaste people were subject. As with the Buddha, who recognized suffering only when he became a young man, the question arises: How could it take him this long? Phule may of course have been shaping his story for dramatic effect. Or perhaps while studying ideas of equality and justice, rationalism and individualism in school, he had lost touch with the realities of his hometown.

Disabused of his social innocence, Phule developed a new clarity of vision. He saw not only that the caste order was an engine of suffering and exploitation, but that the submissiveness of the lower castes contributed some fuel. Providing the unprivileged with a rational education of the sort he had been granted, along with a belief in the possibility of progress against custom, seemed to him necessary elements of a remedy. As he later wrote, 'Without education, wisdom was lost; without morals, development was lost; without development, wealth was lost; without wealth, the Shudras were ruined'.

An aspect of Phule that is neglected today by those who make him a hero of lower-caste politics is his shrewd and swashbuckling interest in Indian history. He would have been aware that he was living through one of his country's key transitional moments. He was born less than ten years after the East India Company defeated the last peshwa of the Maratha Confederacy, which had once controlled vast portions of the western subcontinent. In the following decades, the British moved towards full mastery of India, but the new order was not yet set and alliances were still unfixed. It was a period in which change could be articulated and enacted.

Phule would do both, in pursuit of the values he had imbibed from his reading of the *Rights of Man*. He was barely twenty when, after visiting an American missionary school for disadvantaged girls, he started his first institution for girls and Dalits. His commitment to educating women, and lower-caste ones at that, ranked as scandalous even within his own community. He had taught his unschooled but bright teenage bride, Savitribai, to read and write so that she could teach at his school. It was an assault not just on Hindu stricture, but on family culture. 'Every time Savitribai went on her way to work in the morning to teach in this little school they had started for girls, she would be pelted with mud and stones and garbage,' says Vidya Natarajan, author of an illustrated book about Phule.

> But she was quite matter of fact about it. She would wear a dirty sari on her way to school, get into the schoolroom, change into her clean sari, teach all day, and then change back into her grubby sari to walk home past the same jeering crowds that she ran the gauntlet with in the morning.

Jyotirao was also roundly mocked, and his traumatized father kicked the young couple out of the family house. Leaving home turned out to give Phule and his wife new freedom to be social provocateurs. The small house into which they moved is now a staid museum with mud-coloured walls, fluorescent ceiling lights and displays of scenes from their life. But back then it was the war room for a passionate campaign against social and gender discrimination. By the time Phule was thirty, he and Savitribai were earning praise from the British for their schools, and contempt from conservative Brahmins. Childless (another social scandal of that age), the couple adopted a Brahmin widow's son as their own, which provoked further distaste among leading members of the highest caste.

Phule found even progressive Brahmins suspect, writing that those who 'are called reformed, and who are so clever . . . from time to time commit deeds so evil they would make your hair stand on end'. Still, when Phule and Savitribai set up a refuge for unwanted children and widows, some funding did come from Brahmin friends, as well as European supporters and Phule's own occasional work as a contractor.

Some of Phule's critics thought of him as a crypto-Christian, though unlike many others in his circle, he never converted – influenced, perhaps, by Thomas Paine's anti-clericalism. Other critics considered him a lackey of the British; obsessed with caste injuries, he was effectively conspiring to make Indians embarrassed about the entirety of their culture. One of his ideological opponents put it like this: 'What boldness and what loyalty to government and truth do these tough guys like Phule show in barking at Brahmins and licking their lips.' By attacking Hinduism instead of trying to reform it, Indian liberals contended, he was sabotaging the nascent possibility of Indians uniting to throw off British rule. When challenged about his plans and theories, Phule was rarely diplomatic: he labelled those he disagreed with as 'silly', 'idiotic', or worse. To him, some vague future nationalism led by the upper castes felt far less urgent than immediate, tangible gains for the ostracized.

Phule's feelings about the British evolved in later life as the colonial project changed, and he came to share the critique of colonial economic exploitation held by some of his contemporaries. But Phule was in accord with many among the Indian elites he otherwise opposed in thinking that overall the British had a positive, even providential impact on India. It would have been hard for him to be anti-British, since one of his hopes was to claim for the lower castes the administrative jobs Brahmins held within the government. Good jobs were elusive, then as now; with education, Phule thought that the lower castes might displace so many Brahmins from British posts that they would become a new professional elite.

Across Maharashtra and India today, many government-funded schemes for schools, especially for Dalits and lower castes, bear either Jyotirao's or Savitribai's name, but to remember him only as an educationalist reduces and domesticates a tough, wide-ranging mind. Phule thought it insufficient to set up small islands of education and equality. He wanted to topple the entire caste order. His tireless writing to that end – as poet, playwright, historian and polemicist – contains a social analysis whose iconoclasm still resonates.

In Phule's accounts of the daily lives of the very poor, his language was direct, gritty, and even scatological – reflective perhaps of the everyday cussing of the poor kids he took in. 'At places one finds a line of a child's piss,' he wrote of a peasant household in *Shetkaryacha Asud*, a book whose title translates as 'The Cultivator's Whipcord':

> at some other place a patch of white ash where a child's turd has been
> cleaned up. Several corners of the house are red and dark from

tobacco spit. In one corner sits a large grinder, to be worked by three
or four women, in another there is a large pestle and mortar, and near
the door, under the broom, all the dirt pushed there after sweeping
the floor . . . on top, a rag which was used to clean a baby's arse.

According to Vidya Natarajan, Phule was especially concerned not
to take on 'the snooty linguistic quirks of the Brahmins he was
opposing'. Instead, she says, he was 'embodying in his writing style
what he actually felt about his own people – that what they did
was connected to the earth, therefore important, therefore worth
celebrating – even in his choice of diction and language'.

Phule's writing displayed an acute sensitivity to how the stress and
panic of poverty and discrimination corrodes the mind. The illiterate
man is a mark for exploiters; even when not confused by injustice, he
may think he deserves it. In Phule's view, the inculcation of such help-
lessness was the goal of the Brahmins. As he followed abolitionist
movements in the United States in the years before the American Civil
War, Phule began to think of the Brahmins as slave masters, and the
caste system as an elaborate and effective strategy of human bondage.
He named one of his greatest works, written just after the end of the
war, 'Slavery in the Civilised British Government Under the Cloak of
Brahmanism, Exposed by Jyotirao Govindrao Phule'. *Ghulamgiri*, or
Slavery, as the treatise was known, was dedicated to abolitionists:

> With an earnest desire, that my countrymen may take their noble
> example as their guide in the emancipation of their Sudra Brethren
> from the trammels of Brahmin thraldom.

The book was couched as a work of history, in which Phule imagined
an ancient golden age before the Brahmins, or Aryans, arrived to
subordinate the original Indians, or Dravidians. The Brahmin usurp-
ers invented religious texts and the caste system to give them control
of the land by dividing people who might otherwise have made common cause. To Phule, the Brahmins were similar to the European
settlers who left the native Americans with nothing.

Like Rammohun Roy, with his imagined democratic past, Phule
was inventing a history for himself and his people in the name of

future progress. One aspect of Phule's alternative history that rings true, even today, is the difficulty less advantaged Indians face in coming together to agitate for education or basic resources like water.

In 1873, Phule and Savitribai started the Satyasodhak Samaj, or Truth-Seeking Society, to bring members of various lower castes together in the name of self-improvement. The society gathered, often in their house, to persuade non-Brahmins to educate themselves, to perform their own rituals instead of relying on the priestly caste, and to recognize human equality as a universal value. The Society continued long after his death, as did other aspects of his anti-Brahmin movement, but Phule never became a national figure in his lifetime. Politics then was still local, and would stay so until the foundation of the great pan-Indian movement embodied in the Indian National Congress, in 1885, just five years before Phule's death.

After his death, he was fast forgotten – in part because of his abiding doubt that India's upper-caste liberals would magnanimously devote themselves to the uplift of the lower castes. It was a scepticism that didn't comport with nationalist themes. But in recent decades, with the rise of lower-caste parties in India's democratic politics, and the promise (and uneven enactment) of government policies to improve the lot of the lower castes, Phule has been revived as the forefather of educational schemes for lower-caste boys and girls, who still struggle to obtain the education that Phule knew was the best way out of their subordination. And yet even those who do have education discover that it's not always the powerful springboard Phule imagined it to be.

At Phule and Savitribai's small house in the old part of Pune, the garden around the museum is appropriately well tended. But more significant is the working well in the house's inner courtyard. It is open to all-comers, a practice that the couple began in 1868 in protest against barring the Dalits – said to be impure – from drinking from wells that the upper castes used. Today, as fierce battles are waged between the poor and the powerful over water and other resources, that open well stands as a modest reminder of the wide access to opportunity that Phule was fighting to achieve.

25
Deen Dayal

Courtier with a Camera
1844–1910

In the 1890s, in some circles of the British, European and Russian aristocracies, one manly ritual seemed practically obligatory. Whether viscount or grand prince or dauphin, at some point you had to hie to India and slaughter some tigers. And so, in 1893, an earnest thirty-year-old Austrian royal, Franz Ferdinand, succumbed to his beast-shooting duty and embarked on the Grand Indian Tiger Slaughter Tour. He ended up killing so gleefully, and shooting so often, that he damaged his ears.

Hosting Ferdinand for part of the exotic hunting tour was the Sixth Nizam of Hyderabad, who was among the richest men on the planet and the possessor of some of the world's finest jewels. It was a decade of famine across India, but the diary entries Ferdinand made during his stay provide a glimpse of the other India, the one that drew in the pleasure-seekers of the West.

Mornings, moustaches oiled, Ferdinand and the Indian princes took to the jungles with their rifles. A retinue of servants panted behind them, lugging champagne. At day's end, the party returned to the Nizam's palace, where a lavish formal meal was laid. Opening his diary in the wake of one such dinner, the Habsburg prince recorded irritation at an orchestra whose 'imps' with 'screeching clarinets' utterly mangled the Austrian imperial anthem. More to his liking was a towering cake brought forth by the liveried staff. When cut, it erupted in flapping wings and out came a flock of brightly coloured birds.

Just over twenty years from that evening of spectacle, Franz Ferdinand was assassinated by a young Bosnian Serb nationalist, the act that catalysed the First World War. But in this moment, the world's elites – Eastern and Western – were in relative harmony, and often united by decadent pastimes. The Nizam probably had far more in common with Ferdinand, a duke, and the *bons vivants* of America's Gilded Age, than he did with the unprivileged of his own realm, only a small percentage of whom spoke Urdu, his native tongue.

Sepia-toned photos of Ferdinand and the Nizam, taken by the Nizam's court photographer, stress the two men's affinity. That emphasis was surely no accident. The photographer was Deen Dayal, the country's first master of the camera, possessor of an international reputation of his own.

Early in his career, Dayal's images of the historic monuments and architecture of India – commissioned by the British, and ranging from Buddhist stupas to the Taj Mahal – became a sensation, and a means by which Indian landmarks could be appreciated in the West. Over subsequent decades, Dayal's carefully arranged portraits would open a window on a second aspect of a splendid, idealized India: the lifestyles of the late nineteenth-century elite. Though India had at this high point of the Raj become the world's leading stage for the display of social standing – which often involved shooting – a person's status wasn't quite fixed unless the moment itself was shot, ideally by Dayal.

In that historical idyll, those elites still had control over the images they would display to the world. And like many successful artists before him and since, Dayal became adept at selling his patrons the images of themselves they most wanted to see and share. Dayal's story might be simply the portrait of an artist as a public relations man, if his artistry wasn't so compelling and historically revealing. What he documented caught a cusp moment before the historical change that would sweep away the Austro-Hungarian Empire, spark revolutions, deplete the Raj and princely India, and ultimately pave the way to Indian independence. Today, the work of Deen Dayal – what he showed and what he left out – has become one of our best means of access to the hubristic excess that defined, and helped doom, the class of *fin de siècle* elites.

*

Although high society survives on the labours of good courtiers, the skill of self-effacement is so central to the work of pleasing one's patron that the best of them may be forgotten to history. Dayal, though, was a courtier with a camera. He left no diaries or personal papers, but the vast and carefully catalogued photographic archive he built can help us pull him out from behind the tripod and into the frame.

He was born to a family of Jain jewellers in 1844, in Sardhana, near Meerut in Uttar Pradesh, where the rebellion of 1857 began. As a teenager he would surely have heard of the sepoys who massacred British officers and civilians, and he came of age in a time when the shaken Raj was enforcing what was called 'the smack' of firm government. But Dayal's own encounters with British officialdom seem to have been beneficial. While studying civil engineering in a college that educated both Indians and Europeans, he found several British patrons, and some years after graduating he joined a vast Raj project to expand historical knowledge of India.

Part of effectively governing one's colonies was acquiring the knowledge of what it was, exactly, over which one ruled. A British effort to document the cultural and architectural heritage of India had been long underway by the time Dayal was hired as a draughtsman and head estimator in the public works department of the princely state of Indore. Early interests of the knowledge enterprise had been in topography, geography and disease, mainly because of the risks these posed to British soldiers. The advent of photography gave the project a new dimension. Had Dayal become a civil engineer a generation earlier, he might have spent his career sketching roads and buildings, since drawings or paintings were how European colonizers first documented their holdings. But daguerreotype photography, invented in France around 1839, had come to India by 1844, followed soon after by glass-plate technologies – and by 1874, when Dayal took his first official photos, the business of surveying had been transformed.

The surveyor's eye is present in Dayal's use of high and sweeping vantage points, which give the viewer of his photographs a sense of command over a field rendered with clarity and precision. His gifts for composition and for capturing luminosity are clear even from early photographs of the architecture of Indore, as well as in more propagandistic work, like shots of British military manoeuvres. Most distinctive, though, is his ability to coax an aesthetically satisfying and detailed depth from his photographs through the control of tone, brightness and shade – qualities he mainly achieved through his plate-processing and printing techniques.

You can get a glimpse of a personal sensibility separate from technical skill in an 1882 photograph of the fort at Jhansi (see **23 Lakshmi Bai, Rani of Jhansi**). This time he's shooting from a low angle, using a skeletal tree, rocks, some local men and a camel to depict scale and build volume as the eye moves towards the stepped geometry of rampart castellations. The sky-cut silhouette of the distant fort, set back in a rocky, un-nourishing landscape, gives the image its desolation. You can imagine Dayal silently questioning his patrons, whose forces had defeated the ruler of this once-vibrant fort only twenty-five years before.

More standard architectural work would make Dayal's international name: a commission from a flamboyant Raj official and writer, Lepel Griffin, to document the built heritage of central India. His photographs of temples and palaces, forts and other antiquities – in Gwalior, Khajuraho, Deegh, Orchha and elsewhere – appeared in a celebrated 1886 monograph, *Famous Monuments of Central India*. As one historian put it, the ownership of colonies in the nineteenth century was 'a form of conspicuous consumption on a national scale'. Rulers competed to have the best, and with Dayal's work the British public could properly appraise their assets. They found Dayal's India beautiful and mysterious, far removed as it was from their own industrialized world. Before long, upper-class Londoners were taking European paintings off the wall and putting up reproductions of Dayal's work. His images were printed on Christmas cards, cabinet cards and postcards, and turned into engravings in popular magazines. This success introduced Dayal to multiple means of disseminating his work – something he would become a master of – and galvanized what was already a thriving sideline for Dayal: private portraits of the elite.

Early on, a senior Army officer, Sir Henry Daly, had helped Dayal meet clients, and the photographer had quickly developed enough of a reputation that when the Viceroy of India, Lord Northbrook, and the royal party of the Prince of Wales were visiting Indore, he was the photographer they summoned as a portraitist. He became a master of that form, and soon had so many clients he could start a lavish studio in Mumbai and hire a retinue of photographers to work under him.

Photography was still in its infancy and exposures were long and painstaking, especially in the Indian heat. But British and other European visitors, used to condescending to Indians, were impressed by Dayal's elegant stagings, technique and attention to detail. He's almost as good as his Western counterparts, they reported, amazed. He was equally adept at puffing his patrons up, and maintained a minor rivalry with a fellow patron-flatterer, the painter Raja Ravi Varma, who served the Maharaja of Travancore.

Contemporary critics seeking something distinctly Indian in Dayal's work have come up with little. He was in the international photographic mainstream of his time, moving from Indore to serve bigger patrons. Dayal was the official photographer for several viceroys, shooting their architecture, interiors and guests. And then, in 1894, he was put on a monthly retainer by the Nizam, the richest man in India. The Nizam's patronage gave him the means to refine, experiment, and order special lenses from Germany – not to mention command a cavalry of 2,000 horsemen under his own personal pennant.

Princely states like Hyderabad – big, wealthy and with a reliably obsequious and pomp-loving Nizam – offered the British an essential buttress to their own newly invented imperial order of titles, ceremonies and ornaments. There was also no Indian nationalism at this point to take on the excess and indolence of the princes. So for now, as Rudyard Kipling put it, God seemed to have created maharajas to give mankind a spectacle of jewels and marble palaces.

Newspaper reports about Dayal from 1894 describe the moment he won over the Nizam, after several years of working for the ruler intermittently. One night, very late, Dayal received a summons: the Nizam needed him urgently, for he had just had a spectacular night killing tigers. This, in the Nizam's judgement, was something the world needed to know. Dayal rushed out to the jungle. The resulting shots of the Nizam and his tigers won the Nizam's deepest admiration and secured Dayal a job for the rest of his life. 'So pleased was his Highness with the results of Mr. Lala Deen's artistry,' the *Deccan Budget* of 6 July 1894 reported, 'that before leaving camp he himself proposed a title for his photographer . . . and graced the title with a very pretty and flattering couplet in Urdu recited before the assembled gentlemen in camp.'

Not long ago, art historian Deborah Hutton, of the College of New Jersey, was studying the photos from that crucial jungle escapade for a Deen Dayal exhibition she was curating. Something about the photos struck her as off. A little investigation and expert consultation revealed that faint marks on the two dead tigers were sutures. The tigers the Nizam posed with weren't fresh kill, after all. They were stuffed, pulled off the shelf, as it were, for the photo shoot. So the story of Dayal's career-making race to the jungle seems to have as much image-burnishing in it as the photos of the Nizam with his bounty.

Still, the tiger story reveals the undergirding purpose of portrait photography in that age: less to document reality than to help create compelling and formidable images. The title the Nizam gave Dayal translates as 'Bold Warrior of Photography'. The war he was fighting, for the Nizam and in his private studio, was for the continuation of the halcyon era of the elites, or at least the continuation of the image of a halcyon era, at a time when aristocratic classes were less and less integral to the functioning of modernizing societies.

From the 1880s on, mass production, standardization and steel were creating a frantic geopolitical competition in which states tried to match each other in manufacturing and arms, and traditional power hierarchies were reordered. And the United States, from the Civil War to the turn of the century, industrialized and tripled in economic size, knocking the stuffing out of European agricultural wealth when its western states began to farm. Unified Germany and Meiji Japan were also booming, democratic government became more common, and reigning orders from Britain to St Petersburg came under further pressure in world affairs.

Meanwhile Dayal's photos, reproduced widely, inspired consumption, not production. They were used to help those who could afford it to compete in the international game of having the biggest, the best and the most lavish – from parties to hunting expeditions to home decorations. The high resolution of his work made it possible to see, and imitate, the clothes and jewels. Buckingham Palace's chandelier was huge, so in some acropolitan Gwalior home would be hung one still bigger. It was an international competition in excess that perhaps helped blind its participants to what was happening in a modernizing world and at home.

In India between 1875 and 1900, famine killed a staggering fifteen million people. The recurring famines in the Nizam's own kingdom would remain out of Dayal's frame, apart from a telling album of photos taken by artists from his growing crew of studio workers. The album documented the Nizam's famine relief efforts. In many shots, the starving masses have been posed in straight lines or otherwise theatrically arranged. The photos are moving, sometimes haunting – but the purpose of the commission remains clear: to celebrate a benevolent Nizam who had a tragedy under control.

Viewers of privilege were free to look elsewhere – to see a Russian aristocrat, Grand Duke Alexander Mikhailovich, posing post-hunt with a blindfolded cheetah. To see the Prince of Wales, who would become King George V, carried across a stream by an Indian servant during a hunt. To see the photo of a children's dressing-up party in Hyderabad, the pretty British youth decked in lace and elaborate hats, the girls bearing sceptres topped with flowers and stars.

Still, there are some striking outliers in Dayal's work. Among them is a tantalizing photograph, from 1879, in which a group of Bhil tribals of all ages are set against a hilly landscape, loosely arranged. Some stand, some crouch. Some look boldly towards the camera. Some gaze into the distance. Others seem to want to shrink away. Nothing is known about why he took this photo. A practice shot? Relief from his usual work? All that's clear is that he sees the tribal men as individuals, and with respect. In later years, when occasionally photographing non-elite Indians – circus performers, fakirs – the result was fairground stuff, charged with exoticism, and without the open, humane sensibility of that early Bhil work.

What Dayal made of this world and his subjects – whether he had an explicit politics, or sensed himself living and working at a twilight moment, or sensed the danger of flaunting wealth in a democratizing age – we'll never know. He left detailed records of his photographs and his studio finances, but the only 'life story' we have in his own voice is from a rather wooden account.

Although Dayal's work was honoured in international competitions, including the exhibitions in London of 1886 and 1891, and sold well, his sons were spendthrifts and his Mumbai studio was mismanaged. So, shortly before he died, he wrote letters in a shaky hand, telling clients about being besieged by creditors, and begging them to pay him what they owed. It's one of the few intimate glimpses we have of the emotional life of the man, and it's a painful one.

Dayal was master of a medium that would entirely transform how we see and represent the world, and he seems to have sensed that new technologies might not just serve hierarchy, but subvert it. Among his work are photographs of typewriters and phonographs – machines which, like the camera, would become heralds of the modern democratic age.

Those little girls in his photos bearing sceptres topped with flowers and stars? Before their lives were over, the Raj they had belonged to would be dismantled, princely states abolished, and India would achieve independence. The wealthy would no longer have the means to keep the masses from entering the frame. Dayal's body of work matters for history as much as for art. Without him, we wouldn't understand so powerfully the moment when India was the world's exotic, wondrous playground for the wealthy – before the modern world got in the way.

26

Birsa Munda

'Have you been to Chalkad?'
1875–1900

Who owns India? Who owns the forests and rivers, the farmlands eyed by industry, the slums coveted by real estate developers and airport authorities, the hills and plateaus desired by mining barons?

In roughly a third of the country, this is no idle question. Citizens, governments and corporations are negotiating, sometimes violently, over the answer. The country's tribal belt, which stretches across the eastern and central parts of the country, is where many of these conflicts are unfolding. The people who live in these areas are poor but the natural resources are rich – tempting to corporations and the government.

The nationalists of the twentieth century had a simple answer to who owned the land: Indians did. The British did not. But when the nationalists assembled the jigsaw puzzle of diversities to define the Indian nation, some pieces got left out of consideration. Among those were the original tribal inhabitants of the country, who are now called Adivasis. The Adivasis, taken together, match in size the population of Germany or Vietnam, but they are so various and widely dispersed across the subcontinent that it is nonsensical to speak of them as a single group. One experience many Adivasis do share, however, is the overriding of their rights in the name of development and in the interests of other Indians, especially those with more money. 'It's as if middle and upper classes and castes have seceded into outer space,' the writer and political activist Arundhati Roy says. 'They look down and say, "What's our bauxite doing in their mountains, what's our water doing in their rivers?"'

Although Adivasi efforts to defend their lands date back

centuries, accounts of many of those struggles are lost to history. The life of one nineteenth-century rebel, Birsa Munda, is an exception. Born in 1875 in Chotanagpur, in what is now the eastern state of Jharkhand, and raised in a bamboo hut, the young Birsa herded sheep, played the flute and learned the medicinal power of local plants. In adulthood, he was known as a healer, and ultimately as a defender of his people against the British, their Indian middlemen and Christian missionaries. His was a firework of a life – he was dead by the age of twenty-five – but the embers of his struggle still burn.

When the oppressor wants a horse, the Kol must pay; when he desires a palki, the Kols have to pay and afterwards to bear him therein . . . Does someone die in his house? He taxes them. Is a child born? Again a tax. Is there a marriage or Puja? A tax. Does a death occur in the house of the Kol? The poor man must pay a fine. Is a child born? Is a son or daughter married? The poor Kol is still taxed. And this plundering, punishing, robbing system goes on till the Kols run away.

The Kols are a family of tribes, including Birsa Munda's, that have occupied their land for more than 2,000 years. But the nineteenth-century account above evokes a continuity under threat. The Kols' sense of being exploited and driven away was in part caused by a fundamental change in the British relationship to Indian land.

Until the arrival of the Marquess of Wellesley as Governor General in 1798, the British had considered India a profitable trading post, and had used local zamindars to collect revenues from the peasants. From then on, however, India was a territory to be possessed. Wellesley's land grabs included Mysore, the Maratha Deccan and many densely forested areas that were often amorphously controlled. By the early 1800s, the East India Company had seized pretty much two thirds of India, and over the course of the nineteenth century they pocketed further chunks, including bits of princely India through such dubious legal tools as the Doctrine of Lapse, which was used to dispossess Lakshmi Bai (23).

Birsa Munda's region, Chotanagpur, was seized under the

auspices of a series of laws called the Forest Acts, introduced in the 1860s. Birsa Munda came into the world at a time when tribes could no longer freely forage, collect firewood or graze their livestock in their forests. Meanwhile, the British encouraged Indian outsiders, middlemen and merchants – 'Dikus', the Kol Mundas called them – to settle on the edges of the forests, assigning them rights to land that Kols considered common property. For a young boy exploring the forest, it was a tricky, confusing time.

In his village of Chalkad, Birsa Munda stood out for his fair skin, his height – he grew to five feet four inches, tall by Munda standards – and his liveliness. German missionaries described his features as 'laughing and restless, which told you the moment you looked at him that he was brimful of mischief and nonsense'. They selected him for a Christian education at a mission school in another village – a decision they'd have cause to regret.

Missionaries had been in the region since around 1845, converting more than 100,000 residents, opening schools and adding another layer of psychological complication to growing up Kol. The missionaries sought to suppress native customs like drinking rice wine and dancing, not to mention the worship of the traditional deity, Sing Bonga. Some churches, expanding, also sought to relieve Kol families of their land, a common occurrence in colonial territories around the world. 'Obviously this is not related only to India,' Roy points out. 'They say in Africa, when the colonizers – the white colonizers – came, "We had the land and they had the Bibles. Now we have the Bibles and they have the land."'

Still, many Kols valued the practical aspects of missionary education. Literacy and numeracy made tribes less vulnerable to being swindled out of their land. Birsa was duly educated, though he viewed the Christians with far more suspicion than **Phule** (24) did. Soon after his Christian confirmation ceremony, he argued with the priests and was expelled from school. '*Saheb, Saheb, ek topi hai,*' he now said – all whites, whether British colonialists or European missionaries, wore the same cap.

Returning home to Chalkad, he lived with a family from a Hindu weaver caste, coming under the wing of a Vaishnav monk. He began practising as a healer, and his reputation as a young man with magic in his hands began to grow. His popularity was probably a reflection not just of skill and charisma, but also of the severity of the health needs he was called on to treat. Life was often short in Kol communities, and the 1890s were marked across north and central India by drought, famine and ensuing epidemics. In those circumstances, a healer might seem almost divine. In the words of a later folksong:

> Deep in the wild forest,
> who is clapping?
> Deep in the wild forest,
> Birsa is clapping.
> Birsa claps:
> bears, wild buffaloes, deer, elephants and horses understand.
> But not men.

Other songs told of how 'Deep amidst forest in the village of Chalkad, the Father of the Earth was born'. Soon, 'Have you been to Chalkad?' became a greeting among locals. It was said that in addition to healing illness, Birsa could predict crop failures and other disasters. He could make himself invisible at will. He could turn guns into wood, bullets into water. He could be the Mundas' saviour.

> The beloved son of Sugana Munda, you grazed goats;
> when you were twenty-five years of age, you shepherded the Mundas.

Throughout the nineteenth century, the Kols had periodically tried to expel the British and the zamindars from their lands, most famously in a revolt that began in 1831, known as the Great Kol Rising. Kol territory was a region, in other words, that the government had to work to control. By his early twenties, widely known as a miracle worker, Birsa was involved in agitations against the British, Dikus and missionaries.

Alpa Shah, an anthropologist who has worked among Adivasi communities in Jharkhand, says that Birsa would have acted as a leader across many areas of Munda life. 'On the one hand, he was mobilizing for what we'd see as political causes. But, on the other hand, spirituality was a huge part of how he operated. Spirituality was absolutely central for Adivasis then, as it is today. Religion was not necessarily as we see it now; religion, economics, politics were all part and parcel of the same forces.'

The missionaries in the area were alarmed by Birsa's heathen ways, and resentful of his success at gathering followers. Their fears came to influence the government of Bengal's understanding of what transpired next.

One government informant was Father Hoffmann, a German who ran a Catholic mission. He'd come to the region, he wrote, 'with the one object of working for [the Mundas] to my dying day'. But the vast majority of residents who had earlier converted to Christianity were turning to Birsa Munda, as he noted in a letter. Many extant details about Birsa Munda's activities and the support he commanded come from the missionaries' partial accounts, in letters preserved in colonial archives. By 1895, Birsa Munda's teachings had taken on a millenarian tone. He declared that a fire from heaven would destroy the outsiders, and that those Mundas who did not gather around him would perish. Six thousand people collected homemade weapons and began to climb towards a hilltop camp he had established in Chalkad. The missionaries, unnerved by the human arsenal moving up the hill, reported it to the colonial administrators, who retained memories of the events of 1857.

To Father Hoffmann, this mustering wasn't just a 'mere act of semi-savage foolishness'. 'Under the garb of religion,' he later wrote to the government, Birsa Munda was assuming 'a purely political role of high ambition'. Rumours swirled around that a seditious 'Munda Raj' was beginning, and that Birsa Munda's armed followers would refuse to pay rents or submit to British authority. 'The colonial government thought it was a gathering against them,' says Shah. 'Actually, it seems that people were gathered because they believed that everybody who *wasn't* gathered on that hill was going to die.'

The British arrested Birsa and sentenced him to two years in jail – a term that served to heighten the leader's popular mystique and his antipathy to the government. Soon after his release, he ordered the burning of effigies, made of plantain trees and leaf plates, representing the British Empire as the demon Ravana, and Empress Victoria as Ravana's consort, the demon-queen Mandodari. The following year, in December 1899, he did exactly what the British had feared: he led his people to rebellion.

Father Hoffmann, one of the targets of the uprising, wrote to the government: 'At about 9 p.m. gangs of from 4 to 6 men appeared in all Christian villages, put fire to a hut or two and shot some arrows into gatherings of Christians who were singing their Christian hymns. My companion Father Carbery and myself were lured out by the setting on fire of a shed in front of the Mission house, and as soon as we appeared in the verandah, three arrows were discharged at us. One of these hit Father Carbery in the chest but remained stuck in the lower part of the chest bone, whereas the two aimed at me just missed me by a couple of inches and went into the wall.'

Armed with axes and slingshots in addition to bows and arrows, Birsa Munda's followers attacked the British, Dikus and Christians over the course of the next few weeks. A police squad was confronted; a constable was cut to pieces. By January, the British were firing on mobs, catching innocent people in the crossfire. The uprising, which the Mundas called the Ulgulan, or Great Tumult, did not last long: colonial power crushed a people who had believed their leader's prophecy that British bullets would turn to water. Birsa Munda fled to the jungle, but was captured in March 1900. Three months later, possibly suffering from cholera, he died in his jail cell.

Popular accounts claim that Birsa Munda was insulted by the British even in death, his body cremated by the jail sweeper not with wood, but with cow dung. But he has gained new life in independent India, as a posthumously honoured citizen. Birsa Munda's name now adorns both the airport and the central jail in Ranchi, the capital of Jharkhand. His portrait even hangs in India's Parliament House. Weirdly, the painting is based on a colonial prison mugshot. Birsa's rope handcuffs have been edited out. Official recognition, however, doesn't mean that what Birsa stood for is now respected by the modern Indian state, or by corporations. The battle is still very much on.

In rural Maharashtra, for example, there are nine million Adivasis.

In the Karjat area, they are known, like the Kols, for a will to fight. In 2009, they joined with local farmers to stop Mukesh Ambani's Reliance Group (see 50 **Dhirubhai Ambani**) from acquiring 20,000 acres of land – a David and Goliath story that inspired community organizers countrywide.

But Karjat is also a desirable location for affluent residents of Mumbai and Pune who wish to build holiday homes and villas. What Reliance couldn't do is being achieved by local agents, who buy land from Karjat's Katkari Adivasis and sell it on to developers. 'Relax in natural waterfalls flowing from inside the project,' the ad for a large luxury complex called Elegant says. 'Indulge in farming activities.' It's striking, from the perspective of the Karjat Adivasi, to consider agriculture as an indulgence. In a bitter irony, many Adivasis – Katkaris and others – are now working the numerous brick kilns in the area, firing bricks for the luxury developments being built on their land.

On the roads in and out of the Katkari village of Tamnath, the undulating landscape looks as if it has been shaved before surgery. Call it development, or call it encroachment, the new construction is the main reason why forest cover in the state dropped from 20 per cent to 16 per cent in a decade. Residents of Tamnath now have to travel further and further to find the wood they need. Sitting outside her house in the village, Sita Pawar tells me about the importance of the forest for village families as a source of fuel, food and building materials. 'If we lose the forest,' she says, 'we lose everything.'

Arundhati Roy says, 'If you look at a map of India now, the mineral wealth, the Adivasi population and the forests are all stacked up on top of each other. And the fact that Adivasis still exist is because people like Birsa Munda did stage the beginnings of a battle against the takeover of the homeland.' But for Tamnath's Katkaris and the eighty million other Adivasis, creating opportunitities to participate in India's economic growth, as well as heroes or heroines whose stories don't end with their early death in captivity, is essential work for this and the next generations.

27
Jamsetji Tata

Making India
1839–1904

In the latter half of the nineteenth century, India's first industrial manufacturing boom turned the city of Bombay into a Cottonopolis. Bombay's mills, mostly Indian-owned, supplied cotton goods to the world, and created huge cohorts of skilled workers who over generations gave Bombay a middle class. Today, though, the city's famous mills are history. Visiting the stone-block ruins of one of them, near the financial hub of the Bandra Kurla Complex, is like burrowing into a hollow of the contemporary Indian economy. Just across a waterway from this rat-ridden carcass you can make out international banks and five-star hotels, a condominium designed for what its marketers call 'the ultra-rich', and a private school started by India's wealthiest family, the Ambanis (see **50 Dhirubhai Ambani**), to serve the city's most privileged children. No manufacturing as far as the eye can see, unless cold-pressed juice and pumpkin frappés count.

Rejuvenating India's manufacturing base, and the jobs it creates, is a twenty-first-century government priority: a concern the nineteenth-century owner of the mill would have shared. Jamsetji Nusserwanji Tata created one of India's greatest industrial houses, and showcased an entrepreneurial art in short supply lately: the ability to balance short-term, private interest with a far-sighted sense of public purpose. His story is also something of an anomaly for its times, expressing an unusually global ambition for India's economic growth.

Tata was a contemporary of robber barons such as John D. Rockefeller and Andrew Carnegie and, like the Americans, the origins of his wealth weren't pristine: he was an opium trader and profiteer of British imperialism in Africa. But animated by a faith in free trade and Indian capability, he went on to do more than play a central role in establishing the country's industrial base. He also helped sustain it by creating institutions to produce a better-educated professional, managerial and scientific class.

Born in 1839 into a Parsi family in the small town of Navsari, Gujarat, Tata grew into a short, sturdy man, dressed in the Parsi style, with a white frock coat and turban-like hat. An American engineer later recalled that this strangely dressed fellow with a deep voice appeared one day at his New York office and asked him to help build a steel plant in an Indian jungle. The dubious engineer found himself agreeing, explaining, 'You don't know what character and force radiated from Tata's face.'

But the real source of his power was his entrepreneurialism, not his aura. Although he sought lessons for India in the rapid rise of America, Germany and Japan, he was operating in a colonized country where markets were controlled to serve the interests of the British, and where there was little access to investment capital or technology. He couldn't hope to emulate the path of Western national economies – and he had to be immensely creative in navigating the great global financial crises of his time.

'India was a conquered nation,' the Harvard historian Emma Rothschild observes, 'and the British – believing in freedom and democratic government and free enterprise in the abstract – did not believe in all those things in the particular in India. Yet Tata and his associates were able to get outside that iron constraint of British rule.' In her view, the Tata story is more modern than the iconic legends of American or European titans because it was global from the very beginning.

'Make the world England' was a popular slogan at the height of the British Empire. Today, the companies that sprang from Jamsetji's first concern have made the world more Indian. In 2014, the annual revenue of Tata companies (derived from businesses ranging from power generation and real estate to hotels and IT) was equal to more than 5 per cent of India's GDP. Those great marques of British mechanics, Jaguar and Land Rover, are Tata-controlled – as are Tetley Tea and Corus, the company that was once British Steel.

While the Tata group's archives are an invaluable resource for the history of modern Indian economic life, most of Jamsetji's papers were destroyed by his son Dorabji, for reasons unknown. So we're left to judge Tata mainly by how he was seen by others, and by what he did. We can trace his shift from private interest towards nation-building concerns by following the names of his mills. A factory in Nagpur, opened in 1877, was named the Empress Mills in homage to Victoria, but nearly a decade later, when he set up a more sophisticated mill – now the carcass at Bandra Kurla Complex – he named it Swadeshi, which means, essentially, 'self-made'. Swadeshi was then a fresh term in Indian public life: two decades later, it would become a battle cry against the British in Bengal and, from the 1920s, the banner for Gandhi's mass movement. But in Tata's own time, when independence from Britain seemed not just impossible but imprudent, the mill's name was a gesture in what we might call the era of corporate proto-nationalism: a moderate challenge to Empire waged by an impatient and entitled elite that the Empire itself had created.

Every colonial power requires the aid of a favoured tribe to help administer its outposts. The Spanish in Mexico had the Tlaxcalans; the Dutch in Indonesia had their pijaji. The Raj, in western India, had the light-skinned and often anglicized Parsis. Reputed for their honesty and business sense, Parsis received government jobs and commissions greatly disproportionate to their number. Tata's father, Nusserwanji Tata, was one of the beneficiaries.

Nusserwanji was quick to see economic opportunities in the military and trading needs of the far-flung British Empire. He left his home in Gujarat, and the family's priestly profession, for Bombay, where he set up a trading agency with another merchant and won a lucrative military contract from the British during the Anglo-Persian War of 1856–7. He invested the profits in a new trading partnership, and when Jamsetji, his only son, finished his college education, he was put to work for it – in China.

Unlike caste Hindus, Parsis didn't see travelling abroad as a pollutant. This gave them considerable advantages in trade. Tata's immediate task was to ship opium and cotton to Hong Kong and Shanghai and to send back tea, silk, camphor and gold – a well-worn profit loop in the imperial economy. But as he learned the exigencies of running an Indian business under colonial control, he was also receiving a crash course in world economics.

Not long after his arrival in China, the outbreak, in 1861, of civil war in America radically transformed economic opportunities in western India – for the better, at first. Southern cotton farmers having taken up arms, British mill-owners had nothing to weave with, and global cotton prices rose; Indians quickly stepped in to cover the shortfall. By 1862 India was supplying the vast majority of the cotton used by Britain and France, and Tata's business partner, Premchand Roychand, set up a bank to deposit all the bullion flowing into Bombay.

In the early years of colonization, the East India Company had allowed Indian industries, among them textiles, to stagnate; in a scathing critique of the 1780s, the conservative British politician Edmund Burke accused company officials of ruining India's economy and society. But during the cotton boom, British mill-owners were benefiting, so government policy was inclined to help Indians produce more cotton, and the British took what looked, retrospectively, like a benign disinterest in Indian profits.

Neither the disinterest nor the boom was to last. In 1865, not long after Tata moved to London to manage the firm's cotton business and open a branch of Roychand's new bank, the Confederates were defeated. Ships laden with American cotton soon resumed their transatlantic routes. A Boston merchant working in Bombay described the local reaction: 'I am sorry to say such long faces I never saw on any set of mortals as the English & Parsees put on here. Our success at home is their ruination.'

The bursting of the Indian cotton bubble left Tata in London with so many worthless bills of credit that he had to liquidate his own company. Returning to Bombay, he found his father had sold the family home to pay off more debts. But as many of their counterparts were ruined, old British military connections gave the Tatas a third chance to capitalize on other countries' conflicts.

In 1867, the Negus, or ruler, of Abyssinia imprisoned a handful of British subjects, at which the British sent a force – of, staggeringly, 16,000 men – to free them. The commander-in-chief at Bombay led the expedition, and Tata was among the contractors who received handsome orders to supply it. The incursion ultimately caused a British scandal for costing taxpayers more than £10 million. But Tata was left sufficiently flush that, instead of just trading cotton, he was able to expand into yarn and cloth. He felt that manufacturing at home might help protect his company from future fluctuations in the international market, and in that thinking he wasn't alone. Indians were setting up cotton mills across western India, hoping to profit from the cotton glut that followed the end of the American Civil War. But Tata would set himself apart by dint of his early adoption of international technology.

A habitué of the Great Exhibitions of the nineteenth century, Tata was obsessed with innovation. His home had an electric piano, a cinematograph and other nineteenth-century technological toys. His carriage was one of the first in India to have rubber tyres, amazing bystanders as it rolled silently by. He introduced refrigeration to Bombay and tried to build a business shipping mangoes in cold storage to Britain. And he obsessively upgraded his mills.

He visited England to learn the fine points of spinning technology, then travelled to Egypt to master the cultivation of higher quality cotton. Just as cannily, while his contemporaries relied on family members to run their operations and purchased labour at the cheapest rates, Tata recruited professional managers and sought to maintain a reasonably contented workforce. His prize mill, Swadeshi, was so poorly designed and managed when he acquired it that he had seizures trying to fix it. But after turning it around with new spindle technology and new managers (some of them Westerners), he became the first mill-owner in India to institute a pension fund for his employees. A grain depot, a medical dispensary and a nursery for the infants of women workers soon followed – an early sketch, perhaps, of the model city that his son would later build around the Tata steel plant at Jamshedpur in central India. The prompt for these benefits wasn't soft-hearted generosity. As Tata had learned when travelling abroad, the extras gave skilled workers incentive to stay.

Tata was as much of an opportunist as many of today's entrepreneurs are. If you had money, he'd sidle up to you for financing. He raised funds for his enterprises in France and in French India, and from India's princes; he acquired partners in Switzerland and America. But a harsher British imperialism would soon clip his sails.

By the 1870s, the Raj had begun to put the screws on manufacturers in the colonies, particularly in the cotton industry that had helped it through the American Civil War. Competition was the issue. As Tata and other manufacturers increased exports by penetrating the Chinese market, the mills in Lancashire and Manchester began to suffer, and to protect them, in 1878 the British government imposed higher import and excise duties on Indian-made textiles. This increase came during a fraught decade for India: an era of famines and of periodic riots by cultivators in the western part of the Empire. A reaction was inevitable, but it came about gradually.

Tata was, in many ways, an Anglophile; Gladstone was one of his heroes. But he'd also experienced the less attractive side of British rule. In 1863, he had attended a celebration in Bombay to mark the occasion of the Prince of Wales's marriage; when a British official helped himself to a chair being used by the Tata party, Tata's objections landed him in the city jail. That may have been a mere social slight, but now, in middle age, he was not alone among India's elites in feeling harassed in business and seeing the point of organizing some resistance. Tata's friend and fellow Parsi, the liberal free trader Dadabhai Naoroji, had already begun publishing what would become an influential polemic, based on compendious statistical tabulations: England's policies were draining the Indian economy dry at a time when it needed active support to develop its long-term value.

At the end of 1885, Tata joined seventy-two mostly wealthy men – primarily lawyers and businessmen – in Bombay, at the first annual meeting of the Indian National Congress. Alongside Parsis like Tata there was another group that had benefited from British policies and patronage: the English-educated Brahmins and upper castes. They now populated a restless professional class impatient with the status quo and eager to translate their education into jobs with rank and earnings. In time, the Congress would become Gandhi's mass movement, and then the political party that would dominate the government of independent India for decades. But the first order of business was to push for greater representation in the Raj's administration and legislative councils, in order to secure more equal rights and more government jobs.

Much as his admirers might like to slip Tata into the mainstream of this early political struggle for more self-rule, he's decidedly peripheral in the extant first-hand accounts of the Congress. There is no evidence that he made any intellectual contribution, though a donation of 500 rupees was recorded. Tata's was a different, non-Brahminical strain of early nationalism. It wasn't rights-based; it was focused on skills and essentially practical. He saw a need to expand the range of Indian talent, broadening education and, to some extent, those to whom it was available. It's a strand of Indian nationalism that's often overlooked, if nationalism is viewed purely in cultural and political terms.

In 1892, Tata launched a scheme to send young men to train abroad as future administrators, scientists, doctors, lawyers and engineers. It's possible that he took to heart his friend Naoroji's argument that the drain on India was moral as well as economic: British Indian officials retired to Britain, taking their professional skills back home, as well as their wealth. In time, Tata scholars would number around a fifth of all Indians in the Indian Civil Service.

A grander initiative was reflective of his sense that America, Germany and Japan were growing on the strength of scientific research. With the progressive ruler of the princely state of Mysore (see 33 Visvesvaraya), he created an endowment to establish in Bangalore the Indian Institute of Science (IISc). Although Tata sent his elder son to Cambridge, in planning his own institute he showed himself to be unimpressed by the privileged gentility of Oxbridge: the models that mattered were modern research universities like Johns Hopkins. After his death, the IISc would become a pioneer of Indian scientific research and inspire the creation of other institutions (including more Tata-supported ones). Without those institutions, software India, and for that matter nuclear India, might not yet have emerged. It's as if Tata had been standing on a parallel site to the abandoned mill by Mumbai's Bandra Kurla Complex, considering a hollow in the economy of his own era, and marshalling the resources to fix it.

*

A fascinating aspect of Tata's story, Emma Rothschild points out, is how many failures he was able to absorb. The most politically combative that Tata ever became was in the 1890s, when the British added to their profits by exploiting a shipping monopoly over freighting Indian goods. He sought to break the rate-gouging, and even tried to set up his own shipping line. The British ensured that it failed, though they had to make a few concessions to Tata's cause.

This late-life provocation may be why, as many Indian business and social eminences routinely received royal knighthoods or baronetcies, Tata was bypassed. You could see it as a particularly delicious – and high-minded – form of revenge that Jamsetji's son, continuing his father's enthusiasm for research, was to help fund studies on British poverty and social welfare at the London School of Economics, an act of what Rothschild calls 'reverse imperial generosity'.

Tata's last major obsession was a dream of steel. This would also be a failure, but only in the short term. During a visit to England, Tata had been convinced by the historian and social critic Thomas Carlyle's argument that developing an iron industry was the straightest path to national wealth. In India, though, little was known about where iron deposits might be, mining licences were controlled by the British, and investment capital was hard to come by. Still, Tata toured the mining and steelmaking centres of the United States, recruiting their engineers and technology to scout central India for ore. His son would later hit upon a major lode, steering the Tata companies from cotton into steel and hydroelectric power – resources that would be essential to India's development.

Jamsetji's final project, though, opened just before his death in 1904: the luxurious Taj Mahal Palace Hotel in Bombay, named after the most iconic building in India and now a brand that stands for Indian luxury. During the Mumbai terror attacks of November 2008, when Pakistani jihadists roamed the corridors and lobbies, shooting guests and staff, they still took time to marvel at the opulence before they began to burn it down. But even in old age, Jamsetji was less interested in splendour than in technological firsts: the Taj was the first hotel in India to have lifts and electric lights.

*

Of the institution-building that represented Tata's great philanthropic legacy in India, Tata once wrote, 'What advances a nation or community is not so much to prop up its weakest and most helpless members as to lift up the best and the most gifted so as to make them of the greatest service to the country.' This marks one of the limits of his developmental imagination. Preference for the gifted over the average, already ingrained in Indian society, would become a trait of government policy, continued to this day. Its consequences – among them primary schools whose poor quality has been a consistent feature of modern India – have shackled India's development and kept its benefits firmly within privileged enclaves.

Tata did, though, rightly see that successful business depends on what people nowadays call an 'ecosystem' – to provide trained professionals, to generate new ideas and research, to ensure the entire chain of production is created, and to develop the workforce, the human capital. He recognized that as long as India was ruled by a colonial state, bent on stifling any Indian industry that might compete with British interests, Indian industrialists could not just content themselves with being sharp arbitrageurs. They had to create their own institutions to succeed. Gandhi once said of Tata that he 'never looked to self-interest'. Gandhi was wrong about that. But at some moments – rare historical sweet spots – private business interest and public purpose do align.

Four decades after Tata's death, another industrialist family, the Birlas, provided the compound where Gandhi would spend his final days. A joke went round that it took a lot of money to keep the Mahatma in poverty. But the connection between great wealth and the freedom fight had deeper roots than this. British favouritism helped create an English-educated class of Brahmins and upper castes confident enough to demand, through the Congress, greater political rights and representation. But it had also overseen the rise of a small, ambitious business class confident enough to challenge British trade policies – and, in the case of Tata, to create institutions that substantially expanded India's educated, privileged class. Both of these groups – the educated elites and the wealthy industrialists – would set their stamp on the Congress movement, which, for all its popular fervour, chose gradual capitalist growth over revolutionary temptation.

28
Vivekananda

Bring All Together
1863–1902

The summer solstice is a day that usually passes unnoticed in India. In most parts of the country, it's too damned hot, or wet, for celebration. But in 2015, Prime Minister Narendra Modi spent the morning leading some 35,000 schoolchildren, servicemen and bureaucrats, arrayed in rows on the ceremonial avenue running through the centre of the capital, in a series of yoga exercises. He called this, the world's largest yoga class, 'the contribution from the soil of India for the good of human beings'.

The world had, of course, been sampling this offering well before Modi became the first leader in recent memory to do a competent half-camel in public. In the United States alone, some 15 million people practise yoga, but I'd wager few of them realize that the key text of modern yoga, *Raja Yoga* – one of the first works of Indian philosophy ever to reach a mass Western audience – was written in the US in the 1890s and influenced by the American culture of the time. *Raja Yoga*'s thirty-three-year-old author, a restless, baby-faced monk from Calcutta, had set down his thoughts on yoga's transformative power during the breaks in a lengthy lecture tour of the US.

The monk, Vivekananda, had started the tour with the hope of teaching the West the essence of Hinduism, and counteracting persistent stereotypes of India as a barbarous spiritual vacuum. Late at night, escaping the flashy red robe and saffron turban that increased his mystique at the podium, he dutifully recorded high points of his press reviews for his princely patrons back in India, to reassure them their money had been well spent. 'An orator by Divine right,' said one of the passages he copied out – a review that seems muted in retrospect. By the tour's end, Vivekananda had become, in the words of the political theorist Pratap Bhanu Mehta, 'the most famous brand ambassador for Indian spirituality, culture, yoga, and ideals that our country has ever known'.

When he returned to India in 1897, Vivekananda was given a hero's welcome for having finally engendered respect for Hinduism in the sceptical West and, in certain circles, even a clamour for it. Though he only lived for five more years, dying just before the freedom struggle got underway, his image – arms defiantly folded, soft features hardened by a Napoleonic gaze – could be found in the homes of Indian revolutionaries, Congress leaders, religious men, intellectuals and regional social reformers. Embodying a potent Hinduism that had nothing to apologize for, he gained a pan-Indian appeal that rivalled Gandhi's. Today, he is one of Hindu nationalism's leading spiritual lights.

Modi is not alone in considering him 'a personal inspiration'. Many contemporary Hindu elites in India and abroad celebrate Vivekananda for his insistence that Hinduism is superior to all other religions – and uniquely peaceful and tolerant – 'because it never conquered, because it never shed blood'. They've especially taken to heart his notion that religion is India's 'only common ground, and upon that we shall have to build'.

But when one considers the historical Vivekananda alongside the archetype, the Hindu propagandist enjoying a vibrant afterlife seems like an incarnation that's misplaced one of its dimensions. India's first global guru was a complex and inconsistent man, habitually inflecting his message to suit different audiences and making declarations he'd later contradict. Still, there's a silver thread running through his thought: the imperative to test old grounds of belief and seek out new ones, while grappling with the age-old problem of how to make a moral life a practical one. In this respect, too, Vivekananda resembled Gandhi, who was six years younger. Both men, far from spouting timeless Indian verities, were struggling to convert their own uncertainties into new ways to believe, and be.

Vivekananda's intention was never just to celebrate Hinduism, either in the West or at home. He hoped to motivate his fellow Indians to rework it. 'No religion on earth preaches the dignity of humanity in such a lofty strain as Hinduism, and no religion on earth treads upon the necks of the poor and low in such a fashion as Hinduism,' he once wrote. And he argued that Hinduism as practised was illegitimate because of the dehumanizing effects of the caste system.

His solution was not to turn away from the faith, as the **Buddha** (1) and **Mahavira** (2) had done, and as **Ambedkar** (41) would later do. Instead, he sought the more worldly ends of the philosophy embodied in the Vedanta, the Upanishad scriptures that came after the Vedas, which had been made central to Hinduism by **Shankara** (8). Providing spiritual solace wasn't the main point of the faith to Vivekananda. Rather, in what amounted to a novel and radical argument, he insisted that Hinduism's moral force rested on its capacity to meet society's practical needs.

Vivekananda's short life had a whirlwind intellectual and spiritual itinerary. Among other things, it encompassed Freemasonry, Buddhist meditation, immersion in Thomas à Kempis's *The Imitation of Christ*, readings of Western science and rationalist philosophy, encounters with Western occultism and esotericism and engagement with the organizational energies of American social crusaders.

Born Narendranath Dutta in 1863, he grew up in Calcutta, then the capital of the Raj, where so many currents of European and Indian thought intersected. His father, a successful anglicized lawyer with liberal views, encouraged his three sons to argue and think for themselves. His mother was a practising Hindu. One of his brothers repudiated the faith to become a Marxist revolutionary, but for Narendra, Hinduism, rationalism and social radicalism were ideals that could be reconciled. As a teenager he joined a branch of the Brahmo Samaj, accepting its view of Hinduism as a universalistic religion whose essence was to be found in the Vedanta. He took to heart both the Brahmo Samaj's critique of idol worship and its focus on social reform, inspired by Rammohun Roy's Christian Unitarianism (see **22 Rammohun Roy**).

INCARNATIONS

At college in Calcutta, he seemed to embody a joke that was appearing in Indian periodicals of the time about young Bengali intellectuals dallying between 'Kali and Kant'. Reading European philosophy, he and his friends delighted in trying to solder together unlikely philosophical combinations. One of his companions later recalled an effort to hybridize 'the pure monism of the Vedanta, the dialectics of the Absolute idea of Hegel and the Gospel of Equality, Liberty and Fraternity of the French Revolution'.

As dauntless as Narendra seemed in college, the deaths in quick succession of his Brahmo mentor and his father sent him into spiritual crisis. Following a breakdown, he left behind a family squabbling over his father's property and began spending time on the banks of the nearby Ganga with Ramakrishna Paramahamsa, a hermit in the ecstatic tradition. Ramakrishna was a mystic devotee of the goddess Kali and a practitioner of Tantra and yoga, who had also for a time followed Sufi Islam. His tradition of Hindu worship accepted different paths to God and focused on personal transcendental experiences.

Though Ramakrishna died in 1886, a few years after they met, Vivekananda later described his encounter with the mystic as a spiritual turning point that wiped his soul of earlier influences. On the evidence of his own writings, that's not entirely true; his later reconstruction of Hinduism seems to owe at least as much to his previous intellectual encounters, including those with European ideas, as it does to Ramakrishna. But his religious questing did change in one distinct way. Repudiating the Brahmo Samaj as a '"booby religion"' and taking on the name Vivekananda, 'joyous with knowledge', he began to seek grounds for his religious understandings less in texts and more in personal experiences.

In the late nineteenth and early twentieth centuries, Hinduism was being reconstructed in a variety of forms, both in the West and in India. Theosophy blended Hinduism with esotericism and occultism, to create an arcane philosophy for an elite race (see **29 Annie Besant**). In the hands of V. D. Savarkar, Hinduism was converted into Hindutva, a nationalist ideology that defines Hinduism in terms of blood and territory, and which considers members of religions not 'born' in

India, such as Islam and Christianity, as inherently inferior within
Bharat Mata, or Mother India. Preceding Savarkar into the mix, in
the late 1880s, was Vivekananda.

For several years, Vivekananda wandered India as a mendicant,
carrying little more than a couple of changes of clothes, a rolled-up
deerskin, a water pot and the occasional book. (His interests ranged
from French music to chemistry to history, and he could recite pages
from *The Pickwick Papers* as readily as sutras from **Panini**'s *Ashtadhyayi* (3).) One of his goals during his walkabout was to probe the
nature of Hinduism. As he wandered, he found the faith to be connected in dark ways to the reality he was witnessing in the Indian
countryside.

Ordinary people everywhere were sunk in poverty and ignorance,
while Hindu rulers went off on shooting excursions, he would later
say. Hindu traditions sanctified priests for denying untouchables
their humanity. Seeing the oppression caused in part by Hindu religious practices, Vivekananda felt he was 'being driven mad with
mental agonies'. It became clear to him that the social order, built
around what he called the 'mental disease' of 'don't-touchism', both
mutilated souls and kept people divided. If Hinduism was to have
any moral credibility, and any hope of collective strength, it would
have to address social inequality and degradation.

His anger led to questions. For some time, Vivekananda had been
infuriated by the way Christian missionaries were able to capitalize on
caste discrimination and untouchability by moving in to convert the
lower castes in significant numbers. Were caste hierarchies essential to
Hinduism? What *was* essential? To his guru, Ramakrishna, Vedanta
was the highest expression of eternal religion, or Sanatan Dharma,
which was unchanging and ahistorical. But in its interpretations, Vivekananda began to perceive the shifting, historical hand of religious
authority. For instance, Shankara's interpretation of the Vedanta permitted only Brahmins to study the Vedas and Upanishads. (That
interpretation would exclude Vivekananda himself, because he was a
Kayasth, a scribal caste the British classified as Shudra.) He decided
that Shankara's idea was based on non-authoritative scriptures, and so
rejected it. On similar grounds, he found he could also refuse to accept

other practices he abhorred: for instance, the practice of marrying girls before they had reached the age of puberty, or Vedic rituals like the Ashvamedha that instructed a queen hoping to secure her king's sovereignty to simulate copulation with a dead horse. Vivekananda's re-reading of the Vedas would strike down the bad interpretations and inessential rituals that separated the seeker from deeper eternal truths.

Shankara had interpreted the Vedantist philosophy as showing us the illusory character of the sensory world, and the need to pierce that illusion to achieve oneness with Brahman. Vivekananda took that idea of oneness, but insisted on the reality of the perceived world: one in which the path to oneness was through action. His reconstruction of Vedantist philosophy proclaimed Hinduism as a uniquely practical religion, open to all and directed towards the uplift of society.

His teachings moved Hinduism away from texts as primary repositories of authority and truths and towards personal experience. Gurus or teachers were not essential. Anyone could progress towards truth through exercises and service to the poor and needy – activism that would also restore cultural confidence and pride in Hindu traditions. In fact, he argued, the root cause of all of India's historical wretchedness, including its inability to evade colonization, was that the purest truths of Hinduism had been mangled by obscurantist priests.

Vivekananda claimed that his socially transformative understanding of the place of Hinduism in Indian society was visited upon him whole, in 1892, in the form of a revelation at Kanyakumari, or Cape Comorin, at the southernmost tip of the Indian peninsula. But his letters suggest a project built in stages, embedded in human time. '[W]e must travel, we must go to foreign parts,' he wrote that year to a Brahmin priest who became one of his spiritual guides. 'We must see how the engine of society works in other countries.' By the next year, he was writing to the priest from the United States, where he had begun to enact his idea of activism with a new urgency.

In August 1893, freezing in the New England summer and reeling at the prices of American goods ('a cigar costs eight annas of our money,' he complained in a letter), the thirty-two-year-old Vivekananda visited a Massachusetts reformatory for women. He was amazed to see hundreds of inmates being treated gently by jailors who were intentionally kept unaware of each prisoner's specific crime and were diligently preparing the women for reintegration into society. Such dignified treatment of people of low status was unimaginable back home. 'Oh, how my heart ached to think of what we think of the poor, the low in India,' he wrote to a friend there. 'They have no chance, no escape, no way to climb up . . . They have forgotten that they too are men. And the result is slavery.'

But he wasn't about to share with his new audience the painful light that America had shed on Hinduism's injustices. His commission, funded by maharajas, was to present a gilded version of the religion for Western consumption. The following month he arrived, uninvited, at the enormous World's Parliament of Religions in Chicago, an attempt to create a global dialogue of faiths. Lecturing for days to adulatory audiences, Vivekananda became one of the Parliament's stars.

His agent was now handling details of lectures in other cities, Henry and William James were hanging on his utterances, and rich, ardent American women were inviting him home for tea. It was a bit of a mind-wrench after the meditative barefoot years, and he would later joke that by the end of the tour, he'd succumbed to the biggest of all the temptations America threw in his path: the allure of new forms of organization.

He was fascinated by American social openness, the comparative freedom of women, the ability of people to act collectively in their own interests (labour unions were then gathering steam), and the way state institutions served the practical needs of the people. The secret of Westerners' success, he concluded, was 'the power of organization and combination'. It was a secret that he immediately saw he needed to transmit to his countrymen.

'I give them spirituality, and they give me money,' he wrote with a wink to the Dewan of Junagadh, a minister of one of his princely patrons, in 1894. Funds he raised on tour, as well as inspiration taken from American religious and civic associations, enabled him to set up the Vedanta Society, first in New York and then in London, to promote his version of Hinduism. These would be India's first spiritual missions in the West. After his return to India in 1897, American money would help him realize a key aspect of his revelation at Kanyakumari.

In that same 1894 letter, he had laid out what was, in effect, a charter for his life: a band of religious monks, devoted to social service, would travel India from village to village, educating all tiers of society, including the lowest, 'by means of maps, cameras, globes, and other such accessories' – spreading the light of science, as well as the gospel of religion. Drawing on ideas of social service that he had learned from his late Brahmo mentor, Vivekananda turned them into the organization he would, after his mystic guru, name the Ramakrishna Mission. The Mission had no precedent among Indian religious institutions, and continues to function across India today as a dispenser of education and social welfare.

Other American habits impressed Vivekananda as well, including the country's appetite for beef – which he recommended to fellow Indians as a way of strengthening their physique. He also imbibed American bodybuilding culture, placing exercise techniques at the heart of the practice of true Hinduism. Yoga, breathing and meditation were compatible with everyday life, accessible to upper and lower castes, rich and poor, and Westerners too. If practised sincerely, the exercises would leave a devotee psychologically remodelled. By imparting confidence, discipline and strength, yoga also became a means of changing society and training people to carry out social reform. This is perhaps not the end-goal of the yoga-with-cats classes lately offered in Manhattan, or the 'Stay Woke' yoga-music pop-up in Chicago, where postures are held as the DJ spins, but you never know. Elizabeth De Michelis, who has studied the history of modern yoga, emphasizes that Vivekananda's *Raja Yoga* was itself a novel mix, bringing together loose ideas of yoga, terminology drawn from the *Yoga Sutra* (a text by Patanjali dating from around 400 CE), Indian tradition and occultist and esoteric beliefs he had encountered in America. 'It's not,' she allows, 'very logically tied together.'

As Vivekananda successfully promoted health and strength at the turn of the century, his own health was secretly failing: stomach ailments, heart trouble, loss of vision. He died stoically, in 1902, at the age of forty, three years before the Partition of Bengal.

Unlike Gandhi, Vivekananda lived before the era of mass politics; he always insisted that he was uninterested in politics anyway. But Pratap Bhanu Mehta wonders how or if, had he lived another ten or fifteen years, he would have engaged with the political imagination that came to grip India. Instead, India's political imagination has engaged with him – often assimilating him to nationalist purposes. He's now considered the originator of an aggressive culture of masculinity in Hinduism.

'Bring all together,' Vivekananda once urged. India's different cultures were just emanations of a single principle, and social unity would lead to the achievement of collective purposes. As a hope for change, it's not without merit. But Vivekananda has been turned instead into a warrior-philosopher of a new Hindu pridefulness, invoked today by a political ideology that aims to impose conformity across India's religiously diverse communities.

The irony is that, as much as he wanted to salvage India, whose problems, he claimed, were greater than those of any other country in the world, his writings make clear that he also wanted humans to overcome narrow identities, respect each other and expand their circles of identification. Or at least I think that's what he wanted. One can never be quite sure with the elusive, charismatic Vivekananda. But I rather suspect that many contemporary Indians have mistaken one of their most interesting universalist thinkers for a simplistic nationalist.

29
Annie Besant

An Indian Tomtom
1847–1933

What lingered in the memory was her silvery voice – the most beautiful, some said, they had ever heard. When India's future prime
minister, Jawaharlal Nehru, listened as a child to Annie Besant speak,
he was left 'dazed and as in a dream'. This voice combined with intellectual vigour to make her, in George Bernard Shaw's grudging
estimation, the best orator in England. But it had required real daring
to find. One day in her mid-twenties, unhappily married to a stiff-
backed Lincolnshire vicar, Besant locked herself alone in his church,
climbed into his pulpit and spoke to the empty pews. 'I shall never
forget the feeling of power and delight – but especially of power – that
came upon me as I sent my voice ringing down the aisles.'

Feeling boxed in by Victorian domesticity and the mainstream
Christianity that sanctioned it, Annie Besant soon jettisoned her marriage and put her gift of persuasion to use. She became a polemicist for
a sequence of ideas billowing out of the religious and social crises of
the Victorian age: atheism, workers' rights, women's rights, birth control, free speech, Fabian socialism and Irish Home Rule. By the time
she was forty, critics were calling her 'Red Annie' and admirers were
calling her one of the most remarkable women of the nineteenth century. By the time she had reached eighty, she had become one of the
most remarkable women in twentieth-century India.

Possessed of an ego some thought too healthy for her sex, and
habitually indifferent to convention, she was often made, as she put
it, 'a mark for ridicule'. This mockery began even before her life was
changed by a gimlet-eyed Russian occultist named Madame Blavatsky. Blavatsky claimed to be the London receptor of world-changing

messages received from Hindu sages in the Himalayas. In 1875, along with an American Civil War veteran, Colonel Henry Steel Olcott, and others, she launched the Theosophy movement – a synthetic blend of European esoterica like clairvoyance, elements of Buddhist and Hindu philosophy, and scientism. By increasing its members' spiritual powers, and then their leadership skills, Theosophy promised to create no less than a peaceful world order founded on human brotherhood.

Theosophy was the intellectual flypaper of the Victorian age, capturing the minds of figures from Yeats to Kandinsky to Scriabin to Besant, who took it up with fervour in 1889. Conversion gave her a new past full of incarnations – among them the fifth-century Graeco-Egyptian mathematician Hypatia – and a new proselytizing mission in India: she would engineer a spiritual and political awakening in the land whose religions inspired her new faith.

When she alighted in India in 1893, her first order of business was to build branches of the Theosophical Society, based in Madras, all over the country. In due course, she would also (just a sideline for a very busy woman) help create, through a young man named Jiddu Krishnamurti, the New Age self-improvement spirit of California. But Besant did more for India than import and export mystical fads. Hostile to what she called the 'land-stealing, piratical policy' of the British Empire, whether in Ireland or in India, she became an activist for nationalism, and eventually the leader of the Congress party. More resonantly, she was a catalyst for the intellectual and political elite who would eventually gain freedom and lead a new nation.

Besant grew up in London reading theology; she was raised by a rich evangelical benefactress who took her in after her father's death when she was five. But in Lincolnshire, only a few years after her own marriage, she had to confront the fact that she believed in neither original sin nor the divinity of Christ. Her vicar husband was not best pleased as she let herself loose into London's radical circles.

The Secular Society. The Dialectical Society. The Liberal Social Union. The Law and Liberty League. As Besant wrote later, she now lived 'joyously and defiantly, with sheer delight in the intellectual strife'. And as she expounded on women's rights and workers' conditions, she continued to educate herself, studying Darwinism and new scientific theories, and becoming one of the first women to study for a science degree at University College London. In 1877, not yet thirty, she re-published a 'neo-Malthusian' book advocating population control as a means of addressing poverty and unemployment. Not long after, she wrote her own book endorsing contraception, which no woman before her had ever openly advocated. Already subjected to occasional kicks and stone-throwing for her views, she was now tried for obscenity (an imprisonable offence).

Escaping on a technicality, she was forbidden from seeing her children – causing a personal anguish that seemed to make her even fiercer. In the mid-1880s, her concerns about unemployment and poverty and a faith in social evolution led her to socialism. Joining the Fabians, she organized strikes and was elected to local government. Around this time, she also began to experiment with spiritualism and the paranormal, as did many of her fellow travellers. But Besant went further than the pack after reading Blavatsky, who posited an evolution, rooted in India and Hindu philosophy, towards a higher human race. She went to meet the chain-smoking occultist, looked into her mesmeric eyes, and felt mastered. If Besant found in Theosophy a programme for human fulfilment and self-government even grander than socialism, there was, however, a small snag. Blavatsky considered reincarnation the key to the perfection of the races: contraception blocked such evolutionary upgrades since it was likely to be practised by those of superior intelligence. Without hesitation, Besant withdrew the bestselling book for which she had risked prison and her children.

At the age of forty-six, Red Annie was ready to be reborn as the white-clad Bari Memsahib, transforming the esoterica of Theosophy into practical Indian politics.

It's been said that the dominant narrative of Western colonial engagement is 'We came, we saw, we were horrified, we intervened.' But Theosophy's history in India is an example of what the philosopher Agehananda Bharati called the 'pizza-effect': the adoption by one culture, usually a more powerful one, of some aspect of a foreign culture, which is then embellished and returned home. The Americans did it with Neapolitan pizza; the Europeans did it with Hindu spirituality. Besant and other Theosophists, picking up on the passion of **William Jones** (21) and other 'Orientalists' for ancient Brahminic texts, saw India as the cradle of civilization. With her oratorical genius, Besant proved to be a brilliant re-exporter of this view.

Theosophy spread in part through Besant's steady stream of books, pamphlets and articles. During her time in India, she eventually ran three newspapers herself, and published around a hundred works. But there was also the parlour affability of the weekly Theosophical Society meetings, in which the educated gathered to talk about self-rule and cultural revival, astral travel or voice contact with earlier selves. Besant's enchantment with early Hinduism, alongside her anti-British stance, honed while advocating Irish republicanism, made her a roving *salonnière* of an eclectic flock – princes, progressives and socialists, scientists, artists and politicians, many of whom would play leading roles in twentieth-century India.

Besant took a particular interest in the young in her expanding circle, and one of her early campaigns was to reform Indian education. The Raj's educational system was founded on Lord Macaulay's dictum that Indians must study European literature and history, and not fritter away time on worthless Indian texts. This, combined with missionary activity against Hindu superstition and idolatry, meant that by the end of the nineteenth century, the educated in India had limited access to their own traditions and little reason to value them. Besant's push, ultimately victorious, was to bring elements of western Indology to the curriculum. Later, she established the Central Hindu College, which taught Sanskrit and ancient Indian history in addition to English and British history. It would eventually become part of Banaras Hindu University, an important centre of Indological scholarship. The version of Indian culture propagated, though, was heavily Sanskritized and Brahminized, with little room for the civilization's many other strands.

Besant helped groom a generation of Indian nationalists – the intellectual crack troops of the growing cause. It wasn't enough to give Indians pride in their own culture, she argued: the young also needed to gain the confident knowledge of British culture and manners that would allow them to be taken seriously as an opposition. Her college in Benares held mock parliaments to teach British debating techniques and Robert's Rules of Order. But better, she thought, was education abroad, beginning at a young age – in part so that India's future leaders would not be saddled with the 'chi-chi' accents of those who learned English too late. She campaigned hard to overcome the resistance of high-caste families who thought over-seas travel (believed to be polluting) would cause their children to be expelled from their castes.

In 1901, Besant arranged a Theosophist tutor for Jawaharlal Nehru, the eleven-year-old son of a successful provincial lawyer. Over the next three years, the boy attended Theosophical Society meetings and helped his tutor decipher Sanskrit texts. Recalling science-kit experiments and disquisitions about astral bodies, the Upanishads and the Bhagavad Gita, and Pythagoras, Apollonius of Tyana and other mystics, Nehru said later: 'I felt that here was the key to the secrets of the universe.' He was dejected when, at Besant's sugges-tion, he was sent away, aged fifteen, to study at Harrow.

A different order of grooming was provided for a young Telugu Brahmin whom a colleague of Besant met in Madras in 1909. Besant identified the uncannily beautiful boy, Krishnamurti, as the reincar-nation of Christ and the future World Teacher. The boy messiah was also dispatched to England for education and social polishing (which included regular visits to the gentleman's outfitters Lobb, Asprey and Beale and Inman), in preparation for his appointed role.

It's not accidental that these two young men were both Brahmin. Besant's love of the Aryan and Vedic age led her to see the caste sys-tem as an evolutionary mechanism, reducing ethnic mixing and giving Brahmins brains unrivalled by any other class of people in the world. 'Natural law has been utilised and the result is there before us,' she wrote. Now, these brainy potential world-brotherhood lead-ers just needed a bit of modernization – as the Japanese aristocracy had done, she noted, and the French *ancien régime* had not.

*

As in Britain, Besant's strong views engendered enemies: low-caste leaders who resented her reinforcement of Brahmin superiority; missionaries who loathed her attacks on Christianity; Hindu reformers who found some of her views too conservative; and orthodox Hindus appalled by a white woman's interference in what they saw as their domain. But Besant was famously thick-skinned and, early in the twentieth century, perhaps too impatient to wait for the Brahmins to achieve their destined perfection, she decided to be more political still.

To the viceroy, she said she had come to see that educational reform without political reform was futile. To members of her Theosophical flock, she revealed that she had received a telepathic command from an ancient Hindu sage. But one clear impetus for her shift to politics was the intensifying freedom movement in Ireland. She thought elements of the effective Irish political agitation, including mass public meetings and the clever use of the press and courts, could be emulated by Indians. In a series of 1913 lectures that became a book entitled *Wake Up, India: A Plea for Social Reform*, she argued for (among other things) mass education and foreign exposure, and against (among other things) child marriage. She would explain that 'I am an Indian tomtom, waking up all the sleepers, so that they may wake and work for the motherland.'

Her next move would also rouse up the Raj. In September 1915, she announced her intention to create a nationwide agitational movement for Indian home rule. Built on the back of the Theosophical branch network, its goal was greater Indian self-government. Others started to borrow the idea from Besant: six months later, the Maharashtrian radical leader Bal Gangadhar Tilak launched the Indian Home Rule League, focused on Maharashtra and the Karnataka region. Tilak, who had been forced out of the Congress with the defeat of extremism, and imprisoned until 1914, hoped he and Besant could win control of the organization, which had foundered after the imprisonment of many of its leaders, among them **Chidambaram Pillai** (30). They might have done, and so taken Indian nationalism in a different direction, had not **Gandhi** (38), newly returned to India from South Africa, usurped for his own nationalist purposes the agitational energies stirred by Besant and her followers.

Another of her important moves in this era would not be sustained: the bridging of religious difference. In 1916, in an attempt to gather more supporters and win control of the Congress, she helped to broker an important agreement between Tilak and Muhammad Ali **Jinnah** (39). Jinnah, who would become the first leader of Pakistan, was then a liberal lawyer and politician, belonging both to the Congress and a small organization of elite Muslims, the Muslim League. The issue of how Hindus would share power with the Muslim minority in a more self-governing India had been simmering, and the so-called Lucknow Pact now created a complex formula for electoral representation that would ensure Muslims a base number of seats. That the deal later broke down is sometimes seen as a missed chance to have kept Jinnah working with the Congress, and so to have averted the Partition of 1947.

As Besant aged, her politics became more radical – something young Indians found appealing. After the 1916 Easter Rising in Ireland, the February 1917 Russian Revolution, and the American President Woodrow Wilson's April 1917 War Message to the US Congress defending the rights of small nations, Besant decided to test the boundaries of political expression, as she'd done in London. She wrote a series of articles bluntly denouncing British rule, celebrating the Easter rebellion, and exhorting Indians to let cultural pride rise up into political action. The British, sensing growing discontent, decided she had to be silenced.

In June 1917, the government of Madras interned her – a counterproductive move, as it turned out. In protest, young men across the country mobilized in passive resistance. Gandhi, who credited Theosophy for teaching him the value of Hinduism, arranged a mass petition for her release. Nehru made his very first public speech, in her defence. Besant's Home Rule League multiplied in size to around 27,000 members, as Congress moderates who had previously disdained her signed up. After three months of protest, the British, outmatched, released Besant. In November 1917, her fame never greater, she was elected president of the Congress.

From this peak, there would be a swift fall. Two events ensured the decline of her relevance: the British government's refusal to redeem its promise to give more self-governing powers to India after its people fought in defence of Empire in the First World War, and a British brigadier's decision in April 1919 to open fire on unarmed protesters in Amritsar. Several hundred men, women and children were massacred, and Besant, the British outsider, simply couldn't match the shock and outrage of native nationalists. It was Gandhi's turn now. Besant would live in India until her death in 1933, watching the struggle for freedom from the sidelines.

Among her many legacies in India were two she didn't intend. The first was the rise of an anti-Brahmin movement in the Dravidian south, which would come to split the nationalist movement there. While Besant's views on Aryan virtues and Brahminic Hinduism were embraced by the Brahmin elite of Madras, the counter-reaction against Brahminic revivalism in Tamil India was sharp. In 1916, a new, non-Brahmin political party was formed in Madras, which came to dominate the province's politics for the next two decades. Later, under the leadership of **Periyar** (34), it became the Self-Respect movement. It spoke for Tamil nationalism and Dravidian identity, and after independence pressed for caste-based reservations. It also launched a powerful critique of Hinduism itself, and its political descendants still dominate politics in Tamil Nadu.

The second unexpected legacy emerged in the West, out of her belief that she had found, in the young Telugu boy 'discovered' on the beach, the World Teacher. In 1927, now marginal to Indian politics, Besant bought a large stretch of land in the Ojai Valley in California. It was the other place, apart from India, where she believed a future higher race would emerge. There, she planned to install as World Teacher the young man now known simply as Krishnamurti.

Two years later, however, after a spiritual crisis, Krishnamurti rejected Besant and the entire Theosophical enterprise. 'You are accustomed to authority, or to the atmosphere of authority which you think will lead you to spirituality,' he told a stunned audience of 3,000 in the Netherlands, in remarks directed at Besant and her followers. He added, 'You have the idea that only certain people hold the key to the Kingdom of happiness. No one holds it. No one has the authority to that key. That key is your own self.'

From his base in California, Krishnamurti travelled the world teaching his own secular and radically individualist philosophy, which had little to do with Hinduism. His rise helped California become the New Age and self-help headquarters of the world. It was a pizza-effect boomerang, as people in the West now accepted the British-groomed Krishnamurti as an authentic Indian guru, telling them to believe in themselves.

For all her impact, positive and negative, Besant's Indian sojourn isn't taken too seriously these days. In Britain, it's often seen in spinster-gone-native terms, as eager over-assimilation. For Indian post-colonial critics, she's a favourite whipping girl: lashed for imperial condescension and her part in a revivalist drift in India that shored up a Brahminical, Aryanized view of Hinduism and a hankering for its lost Golden Age. She is as much a 'mark for ridicule' today as she was in Britain during her lifetime.

But through her writings, actions and politics, Besant groomed an elite and created, in skeletal form, a much wider basis for political mobilization of those elites than had existed previously. More subtly, but a strategic legacy nonetheless, she helped perpetuate a global idea of India as the 'mother of spirituality' – essentially gentle and altruistic, with a message for the world.

The image wasn't even consistent with Besant's own experience; one of her frustrations, at the schools and colleges she opened, was that her students were more concerned with material and worldly gains than with spirituality and education. And it would certainly be complicated by the reckless slaughter of Partition. But the perceived moral goodness of Indians promulgated by Annie Besant was that thing we call today soft power. In the next, crucial stage of the freedom movement, Gandhi would use the image instrumentally to draw worldwide support. In time, Nehru would also exploit it, giving a fledgling independent nation, poor and internally riven, an outsized voice in the world.

30
Chidambaram Pillai

Swadeshi Steam
1872–1936

'Long before the World War, all politically conscious people lived as on a volcano,' the Russo-German historian and philosopher Fedor Stepun wrote in the early part of the twentieth century. In the decade before the war, the volcanos had started to seethe. Revolution broke out in Russia in 1905, the Mexican revolution began in 1910, and the revolution ending imperial rule in China took place the following year. In Ireland, the Home Rule bill of 1912 inched the country closer to the free state that would be secured a decade later. And in India during these years, a British attempt to divide the province of Bengal launched a movement that would become more destabilizing to the Raj, economically and politically, than the rebellion of 1857.

In 1905 the viceroy, George Nathaniel Curzon, partitioned Bengal on the stated grounds that it was too big for the British to administer. But there was a political objective too: to isolate the mainly Muslim eastern districts of the province from the irritating political activism of Calcutta's Hindu intellectuals. As Herbert Risley, Curzon's Home Secretary and architect of the Indian census put it, 'Bengal united is a power, Bengal divided will pull in several directions.' Division, it was hoped, would also weaken an increasingly contentious Congress party, which was seeking greater representation in government.

Popular reaction to the Partition was well in excess of the demands the British had wanted to stifle. In the following years, Bengali radicals tried to blow up the train of their governor; later, they tried to shoot him. A tossed bomb missed a notoriously harsh judge, killing a barrister's wife and daughter instead. If the radicals lacked precision in their terror techniques, they didn't lack supporters. Extremism began to spread beyond Bengal. In Ahmedabad, the new viceroy, the Earl of Minto, survived a bomb attack. A revolutionary movement emerged from the Punjab, with outposts in the US and Canada. In London, an Indian student radical murdered a British official at South Kensington's Imperial Institute – an assassination on home soil, rare in the history of the Empire, that shocked and scandalized the British public.

From headlines in Britain, it was hard to make out that violent struggle was only a small part of the uprising. The emphasis was on winning control from the British, and stemming the drain of economic and cultural wealth, by recapturing India's productive powers. Many Indians were losing faith in moderate members of the Congress, an association of upper-caste educated men who wanted to persuade the British to be more open-handed and true to their own professed principles. A new crop of Indian leaders called instead for a boycott of British goods, arguing that Indians must only consume what they produced themselves, and make colonization so profitless that the British would leave. *Swadeshi*, or 'self-made' – the name of Jamsetji Tata's Bombay cotton mill – was now the name of a sweeping political action. Between 1905 and 1908, imports plummeted by 20 per cent.

The southern front of this early struggle for freedom was Tuticorin, in today's Tamil Nadu. Here, a feisty, boyish lawyer named V. O. Chidambaram Pillai was chasing the dream of swadeshi – with ships. Challenging a fabled name in imperial shipping, he tried to regain control of the seas that the south Indians had historically mastered. For a brief time the steamship company he created was one of the Swadeshi movement's greatest practical achievements, and served as a symbol for the agitation as a whole. His followers called him 'Swadeshi Pillai', and he was celebrated for his patriotism across the nation. But Pillai's audacious career would be brief and ultimately founder – like the Swadeshi movement itself.

To read about India's history in the years immediately following 1905 is to feel the possibility that a free India was soon to be formed. Unlike in Russia or China or Mexico, however, the Indian volcano would be capped; independence would not be secured for four more decades. Pillai was only one of the failures littering the long path towards a free India. Many of these stories are now forgotten. But his is worth recovering not least because of what it reveals about the ultimate disappointment of the Swadeshi movement.

Its decline had multiple factors: the variegation of Indian culture; movement infighting; detachment from the concerns of low-wage workers and peasants; and the lack – thankfully – of an Indian Lenin. But great fault lines of Indian society, such as caste hierarchy, also helped keep independence out of reach. Pillai came closer than most leaders to bridging those faults – until he encountered the other element that ensured the movement's failure: the retaliatory hand of the British.

From the British point of view, southern India in the early twentieth century was pleasingly resistant to nationalist politics. As the historian David Washbrook has written, 'Between 1895 and 1916, scarcely a single anti-British dog barked in the streets of Madras.' Tuticorin, on India's eastern coast, would be the southern exception.

The centre of the Indian pearl-fishing industry, and a major port, Tuticorin was prospering when Pillai moved there around the turn of the century. Born in 1872, about thirty kilometres inland, he had come to practise law. He belonged to the Vellalar caste – rich, land-owning, non-Brahmins – and several men in his family were *vakils*, or local lawyers. Serving the English-administered courts, they sometimes found themselves in competition. Once, representing a poor man against a wealthy one, young Pillai gleefully destroyed the opposing counsel – his father. But he was restless.

In India, the path to radicalism often runs through religion. Still in his twenties, Pillai became active in organizations centred on Tamil Shaivite teachings. These 'Shaiva Sabhas' connected Pillai to a politically active circle of writers and intellectuals, who in turn linked him to the work of a man he would soon call his political guru: the legendary Maharashtrian radical and religious popularizer Bal Gangadhar Tilak. Tilak's writings, Pillai later said, 'made me feel that India was my country, that the British were wrongfully retaining it, and that it must be got back from them'.

Tilak emerged after the Bengal Partition as a leader, along with

Lala Lajpat Rai and Bipin Chandra Pal, of a radical wing of the Congress party. Lal, Bal, and Pal, as the trio were known, took up the cry of Swadeshi, then redefined it as a sacred battle against the British for India's cultural unity as a Hindu nation. The political goal of this struggle was *swaraj*, self-rule. To achieve it, they argued, the Congress had to switch from polite constitutional arguments to direct action, even violence. Pillai's deep attachment to Tilak's ideas would soon make Tuticorin the single place in the far south where the protest in Bengal would be replicated.

In British intelligence files, there are glimpses of Pillai before 1905: attending a political meeting, running a short-lived monthly publication on social reform. But after the Partition, the colonial files grew quickly, for he and other immoderate nationalists in the port district acted fast. They embarked on a Swadeshi programme well before Congress, at its December 1906 annual gathering in Calcutta, resolved on a policy of boycotting foreign-made goods and companies. There were Swadeshi emporia and Swadeshi body-building gyms in Tuticorin, just as there were in Calcutta.

Swadeshi employed many agitational techniques that we now associate with Gandhian politics, among them passive resistance and non-cooperation. If these techniques sound anodyne from a distance, they could be rigorous, even intimidating, in practice. For instance, Pillai asked followers to avoid not just British goods, but institutions like schools and the courts. He told them to affirm their commitment to boycott by immersing themselves in a sacred river, and by pledges in the name of the goddess Kali. If they broke their word, he coolly threatened, they should expect to be 'shunned'.

As often as Pillai's movement mirrored Bengal's, freedom-fighting in a place like Tuticorin meant something that it couldn't mean in riverine Calcutta: control of the seas. In 1906, perhaps stirred, as many were, by the Japanese defeat of the Russian naval fleet at Tsushima shortly before the Partition, Pillai turned his thoughts to ships.

The Coromandel coast had been a hub of Indian shipping since the Chola times of **Rajaraja** (9). Well into the nineteenth century, Indians were plying wooden sail ships from its ports. But from the

1870s, British steamers had effectively captured the important Indian routes. Out of Tuticorin alone, the British India Steam Navigation Company was transporting, in addition to cotton and other cargo, some 100,000 people a year, most of them Tamil workers bound for hard labour in Ceylon, South Africa and Malaya.

By 1906, B. I., as the company was known, was a Goliath of colonial shipping, with a fleet of over one hundred ships. It was run by James Lyle Mackay, the most prominent figure in British shipping of the age and a man with such political power in India that he was once informally offered the viceroyalty. Fed up with Tuticorin's nationalist stirrings, he and British officials were already working to develop a new port in a location with more compliant citizens.

Pillai no doubt sensed the dimensions of the corporate-government complex he'd be taking on. Still, through British intelligence, we can see how little he hesitated in setting up a line to compete with Mackay's operations. In April 1906, he met with local merchants to discuss the possibility, and six months later, a joint stock company was on the books. His plan was to raise one million rupees by offering 40,000 shares at twenty-five rupees each – a comparatively low price intended to attract a broad base of investors. The only stipulation was that shares were 'to be held exclusively by the Indians, Ceylonese and other nations of the East'. Calcutta and Bombay activists responded enthusiastically. Funds were also raised in Ceylon. Finding local backers was a trickier business, though.

One British report says some local businessmen were reluctant to participate, on account of Pillai's unnamed 'dissolute habits'. So Pillai and his men went door-to-door to help quell the doubts. His wasn't a chauvinistically Hindu approach, as his mentor Tilak would have preferred. Muslim and Christian merchants worked alongside Hindus at the port, and valued cheap, reliable shipping. He needed them to buy in, too, and some did. The next month, the first steamer launched from Tuticorin.

Named the Swadeshi Steam Navigation Company, it was as irritating to the British as it was celebrated by nationalists across the country. By December, south India's leading newspaper, *The Hindu*, reported keen competition between Pillai's company and B. I.: 'each company lowering its tariff and fare day after day'. The British firm offered promotions like free umbrellas, and hung a board using the word 'swadeshi' to confuse Indians into buying tickets for the wrong line. It allied itself with the British-owned Southern India Railway, and only ticket officials for British steamers were permitted to lure port-bound passengers descending onto the platforms. When a Swadeshi Company official violated the railway ban, he was arrested. The local British administration, under direction from the Governor in Madras, was soon in the fray, delaying medical and customs clearances for Swadeshi line passengers.

Pillai remained defiant. Giving up his first ship, which was leased, he ordered two reconditioned mail steamers, one each from Britain and France, better equipped than the British boats in use. In April and June 1907, those ships sailed into port. They had room for forty-two first-class, twenty-four second-class and 1,300 other passengers, as well as 4,000 gunny bags of cargo. But more significant in British eyes were the ships' colours: the 'Swadeshi flag' – green, yellow and red horizontal stripes, emblazoned with the words '*Vande Mataram*' ('Hail to the Motherland'), a nationalist slogan taken from a famous Bengali poem of the same name. To the British, the slogan – in fact the whole enterprise – was seditious.

As the Swadeshi movement gained traction across India, British administrators scrambled to react and repress. Between the summers of 1906 and 1907, the British prosecuted nine newspapers, and deported several Swadeshi leaders without trial. But this didn't dampen the movement, so in November 1907 a new anti-sedition law banned meetings of more than twenty people. It would be applied widely to protests considered non-constitutional – as Pillai's localized movement was – and place many of Swadeshi's most important agitators in jail.

Around the same time, Pillai finally met his guru, Tilak, at the annual Congress meeting. There, in Surat, a fight broke out between moderates and extremists that descended into haranguing and shoe-throwing, and formally split the party. The extremists, led by Tilak, emerged victorious, and Pillai was given official charge of the South.

Pillai had become a hero of the elite national Congress before he was a local one; his oratory was a bit too lawyerly for popular appeal. But now he was joined in his peripatetic fundraising and swaraj-rallying by a charismatic, once-poor Madras Shaivite preacher and political activist named Subramania Sivam. By 1908, their joint speeches at public meetings were drawing thousands, and Pillai was becoming a genuine political force in the region. Calcutta's radical press compared his deeds to the struggle in the Transvaal, which was led by another Indian lawyer, Mohandas Gandhi.

In Pillai's analysis, the British – 'despicable sinners' – had divided a once-unified India in order to subdue it. As for the religious and caste divisions that predated the British, he felt these should be set aside in the common cause of swaraj. But in the port area, caste divisions were harder than religious ones to bridge. And in south India, where religious observance ran deep, Brahmin power was considerable. By Pillai's time, seven out of every ten university gradu-ates were Brahmin, and they held most of the high posts in the Madras provincial administration. Pillai's caste, though not Brah-min, was also a force in the local district administration. Low-caste Tamils were sceptical of an upper-caste movement dominated by Brahmins like Tilak and Vellalars like Pillai – a movement they guessed might mirror the social hierarchies they inhabited.

Pillai's sharpest challenge on the subject came from low-caste Nadars. Upwardly mobile under the British, they feared a new Indian regime might relegate them to their original work, climbing Palmyra trees and tapping for toddy. According to the British files, one Nadar accused Pillai directly during a speech: 'If you get swaraj, you will ask us to do menial things.' Pillai, who once fretted that Tilak would find him too low caste to dine with, seemed hesitant about any caste inclusion that didn't redound to the benefit of his movement. Like many of the political radicals of the time, he was socially conserva-tive at heart. 'Union does not mean that we should dine together and embrace each other,' he said at another point. 'It will be several years after swaraj is obtained that such things take place.'

Matters of both caste and class – a condescending indifference to the poor, and particularly peasants – hampered the movement nationwide. It took hold in few of the provinces around Bengal, and its epicentres remained in cities like Calcutta and Bombay. But in Tirunelveli, the district that contained Tuticorin, Sivam's passion about worker conditions helped Pillai conceive a broader movement.

In early 1908, the two men trained their focus on low-paid, mixed-caste workers at a prominent cotton mill, Coral, which not incidentally was owned by the same British agency that ran the B. I. line. Sivam, who had closely followed the impact of worker strikes in Russia – 'revolutions always brought good to the world', he said – argued that an increase in Indian wages would do much to make India undesirable to the British. He and Pillai persuaded the mill-workers to strike until they got better terms. It was one of India's earliest labour agitations, and a successful one. Within a few days, Pillai had negotiated a settlement – news that travelled through working-class communities, increased his fame and possibly sealed his doom. The British feared one labour agitation might become many. Within a week of the strike's resolution, they ended their prolonged cat-and-mouse game, and charged Pillai and Sivam with sedition.

The proximate cause was a march the two men had called to celebrate the release of Bengal's leading extremist, Bipin Chandra Pal, from a Calcutta prison. By the police's own accounts, Pillai had instructed his followers to leave at home anything that could be construed as a weapon, even a walking stick; 'if anything goes wrong we must be the injured party and not the offending party,' he reportedly said. Still, the police declared other of his fairly characteristic statements to be illegal and, for good measure, accused him of being an accessory to the seditions of Sivam.

The arrests sparked the very violence the British feared. Protests broke out immediately. The Tuticorin municipal office, courts and police headquarters were set on fire. Panicked Europeans, anticipating a massacre, sought refuge on board a ship anchored in the harbour. A principal of a girl's school later wrote of being told by an Indian teacher, 'The torch is lighted tonight that is to spread from Cape Comorin to Calcutta and nothing can save the English.' Labourers, tellingly, went out on strike. The British, in a state of panic, sentenced Pillai to two life terms in prison.

The harshness of his sentence became a cause célèbre, shaming even some British officials. Funds for his defence were raised all over India, and by Tamils in South Africa too. Eventually, his sentence was commuted to six years, but this didn't entirely ease the popular sense that he was the victim of a great injustice. In 1911, one of his young supporters shot dead the district's British Collector, a man believed to be responsible for Pillai's arrest. It was the only political assassination in the history of colonial south India – and a hollow coda to both Pillai's movement and the larger Indian protest. Curzon's Partition had been rescinded earlier that year. Local strains of radicalism had failed to weave into a genuinely national movement. The surge of national agitation was over, for now.

Tuticorin today is one of those places that reminds you that the 'self-made' has its limitations, and that the desire to extract profit at the expense of public good was not exclusive to colonial powers. Despite sea winds, the port city is the most polluted place in Tamil Nadu. The detritus of copper-smelting and coal-fired thermal power plants mixes with the effluent of chemical factories in a sulphurous, hot, fish-killing sea. Even the salt mined here comes dusted with ash. Ask about Pillai in these parts, and you're as likely to get directions to the port, named after him, as a discussion of a once-famous leader. The cultural historian A. R. Venkatachalapathy notes that he's one of the few nationalist or literary figures in the state who is not claimed only by people of his own caste. But if his appeal remains broad, it's not deep. Periodic calls to build a museum celebrating his swadeshi work have come to nothing. It's as if he's still, all these years later, shy of a mass following.

In the story of twentieth-century freedom across the world, prison can look something like a school playground – a place where heroes are made. Gandhi, Nehru, Ho Chi Minh, Kenyatta, Martin Luther King, Mandela: in each case, the hardship appears productive in hindsight. It forged them into the leaders they became. More often, though, prison is where individuals are broken, and then forgotten. Pillai, in Cannanore jail in Malabar, was doing hard labour, making jute and pressing oil, and comforting himself by writing poetry. In Venkatachalapathy's translation of one of Pillai's *venbas*, a terse quasi-quatrain verse form:

> Chidambaram, who once bestowed largesse
> like the rain to supplicant poets,
> Now, fallen, runs around the world,
> singing *venbas* that don't scan,
> his words and skin, worn thin.

When Pillai left Cannanore jail in 1912, after serving four years, there were no crowds to greet him, no political career about to heat up, nor even a law practice to continue – his jail conviction having effectively disbarred him. Moreover, his shipping concern had collapsed while he was in prison, costing him his base of subscribers' money. Now, a man who thought resisters of his movement should be shunned was shunned himself. Waiting outside the jail was only Sivam, himself recently released from prison.

Surveying the swadeshi years, historians have wondered if more labour agitations might have increased the movement's penetration, showing that swadeshi didn't merely represent the ambitions of an educated elite. But such agitations were only sporadic. In 1908, Lenin, considering a large strike of textile workers in Bombay, had written optimistically that the Indian street had begun to stand with its writers and intellectuals. That it didn't happen on a larger scale can't be laid entirely at the door of those intellectuals. By 1908, the British had deported or imprisoned most of the movement's leaders; many would never return to politics again. Sivam finally died of leprosy contracted in prison. Pillai survived for another two decades, trying to involve himself in various causes, but the world had soured on him. He never had a mass audience again.

That would fall to **Gandhi** (38) to create. The Swadeshi movement – and the acts of terrorism he feared would flow from it – prompted him to write, in 1909, his first serious work about Indian politics, *Hind Swaraj*, one of the aims of which was to dissuade Indians from violent struggle. Six years later, in January 1915, he disembarked in Bombay to begin his decades-long campaign to unite Indians into a national, non-violent and ultimately victorious struggle against British rule.

31
Srinivasa Ramanujan

The Elbow of Genius
1887–1920

> Dear Sir, I beg to introduce myself to you as a clerk in the Accounts
> Department of the Port Trust Office at Madras on a salary of only
> £20 per annum. I am now about 23 years of age.

When a young Indian, seemingly uncertain of his own age, mailed a
letter to a Cambridge don in January 1913, it was a crucial link in a
chain of influence that extended well beyond the young man's lifetime, and will no doubt extend beyond ours.

> I have had no University education but I have undergone the ordi-
> nary school course. After leaving school I have been employing the
> spare time at my disposal to work at Mathematics ... I have made
> a special investigation of divergent series in general and the results I
> get are termed by the local mathematicians as 'startling' ... If you
> are convinced that there is anything of value I would like to have my
> theorems published ...

The young man, who had already solicited two other famous mathematicians in vain, concluded, 'Requesting to be excused from the
trouble I give you'.

The trouble caused by Ramanujan, one of the most gifted mathematicians of the twentieth century, turned out to be vast indeed.
For a century now, his investigations have vexed and inspired mathematical scientists in fields from number theory to particle physics
and even medicine. During most of this time, the weight of emphasis was on 'vexed'. Seen by many as barely fathomable or only
narrowly relevant, the full significance of his work might never

have been recognized had it not been for the tragic romance of his life.

It was a story suitable for novels, documentaries, films or inspirational TED talks: the tale of a deeply religious savant and college dropout ostensibly rescued from a south Indian village and brought to Cambridge by the mathematician G. H. Hardy – the recipient of Ramanujan's letter. After a few years burning bright, Ramanujan died young, his greatest potential perhaps unrealized. The narrative – cut with various quantities of exoticism and the miraculous, depending on the teller – even involves some lost notebooks, dramatically rediscovered, and a cryptic but ultimately revelatory final letter.

In other similar stories, maths is often merely a backdrop. But Ramanujan's work today is recognized as a frontier in advanced mathematics. ('Shiver in ecstasy,' a scientist recently tweeted of a connection Ramanujan made between infinite series, continued fractions, e and pi.) It has proven integral to our highly networked and encrypted digital lives, as well as to cutting-edge attempts to cure cancer and to understand the deepest structures of the universe. Every day, researchers across the world, aided in part by those so-called lost notebooks and Ramanujan's last letter, are sweating to find more applications. Did he hold the key to quantum gravity, which could unlock a unified theory of everything? another scientist recently wondered.

Many questions such as that – about the significance of Ramanujan's work – could not have been asked during his lifetime. The groundbreaking insights in at least one of the papers he published while at Trinity College, Cambridge – the unassumingly titled 'On certain arithmetical functions', from 1916 – remained hidden in plain view for more than thirty years. It took a new generation of mathematicians, armed with three decades of new maths, to see that his results could help solve some of the most intractable problems in mathematical history. Those results even had a role in the biggest mathematical discovery of the twentieth century: the proof of Fermat's last theorem.

If Ramanujan has helped us to understand our universe, the relationship has not been entirely reciprocal. The mathematician Ken

Ono, Professor at Emory University, who has spent the last thirteen years trying to unpack three pages of Ramanujan's handwritten enigmas, says that the more he studies Ramanujan's papers, the less he is able to grasp the mind of the man. Part of this mystery is Ramanujan's apparent indifference to Western mathematical conventions: much of his most far-seeing work doesn't include proofs. Perhaps that was because he learned with a chalk and tablet, erasing figures with his elbow as he moved on ('my elbow has become rough and black in making a genius of me!' he reportedly once remarked). Or maybe he felt – as he sometimes indicated – that proofs would help others steal his work. So his exquisitely terse results, and not his reasoning, are what mathematicians and scientists have to work with: stand-alone puzzles, some of universal dimensions, to which even the occasional scientist has been known to impute a mystical, essentially Indian power.

'I did not invent him,' Hardy famously said, late in life, about Ramanujan: 'like other great men, he invented himself.' But Ramanujan didn't flourish in a vacuum. Aiding his self-invention were the sophisticated south Indian traditions in which he was raised; sources of classical mathematics that he was able to beg, borrow or find; and the encouragement of a determined mother.

Ramanujan's hometown, Kumbakonam, in Tamil Nadu, is sometimes portrayed as the distant, desperate sticks, the better to foreground a Cambridge-bestowed deliverance. In reality, Ramanujan's Vaishnavite Brahmin community, part of a town that had the highest percentage of professionals outside Madras, was the sort **Annie Besant (29)** had in mind when she went all eugenical and talked about superior beings. The Vaishnavite tradition was strict, erudite, ascetic, devout and, crucially, treated with veneration by others in society. Ramanujan was born, in other words, into a hothouse of intellectual self-belief.

Not that status translated into rupees. His father was a clerk, tallying up accounts for a mediocre living, while his educated, self-possessed mother, Komalatammal, taught their only son. A singer of devotional songs in the local temple, she dabbled in numerology and astrology and believed in the spiritual and predictive power of maths. Neighbours considered her a sort of psychic. But when Ramanujan biographer Robert Kanigel went to Kumbakonam and interviewed relatives, he turned up no one before Ramanujan with an unusual gift for numbers.

Komalatammal, strong-willed, noticed early her son's desire for imposing order, through behaviour we might now call 'on the spectrum': when he was barely walking, he aligned the cooking vessels against the wall with absolute precision. Nursing him through several illnesses, including smallpox, his mother noted how quickly he mathematized one of their time-pass games, in order to trounce her. From then on, she became what Ken Ono calls an Indian Tiger Mom.

It is often said that Ramanujan grew up in two parallel but distinct intellectual worlds: the spiritually rich but rationally deficient sacred precincts of the Hindu temple, and the rational but soul-crumbling rote classrooms of the Raj. The reality was less neat. The mathematical culture of the south Indian Brahmin was fundamentally a utilitarian one, using algebra, trigonometry and geometry to make practical astronomical calculations, albeit to regulate religious life. So Ramanujan would hardly have been the first to spend afternoons doing maths in chalk on the floor of the temple where his mother sang.

Nor did the Madras school curriculum of the day conspicuously quash Ramanujan's talent. Though aimed at producing competent and honest junior-level public servants, not geniuses, the system acquitted itself reasonably well when confronted by an adolescent anomaly. Corpulent and hard to understand when he bothered to talk, he could easily have been bullied. Instead, he was recognized both as a star and a practical resource: administrators recruited him to solve such problems as scheduling the movement of 1,200 students through various classrooms across the day.

Once he'd exceeded the limits of his teachers' mathematical knowledge, he studied higher-level textbooks borrowed from a local library and from college students whom his family took in as boarders. After mastering advanced trigonometry from a book by S. L. Loney, around the age of thirteen, he progressed to G. S. Carr's *A*

Synopsis of Elementary Results in Pure and Applied Mathematics (1880), a nineteenth-century compendium of theorems and formulae. In Carr, mathematical facts were stated baldly, without proof or extrapolation; the inner logic was left to the reader to puzzle out. Ramanujan may have absorbed something of that style as he worked his way, problem by problem, through Carr's version of mathematical history.

An obsession with numbers at the expense of everything else brought him the highest honours at matriculation, but also led the protected teenager to his life's first crisis. In 1904 he enrolled on a scholarship at Kumbakonam's small, well-respected Government College. But he lost the scholarship by failing English, and ran away from home in the depths of his shame. Later he tried again at Madras University, where inattention to non-maths subjects caused him to fail his finals *three* times. His school career in India was over. His parents married him to a ten-year-old village girl named Janaki, and now expected him to start earning his living.

Fortunately, as the degree-less, socially awkward Ramanujan struggled to hold down work as a tutor and clerk, word of his intelligence reached the leaders of the newly founded Indian Mathematical Society. One of them, a wealthy district collector, secured him a bursary, even though Ramanujan's work was beyond his ken. An intense period of independent study ensued.

Ironically, given the decades it would take his mathematical successors to appreciate the depth of his later insights, some of the problems he worked hardest on had been solved generations before. When he learned that Leonhard Euler, the legendary eighteenth-century mathematician, had beaten him to a 'discovery' – the series that yielded the basic trigonometric functions sine and cosine – he took no pleasure in having matched one of the greatest minds of the Enlightenment. Instead, shaken and ashamed, he hid some of his results in the roof of the family house.

Where he lurched ahead of even Euler was on the related subject of infinite series – functions whose terms go on indefinitely, but which can often be expressed in unexpectedly simple ways. The ability to grapple almost tangibly with the infinite was becoming a hallmark of his thought. He once told a fellow Indian mathematician, 'an equation has no meaning for me unless it expresses a thought of GOD'. He claimed his most impressive results came to him in a dream, inscribed on his tongue by the Hindu goddess Namagiri, an important force in the life of his family.

This claim has since become a fallback for those unable to account for Ramanujan's genius: a sort of south Indian Hindu longhand for what others call 'intuition' or a power more profound. But I wonder if Namagiri wasn't a way – conscious or otherwise – for Ramanujan to mediate between his family and himself on the one hand, and the demands of his extraordinary abilities on the other. He seems to have felt, partly on the advice of others, that his talents could only be validated and developed in the West. So at the same time that he was claiming inspiration from Namagiri, he was pursuing recognition and mentorship from British mathematicians. And he eventually declared that Namagiri had given him permission to break caste taboos and pollute himself by leaving India to take up the invitation of G. H. Hardy.

Franz Ferdinand was assassinated two months after Ramanujan arrived in Cambridge. At the same time the twenty-one-year-old was caught up in the collective anxiety of war, he was also struggling to absorb shocks of a more intimate scale: aching in a cold he had never before felt, unhappy at letters from home reporting fights between his mother and wife, and miserably hungry in the face of the vile collations that passed in Britain for vegetarian food. Once, overcome with one of the bouts of mortification which he had endured since adolescence, he attempted suicide. Still, he worked.

Given Hardy's renown, the collegial stance he took towards a laden twenty-one-year-old college failure was striking and sensitive, and rooted perhaps in Hardy's own history. He'd been a prodigy himself, and being homosexual had grown up to be a social non-starter in a different way from Ramanujan. On first browsing the young Indian's work, he had had an initial reaction similar to that of some members of the Indian Mathematical Society a few years before: a fraudster was wasting his valuable time. But with deeper engagement in the work, Hardy had come to see a level of confidence and idiosyncratic genius that might be stifled by heavy-handed intervention.

Freedom and collaboration were what Hardy offered instead. With these, Ramanujan would in the course of five years at Cambridge make significant contributions to subjects ranging from probabilistic number theory and hypergeometric series to the distribution of prime numbers and the theory of partitions. On the basis of this work alone, he should be considered one of the greatest mathematicians of his generation. But these were merely the fields in which his contemporaries could grasp the importance of his results.

Experts tell me that it's difficult to appreciate Ramanujan's achievements without a Ph.D. in mathematics or theoretical physics – and even then, noted his biographer Robert Kanigel, it has to be a Ph.D. in the right type of maths or physics. (I'll take their word for it.) But there are a few areas in which the rest of us can glimpse the power of his mind. In 1914, for instance, Ramanujan published work on the irrational number pi, the ratio of a circle's circumference to its diameter. Expressed as a decimal, pi's digits extend onwards for ever in a totally random fashion. For millennia, mathematicians had striven to approximate this number as closely as possible. Until the nineteenth century, the nearest they had got was roughly one hundred digits. Ramanujan eventually tamed the chaos, creating not just one but two beautiful expressions of the value of pi. According to Ono, Ramanujan's innovation was to stop thinking of pi as a decimal, and to conceive of it instead as a complex, but elegant, fraction. Today, supercomputers, using a version of one of Ramanujan's formulae, have calculated the value to more than twelve trillion digits.

Another ancient mathematical puzzle Ramanujan solved at Cambridge – this time with Hardy – has to do with partitions. The partitions of a whole number are all the ways that a number can be added together using positive integers. For example, the number 4 can be partitioned in five different ways: 4, 3+1, 2+2, 2+1+1, and 1+1+1+1. The number 5 can be partitioned in seven different ways. How many partitions would you guess 10 has? Forty-two. What about 100? Nearly 200 million is the answer. In other words, partitions grow extremely rapidly – and unpredictably. Once again, Ramanujan brought this chaos under control, creating a formula that predicted a number's partitions with a remarkable degree of accuracy, and that got better and better as the numbers grew.

If solving such longstanding problems was an extraordinary feat, the greater work would come two years later, in circumstances that had drastically altered.

> I am extremely sorry for not writing you a single letter up to now. I discovered very interesting functions recently which I call 'Mock' ϑ-functions. Unlike the 'False' ϑ-functions (partially studied by Rogers), they enter into mathematics as beautifully as the ordinary theta functions. I am sending you with this letter some examples.

Ramanujan was ill when he returned to Madras. Tuberculosis was the suspect, probably compounded by amoebic dysentery – treatable, had it been diagnosed. He was so enraged by his weakening body that he crunched up thermometers placed in his mouth. This letter, his last to Hardy, was composed in January 1920, on his deathbed. Enclosed with it were the bizarre series of functions that grip mathematicians today.

While some valuable work was done to understand the mock-theta functions in the decades after Ramanujan's death, it wasn't until 1976, when the so-called 'lost notebook' was found buried away in Trinity College's Wren Library, that mathematicians really began to grasp their import. Perhaps the greatest breakthrough only came in 2001. It had taken more than eighty years to catch up with what Ramanujan had been doing.

What mathematicians began to see was that mock-theta functions can be used to reduce different types of infinity down to small, simpler quantities. This allows the infinities to be relatively easily manipulated and studied. In recent years, astrophysicists have realized that when they peer into their models of black holes, what they are seeing, among other things, are Ramanujan's mock-theta functions at work. String theorists, too, rely on mock thetas when trying to describe the most fundamental levels of physical reality.

Ken Ono has often wondered how Ramanujan's maths might have developed if someone other than Hardy had answered Ramanujan's letter – if a different mathematical mentor and collaborator had encouraged Ramanujan's gift in other directions. And what if no one had written back to him? Westerners often remark on how lucky Ramanujan was to be discovered, but some scientists think if he'd stayed in India he might have lived longer and done even more exceptional work – most of it perhaps still waiting to be understood.

If his significance went largely unnoticed in Ramanujan's own day, it's not just that his formulae were gnomic: he was answering questions that wouldn't be asked for decades, or even a century after he died, in areas of mathematics that people didn't even know were important. It's as if he had described the alien inhabitants of a distant planet two generations before we knew the planet existed.

Ultimately, much of what we would like to know about Ramanujan – how he worked, how he understood the meaning of his work, where it was going – seems to have been wiped away, like the notations on his slate. Or perhaps there were never any good answers. I think that even for Ramanujan himself, his process and purposes remained a mystery – so many motes of blown chalk, suddenly forming constellations to those gifted enough to see them.

32
Tagore

Unlocking Cages
1861–1941

In the summer of 2015, I happened to arrive in Washington DC on the afternoon on which the Supreme Court of the United States made same-sex marriage legal in all fifty states. By evening, as supporters of the verdict celebrated in streets and parks across the country, the White House glowed in the rainbow colours of the gay pride flag. As exhilarating as the historic moment was, what struck me more was what came afterwards. A law that would have seemed radical a decade earlier settled almost instantly into the normal state of American affairs. Among liberals, political conversations moved on. It seemed to me a testimony to the deep roots of individual freedom in the United States.

In India, by contrast, a person's freedom to choose the life that he or she prefers is a liberty resting on fairly shaky ground. Section 377 of the Indian Penal Code, a relic of British rule that was upheld by the Indian Supreme Court as recently as 2013, decrees that a single act of same-sex love can land you in prison. And such constrictions are not just statutory, or only for homosexual relations. That Indians have to use the term 'love marriage' to describe a freely chosen partnership between a woman and a man is a reminder that social and cultural pressures operate across the board to arrange the most intimate of human relationships.

At the heart of this weakness – in marriage and in other realms of human choice – is the ancient caste order, which denied individuality in favour of assigned social roles. The idea of treating Indians primarily as members of communities was further entrenched by colonial legislation. Later, the social reform and nationalist movements that arose to challenge caste and empire were focused more on collective freedoms than on individual rights. And it was not as if economics could reel in the political slack: many of the economic processes associated with the rise of the individual in the West, such as a deeply ingrained system of personal property rights, only began to take root in India relatively recently, and even then had to push against collectivist and socialistic currents.

'The history of the growth of freedom,' the restless Bengali writer Rabindranath Tagore said, 'is the history of the perfection of human relationship.' In a nationalist age when many of his compatriots were preoccupied with independence, Tagore, the first Asian to win the Nobel Prize for Literature, preferred to speak of freedom. As he roamed across cultural traditions and genres in a large, often agitated body of work (which included poetry, stories, novels, songs, drama, opera, memoirs, travelogues and essays), Tagore returned repeatedly to this idea. He tested it, says Supriya Chaudhuri, Professor at Jadavpur University, against events, against experience, and against history and politics, to show 'that political freedom is not worth a great deal if one can't free oneself from mental bondage'.

Tagore tried to create a space for individual choice that stood apart from imposed collectives – whether of traditional Indian institutions like caste, religion and patriarchal families, of imperial subjectdom, or of contemporary mass movements for nationalism. The dissolution of personal identity into cultish mass conformity even affected, in his view, the independence movement led by Gandhi. But Tagore wasn't a radical individualist; his conception of freedom was related to expressivity, connection and the deepest human experience – love. Becoming who you are, he recognized, is not something you do on your own.

Tagore was born in 1861 in Calcutta to an illustrious family, and published his first writings before the age of sixteen. A few years later, following a traumatic experience in love, his fiction began sensitively to explore the brutal subjugation of women at the heart of Indian family life. But women weren't the only ones who suffered from the duties of family, society, caste and religion. The subordination of individual hopes and choice to collective demands sent hidden ripples throughout an entire society. India's growth was being stunted by the conformities of tradition.

As political change swept through Asia and Europe in the early twentieth century, Tagore's concern for personal freedom gathered intensity. Though passionately against imperialism, he homed in on a paradox of nationalism: new nations might destroy their civilizations' distinct identity when replicating the patterns developed by the modern European state. He saw, in places like Japan, 'the voluntary submission of the whole people to the trimming of their minds and clipping of their freedom by their government, which through various educational agencies regulates their thoughts, manufactures their feelings,' as he said in 1916. The result was an 'all-pervading mental slavery' masked as national freedom.

This critique of nationalism's military and cultural modes made Tagore unique among anti-colonial figures. But he didn't always walk his own talk. As he shifted forms and avatars, he was given to self-contradiction, while some of his poetry – at least in its English translation – was misty enough to justify Bertrand Russell's exasperated observation: 'The sort of language that is admired by many Indians unfortunately does not, in fact, mean anything at all.'

But Tagore's arguments for the centrality of self-empowerment, or what he called '*atma-shakti*', remained fairly sharp and consistent. The more that people were encouraged to express themselves openly and rationally, the more hopeful Tagore was that divisions might fall away, and that a universal, diversity-respecting humanism might arise. Such language might seem airy and archaic today, a little like the paintings Tagore made late in life. But to embrace it is to see something at the core of Tagore's own thinking, and something we now need.

Great advocates of individualism tend to consider themselves superior to the norm. Tagore, awash from birth in the advantages of multigenerational wealth and education, fits the profile. He came from one of the grandest clans of colonial Bengal, owners of marble mansions in Calcutta and vast *zamindari* estates in the eastern part of the province. Charles Dickens knew Tagore's grandfather,

Dwarkanath, as the 'Oriental Croesus'; he was a man who, when visiting London, sat beside Queen Victoria to review her troops. A friend of **Rammohun Roy** (22), Dwarkanath was an entrepreneur and philanthropist at the centre of the 'Bengal Renaissance'.

Tagore's father, Debendranath, continued the cultural tradition. He was a leader of Roy's rationalist religious reform movement, the Brahmo Samaj, and was a close reader of the Upanishads as well as Persian poetry. He had thirteen children who survived beyond infancy, and he raised them in a lively and competitive, though socially conservative, household. His eldest son was the first Indian to join the elite Indian Civil Service. Another son was prominent in theatre. The youngest child, Rabindranath, felt his historic importance from a very young age. He would later describe himself as containing from early on a perfect blend of cultural confluences – of Hindu, Muslim and European worlds – which he wished the whole Indian nation would embody.

Tagore was educated at home, mainly by tutors, and he never learned to like institutions. At seventeen, having published his first songs to acclaim, he went to England to study and enrolled at University College London. He didn't stick it out to obtain a degree, but he picked up a familiarity with British ways before returning home to a sociability he much preferred: the intellectual companionship he found with friends and family, particularly his sister-in-law, Kadambari. Decades later, in his eighties and nearing death, he would remember how the two of them would sit together in the hot afternoon reading the latest literary reviews from Calcutta, Kadambari fanning him gently. Their attachment was so deep that after Tagore's father arranged his marriage, at the age of twenty-two, to an uneducated ten-year-old, Kadambari was undone. She took an overdose (possibly of opium, according to Tagore's biographer Andrew Robinson). It was a suicide that would mark Tagore for life.

Into his fiction, poetry and polemic came a grave mood of yearning and a theme of injustice. The figure of the young woman married off against her will, fobbed off with the illusion that she would be happy and cared for, became a regular subject. Tagore wanted always to show that 'without love, without a sense of mutual compassion and companionship, marriage is nothing', Supriya Chaudhuri says. Consider the heroine in the devastating 1914 story 'The Wife's Letter', in which a woman explains why she's abandoning a household through which she's long moved, invisible and unheard:

> My mother feared for this cleverness of mine; for a woman it was an impediment. If one who must follow the limits laid down by rule seeks to follow her intelligence, she will stumble repeatedly and come to grief. But what was I to do? God had carelessly given me much more intelligence than I needed to be a wife in your household . . .

Restored to self-worth by the love of a maltreated young girl, the wife realizes that being unmoored and alone in the world, with the freedom to say so, is better than staying in a life in which one will 'die inch by inch'.

For Tagore, the patriarchal imprisonment of women was a crystallization of the way social conventions restricted all forms of individual desire, love and experience. These conventions were a cage, or '*khancha*', that would recur in his poetry and fiction, and would come to seem even more stifling than the political domination of the British. The 'Hindu ideal of marriage has no regard for individual taste or inclination', he complained in a 1925 essay, calling marriage 'one of the most fruitful sources of unhappiness and the downfall of man'.

In his last years, as Tagore glanced back at his life and his writing from early in the century, he spoke of having felt 'the harsh touch of domesticity' in his own life. Marriage he saw as oppressive and constricting; but love he saw as essential, enabling 'human beings to form truly emancipated relationships of interdependence', says Chaudhuri.

This collaborative view of the self – of freedom as interdependence – evolved, intriguingly, during a time of great personal loss. Within a period of six years, beginning in 1902, his wife, his father and two of his favourite children all died. Meanwhile, he married off three of his daughters, barely in their teens. It was almost as if, once the series of deaths began, he was willing himself out of domestic life in one great rush – by demonstrating chilly indifference to his daughters' own choices.

Tagore's characters, like their author, sometimes fail to embody his ideals. The social costs of upholding principle can be too steep, or tradition too seductively convenient. The Marxist critic György Lukács mauled Tagore for being an intellectual proxy for the European bourgeoisie, dismissing him as a pamphleteer whose characters were 'pale stereotypes'. But even when Tagore's novels were political arguments in mufti, the flaws and inconsistencies of his characters made him distinct in the Indian canon – and certainly more complex than doctrinaire.

India's literary traditions have the occasional **Krishnadevaraya** (14) or Allasani Peddana, writers who explored interiority and personal choice. But until late in the nineteenth century, individual lives were worth bothering about only when they were exemplary and morally improving. Tagore's sympathy extended to the imperfect. For instance, in 'The Broken Nest' – the story of a Kadambari-like young wife who falls in love with her cousin-in-law, a writer – the wife's distracted husband, a struggling newspaper editor, could easily be a villain. Instead, Tagore gives this secondary character equal complexity, and a parallel heartbreak in the end. In Tagore's world, fate follows the logic of specific choices, made by people with specific natures, encountering specific historical conditions; it has nothing to do with supernatural powers or caste destiny.

That this emphasis was innovative in the early twentieth century reminds us how underdeveloped the idea of individuality was in Indian literature. Tagore's contemporary, Chekhov, grew up with the interior fiction of Dostoyevsky and Pushkin, not to mention the work of Gogol, who was already so bored by Russian psychological inwardness in the first half of the nineteenth century that he wrote against it. In India, Tagore lacked such shoulders to stand on.

So he became those shoulders for other writers – and for more than interiority. He also allowed his successors to envisage an Indian self that was broader than any one of the subcontinent's many religious and cultural traditions. Tagore's writing certainly has a strong sense of place – the natural landscape and culture of Bengal are intensely present and studied. But his cultural net was large, drawing in elements from other traditions, high and low. There are allusions to the Upanishads, Buddhism, the songs of the Bauls (a community of roving folk singers from eastern India), and more. In Tagore, such cultural elements inflect natures, but they don't define them. Always, there is room for human idiosyncrasy.

One of Tagore's most celebrated verses begins:

> Where the mind is without fear and the head is held high;
> Where knowledge is free;
> Where the world has not been broken up into fragments
> By narrow domestic walls . . .

These are lines many Indian schoolchildren will recognize, and it's as close as Tagore got to a political poem. Written in 1901, it ends with a wish for his country to awake to freedom. That would not take place until after Tagore's death, but nevertheless his poem became well known during the years of the Swadeshi movement in Bengal. The nationalist agitation had begun during his period of personal loss: early on, perhaps as a distraction from his grief, he brought his many talents to the cause. He composed patriotic songs, among them one that became the national anthem of Bangladesh. (A few years later, he wrote what eventually became the Indian national anthem.) He invented festivals to instil brotherhood among his fellow Bengalis. He led marches. He used some of his family lands to try to develop a model rural community, inspired by the ideas of Armenian nationalists in Russia. And in his indignation – shared by many – at British dismissals of Indian culture, he wrote in celebration of a glorious Indian past.

His revivalist view of Indian history was considerably more expansive than some of his brethren's. In part because of an infatuation with Japanese culture (though later he would reject and fear Japan's nationalist politics), he cultivated for a time the idea of a mystical unity of Asian civilizations. Western humanism and the Enlightenment, too, were gathered up and brought into his opening of the Indian mind. But as Tagore went broad, the Swadeshi movement narrowed. By 1907 it had become more of a Hindu movement, and its strategy drifted from public agitation towards clandestinely plotted violence. Nor was that violence exclusively directed at British targets: Bengal's Hindus and Muslims also began to attack one another.

Tagore's enthusiasm for Swadeshi promptly lapsed. He valued the living pluralities of Indian civilization more than the speculative idea of a tidied-up Indian nation. Instead of political change, he subscribed to a belief in self-improvement not unlike that of his contemporary Booker T. Washington in the American South: *instead of attacking the oppressors, edify yourself.* In an article of 1909, following a series of terrorist incidents, Tagore wrote, 'The British Government is not the cause of our subjection; it is merely a symptom of a deeper subjection on our part.' India's own laws, customs, and religious and social institutions were holding its people back, he believed.

Although this tendency towards critiquing his own nation was in line with Gandhi's temperament, **Gandhi** (38) had little use for Tagore's belief that individual freedom and expression were the drivers of social change. The men's respective views on education illuminate the difference. Tagore felt a broad liberal education, encompassing Indian ideas and traditions as well those from Europe and Asia, was central to self-development and the sound exercise of personal judgement; he argued that the British had set Indian development back decades by providing a small segment of Indians with a flimsy and entirely Anglocentric education that prepared them simply to be cogs in the colonial administration. Meanwhile, Gandhi, for all his concern for the masses, possessed a view of education almost as limited as that of the British: among other things, he believed that literacy wasn't necessary unless it was practical for work. (Views like Gandhi's prevailed, which left primary education to be the poor relation shunted to the corner of the modern Indian state.)

In Tagore's conception, freedom should not be subordinated to the expediencies of nationalism or of politics. 'Those people who have got their political freedom are not necessarily free,' he cautioned. 'They are merely powerful.' He felt that Gandhi's authoritarianism boded ill for India's future. In 1921, at the height of Gandhi's movement of non-cooperation with the British, Tagore wrote of how, across the country, he sensed 'a spirit of persecution, which is not that of armed force, but something still more alarming, because it is invisible'. The use of reason was being shut down. 'It was only necessary to cling to an unquestioning obedience,' he went on, 'to some mantra, some unreasoned creed.'

Another sharp conflict with Gandhi blew up in 1934, when Gandhi declared that an earthquake in Bihar was 'divine chastisement' for the 'sin of untouchability'. Tagore's views on personal liberty had made him an opponent of untouchability well before Gandhi was, but as much as he loathed the institution, he was repulsed by how Gandhi exploited superstition to turn an event with a scientific explanation into an ethical homily. Instead of correcting popular unreason – which was, in Tagore's view, 'a fundamental source of all the blind powers that drive us against freedom and self-respect' – Gandhi was fostering it.

Tagore's resistance to Gandhi's charms and his scepticism of nationalism made him unpopular. Some of his enemies considered him treasonous to the nationalist cause, and it was not uncommon in the 1930s for India's sole winner of the Nobel Prize to be lampooned in the press. Abroad, the Japanese and Chinese dismissed his cautions against nationalism's dangers as the pleadings of a colonized mind. (Mussolini, though, welcomed him warmly in the early 1930s; Tagore's appetite for praise overcame his scruples on free expression, now that he was less loved at home.) In his last two decades, the famous educational experiment begun at Shantiniketan, outside Calcutta, became the focus of his attention.

In his poem imagining his whole country waking to freedom, it's telling that Tagore wrote of a world beyond 'narrow domestic walls': our larger freedom, he's saying, begins at home. Making and sustaining that connection between the freedom of the individual and of the collective, and recognizing their indivisibility, has been a struggle in India. Tagore had been dead six years when Nehru, who considered Tagore his intellectual guru, became free India's prime minister, and he was nine years gone when the Indian Constitution was enacted, in 1950. That document installed a conception of equal freedom as a promise to all Indians; but it also conceded to state power and to social interests many opportunities to constrict those freedoms in an array of hedging qualifications made in the name of state security and collective rights.

Menaka Guruswamy was one of the lawyers who argued in the Supreme Court against the constitutional legality of that part of the Indian Penal Code that criminalizes consensual gay sex. She lost – in a setback not just to the rights of a minority, but to the Constitution's promise of freedom to every Indian citizen. 'If you do not recognize the ability of a human being to freely love, or if you do not recognize the ability of a human being to have freedom of thought and expression,' Guruswamy says, 'then you are doing something to freedom . . . And there is nothing intrinsically more powerful in the quest for freedom than being able to love whom you want to.' It's hard not to think Tagore would agree.

33
Visvesvaraya

Extracting Moonbeams from Cucumbers
1860–1962

If the Netflix streaming service had a category entitled 'twentieth-century industrialization porn', alongside the Soviet backlist there should by rights be the 1972 Kannada-language blockbuster film *Bangarada Manushya* ('The Golden Man'). In it, the legendary south Indian actor Rajkumar plays a relocated urbanite bringing technology to a droughty village. In one exuberant song, ragged farmers watch in awe as dynamite shatters a rock mass, hydraulic drills create bore wells, and ploughs upend tree after tree. (Environmentalist viewers may want to cover their eyes.) Not long after the denuded terrain floods with water, villagers are shown staggering about under the weight of magnificent harvests. The climax of this sequence isn't the seductive close-up of a tractor sputtering across a field; it's the moment when the director briefly cuts away to a clip of newsreel: a be-turbaned, unsmiling, hawk-faced engineer named Mokshagundam Visvesvaraya, bending to receive a medal. The song moves to its climax: without his work, 'would this precious land have harvested gold?'

MV, as he was widely known, was an unlikely celebrity – a frail bureaucrat who walked stooped over, as if the burden of state-building literally pressed down on his shoulders. But in the popular imagination he turned an engineering degree into a superhuman world-fashioning prowess. Austere to the point of dourness, but audaciously hopeful, he sought to frog-march India into modernity.

In the early twentieth century, Visvesvaraya became the chief administrator of the princely state of Mysore. His well-tended state – now part of Karnataka – stood as a rebuke to other princely domains run down by decadent or incompetent maharajas. A state in which efficiency and technological innovation mattered; a state in which meritocracy, not patronage, reigned – that's how even the British spoke of Mysore. Its image of correct and diligent self-improvement was so carefully crafted by Visvesvaraya that it would not be matched again until twenty-first-century Gujarat.

Though the myth of MV's accomplishment is a bit too polished to be believable, this much is true: moving across the towns and princely capitals of south and west India, he left in his wake enduring improvements for millions of people. He innovated in sanitation, statistics, flood control, drainage and irrigation – though all those water-management leaps aren't the only reason I occasionally think of him while in the shower. As he worked to support cottage industries, he also founded the factory that makes my favourite Mysore sandalwood soap.

Visvesvaraya's plans for economic growth struck some as vain and overly ambitious; one south Indian newspaper derided them, in a twist to *Gulliver's Travels*, as 'promises to extract moonbeams from cucumbers'. He would have extracted those moonbeams if he could, as they would have lowered Mysore's electricity costs. But such technocratic strong-headedness had its weak points too. Visvesvaraya was quick to construe democratic processes as an irritant, and often saw social and local diversities as problems that more uniformity could solve. Both his technical vision and his ideological blinkers brought him into conflict with other patriots, and ultimately his favoured path for India's development was not taken by Nehru and his successors. Indeed, he was embittered when Nehru's plan for the new nation absorbed only a smattering of his economic ideas.

Visvesvaraya's century-long life spanned a fundamental shift in conceptions of the Indian economy: from fatalism about India's economic prospects (seen as fragmented by geography, and trapped by social and cultural attitudes) to a post-independence faith in state-led industrial growth and redistribution. In the decades since his death, that post-independence faith has dwindled, as a planned and protected economy failed to fulfil its promise. Today, as India seeks to become a global economic power, some of Visvesvaraya's views on economics and governance have been recycled back into fashion. The new faith is in technocratically managed growth, and in the example of competitive success. Laggards, current wisdom says, will learn: they will have to get on their bike. It's a stricture Visvesvaraya would have endorsed. But the tensions between an efficient, fast-growing economy and an inclusive one remain as acute in our time as they were in his.

In still portraits, he seems almost masked, as unreadable and hieratic as a face on a coin. But MV's wilfully depersonalized, industry-standard self – every day the same ritual, the same outfit – was consistent with his social vision. Quirks, charm and connections should have nothing to do with an individual's ability to ascend the social ladder: what counted was discipline, honesty and expertise at the role you were given. He self-consciously modelled these practices, and underplayed how his own life embodied that other means of social ascent – dumb luck.

Visvesvaraya was born to a poor Brahmin family around 1860, in the Mysore village of Muddenahalli. At the time, the British controlled the state, the royal family having been disempowered on the grounds of maladministration. Visvesvaraya had already attended a mission school and excelled at college in Bangalore when luck hit: a new maharaja, Chamarajendra Wadiyar, came of age.

Wadiyar was a princely exemplar of Macaulay's class of men: 'Indian in blood and colour, but English in taste, in morals, and in intellect.' In 1881, confident that he was up to managing the state, the British ended fifty years of their own rule in Mysore. The newly empowered maharaja, intent on governing so judiciously that the British would stay out of his business, promptly launched a series of democratic and educational reforms. One of the latter sent the diligent twenty-year-old Visvesvaraya off to get an engineering degree at the College of Science in Poona (now Pune). He topped his class, and for the next three decades honed his skills and reputation in western and central India.

Working for the Raj's Public Works Division in Bombay Presidency, Visvesvaraya swiftly demonstrated a capability well beyond inspecting minor irrigation projects and supervising repairs. Instead, he built a water pipeline system in Nasik; concocted an efficient way to supply potable water in Sukkur; and devised in Pune new ways of controlling floods and capturing the rain that was historically wasted during the monsoon, with a system of sluice gates that was soon imitated around the world. It could have been another Rajkumar song sequence: Super-Engineer of Mysore, zipping across India, bettering lives.

As one of his private secretaries would later remark, 'In action he was a great autocrat, else he could not have achieved so much.' That he got a patent for those sluice gates, but chose to give up the royalties, illuminates another aspect of his nature. He wasn't motivated by money, and was intolerant of the excuses other bureaucrats made to justify their corruption. Public credit mattered to him more – and the credit-dispensers he worked for were the British.

By 1907, as he upgraded the water supplies in Aden and in Kolhapur, the Swadeshi movement was in full swing elsewhere in India. But while Visvesvaraya wanted independence, and quietly engaged with liberal progressives like Mahadev Govind Ranade and Gopal Krishna Gokhale, he was nervous about being linked to anti-government agitators. After all, his career was flourishing. By 1908, when Swadeshi lost steam, Visvesvaraya had, by merit, superseded eighteen of his seniors.

But now he bumped up against a ceiling that talented Indians before him had hit. The crowning position in the Public Works Department of Bombay – the title of Chief Engineer – would never be given to a brown man. Too disciplined to publicly air his frustration at his employer, MV resigned to accolades and honours, then hightailed it to Europe, Russia and America to study sewers, irrigation techniques and dams. Back in India, he applied his expertise to Hyderabad after a devastating flood, trying to ensure it didn't happen again. And by the end of 1909, he received from the Maharaja of Mysore the job the British in Bombay wouldn't give him: Chief Engineer. Within three years, local politics advanced him even further, to the role of dewan, or prime minister, of the entire princely state.

*

Since the Mysore royal family's return to power in 1881, they had selected their dewans from outside the state to avoid factionalism. But by 1912 the clamour for a Mysorean to be chosen was so loud that a new maharaja, Krishnaraja Wadiyar, had to bow to public opinion. His eye turned to his Chief Engineer, whose aloofness from court politics was matched by an interest in methods of economic development. To one Mysore sceptic, placing an engineer in charge of government was only marginally wiser than appointing a wood-cutter: the era of the technocrat as the guide and saviour of society and public life had not yet begun. In fact, Visvesvaraya, who imme-diately set to work applying the statistical precision of engineering to the development of the state, was one of those men whose careers established in India the technocrat's halo.

While other rulers of princely states embarked on study tours of European casinos, Visvesvaraya was drawing heavily on lessons of development from the United States, Sweden, and especially Japan, which had modernized swiftly in the wake of the Meiji Restoration, combating the cliché that efficiency and good governance were syn-onymous with the West. Among the Japanese lessons Visvesvaraya applied to Mysore was that fostering industry and creating jobs would help the poor in the long run more than weaving social safety nets. This stood in contrast to other princely states, where dole money and fruitless public works projects were offered against mass hunger.

But for all their practical-mindedness, technocrats need theories as well as examples. In the air of Mysore were also the mercantilist ideas of the nineteenth-century German political economist Frie-drich List, which had gained favour in Indian liberal intellectual and progressive princely circles. List advocated state protectionism for infant industries in the weaker national economies that hoped to compete with powers like Britain – a position that Visvesvaraya would adopt as well.

At a time when the Indian economy's growth rate was barely a number, and when the Indian literacy rate was just over 10 per cent, Visvesvaraya also grasped that sustained industrial growth required a more skilled and literate populace. Nurturing Mysore's revenues to an increase of 50 per cent in six years, he invested the surpluses in infrastructure and education. Mysore became the first state to make primary education compulsory, the first princely state to have its own university – and an engineering college, of course – in addition to a network of public libraries. And Bangalore became the site where Tata's (27) ambition to build a research university was fulfilled, with the founding of the Indian Institute of Science in 1911.

Visvesvaraya also developed the sandalwood oil and soap, tourist and sugarcane industries; founded the Bank of Mysore; and commissioned what was then India's biggest, most expensive dam. Built across the Kaveri river over twenty years, the Krishnaraja Sagar Dam allowed 100,000 acres of previously arid land to be irrigated – the feat that inspired the film tribute in *Bangarada Manushya*. Meanwhile, the electrical power the dam produced jumpstarted the state's industrialization and electrified Bangalore, several years before the electrification of Bombay.

Mysore's Tamil neighbours complained about the dam (they said its height deprived them of their rightful water), and local critics sniped that the flinty Visvesvaraya recouped the state wages of dam-builders by selling them alcohol at the end of the day, according to social scientist Chandan Gowda. As MV's tenure as dewan progressed, there were other, more substantial grumblings. At a time when the state was nominally increasing legislative representation, MV's dictatorial style offended many. The cost of his schemes rankled too. The dewan who advocated fiscal discipline and statistics as a means of making government more analytical and accountable saddled Mysore with an exquisitely enumerated – and alarmingly large – public debt. It wasn't until the dawn of the Second World War that his most financially and technologically ambitious project, the Bhadravati Iron and Steel Works, would turn a profit.

Still, under Visvesvaraya, the national image of Mysore flourished. In addition to pulling off feats like the dam, he made canny investments in trophy projects, like the graceful fountain and gardens attracting tourists to Mysore city's Brindavan Gardens, a forerunner of beautifications such as Ahmedabad's Sabarmati Riverfront. Even the loss-making steel works had its defenders. Gandhi, for all his anti-industrialism, declared it an instance of a 'top to bottom' Mysorean enterprise, revealing Indians to have 'practical genius'.

So it was something of a surprise when the maharaja, who shared Visvesvaraya's appreciation for efficiency and welcomed Mysore's status as a model state, began losing faith in his dewan's judgement.

In Mysore, as elsewhere in India, Brahmins like Visvesvaraya – though a statistical minority – held the preponderance of government jobs. And elsewhere in India, including next-door Madras, movements against Brahmin dominance were gathering pace. The maharaja had been following these developments and, under pressure from local leaders, decided in 1917 to improve the position of Mysore's non-Brahmin castes.

Visvesvaraya had little patience for engineering social change through policy. Moreover, from the limited exposure he'd had to the Mysore masses, he had come to believe that a fair share of Indian poverty was caused not just by a lack of employers, but by the failure of individual noses to bend to the grindstone. Americans, he said, had much more hustle. (Now that stereotypes of American and Indian workers are reversing, it's amusing to see a quote attributed to Visvesvaraya being bandied about in American conservative circles: 'Ignorance, dependence, inefficiency, laziness, want of the spirit of enterprise are the real causes of poverty.')

When the maharaja instituted scholarships for non-Brahmin students, Visvesvaraya acquiesced. But then the maharaja wanted preferential allocation of educational places (what in later Indian policy would be known as affirmative action or 'reservations') for non-Brahmins. This was hardly common practice among the princely states, and Visvesvaraya was affronted. As he later wrote, 'By ignoring merit and capacity I feared production would be hampered and the efficiency of the administration, for which we had been working so hard, would suffer . . .' Growth could efface caste handicaps, in his view. Trying to correct the problem in the short term was a waste of state and social energy, as well as wrong in principle.

Variations on this argument – ideals of growth and meritocracy versus those of inclusion – continue heatedly today, as disadvantaged groups demand that affirmative action be extended into new areas of employment, including India's dynamic private sector. Back in the 1910s, the maharaja and his dewan conducted their skirmish via courteous memo, stony silence and sneaky press leak – until Visvesvaraya provoked the maharaja by putting forward suggestions for members of a government commission. The commission was meant to assess the plausibility of caste-based proportional representation in public service. Every name Visvesvaraya recommended was Brahmin. When the exasperated maharaja insisted that at least half be non-Brahmin, Visvesvaraya offered his resignation – probably as a bluff to get his way. To his surprise, the maharaja let his state-shaping prime minister go.

To MV's slogan, 'Industrialize or Perish!', Gandhi had once responded: 'Industrialize – and Perish!'. But in the 1930s and 40s, as the horizon of independence drew nearer, Gandhi's became a recessive voice against a political and business elite whose visions converged in an industrial future. The details of that future, though, were contested.

The successful industrialists of western India hoped to secure favourable conditions for their own profitable textile and consumer industries: they wanted the state to invest in infrastructure and heavy industries, and protect them from foreign competition. They had little interest in policies of inclusion, still less in redistribution. But among the ambitious politicians of the Congress party were progressives who believed that a state-owned industrial base, built by economic planning and combined with reforms of India's concentrated land holdings, would eliminate poverty and create a less hierarchical society. They had little interest in private enterprise, still less in private profit. MV's own views, like those of other technocratic administrators of his era, fell between stools. He wanted both Japanese-style state investment and industrial strategy as well as American hustle and enterprise.

Nehru was not persuaded. He doubted that what had been done by an autocrat in a state of immense princely wealth could be replicated elsewhere in a poor democratic nation. Moreover, he worried that under Visvesvaraya's plan, India's already yawning inequalities – both regional and individual – would widen further. And Nehru, unlike Visvesvaraya, was answerable to parliament and had elections to fight.

After independence, Nehru did incorporate into the model of national planning the Mysorean's faith in the idea of a central intellectual 'brain' for society: a council of expert economists, technocrats and businessmen who could determine policy goals (Nehru was less willing to induct business instincts into this national economic cerebrum). To Visvesvaraya this was hardly enough. In the 1950s, when Nehru conferred on him India's highest civilian award, Visvesvaraya remained his crotchety, unbending self: 'If you feel that by giving this title, I will praise your government, you will be disappointed. I am a fact-finding man.'

Today, India's 3,500 or so engineering colleges train a million and a half graduates annually. The esteem with which they're held has something to do with the brand Visvesvaraya left on the profession. The work he did to help bring clean water and power to his part of the world, and to reduce catastrophes like monsoon flooding, would have been a substantial legacy even if he hadn't done more than anyone to lay the foundations of Bangalore, whose professional class has probably drawn more wealth to the nation than that of any other city.

But what he failed to achieve is almost as intriguing. Visvesvaraya died in 1962, at the age of a hundred and one. Nehru followed two years later. In less than a generation, it became clear that the planned economy was stifling Indian potential. By 1991, over one third of Indians were below the poverty line; economic growth had dipped to just 1 per cent; and the country's finances were in a mess. Nehru's political heirs were compelled to open India's economy to the world, and embrace, even if warily, global capitalism and private entrepreneurship. It's tempting to believe that if Visvesvaraya had got his way, India would be far more developed today – and a real rival to economies like Sweden and Japan. But against this flight of speculative inquiry, it's been argued that in the early years of free India, a laissez-faire attitude to urgent social inequalities would have triggered caste and class conflict.

Oddly enough, twenty-first-century India now offers something close to a test case for the Visvesvaraya model. A good deal of the economic revitalization plan Prime Minister Narendra Modi promised in return for the mandate he won in the 2014 national elections parallels what Visvesvaraya advocated: development of large-scale industries, greater power to the states, decentralized administration, efficiency as a primary value of governance and harsh responses to corruption. Modi also shares Visvesvaraya's lack of patience for social questions. The weakness of human development indices do not perturb him greatly, and his government has cut funding for schemes to improve them.

In Modi's conception, model states of the sort Mysore once was might temporarily exacerbate inequality, but they'll inspire India's poorer states to join in a race to the top. Competitive federalism, the new catchphrase, reminds me of something Visvesvaraya once said: 'Take care of the pieces well. The whole will take care of itself.' It's a good line, widely quoted nowadays, but one which raises a question of political judgement – the kind of judgement neither Visvesvaraya nor his modern incarnations consistently excel at. If just some pieces do well, at what point will the whole begin to wobble?

34
Periyar

Sniper of Sacred Cows
1879–1973

Imagine, if you will, that Indian women were a country unto themselves – the Women's Republic of India. At around 600 million people, the new state would be the world's third largest, a little smaller than the misruled territory of Male India. On the 2014 UN Human Development Index, it would rank between Myanmar and Rwanda. Now home in on mean years of schooling. Our Democratic Republic of Indian Females would be, at 3.2 years, neck and neck with Mozambique. As for per capita, inflation-adjusted income, hold onto your hat as Ivory Coast and Papua New Guinea leave our new nation in the dust. It's sobering to see what a tripling of India's GDP since 2000 has *not* done for its women.

In fact, we don't have to cross borders to imagine an environment less crushing of Indian women's capacities. In the states of southern India, development indices and daily freedoms have long been different from those across the northern states. In the north, for instance, the majority of women marry before the age of eighteen; in the south, the number in some states is as low as 15 per cent. One result is that fertility rates in parts of the south are half what they are in some northern states. You'll find parallel differences in women's illiteracy, and in female rates of participation in the labour force (over 50 per cent in the south, just 36 per cent in the north). Such variations are arguably at the heart of a North–South divide that is often cited as one of India's major economic and social faultlines. Surprisingly, that divergence has something to do with a primary school drop-out named E. V. Ramaswamy Naicker, who was born nearly 140 years ago.

Ramaswamy Naicker is best known in India as an anti-Brahmin activist, rationalist and take-no-prisoners orator – an iconoclast who joined Gandhi's Congress but became a famous enemy of the Mahatma. In the mid-1920s, Naicker founded the Dravidian Self-Respect Movement, whose followers called him Thanthai Periyar, the Great Man – a self-conscious dig at Gandhi, the Great Soul. Though he never ran for office, Periyar left a massive imprint on modern Tamil politics; the political parties that emerged from his movement have governed the state since the late 1960s. Nationally, his advocacy of the Tamil language and his refusal to accept the nationwide imposition of Hindi influenced India's post-1947 policies of linguistic pluralism, while his views on caste helped to create an atmosphere that favoured legislation on affirmative action in the early days of the Constitution. He was also the first leader of his time to argue forcefully – without the paternalist condescension many Indian men are given to when they speak on this subject – for the freedom of women in a country where the wagons are always circled around the patriarchal family.

Periyar mocked the 'stupidity' of Sanskrit epics that celebrated self-sacrificing women as if they were chaste footstools. He advocated girls' education, love marriages, divorce if those marriages didn't work out, women's property rights and – most radical of all – respect for women's sexuality and ability to control conception. Women shouldn't passively wait for rights to be bestowed upon them, either, Periyar said. In an essay in which he called for manhood to be destroyed in the name of female freedom, he famously wrote, 'Have cats ever freed rats? Have foxes ever liberated goats or chickens? Have whites ever enriched Indians? Have Brahmins ever given non-Brahmins justice? We can be confident that women will never be emancipated by men.'

Periyar was making his case in a region with more than its share of ancient warrior queens and powerful goddesses, a lower fertility rate and, in some communities, an existing tradition of birth control – and this probably intensified the twentieth-century statistical face-off between South and North. But the more I learn about this gruff idol-breaker with a stiletto tongue and a furnace of a brain, the more I wonder: if only other regions of India had had similar legacies, would our Democratic Republic of Indian Females be in better fighting shape today?

> There is no God. There is no God.
> There is no God at all.
> He who invented God is a fool.
> He who propagates God is a scoundrel.
> He who worships God is a barbarian.

For decades Periyar made a habit of beginning his mammoth meetings of the Self-Respect Movement with that incantation. He spoke rhythmically, and watching him on video – a bulky man in a black shirt with a bald head, untamed white beard and, beside him, a little pet dog to scare away Brahmins, who consider dogs unclean – I feel as if I'm in the company of a beat poet. He was in many ways as wild-spirited, though his words were never mystical. He was a scorching critic of anything and everything he considered irrational, beginning with caste and religion.

Periyar was born ten years after Gandhi and grew up in the town of Erode – known for its textile-making and little else – in Coimbatore district, Madras. His caste was a middle one, of agrarians and traders, but his father's prosperity as a trader protected him from slights. As a child, the boy had a good house, with servants, and could afford to be a little rebellious.

Early on, Periyar would needle the sadhus and Brahmin priests hired by his socially aspirant father to instruct him in Sanskritic ways. The religious men couldn't take it, and stopped coming, leaving the young Periyar unconvinced by their teachings. But he remained enough of a Hindu to make a pilgrimage to Hinduism's Brahminopolis – Benares. Here, in his early or mid-twenties, he had what is always recounted as his decisive moment, a counter-Damascene one. He wrote and spoke of it frequently afterwards. How he'd fled to Benares after interrupting a big Brahmin feast hosted by his father. How he'd been repulsed by the money-grubbing Benares pandits and their aggression towards non-Brahmins. How he couldn't get a meal at any of the Benares feeding stops because of his caste. How he wouldn't have survived without charity – eating, on one occasion, food scraps used as offerings in death rituals.

Contrary to the myth, the experience didn't immediately change his life. But it implanted in him a slow-burning, private rage against the Brahmins, and he seems to have begun, in his twenties, a long process of reading and self-education. As the Cambridge historian of south India David Washbrook notes, since the 1880s Madras intellectuals had debated back and forth whether it was possible to reconcile Hindu belief and practices with modern, scientific thinking. **Annie Besant's (29)** Theosophy, with its rationalist demolition of missionary Christianity and scientistic defence of Brahminic Hinduism, was a godsend to the South's upper-caste intellectuals. They could now defend their religious and caste practices in a modern idiom. But Periyar, without a high-caste status to preserve, was free to follow a logic unshackled by prejudice: 'He liked to joke, "I've got no personal problem with God – I've never even met him, not once",' says A. R. Venkatachalapathy, a leading Tamil cultural historian now working on a biography of Periyar.

Periyar's logical consistency was usefully supported by his material position. His hostility to Brahminism reflected something we've seen as far back as **Mahavira (2)** and **Buddha (1)**: it wasn't impoverished low-caste individuals, but men who were effectively bourgeois – higher on the caste ladder, with some wealth – who were most willing to confront India's oldest form of hierarchy. A person of Periyar's means was also more free to be provocative. Consider one of his most famous wind-up lines: 'If you see a snake and Brahmin on the road, kill the Brahmin first.' If a Dalit spoke publicly like that in the early 1900s, most likely he'd have been the one killed.

But in his twenties and thirties, Periyar wasn't shouting that critique in the streets, nor was he swept along by the first wave of mass nationalism, which broke soon after he returned from Benares. Instead, he was married with a family, engaged in successfully expanding his family business into one of the largest merchant trading houses in Coimbatore. By 1918, respected for his managerial prowess, he became the chairman of the Erode municipality, considering budgets, pipes and drains.

*

Kerala's Kottayam district is today one of India's most socially pro-gressive places; literacy rates are high, above 90 per cent, and some years ago it declared itself India's first tobacco-free district. One of its oldest shrines sits at the centre of a lattice of roads in the town of Vaikom: a wood-pillared Shiva temple controlled by a priestly South Indian caste of extreme orthodoxy, the Nambudiri Brahmins. Those roads would lead Periyar, approaching forty, into politics.

The Nambudiris had for centuries forbidden untouchables and low castes not just from entering the Mahadev temple, but also from walking on the surrounding roads. In the early 1920s, a low-caste movement arose, calling for the ruler of Travancore state (as Kerala then was), to open temples to all Hindus. Otherwise, they threat-ened, they would convert to Christianity or Islam. The Vaikom temple became the epicentre of the movement's agitations. By 1924, Gandhi had been drawn in – the first occasion on which he made untouchability a cause for public protest.

At the time, Congress politicians were becoming increasingly embarrassed by how few lower-caste Tamils held senior positions in the party; to dampen the criticism that it was Brahmin-dominated, it was searching out new leaders. Rich, confident and smart, Periyar had been convinced shortly before the Vaikom protests to join the party, after a chance meeting with two leading Tamil Congressmen on a railway platform. Now Congress needed someone of lower caste – a figurehead perhaps – to lead the Vaikom cause. Periyar was their man.

He took to nationalist politics almost instinctively and, initially, with hope. He thought Gandhi, mid-caste like himself, might share his opposition to Brahmin control of the Congress leadership – that the interests of nationalism and of caste fairness might be reconciled. Travelling around the conservative state, Periyar was too independent-minded to stick to Gandhi's view that only the roads around the temple should be opened to all. He supported the protesters' demand that the temple itself be opened to everyone – even though he told his audiences that they were idiots to want to worship there. He was so effective in galvanizing the movement that he twice wound up in prison.

While Periyar was in jail, Gandhi negotiated gently with the Nambudiri priests. (The low castes, one of the Brahmins said, had to be excluded because they were 'reaping the reward of their karma'; no doubt, Gandhi agreed, but asked, 'Who are we human beings to take the place of God and add to their punishment?') Ultimately, in 1925, the new Maharani of Travancore worked out a compromise: some of the roads surrounding the temple were opened, but the main entrance stayed accessible only to Brahmins. The demand that lower castes be permitted to step over the threshold into the temple compound and shrine wouldn't be met until 1936.

To the Congress, the Vaikom Satyagraha was a model success, a breaching of the barriers of orthodoxy. To Periyar, it was an exercise in high-grade deception: Gandhi had sold the lower castes out. Over the next two years he gradually detached himself from the Congress and Gandhi, whom he never forgave. With his family money, he began the Self-Respect Movement. His arena was the Dravidian-language-speaking South – Tamil Nadu as well as Andhra, Karnataka and Kerala – and his agenda sometimes the very opposite of Gandhi's.

Where Gandhi and his followers wore white, Periyar instructed his supporters to dress in black. Where Gandhi massaged the religious beliefs of his audiences, Periyar called his listeners fools, insulted their beliefs and caste practices, and threatened to thwack their gods and idols with his slippers. And where Gandhi wanted to build a national movement, Periyar revelled in the Dravidian South.

As with many autodidacts, it's tricky to trace precise philosophical antecedents for many of Periyar's ideas. Venkatachalapathy, who has spent years with his papers and letters, notes his habit of referencing sources, *ex post facto*, for what seem to be original ideas. But in the case of his radicalization on the subject of women, it's clear his thinking was affected by the controversy over a notorious book published in 1927 – a work that Gandhi and the Congress officially despised.

Mother India was the American journalist Katherine Mayo's muckraking exposé of Indian life, and particularly of how Hindu traditions exploited women. Mayo laced her polemic with dismaying statistics on child marriage, venereal disease and the treatment of widows, along with official commentary justifying traditions like marrying girls before the age of fourteen. While some Congress leaders were actively pressing for reform on these same issues, this influential critique from America – a case of 'concern-trolling' *avant la lettre* – implied that Indian self-rule would be catastrophic for women. (One Indian suspicion, which proved correct, was that Mayo had the counsel of British Intelligence in India.) Congress leaders chose to close ranks, affirming Hinduism as a noble protector of women.

Periyar saw the ideas in *Mother India* differently. Of course he delighted in the attack on Hinduism, but he also recognized, in the social issues kicked up by the controversy, connections to what he had been learning about feminist movements in Europe. Starting in the late 1920s, the issue of Indian women's rights became a significant part of his Self-Respect campaign. He pressed it in his oratory and in a weekly magazine he founded, each as direct, unpretentious and outrageous as the other.

In centuries-old Tamil folksongs, women sometimes protested that they were expendable servants of men and nurses of children, and that neither married women nor widows had any property rights. ('If a son had been born in my womb/The son would have got his rightful share/We would have had justice in the courts of Madurai . . .'). Part of the problem, Periyar believed, was that their marriages were essentially enslavements: loveless financial barters among elders of the same caste, in which the volition of the bride (often a child) was immaterial.

Periyar's dramatic, colloquial public voice had extended his movement from the urban classes, with whom his rationalist rhetoric was most compatible, across the Tamil heartland. In 1928 or 1929, under his auspices, rural men and women began having what were called Self-Respect Marriages: often inter-caste love weddings, conducted without Brahmin priests or mantras. Against elaborate, multi-day traditional weddings, a Periyar-inspired ceremony was fast and simple by design; he thought money lavished on ritual was better directed towards educating a couple's presumptive children. At the same time, there was no pretence in the resulting unions that sex was just for procreation.

Officially, Self-Respect had five aims: 'no god; no religion; no Gandhi; no Congress; and no Brahmins'. Abolishing patriarchy was ancillary. But over time, Self-Respect Marriages, in which the equality of bride and groom was explicit, became important, movement-defining occasions. They were a way to shake the bedrock of Hindu society (which depended on family rituals, conducted by Brahmins), to spread Periyar's ideas village by village, and to demonstrate one of his ideals: rational argument and frank exchange among men and women.

To Periyar, the evil of arranged, caste-sanctioned marriages perpetuated the widespread illiteracy of girls: parents wanted daughters to be more ignorant and helpless when married off to strangers. He called instead for girls to be trained intellectually and physically, through active sports. Once those girls were grown and married – preferably to men they chose themselves – he wanted them to know how to control their childbearing capacities. This wasn't the sort of prescription for health and population control that is now vaguely in the air; it was about women's (and men's) autonomy, in sexual activity and, through that, in other domains of life.

The Tamil press went after him for peddling immorality. Periyar responded, in one wedding speech, with cool logic:

> If a wife has to obey her husband, then why should a husband not have to obey his wife as well? If a woman has to obey her in-laws then why should a man not have to obey his? For if there is no reciprocity, then it is as though a slave girl has been bought to do the housework or for sexual enjoyment. We should not allow this kind of marriage in our land for even half a second.

Over the course of the 1920s, Periyar had become interested in the social experiment underway in Communist Russia, and in late 1931 he travelled there and across Europe to see for himself. He spent almost a year abroad, and it removed him further from the Indian mainstream. In Berlin, he delighted in visits to nudist camps – he later asked, futilely, that his authorized biography include a photo of him *au naturel* – and he came home more convinced than ever that science, technology, medicine and contraception were needed for Indians to advance.

He was particularly interested in how Soviet policies relating to divorce and to state support for children were changing the nature of the family, making it less essential. He was also intrigued by some of the economic ideas he encountered, and on his return he introduced notions of employee share ownership and partnership companies into the family business – giving workers a share of profits, for instance, instead of paying wages.

It's often said that Periyar imitated his nemesis Gandhi in seeking to shift social attitudes and sway public opinion without aspiring to political office himself. It's also noted that his following was significantly diminished when in 1948 Periyar, now a widower, married a much younger woman. A faction of young Self-Respecters cooked up a scandal around the marriage and went off to create a rival party, the Dravida Munnetra Kazhagam (the Progressive Dravidian Federation), which, along with another offshoot of Periyar's movement, has dominated Tamil politics for approaching half a century.

But in fact Periyar exercised a good deal of influence in independent India's electoral politics. For decades, he appeared as the star campaigner on behalf of candidates, and his mass appeal kept him a kingmaker. He was thus able from the outside to exercise pressure on governments and on legislation – a position of some power and no responsibility which didn't seem to trouble him.

Unlike **Ambedkar** (41), Periyar never generalized his critique into an all-India one. He was too deeply rooted in the Dravidian culture of the south. As his ideas seeped into that culture, the legendary sniper of sacred cows became, over time, something of a sacred cow himself. Even politicians who tried to marginalize Periyar for twenty years, after the 1948 controversy, later pretended otherwise. He died in 1973, and today, David Washbrook says, 'No major Tamil political leader doesn't claim a lineage of descent from Periyar – even while doing things he'd detest.'

Demographers and historians of science and medicine are right to protest that Periyar shouldn't be over-credited for the progress that south Indian women have seen in their health and well-being; many of these changes stem from trends that began well before he was born. But the fact that fertility rates in the Tamil region declined markedly during the interwar period suggests that his rhetoric on contraception had influence. If nothing else, he interjected the idea into debates, and lodged it in people's minds. It would be foolish – to use one of Periyar's favourite adjectives – to think that this passionate leader with a mass rural and urban following for over five decades was extraneous to the improvement of women's lives.

In Tamil Nadu today, the social progress of women as measured by development indicators seems to have stalled, despite the propitious legacies. Meanwhile, states in the historically poor, tribal north-east of India have made significant, if under-reported strides. It's startling to see, in the tables of the 2011 Census, that tiny Sikkim, a remote Himalayan state, has surpassed Tamil Nadu in female literacy. Since 2007, more Sikkim girls than boys have been enrolled in school at every level.

The causes of the narrowing gender literacy gap, and the obliteration of the schooling gap, are surely multiple, but one of them is sustained, obsessive campaigning: women's rights advocates banging the drum not just until victory in the next election, but year after year after year – as Periyar did. Persistent, public advocacy may not change lives quickly, but in the long run, the Women's Republic of India will register the difference.

35

Iqbal

Death for Falcons
1877–1938

Whose law should we show allegiance to – God's or the state's? It's an old question, and a bloodstained one too. Although it might have seemed exhaustively debated in Western societies, it is once more exercising a significant proportion of the planet's people.

Its bluntest formulation these days comes from a Muslim leader with an international following. In 2014, he announced that there was a state that would give Muslims dignity and rights, a state that transcended racial or ethnic boundaries, 'where the Arab and non-Arab, the white man and black man, the easterner and westerner are all brothers'. It sounded like the progressive vision of a non-racial society.

The speaker was Abu Bakr al-Baghdadi, the self-proclaimed Caliph of the Muslim world and leader of ISIS, the Islamic State in Iraq and Syria. The state he imagines not only seeks to efface social divisions, it also intends to abolish political boundaries. 'The earth,' al-Baghdadi said, 'is Allah's.' His vision of how to reconcile identity and authority is particularly malign. But the problem he is addressing is one many Muslim statesmen and thinkers have grappled with since the dawn of nationalism and the territorial state. As they have done so, many have looked to the same lodestar – the Indian poet and philosopher Muhammad Iqbal.

It's fitting that the afterlife of a thinker who was dismissive of nationalism and iconoclastic towards national borders can't be contained by geographic boundaries. Both Shia-dominated Iran and Sunni-dominated Pakistan claim Iqbal as their founding spirit. One of India's most patriotic, eloquent panegyrists, he is also celebrated as Pakistan's national poet. Like al-Baghdadi, Iqbal believed that the ideal ethical, political and legal order that Islam represented stood above all national identities, but accepted that it might require a state of its own to realize those ideals – though not, for Iqbal, through violence. To concede the necessity of the state, of course, was to be plunged back into the realm of man-made and state-dispensed law – to be subject to human judgement, free to turn its back on the divine.

Muhammad Iqbal was born in Sialkot, in the Punjab, in 1877. His family was descended from Kashmiri Hindu Pandits who had converted to Islam in the seventeenth century, and he stood in many ways at the confluence of the two belief systems. As he put it in a poem, 'though a Brahman's son I be,/Tabriz and Rum' – intellectual godfathers of Sufi Islam – 'stand wide to me'.

Though he exuded an air of poetic melancholy, and was often prone to tears, people flocked to his home in Lahore, for he was, as one visitor put it, a 'performing artist of conversation'. He held a gracious court, reciting his verse in flights of inspiration. His son Javid learned to detect when an idea took hold of his father: 'the colour of his face changed, and he gave the impression of suffering from physical discomfort'.

Iqbal authored a dozen collections of poetry, in Persian and Urdu, as well as numerous essays, speeches and volumes of correspondence. One of his works, the *Javid Nama* (1932), or 'Book of Eternity', has been compared to Dante's *Divine Comedy*, with Rum – the thirteenth-century Sufi poet Jalal al-Din Rumi – playing the role of Virgil. In his spare time, Iqbal wrote one of the first Urdu textbooks on economics; earned a doctorate in philosophy, which he studied in Lahore, Cambridge and Germany; and became a barrister in London.

Herman Hesse once remarked that Iqbal's 'tremendous work' belonged to three domains: 'the worlds of India, of Islam, and of Western thought'. R. A. Nicholson, one of Iqbal's tutors at Cambridge, called him 'a man in disagreement with his age'. He was; but he was also deeply engaged with the histories, themes and conflicts embedded in Islamic thought and in the literary traditions that fired his imagination. Most pressing, for many of those who came into contact with his thought, was the way he intervened in the global debate between those conceptual edifices the East and the West. This was an exchange about the form that individual lives and entire societies should take – one that had become particularly acute in Iqbal's day through the intellectual and political convulsions of Europe in the years during and after the Great War. But it also reflected a personal struggle between the imperatives of Iqbal's heart and the cultural expectations into which he was born.

In the late 1920s, Iqbal became embroiled in a distinctly Indian version of the argument over the relationship between religious identity and the territorial state. As India moved gradually from the imperial dispensation established by the British towards national sovereignty, a serious debate erupted over the shape of a self-governing India. How should the state reflect the religious variety (and related social conditions) of its citizens? Given the depth of those differences, how – if at all – could they be arranged in a single political order?

Other nations have faced similar questions about the relationship between religious diversity and political power, but none had faced the issue on the colossal scale that India did in the middle of the twentieth century. 'If an effective principle of cooperation is discovered in India,' Iqbal once declared, it would 'solve the entire political problem of Asia' – and, one might add by extension, the world. As with several other Indian thinkers of his era, including **Tagore** (32) and **Gandhi** (38), there was nothing modest about how Iqbal saw the stakes and the implications of his own engagement with his times.

Though Iqbal occasionally tried to answer these questions in bald prose, poetry was his natural medium of thought and expression. His poems bear all the marks of a struggle to balance an idealizing account of human nature with the political realities of Asia. As the historian Rajmohan Gandhi put it, Iqbal 'sang with impudence and acted with prudence'. Iqbal himself put it more loftily, and perhaps more accurately: he was a 'visionary idealist', he said, who often had to yield to 'the force of those very limitations which he has been in the habit of ignoring'. Many of his most daring propositions seem like remedies to counteract the poisonous effects of his era. Against the dehumanizing consequences of materialism and totalitarianism he celebrated the individual's spirit and capacity for self-determination. Against the spectre of total war he sought to imbue modern politics with the force of love. And against fascist discourses of racial and national superiority, he advocated submission to a far higher power.

He began with the devil. Though Iqbal's verses are included in many a Pakistani bride's trousseau, he was perhaps the devil's most sympathetic ventriloquist since Blake:

> For a falcon, living in the nest spells death.
> You do not yet know this,
> But with union comes the end of longing:
> What is eternal life?
> To burn – and keep on burning!

Like his devil, Iqbal urged man to 'Keep desire alive in thy heart,/ Lest thy little dust become a tomb./Desire is the soul of this world . . .' Indeed, the devil was his ideal image of man – in all but the most crucial respect. It was a conviction that seems to have taken hold of him while he was in the West, before becoming the basis of an ardent critique of Western society.

Iqbal arrived at Trinity College, Cambridge, in 1905, during the philosophical heyday of A. N. Whitehead, G. E. Moore and Bertrand Russell; but the biggest impact on his thought was made by the English Hegelians, philosophers like J. M. E. McTaggart, and by the atmosphere of social freedom. Although his parents had arranged his marriage after high school, in England he fell for an intellectually daring, aristocratic Indian Muslim, Atiya Faizi, who had been educated in London and went around without the veil. Their relationship may have remained at the level of conversations and correspondence, but it would haunt Iqbal for life.

Much of the poetry Iqbal composed during the three years he spent in Europe was about love. But love and desire for him were confusing categories – part sensual, physical, heterosexual; part Keatsian in its idealistic regard for a fleeting yet eternal Beauty; part piously metaphysical, an illuminating love from God. One focus of this poetry may have been Faizi; another was certainly Allah.

At the same time that Iqbal had the freedom to form an intimate bond with a woman he chose (something next to impossible back in Lahore), he was also gathering impressions for an Islamic critique of Western society that would eventually become famous in Europe, India and the larger Muslim world.

'Pleasure is the only effect of the West's wine,' Iqbal wrote of the materialism he saw in Europe. Another lyric from this time strengthened the theme and became one of his most well-known verses on the subject:

> O Western world's inhabitants,
> God's world is not a shop!
> What you are considering genuine
> Will be regarded counterfeit.
> Your civilization will commit suicide
> With its own dagger . . .

Later, after the horrors of the First World War had swept aside the belle époque and many of the intellectual certainties of the age of Empire, Iqbal crystallized this critique. By 1930, he was able to say that Western societies since the time of Luther and the Protestant Reformation had been ceding the universal ethics of Jesus to a parochial ethics of nationalism that posed 'the greatest danger to modern humanity', engendering 'mutually intolerant democracies whose sole function is to exploit the poor in the interest of the rich'.

To Iqbal, the West's problem was one of love and desire. Like the devil, the West seemed consumed with an insatiable appetite. But the devil's failing, like that of Milton's Satan, was that he 'declined to give absolute obedience to the Almighty Ruler of the Universe'. In the same way, the West, by turning away from God and the human brotherhood preached by Christ, had created a terrible inversion of the ideal society. Its desires, severed from the highest things, had become purely material. Islam presented an alternative, Iqbal felt, because it did not 'bifurcate the unity of man into an irreconcilable duality of spirit and matter', but put God at the centre of man's desire.

Nevertheless, individuals retained a devilish freedom, and it was up to them to choose God if they saw fit. 'Man is a free responsible being, he is the maker of his own destiny, his salvation is his own business,' Iqbal wrote. The most important part of this freedom was *ijtihad*, or forming independent judgements, particularly on matters of Islamic law. It's a deeply contested concept in Islamic thought, and the ulema or religious scholars claim prerogative over its exercise; but for Iqbal its presence at the core of Islam meant that 'There is no mediator between God and man. God is the birthright of every man.'

Iqbal's analyses – of the West and of the self – were founded on a crippling irony. In a letter to Faizi, Iqbal wrote about his frustrations at being forced into marriage, adding, 'As a human being I have a right to happiness – if society or nature deny that to me, I defy both.' This may have been true in spirit, but in his actions he capitulated, and that capitulation, Faizi thought, determined the character of his life:

> Iqbal, as I knew him in Europe, was never the same personality in India . . . In India his brilliance was blotted out, and as time went on this blot permeated his entire consciousness. He moved and lived dazed and degraded in his own mind, for he knew what he 'might have been'.

So, Iqbal, who had not felt himself free to shape his own life, imagined for human beings a nature, full of agency and desire, that was free to love God in its own way.

For the next three decades, after his return to India in 1908, Iqbal would continue to practise the law with one hand and write poetry with the other. In the mid-1920s he entered politics, serving as the Muslim League's president in 1930 and 1932, and becoming a sort of moral preceptor to Muhammad Ali **Jinnah** (39) and the League's leadership. As he wrestled with political developments, he expanded his critique of the West, and his vision of human nature, into a striking – and ultimately problematic – vision for Indian society.

I've sometimes wondered whether Iqbal is a good but also cautionary example of what happens when poets venture too wholeheartedly

into politics – and politicians in turn embrace them. Did he aestheti-
cize and idealize politics, in a way that bore little relationship to
reality but had very real effects? At what cost, to himself and to the
subcontinent's Muslims, did he let his ideas get diverted from poetry
into politics?

In 1932, Iqbal warned the All-India Muslim Conference that the
people of India were demanding the very secular institutions which
he considered the downfall of the West. At the same time, he objected
to the ethnic chauvinism of the 'Arabian Imperialism' that characterized earlier periods of Islam. Islam should be above the building
blocks of blood and soil with which Western and Arab nations had
been constructed and by which their people had become walled off
from one another.

> Our essence is not bound to any place . . .
> Neither is our heart of India, or Syria, or Rum,
> Nor any fatherland do we profess except Islam.

That fatherland was rightfully governed by what he called the
'Muslim political constitution'. This was a somewhat illicit construct, which slid between notions of law and character. It had two
pillars, one of which was a belief in the 'absolute equality of all the
members of the community'. Because of this belief in equality, Iqbal
held that the 'best form of Government for such a community would
be democracy' – though not Western democracy, based as it was on
counting numbers, and for which he had nothing but contempt. It
ended up trying, he said, to extract the thought of 'one man from the
brain of two hundred donkeys'. Nor did he have time for the version
of secular democracy that Nehru and others envisaged: the other pillar of Iqbal's political vision was that 'the law of God is absolutely
supreme'.

A spiritual democracy, Iqbal wrote, was the ultimate aim of Islam,
designed to solve the problem of 'how the many can become One
without sacrificing its plural character'. Indeed, Iqbal felt his political vision *was* Islam, which he convincingly maintained was not a
private religion but what he called a 'polity': 'a social structure regulated by a legal system and animated by a specific ethical ideal'.

Bound by love among equals, it was a polity that could transcend materialism and national borders, infusing the entire world, he wrote in one of his verses, with the 'the light of God'.

To achieve this enlightened community, Iqbal sought to transcend the dogma that had encrusted Islamic thought and practice. He challenged the strict literalism of the ulema's interpretation of the sharia and instead endorsed 'the freedom of Ijtihad . . . to rebuild the law of Shariat in the light of modern thought and experience', imagining legislative assemblies that would exercise this freedom collectively, through a process of scholarly consensus. The truth of the Qur'an, unfolding through history, must be left open and available so that 'each generation, guided but unhampered by the work of its predecessors, [is] . . . permitted to solve its own problems'.

It has been said that Iqbal saw Islam as the only alternative to the two other ideological systems dominant during his lifetime: nationalism and communism. But for Iqbal, who wrote that 'Islam itself is Destiny, and will not suffer a destiny', it had a sort of history-ending inevitability.

Though his profoundest hope was for a global Islamic society, his immediate proposal was for a federated India in which Muslims would have a territorially unified, semi-autonomous state where they could freely enact his Islamic polity. India's very diversity, Iqbal believed, could make it the paradigm of such a society. Its Muslims were not all Arabic, or all Turkic, but also Bengali, Andhra, Punjabi, and more. If they were able to 'sink their respective individualities in a larger whole' in favour of an Islamic moral consciousness, and if they were given their own territory, Iqbal believed that Muslims – who already formed a significant part of the military – would in turn defend the rest of India.

Iqbal's vision inevitably brought him to loggerheads with those, including the British government and the Congress movement, whose aspirations for India did not extend to an ideal Islamic polity. Partly as a result – although he died almost a decade before Partition – Iqbal's work has often been read as an argument in favour of Pakistan. This is not quite right; as the journalist Aakar Patel has wryly put it, Iqbal authored 'the thought that produced Pakistan' but wouldn't want his byline on the country itself.

Today, that Islamic republic, far from the dream of a polity founded on fearless self-determination and love, and even of submission to the law of God, is arguably one of the world's great oppressors of Muslim individuals and communities (to say nothing of ISIS). Of course, India can also be a harsh, alienating, even deadly home for Muslims. But, in his pursuit of poetic unities, perhaps what Iqbal missed was that a messy, multi-religious democracy, backed by a secular constitution, even in a Hindu-majority society, might – just might – be a better bulwark against the horrors of Western modernity, and a better buttress for the practice of a loving, energetic Islam, than a state devoted to upholding a single creed.

Though he defended a relatively strong conception of individual judgement in the form of ijtihad, for Iqbal freedom was, in the end, possibly too redolent of the devil's party. If his ideal democracy was to function, individuals would have to abjure an open-ended freedom in favour of submission to the law of God. Iqbal's political beliefs, rooted in his poetic vision, asked his co-religionists to trust in one another and in their leaders. But in politics, trust beyond a certain point becomes credulity. Men are not angels, and government is necessary.

In India, where the argument over the relationship between religious identity and the state has been constitutive of the country's politics, there was recognition, after 1947, of the need to create democratic institutions. Suspicion and mistrust had to be built into the Constitution; citizens could not entrust themselves to one another's moral goodness, let alone to the moral qualities of their leaders. Keeping the debate alive has on balance given individuals of all religions more freedoms than a homogeneous Pakistan has managed. In India, too, people now wish to bring that argument to a close: to replace the ruckus of politics with the moralized ideology of Hindutva. But as Iqbal himself said, man and society are like a wave: 'When I am rolling, I exist,/When I rest, I am no more.' What would it mean to bring the argument to an end? As the devil suggests of the falcon, such unity would signal death.

36
Amrita Sher-Gil

This is Me
1913–1941

'God please save me from the magnetic pull of this journey.'
Amrita Sher-Gil, 1933

From van Gogh to Dash Snow, an artist's premature death may impart a bankable aura, especially if the persona of the corpse is as compelling as the canvases. The painter Amrita Sher-Gil – twentieth-century India's first art star – became a prized commodity when, after a convention-flouting life, she died under shrouded circumstances at the age of twenty-eight. When the artist **M. F. Husain (49)** later noted her standing as 'the queen of Indian art', it was not without a certain edge; while alive, Sher-Gil was sometimes belittled by male contemporaries as merely an ambitious provocateur. '[R]ather self-consciously arty,' noted the journalist Malcolm Muggeridge, with whom she had a brief, intense affair – a line that to my ear begs the question, what else can a working artist be? To me, her glamour and her tragedy are footnotes – if substantial ones – to the fact that she could really paint, and remains one of modern India's great depicters of the jagged and imperfect self.

Frustrated by notions, like that of 'the masses', that blotted out individuality in society, Sher-Gil paid particular attention throughout her career to the poor, from Hungarian gypsies and Parisian consumptives to Indian peasants. But she believed firmly that it was the art, not the subject, that mattered most. Drawing on Western artists like Cézanne, Gauguin and Brancusi, from Indian ones like the Ajanta fresco painters (see **1 Buddha**) and from the Indian tradition of miniature painting, particularly in the Pahari style (see **20 Nainsukh**), she managed to do something doubly radical within India: to declare her own vision vital in the history of art, and to do so as a woman. Thus she endowed successive generations of Indians with something scarce in the culture: an example of an autonomous, creative female.

While some women artists and writers struggle in the well of depression before finding a voice, Sher-Gil worked from a seemingly innate belief in the validity of her first reactions. '[Y]ou will say that I am a self-opinionated monkey, but I stick to my "intolerant" ideas and to my convictions,' she wrote to her mother when she was twenty-one and already gaining recognition. Reflexively truthful and intellectually curious, she made her work to satisfy herself.

As usual in India, her gift was enabled by privilege. The daughter of a sophisticated Sikh aristocrat, she developed as an artist with the aid of her Hungarian mother, whose own artistic enthusiasms had devolved, after marriage, into parlour entertainments. Raised in both Hungary and India, Sher-Gil's skill with a brush was refined in Paris, and early on she chose women's sensuality, labour and relationships with each other as her subjects. Her many early self-portraits, often nude, would prove important images for others, too – made, as they were, in a time when women's lives and feelings (including erotic feelings) were systematically shamed and denied.

'You can take those stories if you like, and you can run with them,' the prominent contemporary artist Bharti Kher says about the many tales and myths that encircle Sher-Gil's life,

> But you have to look at the work. It's essentially very powerful because she was a powerful woman, but still, she allowed her own vulnerability to come through ... In the self-portraits, you see in her eyes a deep longing. She has a search in her, and she wasn't afraid to show that, to actually show her body, to expose herself as vulnerable. To say, 'I'm naked. I'm here. This is me.'

> *'Poor little bride, you little know that perhaps you might live only a year. You are doomed and yet you don't realise ...'*
> Diary entry of Amrita Sher-Gil, aged twelve,
> on observing a wedding

For all her sensitivity, even as a child, to the difficulties inherent in the lives of women, Sher-Gil saw herself as a member of no group and was known to slag off other women artists as 'sentimentalists' lacking 'passionate souls'. Nor was she interested in being a role model or cultural hero. 'Pomposity or exhibitionism' is how she dismissed exemplary stories of important figures in a letter to her friend Jawaharlal Nehru. So it's an irony that, as her fame grew after her death, she became so much an icon that some of today's artists find her an oppressive, almost establishment figure.

Sher-Gil inherited from her parents both an artistic sensibility and a temperamental unconcern for the censorious reactions of conventional people. Her father, Umrao Singh, sometimes forgot his own controversial past when berating his daughter for shaming the family. A close friend of Muhammad Iqbal (35), Singh was a Sanskritist, philosopher and photographer of sometimes risqué subjects in experimental styles; he also maintained a radically anti-British politics that swung between socialism and Tolstoy-style anarchism. Meanwhile, his emotionally troubled wife, Marie Antoinette Gottesmann-Erdobaktay, loved bourgeois luxuries and was given to great public dramas. To offend was as natural in Sher-Gil's childhood as to draw.

Precocious and acutely analytical from a young age, she spent her first seven years in and around Budapest, and endured the First World War in a cultured milieu where she was both the subject of art (her father's photographs) and a maker of it. The contemporary artist Shilpa Gupta sees a superb draughtsmanship even in Sher-Gil's juvenilia, and believes she was well served, intellectually, by her plural upbringing: 'What sorts of choices do you make? Where do you belong? Are you local, are you international? In terms of the family she's born into, by default she's born into a situation where she could pick and choose what she was interested in.'

As Hungary after the First World War suffered partition, economic collapse and violent extremism, Sher-Gil's father repeatedly petitioned the British, who were nervous about his underground political alliances, until the family was permitted to return to India. They settled in the British summer capital of Simla, in a house that was built for a viceroy. There, the family became prominent in the Indian equivalent of the Happy Valley set: her mother at the piano of an evening, singing Rimsky-Korsakov, her father taking photographs. When she was about eleven years old, Amrita won her first prize – fifty rupees – for a painting. Before long, she would be assuredly telling her parents that she was giving up her many other talents to focus on the one in which she could be great.

Her art was erotic and dark from the beginning. Barely twelve, she painted a woman enraged, her filmy gown rent to reveal bare breasts, a dagger clenched in her fist. Each time I see that painting, I change my mind about whether the dagger is bound for someone else's heart, or for her own.

Another painting from her early adolescence shows a nude young woman on a bed, turning away from a Christian cross. Sher-Gil developed an intense distaste for European Catholicism, along with a love of Italian Renaissance masters, after her mother pursued a paramour to Florence, with Amrita and her sister in tow. Lodged in a convent school she found repressive, Amrita was relieved when the affair ended and they returned home. '[A]ll art, not excluding religious art, has come into being because of sensuality: a sensuality so great that it overflows the boundaries of the mere physical,' she later wrote to a friend.

Her mother saw that Simla wasn't the place for an artist as ambitious as Amrita. So at sixteen, after her atheism got her expelled from a Simla convent school, she became the rare Indian girl whose family dropped everything to bring her to Europe to study art. At Paris's École des Beaux-Arts, under the low-key tutelage of the post-impressionist painter Lucien Simon, she continued to explore erotic themes, as well as the relationships between young women.

The artist Krishen Khanna, now in his nineties, says Parisian studio-based training made a deep impression on Sher-Gil's work. As the students painted models or arrangements of objects, the relationship between the eye and the hand became vital. 'The communication, the correlation, between the two is very important in European painting,' according to Khanna, 'whereas in India you see something, you brood on it, it stays in the mind, and distortions happen there.'

In 1932, three years after arriving in Paris, Sher-Gil painted her first large canvas, the boudoir-set *Young Girls*. Its composition and mysterious tension remind me of Balthus, although in Sher-Gil's hands the knowing intimacy of two girls – one with golden tresses, déshabillé; the other neatly dressed, dark hair slicked, a bowl of cherries on her lap – feels natural rather than voyeuristic. The acclaim for this picture made Sher-Gil the youngest, and some say the first Asian, painter to be elected an associate of the Grand Salon. But her intense work in these years was occasionally interrupted by personal trauma.

Vivacious and sought-after in artistic and intellectual circles, she contracted venereal disease from a Muslim aristocrat whom her increasingly unstable mother had considered a prospective son-in-law. Sher-Gil's cousin – and lover – Victor, who was training in medicine, was summoned to treat her and then to perform an abortion. Around this time, she sent him a series of letters that seem almost written to herself, one of which focused on what she called her parents' prophecy: that because of her rude, ungrateful, isolated and otherwise 'odious character', she would find no happiness in love. She saw already the difficulty of reconciling a life of painting with stable companionship. 'But little by little,' she said in another letter, 'I realize that every person carries within herself a calling against which it is hopeless to fight.'

Bharti Kher sees in Sher-Gil's teenage work the struggle of a young woman 'desperately trying to understand her own body and her own sexuality through her own painting'. Shilpa Gupta dwells on the way she treats the body:

> It's very still, but it's not over-romanticized. There's a kind of objectivity to it. There is space, the outlines are very thick. The object blurs. I like that style in Cézanne's work, and I feel a bit of that is in Amrita's work: you can look at the object from the outside. The inside is there, in any case, but there's an external part to it.

For all Sher-Gil's love of Cézanne, Brueghel and Gauguin – particularly the latter's ability to rework the archaic in contemporary ways – at the age of twenty her interest in Europe and its culture started to wane. 'I began to be haunted by an intense longing to return to India,' she later recalled. Her father discouraged her from coming back, in part because her free sexuality would bring shame to the family, and in part because he felt her knowledge of Indian culture was shallow. But this was just the goad she needed. 'Modern art has led me to the comprehension and appreciation of Indian painting and sculpture,' she protested in a letter home. 'It seems paradoxical but I know for certain that had we not come away to Europe I should perhaps never have realized that a fresco from Ajanta or a small piece of sculpture in the Musée Guimet is worth more than the whole Renaissance!'

Before long, confident to the point of intoxication in her Indian project, she was dismissing every other Indian artist of the age. 'Europe belongs to Picasso, Matisse, Braque and many others. India belongs only to me,' she would say in a famous provocation in 1934. Only when revisiting the wall paintings at Ajanta's caves did she feel genuinely silenced by the tradition she had re-entered. She wrote to her parents, 'I have for the first time since my return to India learnt something from somebody else's work!'

> 'It is slightly irritating to be always labelled as a "great promise" ...'
> Amrita Sher-Gil, 1937

Sher-Gil once wrote that she responded artistically to sadness more than to contentment and joy, but the best of what she made of that response in India was not sad. Among my favourite of her Indian paintings is *Haldi Grinders*, a late work – though late is an odd term to apply to a woman who died at twenty-eight. In flat, bright colours, and with brilliant sensitivity to the fall of light, she paints a scene framed by dark trees: women at work, pulverizing turmeric. An old woman dozes in the background; a young girl, in the foreground, is clad in bright red. Faces can barely be discerned, though there's eroticism in a flash of painted toenails. The power of the painting resides in the physical posture of the women grinding, their tensile strength. The work the women do reveals their essences as individuals.

It seemed natural to her to be painting labourers, beggars and tribal women as she had earlier painted gypsies and consumptive art models. The work didn't sell, nor did it win over critics, and some later artists glimpsed in the paintings of humble Indians a touch of the empty European sentimentalism she claimed to abhor. Krishen Khanna dismisses one of her most celebrated paintings, *South Indian Villagers Going to Market*, as essentially 'a lie': her servants propped up in a studio so she could paint them.

In her own view, she was responding to criticisms of the Bengal School, which was led by Abanindranath Tagore and Nandalal Bose and inspired by folk art and Mughal miniatures, as well as by Asian traditions from Persian to Japanese. The Bengal School had dominated Indian art for decades and became after Independence the house style of the new nation. (Nandalal Bose would be invited to illustrate the text of the Constitution.) To Sher-Gil, the romanticism and over-complication of many of their paintings had a 'cramping and crippling effect on the creative spirit'. Much of what was depicted was not essential, she felt, and the overall impression was of empty 'shells' compared to the 'kernel' of ancient work like the Ajanta paintings, or frescoes she'd studied in south India in 1937.

The form and technique of some of the wall paintings in Cochin's Mattancherry Palace – 'the drawing perhaps the most powerful I have *ever* seen', she wrote to her sister – were driven by the anonymous artists' intense powers of observation, and their sculptor-like formal confidence. Copying them, she felt she'd discovered a lost treasure whose value was infinitely greater than the enduringly popular heavy oil work of the Raja Ravi Varma School, with its glossy portraiture, mythological figures and rubicund maidens on swings. *Bride's Toilet*, which Sher-Gil later called her 'best thing so far', was made in the following months, as part of what would become her famous 'South Indian Trilogy'. Intent on a new simplicity, and embracing the region's local colour palette, she struggled with the painting, finding flaws after she thought she had finished and reworking it substantially. But the scene, of a fair-skinned, melancholy woman in a deep red sari having her hair braided and henna applied to her palms, is a triumph of form, the thing Sher-Gil cared about most.

That she felt impelled from within was more necessary than ever now, for few collectors were buying her work. Malcolm Muggeridge, her transitory lover in the mid-1930s, was fascinated, as many before him had been, by 'her vivid, forceful, direct reactions to life'. But he also described the Amrita of this time – a woman not as successful as she felt she should be – as wearyingly petulant, egocentric and vain. When one or another of her paintings *was* recognized, she'd inevitably complain that it was the least interesting of the work that she'd done. Her frustration eased only slightly after an exhibition in 1936, in Bombay, gave her her first real critical success in India. Among her new champions was Karl Khandalavala, an influential critic and collector (not to mention a renowned lawyer) whose belief in the originality of her paintings would become her ballast in her final years.

By this point, with her parents' finances in decline, she found herself making a 'sugary' self-portrait in hopes of getting paid portrait commissions from 'that rotten paper', the *Illustrated Weekly of India*. In 1938, she finally married her cousin Victor, now a doctor with an uncertain career. She chose him because she had nothing to hide from him, and could live the artist's life she wanted. The choice unhinged her mother. After having invested heavily in the cultivation of her daughter's talent, Marie Antoinette considered it Amrita's duty to find a wealthy husband.

Unwelcome in the family home, Sher-Gil and Victor moved between cramped quarters in Hungary and India, in search of a base for Victor to set up his medical practice. During this stretch of dislocations and tension, she could no longer reliably turn to her brush as a lifeline. Blocked artistically, she occasionally lashed out at Victor for his merely perfunctory interest in her work. Whatever the cause of her sapped inspiration, it was a true blow to a woman who had for a lifetime painted almost as she breathed.

Her plaintive letters from this period seem to be those of an exhausted artist in mid-life crisis. It's shocking to recall that she was only in her twenties. A stay in Saraya, a village in the United Provinces, helped her recover her instinct to paint. Against the appreciation of labour evident in the *Haldi Grinders*, I often recall one of her more celebrated but troubling works: that of an idle, languorous woman on a charpoy, hand lying inertly on her belly as a servant fans her.

In the autumn of 1941, Sher-Gil and Victor finally decided to settle in Lahore, where an earlier exhibition of her work had caused a sensation in the lively artistic community. Before the year's end, though, she died suddenly at home, under Victor's care, as a result of either food poisoning or a botched abortion.

Bharti Kher mourns the fact that Sher-Gil survived what are often the most arduous years for a woman artist – finding her identity as a young woman in a patriarchal art world, and then achieving some stability in her family life – but failed to reach the sustained period of focused creativity that the second half of a woman's artistic life often allows. Sher-Gil was denied the chance to come into her own.

Some say she had a premonition of her early death, but I'm sceptical. All serious artists consider mortality. In her last works, though, I sense a new respect for the power of nature. In *Elephant Promenade*, the background has the formality of a Mughal miniature: a courtyard, white chattri and ramparts. But coming implacably towards this man-built world are elephants. It's as if they are herding the brightly dressed folk who ride and tend them, not the other way around, as the sky shivers on the verge of a violent storm.

37
Subhas Chandra Bose

A Touch of the Abnormal
1897–1945

In a backwater town 300 miles from Calcutta, a bright, protected eight-year-old boy caught no echo of the popular agitation against the Partition of Bengal, which prompted the Swadeshi movement in 1905. But by early adolescence, his insulation from the world had become thinner and he was cutting out newspaper pictures of Bengali revolutionaries and tacking them onto the walls of his home. His father, a minor servant of the Raj, nervously tore them down.

'I had in some respects a touch of the abnormal in my mental make-up,' Subhas Chandra Bose admitted later. You can see it in a letter to his mother, written when he was fifteen: 'Will the condition of our country continue to go from bad to worse – will not any son of Mother India in distress, in total disregard of his selfish interests, dedicate his whole life to the cause of the Mother?' Not long afterwards he became a freedom fighter whose patriotism Gandhi himself would term 'second to none'.

Bose built such a formidable political base in the Raj's most populous province, Bengal, that from his mid-twenties British officials were extending their usual backhanded tribute to an Indian's political influence – detaining him at His Majesty's Pleasure again and again. Once, to remove him from circulation, officials sent him to Mandalay; another time he was shipped off to Europe. But in the summer of 1940, for his eleventh incarceration, the two-time President of the Congress was holed up in Calcutta's grim Presidency Jail. Among the few amenities granted him was access to radio and newspapers, through which Bose followed the dramatic developments of the new war in Europe.

Paris had fallen to Hitler's armies, and that summer Britain teetered on the edge, as the German Luftwaffe bombarded British airfields, ordinance factories, and whole cities. Bose found himself thrilled and inspired. Gandhi and Nehru had been pressing towards freedom too demurely, in his view. To turn the distant vulnerability of Britain to India's local advantage required action, not passive resistance. To expel the British once and for all, Indians should collaborate with Mussolini and Hitler.

Britain's enemies were no abstraction to Bose. During his European exile, in the 1930s, he had befriended Nazi officials and met Il Duce. Bose was a man of immense self-belief, who thought he could persuade the totalitarians to help him gather troops and direct, from Europe, the decisive war for Indian independence. First, though, he had to get out of this jail. Fortunately, as a regular tenant of such institutions, he had learned that the system could be manipulated. If his health was at stake, he calculated, the British might transfer him to internment at his home. At this fraught moment in the freedom movement, the British didn't want heroes perishing in prison. 'The blood of the martyr is the seed of the church,' Bose wrote to the authorities, invoking Tertullian to tell them he was going on a hunger strike. Within a week, the agitator had been shifted to house arrest at his three-storey Calcutta mansion, ringed by multiple layers of security.

Bose and his family discreetly analysed the movements of the armed guards, waiting for a window of opportunity. Just after midnight, on 17 January 1941, he pulled off one of the boldest political escapes of the twentieth century. Swapping his owlish, black-rimmed signature spectacles for an old pair, and donning a false beard and fez, he jumped into a waiting car in the disguise of a Pathan Muslim merchant. He was in Peshawar, heading for Kabul, before the British had realized he was gone. Then it was on to Moscow and, in a second disguise (as an Italian businessman), to Berlin. Now he could seek out Hitler, raise an army, and start a war.

In the four years that followed, Bose's life would have as many twists and turns as the caper that brought him to Berlin. But it would end in failure: death in a plane crash, just days after the surrender of his final ally, Japan.

George Orwell felt the world was well rid of him, rating Bose as a quisling comparable to the French politician Laval, whose Vichy government welcomed the Führer. But Bose, who had been driven by magical thinking, also inspired magical ideas in others. Outside India, the reputation he had gained seemed decidedly off: a man who sought to work with the Nazis, and who later chose to fight alongside the Japanese Imperial Army, rates today as a national hero, his name affixed to airports, schools and stamps. The vitality of his hold on the national imagination is manifest in other ways too: after his death he was periodically 'discovered' alive – as a prisoner in a Soviet concentration camp, as a Chinese military officer, or as an Indian sadhu, a holy man with miraculous powers. It took three official commissions, the last one in 2006, to certify that he actually died in 1945.

Nor did Bose's influence on India's international choices cease with his death. Enduring lessons of his war – about political realism, great power strategy, and India's place in the hierarchy of states – were absorbed and implemented by India's first prime minister, Jawaharlal Nehru, and by his diplomatic adviser, **Krishna Menon** (44), to produce a more subtle Indian stance towards the world.

When Bose's father named his ninth child Subhas, meaning 'one of good speech', he wasn't imagining that the boy would apply an oratorical gift to fervent radicalism. But in Bose's telling, he was changed by the work of **Vivekananda** (28), whose teachings of sacrifice, service and religious scientism he encountered as a teenager. While his parents' household tried to keep a cordon sanitaire around popular politics, this aspect of the era's cultural revivalism couldn't be kept out. When he moved to Calcutta to attend Presidency College, he could more freely follow his interests. He read German idealist philosophy and Henri Bergson, and came directly to politics through the works of the spiritual nationalist Sri Aurobindo Ghose. Aurobindo, twenty-five years older than Bose, was a hero of Calcutta's radical youth. He had abandoned the Indian Civil Service to become a leader of the Swadeshi movement until, disillusioned by its moderation, he turned to plotting terrorist acts. 'It was in the voice of

Aurobindo,' Bose later said, 'that we heard the message of political freedom for the first time.'

Aurobindo and other Bengali thinkers made Bose confident in the face of British racial arrogance. In 1916, having retaliated physically against a British professor's maltreatment of a classmate, Bose was chucked out of college. Still, after getting his degree at another college, he travelled to the dark heart of England to cram for the Indian Civil Service examinations. It was his father's idea, and while he derived some pleasure from the experience – 'Nothing makes me happier than to be served by the whites and to watch them clean my shoes,' he wrote to a friend – he resigned from the Service just weeks after securing a coveted post.

'Life loses half its interest if there is no struggle – if there are no risks to be taken,' he wrote to his brother Sarat, before returning to India in 1921. Fortunately for him, he was stepping into a new phase in India's history, defined by Gandhi's invention of Indian mass politics and marked by disillusionment with the Raj's post-World War policies. He'd have no shortage of interesting struggles – with the British, and with **Gandhi** (38) – from now on.

'No taxation without representation' had been the banner of another historic anti-British uprising. In the years following the Treaty of Versailles, 'No loyal service without representation' was the Indian equivalent. One million Indians had served the British in the First World War, during which they were treated as second class, and now it rankled that they had no more say than before in the decisions of the colonial government. The freedom movement, led by Gandhi, who had loyally run an ambulance unit in the war, gained momentum.

Gandhi liked to call the Congress a family, with all the internal tensions the term implied. He was, of course, the father surrogate – a slightly embarrassing, dictatorial one in the opinion of Bose, who joined the party in 1921. As much as he admired Gandhi's ability to enthuse huge crowds, he was infuriated by the older man's religiously inflected speech and habits, his love for artisanal simplicity and, above all, his willingness to compromise with the British. 'The younger generation in India are all impatient,' he told a German admirer in 1930s Berlin. 'They think with me that Gandhi is too good – too moderate – in his ideas and actions. We want a more radical and more militant policy.'

In Nehru, Bose initially found an ideological brother: committed to socialism and industrialization, to secular politics, and to building India's international profile as a progressive state – and also, Bose thought, in a hurry. In the late 1920s, the two emerged as the voice of a new generation in Congress. Until then, the organization had demanded from the British only Dominion status – equal to the settler colonies of the Commonwealth, such as Canada and Australia. Over Gandhi's objections, Bose and Nehru got the Congress to dedicate itself to the cause of full independence for India, which included sovereign powers over military affairs.

But virtually no other pre-independence Indian leader, including Nehru, considered hard power as essential as Bose. He hadn't fought in the Great War – his bad eyesight rendered him fit only for a student defence force, where he developed an abiding taste for uniforms and parades – but he took what he saw as the conflict's lesson to heart. 'The war had shown,' he wrote, 'that a nation that did not possess military strength could not hope to preserve its independence.'

Even in the years when he was closest, emotionally, to his Congress colleagues, this difference kept him somewhat aloof. In a photograph taken at the 1928 Congress session in Calcutta, amidst a rank of party leaders dressed in Indian styles (kurtas and dhotis, sherwanis, turbans and Gandhi caps), stands what looks like a well-decorated officer of the Japanese Imperial Army. It's Bose, in the jackboots, jodhpurs, buckle, cap and baton that – in addition to his spectacles – would become his trademark. The outfit evoked the combat he longed for but had not known. It would take another war for the costume role to become real.

In 1942, Joseph Goebbels, the Nazi chief of propaganda, made an excited if somewhat under-evidenced entry in his diary: 'Bose's appeal has made a deep impression on world opinion.' Bose, now in Berlin after scarpering from his Calcutta house arrest, had just given his first shortwave radio broadcast, telling listeners in India and elsewhere that the 'enemies of British imperialism are today the natural allies of India'. He added, 'we shall heartily cooperate with all those who will help us in overthrowing the common enemy.'

What had happened in the 1930s to drive him here? Bose, who wasn't a Nazi, recognized that Germany might be 'fascist or imperialist, ruthless or cruel', but he was desperate for action after a decade of jail, exile, incrementalism and Congress infighting, which had given him a taste of power and then withdrawn it. He'd had enough talk of non-violence and passive resistance.

Bose had broken formally with Gandhi in 1933, co-authoring a political manifesto urging the Congress to find a new leader, a new principle and a new method. Gandhi responded in the way he did to most of his occasional challengers: asphyxiate the opponent with compassion and accommodation, then bring him back into the fold. When Bose finished a prison stint in 1937, Gandhi arranged his election as Congress president, at a moment when Indian political representation had markedly increased. In the middle part of the decade, Britain had expanded the Indian franchise six-fold and created eleven elected provincial assemblies with legislative powers. By 1938, Congress had formed governments in seven of these.

With these legislative levers in Indian hands, there seemed to Bose to be a genuine chance to pursue his political agenda – to press for sovereign powers, industrialization and population control. But his leftist calls for land reform and labour rights had unsettled the big landowners and industrialists – men like G. D. Birla – on whose support Gandhi and Congress depended. That year, Bose won re-election despite Gandhi's opposition, but in 1939 Gandhi orchestrated his removal, describing him in one letter as the Congress family's 'spoilt child'. Bose, militant as ever, was further sidelined by another stint in prison, where he was appalled, if not surprised, by Gandhi's pacifist reaction to the Second World War.

Bose believed that, after his private war expelled the British, Free India would achieve a historical synthesis of Fascism and Communism, the two progressive currents of modern times. Installed in Berlin, he admired German discipline and planning, especially its ability to strike with lightning military speed. But what he couldn't see, through his patriotism and self-belief, was that India's insignificance as a global entity was part of the reason his war had not yet begun.

He had intended to cull troops from around 15,000 Indians captured by the Germans, but so far only a few thousand captives agreed to join his Free Indian Legion and swear allegiance to Hitler and himself. Meanwhile, he waited for Hitler to meet with him or declare his support for Indian independence. Instead, Hitler invaded Russia in June 1941 – a disaster for Bose's plans. As Bose knew, in a war between Germany and Russia, Indians would side with Russia, whose ideology was more attractive to a poor, colonized people. His hopes of marching by land across Afghanistan and to India evaporated.

So where did that leave Bose in Berlin? Instead of leading a beautiful struggle, he was a minor propaganda tool: Lord Haw Haw with a Bengali accent, a role he was tiring of but would have to endure for another two years. A visitor to his hotel room in the summer of 1941 found Bose sitting in the lotus position, deep in gloom, peering down at a map of the world. His eyes swivelled to Japan.

To get to Japan undetected, the only way was under the seas. He convinced the Germans to put him in a U-boat for half the journey, then transferred mid-ocean to a Japanese submarine. British intelligence was following the craft as it powered towards Tokyo, but chose not to intercept it. They were after bigger fish, and didn't want to reveal to Japan that its code had been broken. Bose had escaped again. His new incarnation was leader of the Japanese-supported Indian National Army. This time, his troops awaited him: Indian prisoners of war who had been captured when the British garrison of Singapore fell in February 1942.

The following year, Bose launched his new campaign: *Chalo Delhi* ('Onwards to Delhi'), an echo of the sepoys' cry of 1857. The Malay peninsula contained a large Indian diaspora, and an ornately uniformed Bose toured it in an open-topped Dodge, addressing vast audiences, raising money and recruits, his men intimidating and occasionally torturing those who denied him. The destitute agricultural workers who joined him became known as 'rice soldiers'. He also raised a several-hundred-strong women's regiment, named after the Rani of Jhansi (see 23 **Lakshmi Bai**). Overall, his army grew to somewhere between 30,000 and 50,000 fighters – men and women who probably didn't realize their charismatic, uniformed leader had no military experience at all.

By now, India had become a prize in the war, and interest in Bose increased accordingly. For the Axis powers, the conquest of India would enable the Japanese and German military theatres to come much closer to connecting. For the Allies, with the collapse of Britain in South East Asia, holding onto India was vital; it was a base from which to provision Chiang Kai-shek in China, guard supply routes up to Russia, and otherwise hinder further Axis expansion.

Back in India, the entire senior Congress leadership was in jail. Gandhi had rejected British entreaties to support the war, instead launching the Quit India movement in 1942 – a collective 'do or die' effort to throw the British out. The arrests aborted Gandhi's satyagraha, or passive resistance, and left Bose, for now, the only freedom fighter standing – on Japanese-held soil. He declared himself the head of Azad Hind, an Indian government in exile, and began planning his future state, from provincial structures and taxation down to table manners. He envisioned battling his way to India, and taking control, in about a year. His arguments helped convince the already over-extended Japanese to push into India from Burma, through Arakan and across the Imphal plain. When he reached Bengal, he told them, he would be able to incite a revolt that would destroy the British Empire.

But Bose's blindspot had travelled with him. Here, as in Berlin, he was less a leader than a persuasive power to be exploited. Although he imagined his army spearheading the campaign into India – according to the historian and strategic analyst Srinath Raghavan, Bose 'insisted that the first drop of blood which should be shed in the course of the offensive should be Indian' – the Japanese considered his soldiers poor fighters, useful primarily for building and repairing roads and bridges, and carrying supplies. Only a modest 'Bose Brigade' was allowed at the front, while operational command remained with the Japanese. With Bose sidelined in Rangoon, his soldiers – poorly supplied, poorly equipped, then split between battalions – now marched towards the worst land defeat ever suffered by a Japanese army.

Even as Bose's soldiers succumbed to death, disease, starvation, desertion and defection to the British, they didn't quite extinguish his hope of governing India. Congress leaders were now free, negotiating again with the British and Muhammad Ali **Jinnah** (39). Bose understood there was no going back to the family – unless, just maybe, he approached the problem from a different direction, with the help of another great power.

The fascists having failed him, he decided to escape to Soviet Russia. A few months later, just days after the Japanese surrender, and with the Soviets now also at war with Japan, he boarded a plane heading for Russian territory (exactly where remains unclear). But as it took off after a fuel stop in Taipei, it crashed and burned.

If Bose is today regarded as the most formidable military leader of the nationalist movement, it's because he was the only one. Nationalist hagiography abhors a vacuum. But the historical record shows no particular gift for military strategy or leading troops; instead, he possessed courage, moral myopia, and a capacity for outlandish reinvention that rivalled his nemesis Gandhi's whenever faced with an impediment to the goal of independence. He was a single-minded instrumentalist, in pursuit of great powers to serve his ends, but underestimating always the peripherality of his goals to their own.

Nevertheless, his unpredictability became a tangential pressure in the British decision to resume negotiations with more moderate leaders instead of keeping them imprisoned. A wild-card warrior like Bose made a Nehru seem as manageable as a houseplant. And so, in this way, Bose enabled the final thrust towards a freedom he would never see.

But India may have benefited even more broadly from its own renegade Trotsky. Bose's years of arguing against the conventional wisdom did much to clarify the thinking of his Indian opponents. And his decision to partner with two of the titanic powers of his time – with the Soviets seemingly next – helped entrench a post-independence resistance to military pacts and great-power alliances.

Nehru had been dismayed by his old friend's pact with the Nazis, saying, 'It is a bad thing psychologically for the Indian masses to think in terms of being liberated by an outside agency.' As he followed Bose's course from Berlin to Tokyo, Singapore and Rangoon, he saw the strategic shortcomings too. The concerns of a poor, militarily weak nation didn't really rate in the eyes of the leading powers. In any divergence of values or goals, the interests that prevailed would not be India's.

That scepticism – the inverse of Bose's magical thinking – was turned into policy when Nehru became the first prime minister, giving the life of Bose one of the great ironic codas in modern Indian history. In the end, the convinced aligner and advocate of hard power helped underwrite independent India's commitment to the accumulation of soft power and to staying resolutely non-aligned.

38
Gandhi

'In the Palm of our Hands'
1869–1948

Gandhinagar, the capital of Gujarat, is named after the region's most famous son, Mohandas Gandhi – the Mahatma. It's a new, well-planned city, spacious, with good infrastructure, and some years ago I happened to watch a film there about the plot to kill Gandhi. As the screen assassin pumped bullets into Gandhi's body, the audience erupted into wild applause and cheers.

In many parts of the world, Gandhi is virtually a saint, an icon who transcends political and national divisions. In 2015, a hundred years after Gandhi began his campaign against British rule in India, a statue of him was put up in London's Parliament Square. He seems to be gazing almost idly at the buildings from which the world's largest empire was run – the one he helped to bring down.

Protect me from my friends, flatterers and followers, Gandhi once said. But these days he has as many foes, especially in India. Hindu right-wingers, whose glee I heard that evening in the city that carries his name, despise him as an appeaser of Muslims, and blame him for India's Partition. Others regret his induction of Hindu rhetoric and symbols into Indian nationalism, revile him for his refusal to disavow caste, believe he betrayed the labouring classes, and are appalled at his views on women. Modernizers and advocates of Indian hard power dismiss his anti-industrialism and pacifism.

It is right that Gandhi should have enemies, and unsurprising that he provokes so many angles of attack. I can't imagine he would have expected otherwise. He never saw himself as a model. He saw himself as an incitement. His entire life was an argument – or, rather, a series of arguments – with the world. That life stretched across three continents, and a third of it was lived outside India. It also spanned the most murderous decades in human history: Gandhi lived through the Boer War and the suppression of African rebellions, through two World Wars, and the Partition of the Indian subcontinent – with some personal experience of all of them.

Gandhi's eccentricities make it hard to get his measure. It's clear to me that he was a political figure who ranks beside a very small number of his contemporaries: Lenin, Stalin, Hitler and Mao – men who remade the modern world. Except that Gandhi, unlike the rest, chose to try through non-violence. Also unlike those men, Gandhi never commanded a state, and his leadership of the Indian national movement was episodic. He was at the centre of agitations, or led negotiations with the British, only for brief periods: from 1920 to 1922, when he launched his first Indian civil disobedience campaign; during his Salt Satyagraha of the early 1930s; and in the years leading to his final mass protest, Quit India, in 1942. Each of these mobilizations was followed by spells in prison, and in between there were long periods when he retreated to one of his several ashrams.

Yet in a society with no history of large-scale collective action, where politics was for most a domain of distant and spectacular power, Gandhi made people believe that they could make a difference. He built a movement, shaped a nationalist imagination, and expanded the world's repertoire of dissent, protest and peaceful disagreement.

His achievement in part had to do with the force of his own personality: Gandhi had a voracious appetite for self-improvement (however quirky), an openness to experiment with ways of living, and a remarkable imperviousness to embarrassment. He was a quick assimilator of elements from other cultures and traditions, repurposing them to express himself in direct and startling ways.

His impact also had to do with the nature of his opponent. British imperialism justified itself in terms of a liberal ideology of constitutional government and the rule of law. But the Raj, though cloaked in British ideals, was premised on the routine use of draconian 'emergency' powers and coercive force to control dissent and opposition. Gandhi became a master at revealing the faultlines and contradictions of the liberal imperial state, subverting its pretensions and showing it to be a violence-dispensing machine.

There was a third element too: his command of the media, Indian and global. Europe and the subcontinent became linked by the telegraph just around the time of Gandhi's birth, and his life coincided with the rise of a new type of political power – public opinion. In the West and many parts of Asia, as states raced to amass military might, they also recognized the need to develop methods of propaganda. Gandhi became a master of using his own image, body and words to shape global opinion in a way that undermined imperial self-justifications.

What would India be if Gandhi had not lived? It would still have gained independence from colonial rule, but it would have taken a more violent and divisive path, leaving legacies yet more bitter than they are today. Gandhi made himself into a unifying ideal for Indians, established discussion and negotiation as the way they did politics (though he'd resort to coercive fasts unto death when negotiations weren't going his way) and did much to lessen their sense of victimhood.

The India he left behind remained a flawed place. It is true that he did not abolish untouchability. But he did delegitimize it. It is true that he failed to bring about unity between Hindus and Muslims. But he did make many Indians feel shame when religious violence and killings occurred. Unlike a Stalin or a Mao, who tried to change the imagination of their people by wielding state power, Gandhi used imagination to try to change the nature of power and the state.

The most famous modern Indian might not have become famous if he had stayed in India. His years abroad, especially two decades in South Africa, enabled him to break free of many social conventions, to explore different kinds of intimacy, and to build political associations across religious and caste divides. He would draw upon this experience to invent, back in India, a different way of doing politics.

When Gandhi arrived in Bombay in January 1915, an Indian politician described in a letter to his brother the impression he made: 'modest downward face and the retiring speech', with 'one front tooth missing on the left side'; eating only 'queer food' – no salt, milk, ghee – just 'fruits and nuts'. To most who met him in those early days of his Indian homecoming, the forty-five-year-old Gandhi was an oddity. He didn't exude the glamour of power. 'I should have passed him by in the street without a second look,' a viceroy later said of him.

Gandhi was born in 1869 and raised in relative privilege. His father served as a senior official in several of the small princedoms of western Gujarat – though the family was of the Bania caste, a trading community an order below the Brahmins and Kshatriyas. That subordinate position made Gandhi sensitive to social rank and power and aware that his own rank was not much to exploit.

Breaking the rules of his caste against travel abroad, he decided as a nineteen-year-old to go to London to qualify as a lawyer. In his two and a half years there he revelled in a freedom that led him to discover vegetarianism, the Bhagavad Gita, and the Victorian ethic of self-help. But he failed to master a fear of public speaking and, unable to establish a legal career in India, accepted a brief that took him to South Africa in 1893.

There, he befriended Muslims and Parsis, European Jews and Christians; worked with Chinese, Tamils, lower castes and indentured labourers; and emerged as the leader of Indian immigrants who used political lobbying and peaceful resistance to fight against racially discriminatory laws. He came to believe that he could see the world from the bottom up, that he understood the oppressed and could speak for them. This became a powerful source of his own self-belief, though it was never as well founded as he liked to put about.

Throughout his time in South Africa, he never made common cause with Africans, who were subject to far worse discrimination than any Indian was. His own racism was to blame, compounded perhaps by caste-derived reflexes that he never escaped, however long or far away he was from India. His efforts went into getting Indians classified and treated differently from Africans – to improve their position within the racial hierarchy, not to do away with the hierarchy altogether. If that required showing loyalty to the British Empire, he didn't shirk from it. Signing up as a stretcher-bearer when the

British crushed a Zulu uprising in 1906, he wrote: 'It is not for me to say whether the revolt of the Kaffirs is justified or not.' It's an instance of the limits of Gandhi's vision, a sign of how his convictions could slide into dogmatism and prejudice. In India, that dogmatism would alienate some of his interlocutors, notably Muhammad Ali **Jinnah** (39) and Bhimrao **Ambedkar** (41), with immense consequences for the country's history.

Far more radical than his public politics were his experiments in living, which led him to dispense with that bedrock of Indian society, the family. Gandhi loved domesticity, but despised the family. It's not just that he didn't much care for his own. He came to see the family in general as a carrier of caste and religious bigotry and as the progenitor of material acquisitiveness. So he set up communal farms that became laboratories for new types of domestic relations, and tried other inventive ménages, including some with men only.

Gandhi had tried several times, from South Africa, to join Indian public life. When he was finally able to return to India in 1915, he pledged to his mentor, the liberal Congressman Gopal Krishna Gokhale, that he would observe a year's political silence as he reacquainted himself with the country. Travelling across India, he saw how distant the power of the state was from the lives of most Indians, and also how divided the society was by caste, language and religion. He began to search for ways to bridge divides in a society saturated with signs of discrimination – to find causes and symbols that could unify.

He started with clothing, an immediate marker of community identity. (The politician who described Gandhi immediately after his arrival in 1915 – before he began his dress experiments – went on to tell his brother that Gandhi was 'dressed quite like a bania'.) Gandhi spent months pondering his headgear, trying turbans in all styles, before inventing the Gandhi cap; he rid himself of garments down to the bare minimum, thereby conveying asceticism, but even more importantly communicating a social neutrality, a degree-zero of caste, religious and regional belonging.

This was a new way of being Indian, and he combined it with new ways of doing politics. Gandhi, in the early years of his return, tested his methods of boycotts and peaceful resistance in the Indian countryside, leading agrarian protest movements in Gujarat and Bihar. He recruited to his cause local politicians who later served him well in his effort to control the Congress party. He conciliated a textile workers' strike, which gained him the trust of industrialists and businessmen like Ambalal Sarabhai, who began to subsidize him. With these resources, he built himself up in the Congress, coming to dominate the fractious party, and reorganizing its structure and membership to expand it beyond its core of English-speaking elites.

For all his radicalism, Gandhi remained loyal to the Empire for the duration of the First World War. But that loyalism was shattered in 1919 by the shooting in Amritsar of unarmed men, women and children who had gathered to protest against the continuation of draconian wartime detention powers. What particularly outraged Gandhi and others was the refusal by the British authorities to punish the officer who ordered the killings. Gandhi was ready now to take the battle to the British.

As it happened, in order to build his first national campaign of civil disobedience, he seized upon an issue quite remote to India. Victorious in the First World War, the Allies were negotiating the break-up of the Ottoman Empire, which would end the Ottoman sultan's rule over Mecca and Medina and bring about the collapse of his Caliphate. Muslims in India and across the world were outraged. Gandhi decided to pledge Congress support to the movement, led by conservative Muslim *maulvis*, to preserve the Caliphate. He convinced Hindus across the country to unite with their Muslim brethren, to the horror of liberals within the Congress, including Jinnah, who feared that Gandhi was releasing religious passions that would be impossible to retire. Nevertheless, Gandhi managed, for a brief moment, to bring together Hindus and Muslims. He had begun to unnerve the Raj – and he was doing it through non-violent confrontation.

In 1897 in Durban, Gandhi was beaten bloody by a white mob that had planned to lynch him. In 1908, in Johannesburg, he was assaulted by a group of Pathans. During the decade between these attacks, he read Tolstoy on passive resistance and began his experiments with the practice he later called satyagraha – 'truth force'. But he really started to think deeply about violence after encounters with young Indian terrorists and revolutionaries.

In 1909, Gandhi travelled to London on one of several visits to lobby the cause of South Africa's Indians. The city had become a way-station for disaffected young Indians. (Just before Gandhi's arrival, an Indian student had shot dead a British Indian Army officer in South Kensington.) Gandhi made it a point to speak with these radical nationalists – he met 'every known Indian anarchist' in London, he later said – including the Hindu-nationalist ideologue V. D. Savarkar. He became fascinated by their schemes and plots, and admired their willingness to die for the cause of India's freedom, but was troubled by their readiness to kill. He began to muster arguments against what he later called this 'Indian school of violence'. That, in turn, led him to a critique of modern society and civilization, which he articulated in a short, burning text written in an eye-blink on the boat back from Britain to South Africa, in 1909 – *Hind Swaraj*, or *Indian Home Rule*.

The book took the form of a dialogue between an Editor, representing Gandhi's views, and a Reader, representing the views of a nationalist warrior. 'We will assassinate a few Englishman ... we will undertake guerrilla warfare, and defeat the English,' says the Reader, who argues at another point, 'As is Japan, so must India be – we must own our own navy, our army ... then will India's voice ring through the world.'

This was exactly the path that so many twentieth-century anti-colonial and nationalist movements would take, exactly the ambition that would animate so many new nations and their peak-capped leaders. Gandhi resisted it. 'What is granted under fear can be retained only so long as the fear lasts,' he told the advocates of violence. What they were fighting for was a free India in the pale image of other nations – not true swaraj, merely 'English rule without the Englishmen'.

'What we need to do,' Gandhi went on to say, 'is kill ourselves.' He liked to argue by inversions and reversals of commonplaces; this is one of his most puzzling and provocative. In a counter to the terrorists, eager to kill in order to challenge the state's sovereign power over life and death, Gandhi proposed the figure of the satyagrahi – the trained non-violent resister, who, by his or her willingness to die, subverted that power. By asserting control over his own life and death, the satyagrahi was able to possess a different, more intimate kind of sovereignty – over his own person.

Violent rebellion could always be easily suppressed in India, as it was during the uprising of 1857. The balance of coercive power lay with the British. But Gandhi's conception of non-violent action was not merely a tactical one. He was making a fundamental point about power's dependence on legitimacy. It's not just that the more powerful could retaliate against the less powerful by the use of force, and do so more effectively; it's that they were always in a position to justify the use of retaliatory force. 'The show of violence always gives the privileged group, the holder of power, the opportunity of using a much more potent weapon than any military force,' the German-American theologian Reinhold Niebuhr noted in a perceptive essay on Gandhi in 1931. 'That force is the identification of its own interests with the necessities of law and order.' Niebuhr recognized that Gandhi was waging a battle over beliefs, the ultimate source of power. Gandhi was delegitimating power – robbing 'the privileged group of its moral pretensions', as Niebuhr put it.

Niebuhr's essay was written in the wake of Gandhi's most famous act of non-violent resistance – the Salt Satyagraha of 1930. It's often held up as an exemplary instance of Gandhi's spontaneous, even naive style – a testimony to his sheer determination. But Gandhi didn't just lead the campaign. He managed it down to its minutest detail, making brilliant use of a new instrument for shaping belief: the global media.

In the spring of that year, Gandhi came to Dandi, a small village on the Gujarat coast. He had walked at the head of a band of followers for twenty-four days, travelling some 200 miles from his ashram near Ahmedabad. The reason for the march? To pick up a handful of salt from the sea shore, so defying a British tax on the substance. Gandhi would later say that the decision to make salt the focus of his agitation was a flash of inspiration.

Perhaps. Gandhi recognized that the British Empire, and especially the Raj, was, in the words of nineteenth-century British observers, an 'empire of opinion'. In weeks of meticulous planning for the campaign, he set about reinventing an ancient practice, the pilgrimage, for the modern media age.

The seventy-nine marchers who accompanied him were each chosen and vetted by Gandhi himself. He wanted a small enough number for him to personally manage the procession; a representative from each part of the country; and marchers who were dedicated but relatively unknown – no political colleagues who might dilute the attention centred on him. He carefully designed their outfits – no political insignia or markings were allowed: he wanted his satyagrahis to convey a timeless, elemental quality – and made sure that he was the only one to carry a stick. To secure the vocal support of townspeople and villagers along the route, he dispatched his lieutenants to visit stopping points in advance and rustle up excitement.

He did all this because he had also arranged for the world's press to come along, and he wanted to minimize the unexpected. In the weeks before the march, he invited journalists, both Indian and foreign, to his ashram on the banks of the Sabarmati river. He allowed them to write up what he said at his public prayer meetings, and also in his private conversations with visitors and ashram members. Gandhi used the prayer meetings to build the drama, telling his listeners that for the marchers this would be their last fight. Meanwhile, in the audience, mill-owners mingled with the poor and lower castes so that Gandhi could convey the breadth and unity of his supporters. The journalists dutifully took it all down, then published it internationally.

Most importantly, Gandhi invited photographers and film crews to accompany him on the trek to Dandi. They did so, in motor cars. The jiggly footage they shot of Gandhi's fast-paced walk – he quickened his stride at certain strategic points – was seen across the world. The image of the Mahatma striding across the dusty plains ahead of his band of followers was now burned into the imaginations of millions: the tiny stick man with teapot ears, showing up the imperial blimps. Some months later, *Time* magazine drew him for their cover.

Annie Besant, c. 1897.

Kappalittiya Thamizhan (*The Tamil Who Launched a Ship*), 1961, a Tamil film celebrating Pillai's achievements.

Srinivasa Ramanujan, 1919.

Rabindranath Tagore in Japan, 1916.

Muhammad Iqbal, c. 1930.

A still of Thanthai Periyar (and his Brahmin-repelling
pet dog) from the 1960s.

Amrita Sher-Gil, *Self-Portrait in Green*, 1932.

Satyajit Ray directing Sharmila Tagore and Soumitra Chatterjee in *Days and Nights in the Forest*, photographed by Nemai Ghosh, 1969.

M. F. Husain, *Self-Portrait with Horse*, 1995.

He was cleverly shown studying a newspaper, reading perhaps of his own exploits.

Swaraj, Gandhi had written in his 1909 book, lay 'in the palm of our hands'. It was another of his arresting inversions. For those committed to using violence, freedom lies in the capture or destruction of a distant object, the state. But Gandhi challenges us to shift our attention away from the state. That's not because he is essentially an anti-political thinker, a moralist, as many think. It's because his view of politics was expansive.

Gandhi saw the modern state as a usurper of duties that we as individuals should rightfully retain. We had lost the capacity to restrain and control our own desires; we were no longer masters of ourselves. That breakdown created the necessity for an external apparatus of control: the state, with its concentrated powers of coercion, its calculus of law and punishment.

According to Gandhi, terrorist revolutionaries and constitutional nationalists laboured under too narrow a conception of politics, obsessed as both groups were with the state. For them, freedom was a goal in the future, achieved either through the violent capture of state power or by gradual entry into government through electoral means. Instead, Gandhi wanted us to see freedom as something there to be seized in the present moment, through everyday activities that had nothing to do with the state – by spinning thread to make your own cloth, gathering your own salt, tending your own health, resolving your own conflicts. These were fundamentally political acts that could restore Indians to mastery over their habits of mind and body, and so give them freedom.

There's something solipsistic about this conception of freedom, but it's also a challenging one. It asks us to think of a politics beyond the imaginative confines of the state. Politics had become all-pervasive and inescapable, entrapping us 'like the coil of a snake', Gandhi said. If politics pervaded every aspect of our lives, it also meant that our most intimate acts had political significance. Gandhi didn't renounce politics, he redefined it.

*

To make politics intimate was a form of power against an empire built on distant majesty and intimidating impersonality. The march to Dandi to pick up a handful of salt showed that it was possible for an individual to stand up to power by a simple act. It was an act of political enchantment that made politics personal again.

But it was also an act of provocation – and not only to the British. Gandhi's assassin, Nathuram Godse, a Brahmin from the Pune region of Maharashtra, was directly inspired by the ideas of Savarkar, the young terrorist and ideologue of Hindu nationalism with whom Gandhi had argued with in 1909. Godse was angered that Gandhi, with his 'eccentricities, whimsicality, metaphysics and primitive vision', his 'childish insanities and obstinacies', was nevertheless able, as if by magic, to mobilize hundreds of millions of people. Gandhi's movement might succeed or fail, Godse said, 'but that could make no difference to the Mahatma's infallibility'; Gandhi had become 'formidable and irresistible'. And his actions, Godse believed, had fed the demands of India's Muslims, leading to India's holy territory being split into two.

In the weeks before Godse pulled his gun, there were several attempts on Gandhi's life – including, just ten days earlier, a bomb attack at one of his Delhi prayer meetings. Gandhi knew there was a conspiracy, yet he refused extra precautions. He told those assembled at his prayer meetings that, even if a bomb were thrown into their midst, they must not budge. I want to keep saying the name of Rama, he said, even if there is shooting around me. And that is exactly what he did when, on the evening of 30 January 1948, Godse shot him dead.

39
Jinnah

The Chess Player
1876–1948

In his lonely teenage years in London, apprenticed at a trading firm while precociously reading for the Bar, Muhammad Ali Jinnah steeped himself in British liberal democracy. Days off from the office were spent at Hyde Park listening to the soapbox speechifiers, or to Gladstone at the House of Commons. It was cheaper than his other favourite diversion: Romeo, Hamlet and the Shakespearean lot at the Old Vic. Still, had some prophetess informed this anglicized budding lawyer – a person with no religious convictions whatsoever – that he'd spend the final years of his life creating the world's first and largest Islamic state and becoming its Quaid-i-Azam, or Great Leader, he might not have laughed. He was fashioning himself for political achievement.

As a young man, Jinnah vaguely shared the idea that would be an article of faith to Gandhi, Nehru and the national movement: that India was a single civilization containing within it many varieties of belief. But by the late 1930s, as president of the All-India Muslim League, he had come to fear for the prospects of minorities – like his own – in a post-imperial and democratic India. British India's Muslims made up a quarter of the subcontinent's population, forming the largest body of their co-religionists anywhere in the world, and dominated five of the country's eleven provinces. But Jinnah doubted that they would share equally in the new freedoms of an independent India.

In 1939, Jinnah told the *Manchester Guardian* that it was 'impossible to work a democratic parliamentary government in India', where the bulk of voters were 'totally ignorant, illiterate and untutored, living in centuries-old superstitions of the worst type, and thoroughly antagonistic to each other, culturally and socially'. The following year, he went further. India isn't really a country, he wrote to the man he saw as his rival, Gandhi. 'It is a sub-continent composed of nationalities, Hindus and Muslims being the two major nations.' A few months later, he unfurled that view at the Muslim League's general session in Lahore, in a speech that electrified Muslims across the subcontinent and would build to the most momentous decision taken in 300 years of British rule over India.

On the morning of 3 June 1947, before a phalanx of photographers, Jinnah, in a white linen suit and striped tie, posed around a table with Nehru, the Sikh leader Baldev Singh, and the Viceroy of India, Louis Mountbatten; behind them was a map of India, shortly to be divided. The photo opportunity had come after months of bargaining. Now, they publicly assented to a partition that, carried out in haste, would give roughly half of India's Muslims political autonomy, cause around a million deaths, displace some 14 million people, and transform the geopolitics of the world – a decision that has, in the opinion of the historian Perry Anderson, 'a good claim to be the most contemptible single act in the annals of the Empire'.

No one around that table was blameless for Partition, but that the subject was on the table at all was down to Jinnah. Like Lear dividing his kingdom, he saw Partition as a form of inoculation – 'that future strife/May be prevented now'. Scholars today still argue over why this was so. Some say he was forced into this position after failing to secure a liberal India in which Muslim rights were protected. Others believe a liberal Islam, in a separate society, was his true desire. That he didn't get what he wanted either way – that's obvious. Less obvious, perhaps, is the kind of leader Jinnah was trying to be.

In social background and cultural habits, Jinnah was what the Oxford historian of India, Faisal Devji, calls 'multiply marginal'. British India's 70 million Muslims, spread as they were from the North-West Frontier to Assam, from Kashmir down to Kerala, were the world's most diverse group of Muslims. They encompassed all the major theological schools and sects, from syncretic Sufis to purist Wahhabis. They ranged from the big landowners of the northern

United Provinces to landless labourers in Bengal, from highly literate to uneducated. Jinnah's family were Ismaili Khojas, a sect of Shia Islam known for its liberal and pragmatic views, and considered little better than heretics by many of the Indian subcontinent's dominant Sunni Muslims.

It was only in Jinnah's lifetime that India's Muslims began to have a sense of themselves as a single community – but, ominously, one relegated to the status of a minority by the new political language of numbers. Driving this new self-conception was the juggernaut of the Raj's knowledge project. Beginning with the first decennial census in 1871, officers of the Raj surveyed towns and villages, frequently encountering people who thought of themselves as simply belonging to local sects, or others who were comfortable worshipping at temples and shrines as well as mosques. The instrumentalities of the modern state have a low tolerance for ambiguity, though. For enumerative purposes, the census asked individuals to caption themselves more abstractly: Hindu, Christian, Sikh or Muslim. So plural identities narrowed and became countable; and people began to have a sense of themselves as belonging to either political majorities or minorities.

Jinnah grew up far from the heart of British India's coalescing Muslim politics, which lay with the Urdu-speaking landowners in the United Provinces. Shortly before he was born, his father, an unsophisticated but ambitious trader, moved from Paneli in today's Gujarat to the port city of Karachi. Politically marginal though Karachi may have been, the place was booming after the opening of the Suez Canal in 1869. Jinnah's sister Fatima recalled that even on the playground, shooting marbles, Jinnah had a sense of importance and superiority. He would take it with him, aged sixteen, to London.

During his London apprenticeship, Jinnah learned of the death of his beloved mother in childbirth, and the start of the collapse of his father's business. Around this time, he began, almost theatrically (for this was a teenager who longed not just to see Shakespeare, but to play the hero before the audience), to craft a new sense of self. Studying the lives of important English public figures, he realized many had legal training. Though it angered his father, he began to study law. He changed his name from Jinnahbhai, a Gujarati form, to Mr Jinnah and, in 1896, became the youngest Indian to be called to the British Bar.

Upon returning to India, Jinnah abandoned Karachi for Bombay. In the words of his sister, 'He wanted to discover himself on the highways of eminence and fame.' Wearing bespoke suits, speaking cut-glass English, smoking languidly, and even eating pork, he became a familiar sight in Bombay's elite clubs, where he cultivated legal clients and mixed easily with the city's Hindus, Parsis and Christians. This distance from orthodox Muslim practice wasn't something he viewed as illicit. This was Bombay, after all. And this was his career. Although some accounts say he was the only Muslim lawyer in the city, he wouldn't have the fame he sought if he settled for a Muslim-only practice.

Politically, however, Jinnah would eventually come to represent Muslims alone. That he didn't stand for any one of the major sects or regions actually served him well, permitting him to position himself as spokesman for all India's Muslims. In 1904, he joined the Indian National Congress, which from its inception had thin Muslim support. (Of almost 14,000 delegates who attended the annual Congress gatherings between 1892 and 1909, less than a thousand were Muslims.) Jinnah promptly aligned with the moderate, constitutionalist wing of the party associated with Gopal Krishna Gokhale. Both men believed in gradual, negotiated reforms, not boycotts or radical action against the British, and in 1910 both were elected to the newly created Imperial Legislative Council, another step in the Raj's piecemeal invitation to Indians to enter the portals of self-government. Entry to the council was by separate electorates, whereby different religious groups and some caste groups voted for candidates drawn exclusively from their own communities. Jinnah, elected as the Muslim member from Bombay, was still holding that seat in 1946.

One of around only fifty Muslims in the Congress, and already distinctive in his political style – sporting a monocle, for instance, in imitation of Joseph Chamberlain – he set himself to be a bridge-builder between India's Muslims and the Congress party. By 1916, it seemed to many that he had achieved that. Working with **Annie Besant (29)** and with the extremist Congress leader Bal Gangadhar Tilak, Jinnah secured a historic agreement between the Congress and the then small Muslim League, which had been formed a decade earlier by a group of conservative notables and landowners from the United Provinces and Bengal. (Jinnah had joined the league in 1913, while remaining a member of the Congress.) The Lucknow Pact, as it became known, guaranteed separate electorates to Muslims and political representation slightly in excess of their population size. It embodied the kind of constitutional deal-making that Jinnah excelled in, and also gave him the approving audience he'd longed for.

With the Congress and India's main Muslim party now pledged to work together to further self-government, Jinnah, at the age of forty, seemed set to become a major figure within Congress nationalism – the leader to fill the gap left by Gokhale, who had died the previous year. But 1915 was also the year that Gandhi returned to India, ready to protest in defiance of constitutional limits and use religion as a way to bring Indians together.

Gandhi built his first popular movement in 1920 by shrewdly adopting an issue peripheral to the primary agenda of Indian politics but important to many Indian Muslims. The defeat of the Ottoman Empire, and subsequent negotiations by the Allied powers over its future, gave reason to fear that the Ottoman Sultan would be deposed and his overarching Muslim Caliphate abolished. Indian Muslim religious leaders had launched protests against the British to demand the Caliphate's preservation, and Gandhi decided to throw the support of the Congress behind what became known as the Khilafat movement, hoping he could in return cull Muslim support for his party.

To Jinnah, this was a provocation. It undercut his own efforts to broker constitutional agreements between Muslims and Hindus and weakened his role as the 'Ambassador of Hindu–Muslim Unity'. To Jinnah's lawyerly and constitutionalist way of thinking, it also changed the standing of Muslims in the political process. In the nationalist cause, he saw Hindus and Muslims as contracting parties – abstract political entities, each with equal rights, entering into an agreement almost as if they had the status of nations. And hadn't Muslims dominated the Indian ruling classes for over 500 years, before the British? Yet here was the non-Muslim Gandhi appealing to Muslims in their full religious being, participating with them in a religious movement – methods which Jinnah thought diminished Muslims' power. Defined as a political category, he believed, Muslims could claim at least an equal status; but if defined as a religious community, Muslims in India would always be numerically second – the 'largest minority'.

Through his Khilafat movement, Gandhi established control over the Congress at the party's annual meeting in 1920, a meeting one Congressman found akin to a 'religious gathering celebrating the advent of a Messiah'. When Jinnah, hoping to voice his dissent against Gandhi's strategy, stood to speak, he was shouted down and booed off the stage. He quit the party within the year. By the end of the decade, unsure that his own style of liberal constitutionalism had a future with the Congress and uncomfortable in the orthodox conservative milieu of the Muslim League, he had returned to London, concocting another self. He became the epitome of the successful London barrister: chambers in the City, mansion in Hampstead and a chauffeured Bentley in the driveway. Or maybe he'd be Achilles in the shade.

Early in his Bombay legal career, Jinnah, invoking the influential Congressman who had mentored both him and Gandhi, said he wanted to be the Muslim Gokhale. Gokhale's liberalism, like its Western counterparts, recognized minority rights and had a strong sense of injustice, but it also took community belonging and group identities seriously. Which Indian politician could ever afford not to? Jinnah had tried to reconcile this liberalism with Islamic thought and Muslim realities, until he decided it simply couldn't be done in his homeland.

For many of India's Muslim intellectuals and educated classes, the prospect of an undivided India governed through democratic institutions had long been a source of anxiety. The theoretical axioms of Western liberalism bristled with warnings for a multicultural society like India. 'Free institutions are next to impossible in a country made up of different nationalities,' John Stuart Mill had written in 1861,

' . . . each fears more injury to itself from the other nationalities than from the common arbiter, the state.'

You can sense Mill's thought burning brighter in the minds of Muslim intellectuals from the late 1920s, as British-managed constitutional reforms advanced in response to growing nationalist pressure. Muslim intellectuals were also watching liberal democracy unravel across interwar Europe. As empires dissolved, groups suddenly defined as minorities became vulnerable to persecution, mass exile and death. Simultaneously, the language of nationalism spread, with groups claiming treatment as nations, deserving of their own states. The alignment of identity with territory seemed the answer to the problem of social differences.

Even the visionary **Iqbal** (35), who, with **Tagore** (32), was one of the sharpest Indian critics of European ideas of nationalism, began to advocate separate Muslim territories. '[I]t is necessary to redistribute the country and to provide one or more Muslim states with absolute majorities,' he wrote to Jinnah in 1937. But the concept of the state was highly unstable in Indian debate during these years and, in a letter the following month, Iqbal seemed torn between the idea of a 'federation of Muslim provinces' and that of a separate state.

Iqbal was writing in the wake of the most significant expansion to date of Indian self-government, achieved through a new, British-designed Constitution. The expansion, introduced in 1935, had convinced Jinnah to forsake London and return to India to head the Muslim League. Under the new constitutional arrangements, the British created provincial assemblies elected on an expanded franchise of some 10 per cent of the population, though voting still in separate electorates. The Congress, setting aside an earlier boycott, decided the terms were good enough to contest in the assembly elections of 1937. Knowing it had little Muslim support, the party signalled its willingness to form coalition governments with the Muslim League. But, in the event, the Congress won big and shelved the deal, forming governments in seven of the eleven provinces largely on its own (including in the Muslim-majority North-West Frontier). Nehru, speaking for Gandhi and many Congressmen, famously and perhaps fatefully declared that there were now only two political forces in the country, the nationalist Congress and the imperialist Raj.

Jinnah was left shocked and embittered. The liberal model that was supposed to protect minorities seemed instead to disenfranchise them. Neither constitutional features like separate electorates nor trusting in Congress had put Muslims in power, or even on an equal footing. With almost all the Muslim legislators on the opposition benches, the Congress looked exactly as Muslims had feared: a Hindu majority governing over a Muslim minority, even as it called itself plural and inclusive. If liberal theory was not workable in the conditions of the subcontinent's diversities, the way to make self-government possible, Jinnah began to think, was to change the subcontinent's frontiers.

'The Mussalmans were in the greatest danger,' Jinnah said in a speech to students at Aligarh Muslim University in 1938, explaining why he had come back from London. 'The majority and minority parties in Britain are alterable, their complexion and strength often change,' he went on. 'But such is not the case with India. Here we have a permanent Hindu majority and the rest are minorities which cannot within any conceivable period of time hope to become majorities.' Hindu governments might interfere in minorities' religious practices and laws – or worse – while doing little to support their economic and social interests. The only hope for minorities, he concluded, was 'to organize themselves and secure a definite share in power to safeguard their rights and interests'. That meant redefining Muslims as a nation that could make equal claims on the British and against the 'Hindu Congress'.

Jinnah was already wounded politically when he decided to raise the cry of danger in his Aligarh speech. In the wake of the Muslim League's electoral failure in the 1937 elections, Nehru was leading a mass campaign – a 'massacre' campaign, Jinnah complained – to win Muslims over to Congress by appealing to their economic interests. One prong of the campaign was to convey to the poor majority of Muslims that Jinnah and the rich landowners of the Muslim League didn't have their interests at heart.

Politics, Jinnah would often say, was a chess game: it had to be won with the pieces you had left on the board. Iqbal had warned him of the need to combat the 'atheistic socialism' of Nehru, and now, with greater regularity, Jinnah began to reach for the queen – religion. According to the historian Venkat Dhulipala, at this point Jinnah had 'no qualms in using religious ideology for his politics'. By 1937, having dropped his suits for sherwanis and a karakul hat (which came to be known as the 'Jinnah cap'), he was describing the Muslim League flag as a gift from the prophet. By the 1940s, he was publicly imagining Pakistan as a kind of Islamic state, with sharia law.

But his most influential statement – to the Muslim League at Lahore in March 1940 – played down any explicit religious appeal, in favour of the language of nationalism. He claimed that trying to fit Hindus and Muslims into a single state, 'one as a numerical minority and the other as a majority, must lead to growing discontent, and final destruction of any fabric that may be so built up for the government of such a state'. It was a direct echo of Mill's caution – and, taken up, it would produce the very violence about which Mill had warned.

In 1939, the provincial Congress governments had all resigned in protest after the viceroy took India into the war without consulting them. Then, from August 1942, the entire Congress leadership was imprisoned by the British after Gandhi launched his Quit India movement. In the political vacuum, Jinnah became the sole interlocutor between India's Muslims and the British. By the time most of the Congress leadership was freed, in 1945, Jinnah was established as the leader of all India's Muslims, and primed to be the man in the viceroy's study in the summer of 1947.

In the light of Pakistan's post-1947 history (its own partition in 1971, with the secession of East Pakistan, which became Bangladesh; the long dominance of the military; and the unending spread of religious sectarianism and violence) it's become common to say that Pakistan was from its inception a country 'insufficiently imagined' – or, as a sceptical American intelligence officer put it in a 1943 report, 'a kind of Muslim Never-Never Land, a fairy tale Utopia'. It's a view that takes support from historians who argue that Jinnah never intended to see India divided into two states, or to create Pakistan. He was engaged, they claim, in an elaborate endgame with the British and Congress, and used the demand for Pakistan as a psychological manoeuvre in order to secure guarantees for Muslim interests and more autonomy over their own affairs. An impatient Congress, hungry for power, called his bluff.

That argument has the merit of annoying both Indians and Pakistanis, since it makes the Congress leadership responsible for Pakistan. Yet it underplays the self-confounding rigour of Jinnah's intellectual project: his aspiration to a kind of liberal perfectionism, beyond the realities of social difference, which used religious feeling to forge national homogeneity. Jinnah was an idealist who thought he was a realist, suggests Devji: 'Jinnah seems to have had almost no sense of history, of memory, and of the possibility of trauma. He thought that one could just socially engineer this thing, and that people would forget.'

The history of the Indian subcontinent over the past century and more contains an encyclopaedia of identifications, from Shakta to Tamil to Syrian Christian to Deobandi to non-beefeater to LGBT, by which people have sought to act collectively. Jinnah's Pakistan was premised on the idea that there was one key identity: religion, which could lock in all the others. But even in Pakistan, created on the principle of religious homogeneity, Muslim or Islamic identities have always had to compete with other forms of identification, their relative attractions shaped by politics. East Pakistan's transformation into Bangladesh in 1971, and the continuing struggles of Baluchis and Sindhis to assert their cultural autonomy against a national Pakistani identity, bears this out. Even the effort to sustain a singular Muslim community has faltered, blown apart by the regular clash of sectarian groups.

And it's not just Pakistan: India, too, is hardly immune to ideologies that wish to cure it of its own internal differences, and that dream of a more perfect alignment of identity with territory. To many Indians today, living in a growing and increasingly world-important economy, the chasm that separates them from the country Jinnah conjured appears reassuringly unjumpable. But contrary to what Indians may wish to think, it's no protective moat. India can't fix Pakistan, but neither can it ignore it. It's not just that what brews in Pakistan bubbles up in India; it's that Pakistan remains a mirror to what India might have been, and might be – if it goes in search of a singular, neat national identity of the type that Jinnah believed he could master.

No religion, no nation, no community, no individual, even, is ever one. From the nation all the way down to the individual, identity is prone to be secessionist. Jinnah articulated one powerful strand in the dreams of modern nationalism: for homogeneity. But every dream of homogeneity stares at an infinite regress: there's always some aspect of identity, some sect, some culture or language, that doesn't fit. To pursue homogeneity is to enter an endless life of purging, secession and self-destructive violence.

40
Manto

The Unsentimentalist
1912–1955

For all the accounts I've read about the Partition of 1947, it is passages from fiction, not history, that thrum in the back of my brain when I try to fathom the depth of the loss. Perhaps the deepest thrums are lines from India's master of the short story, Saadat Hasan Manto.

The first startlement of the art of the great twentieth-century Urdu writer is that, when his lens zooms in, you feel the horror opening out. In 'Khol Do' ('Open It!'), an old man who has travelled by train to Lahore returns to consciousness after being assaulted. Through his frayed mind, Manto distils, in half a dozen words, twentieth-century South Asia's greatest nightmare: 'Loot. Fire. Stampede. Station. Bullets. Night.' This list is followed, chillingly, by the name of the old man's daughter, who is missing.

This brings us to the second surprise of the art of a Manto story: for all the velocity that his economy of language creates, the pressure of a story builds quite slowly. You're never quite prepared for the moment that blasts off the emotional roof. His sentences etch a groove in the mind not because he saturates his truths about atrocity in lurid colour, but because he delivers them off-hand, even elliptically.

Manto didn't fuss much over his sentences. He wrote in a rush, at hack speed, for money – and often legless drunk. His visceral response to experience matched a historical moment that needed it. In a divided country that Manto thought possessed 'too few leaders, and two many stuntmen' (one of many instances in which he jibes at ascetics like Gandhi), his sentences asserted, plainly, the human facts, not the moral or political motives that produced them. 'Don't say that a hundred thousand Hindus and a hundred thousand

Muslims have been massacred,' he writes in his story 'Sahai'. 'Say that two hundred thousand human beings have perished.'

The sensibility that Manto brought to that violence had been in the forge for years. He spent his childhood in Amritsar, where colonial brutality upturned his childhood. Young adulthood spent in the glitter and seediness of 1930s Bombay intensified his empathy, his cosmopolitanism and a sexual frankness that even multiple obscenity charges did not thwart. 'If you cannot bear my stories,' he once said about those charges, 'then this is an unbearable time.'

And it was, especially in 1947. As communities across the country broke up along religious lines, he was one of the roughly 14 million who made the wrenching decision to leave home for life in a new country – in his case, migrating from Bombay to Lahore. There, in his famous *Letters to Uncle Sam*, he developed a near-prophetic sense of what the future of Pakistan would look like, from the censorious mullahs to the military state.

But to construe Manto merely as a note-taker of the bohemian corners of a society, or as an eyewitness to Partition and the early years of Pakistan, slights the power of his style and his voice. He had the capacity to turn the heard phrase into aphorism, the seen moment into parable. In January 1955, a friend discovered him shivering in bed and rushed him to the hospital. The doctor on duty felt for Manto's pulse and said casually, 'You have brought him to the wrong place. You should have taken him to the graveyard. He is dead.' It could be a line from one of Manto's stories – tales that sprung immediately, unsentimentally, from life.

Manto claimed that 'I write because I'm addicted to writing, just as I'm addicted to wine. For if I don't write a story, I feel as if I'm not wearing any clothes, I haven't bathed, or I haven't had my wine.' We are the better for his compulsion, because although he churned out a lot that didn't hold up, he produced enough of quality to help underwrite the late twentieth-century blossoming of fiction in India and in Pakistan.

In the winding trek towards the creation of a free India, the most decisive single day was probably 13 April 1919. At Jallianwala Bagh,

Amritsar, protesters had gathered in anger at the arrest of two of their leaders, held under wartime detention powers that the British refused to rescind. Brigadier General Reginald Dyer entered with 140 troops and ordered them to fire. Hundreds of men, women and children were killed, and more than a thousand injured. It was a massacre that fundamentally changed the way a generation of elite Indians understood the intentions of the British – especially when an official investigation cleared the general of any wrongdoing. **Tagore** (32) returned a knighthood he'd been given; **Gandhi** (38) withdrew his loyalism to the Empire; Nehru and **Bose** (37) lost any dreams they had of serving the Raj.

Manto was seven years old when the killings devastated the city he lived in. His memories of the massacre inflected one of his earliest published stories, '*Tamasha*'. Tamasha – a trivial or foolish commotion – was the word the fictional boy's protective father used to explain away the gunfire they could hear from their house. The boy can't understand why they can't go and join the fun. From his window, he watches, bewildered, as another boy bleeds to death on his street.

The experience turned Manto vehemently against the British; as a teenage 'armchair revolutionary', he longed for the populace of Amritsar to take to the streets as if this were Moscow in 1917. His intense desire to overthrow the colonial rulers was a position that would have alienated him from his barrister father, had the two not already been estranged. His mother was the second wife, a woman of lower status and treated accordingly. Manto's anger at her treatment, and his own denigrated position in the family, may have seeped into the ironic, often cutting tone of his writing.

In 1936, after studying at Aligarh Muslim University, Manto left Amritsar for the more glamorous and squalid precincts of Bombay. It's telling that, less than twenty years later, hallucinating and with cirrhosis in a Lahore hospital, he believed he was back in Bombay – the place where he'd found his voice.

Bombay's middle-class Byculla neighbourhood is majority Muslim, and far less diverse today than it was in Manto's time. Then known as the Jewish quarter, it had Iranian cafés and Parsi chawls; it took all comers, including a financially strapped writer eager to explore the city's culture, high and low. 'You can be happy here on two pennies a day or on ten thousand rupees a day, if you wish,' Manto would later write of how the city beckoned him. 'You can also spend your life here as the unhappiest man in the world. You can do what you want. No one will find fault with you. Nor will anyone subject you to moralizing. You alone will have to accomplish the most difficult of tasks and you alone will have to make the most difficult decision of your life.'

Manto became a member of the Progressive Writers' Association, a group of leftist intellectuals who felt literature should engage more usefully, and politically, with contemporary life. But his Bombay writings were only obliquely political. To make a living, he hit upon the film world, a subject with enough popular appeal to just about support the wife he married after his arrival there, and later their children. Many of his sly weekly dispatches from the film line – recounting the naiveté of the actress Nargis, or the reclusiveness of the actor Ashok Kumar – hold up today. Funny, full of unexpected-ness ('In the beginning, he used to look like someone made of chocolate . . .') and acid with insight and gossip, this was hackwork of a high order.

He was also developing his fictional voice, having refined his skill in Amritsar by translating Chekhov, Oscar Wilde and Maupassant, that master-excisor of extraneous detail. Soon his own stories were creating a tamasha. In 'Bu' (Smell), for instance, a young man calls inside his house a much poorer girl who has been drenched in a sud-den downpour. With few words, he strips her of her soaked clothes and they have sex. He becomes transfixed by the smell of her arm-pits, her breasts and her navel – an erotic immersion so intense that later the memory would render him cold to his wife. The writer Aakar Patel, who calls the story 'the most sensual thing I have read in any language', came across it at the age of thirteen and was enrap-tured; many other writers will tell you first-encounter-with-Manto stories that are reminiscent of Keats on Chapman's Homer.

'Bu' inspired a judge to charge Manto with obscenity. Other obscenity charges would follow – but they seemed only to incite him to stretch the boundaries further. In addition to editing film week-lies, contributing to All-India Radio and writing screenplays, he kept producing stories of uncommon style and provocation.

Perhaps my favourite of the Bombay stories is 'Ten Rupees', an account – this one not erotic – of a child prostitute sent with custom-ers on a car trip, beautifully translated into English most recently by the writer Aatish Taseer. Consider the spare simplicity with which Manto conveys the web of relationships within the chawl where the exploited girl is growing up. In reference to a sad anecdote that the girl's mother tells her neighbours, he wrote: 'In any case, it didn't evoke any compassion for her in the chawl, perhaps because every-one there was also deserving of compassion. And no one was anyone's friend.' There's no pity here, nothing softening about life in a stress-ful, impoverished community. Rather, there's a felt sense of that world as it is to those who live there, transmitted with stunning efficiency. Like most of Manto's characters, the childprostitute is decidedly individual, finely realized instead of stereotyped – permitted both a sense of delight and dignity.

Stories like this one provoked readers on the left, just as stories like 'Bu' provoked conservatives. Social reformers thought his depic-tions of social ills like child prostitution should breathe outrage, and condemn more explicitly, while also proposing means of social cor-rection. But Manto, who couldn't fix his own slide into alcoholism, didn't presume he could fix society. No sentence he wrote could be mistaken for one in a pamphlet.

Sometimes, in the Bombay stories, we pull close to Manto himself. In one, a father is stricken by the sudden severe illness of his beautiful young son. Descending into paranoia and obsession, he exacerbates the panic of his desperate wife. As the illness worsens, he disappears – wilfully absent when the boy breathes his last. Manto, a vexing husband, was also a loving parent who lost his own son to pneumo-nia, and he wrote his harrowing fictional portrayal of parental love and paranoia with that history in mind. Here, as in his more explic-itly non-fiction writings, Manto avoids playing victim – or judge.

This helps explain why Manto, who had longed for freedom from colonial rule since childhood, shuddered at the movement incarnated by Gandhi. He had no use for Gandhi's moralism and sanctimony. Men's natures are often bad, in Manto's cosmos, but they can't long be denied. One of Manto's fictional descriptions of Gandhi's followers in the ashram showed men 'as blanched and lifeless as the udders of a cow from which the last drop of milk has been squeezed out'.

These joyless, self-denying men ultimately helped make India free, of course. But when that freedom came with Partition, the religious tensions that had begun to flare up during Manto's lifetime exploded. Religion was a garb he had always worn lightly – in Sikh Amritsar, in Bombay's Jewish quarter, among his seemingly infinite number of Hindu friends. In January 1948, he shocked many in his circle by choosing to go to the other side of the new border.

One long-time friend, with whom Manto had a falling out over Pakistan, wrote that his interests were base: he wanted to claim one of the nice Lahore houses from which Hindu families had fled. But it's also clear he was shocked by anti-Muslim actions at his day job at the Bombay Talkies film studio. If communal hatreds that had quickened on the streets were poisoning even this haven of sophisticates – breaking up old collaborators because of religions they barely practised – perhaps he felt the Bombay he loved was done for.

Joining his wife and children there, his drinking worsened, as did his tendency to pick fights with his wife. A close friend in Lahore noted that even though Manto was not pessimistic by nature, his private life was 'very bitter'. Personal distress mixed with political anguish, and his writing became more edgy and more haunting.

In late 1948 he published *Siyah Hashiye*, or 'Black Margins', a series of connected, pointedly arrhythmic fragments on Partition, some of which were only a few urgent sentences in length. None of the participants in violence is identified by religion, because to Manto the distinctions were arbitrary and the guilt had to be shared. This experiment in form, reflective of the shattering of a country, was followed by a longer story, about the psychological effects of committing rape, that brought him a new obscenity charge. In Pakistan the stakes of conviction were high: up to thirty-six months in prison. Manto, financially strapped, spent the next three years fighting the charge, and enduring police searches of his home and surveillance of his movements, before the conviction was overturned on appeal.

His work in this period was uneven, but some of it ratifies that cliché of prose, 'unforgettable' – even when you might wish to forget. In 'Khol Do', the old man eventually finds his daughter in a hospital – dying, barely conscious. When she hears a doctor request that a window be opened – 'khol do' – she reflexively parts her legs. The doctor, understanding the implication, is left in a cold sweat. And that's the end. Manto won't let a wall of words distance his reader from a terrible image. This had happened, this was life now, and it had to be confronted with realism, lacerating economy and black irony to be made endurable.

Manto was, by the early 1950s, barely enduring himself. 'This country, which we call Pakistan and which is very dear to me, what's my place in it? I haven't found it yet,' he wrote in an essay. 'This makes me restless. This is what has sent me sometimes to the lunatic asylum, and sometimes to the hospital.' What he hoped (and sometimes worried was merely delusion) was that he was making a name for himself in Urdu literature. But neither drying-out hospitals nor asylums could cure him of his thirst. So Manto's time in Pakistan proved not just miserable, but short.

After his death, at the age of forty-two, Manto's reputation attenuated. In Pakistan, he fell out of fashion for moral reasons, in India for punitive ones. Access to his work in India was diminished twice: first because he had fled, and then because Urdu, still the mother tongue of many north Indians, lost some of its literary prestige in the face of Hindi revivalism and policies of linguistic nationalism.

But sensitive readers and writers on both sides of the border kept his stories in circulation, aided before long by English translations, the best known of which were Khalid Hasan's somewhat sanitized versions. For many South Asian writers, the Partition stories, coming as swiftly as they did after the birth of two new countries, were important legitimations of the literary form. They instanced fiction's ability to capture with clear eyes immediate aspects of life in the two nations that the conventions of South Asian non-fiction and nationalist history obscured. Salman Rushdie, who himself brought Partition to life in *Midnight's Children*, rated Manto as unmatched in India in the form of the short story – an enthusiasm that helped Manto's reputation spread further in the West. Mohammed Hanif and other Pakistani writers also took up his cause. And in 2012, moral issues set aside, the civilian government of Pakistan commemorated his birthday. Today, as his popularity surges, and new translations clarify more of his technical and linguistic inventiveness, there's a risk that he will be seen in the twenty-first century as the *only* fiction writer of the Partition era. Manto, of course, would have liked that.

41
Ambedkar

Building Palaces on Dung Heaps
1891–1956

'A society, almost necessarily, begins every success story with the chapter that most advantages itself,' the American public intellectual Ta-Nehisi Coates recently argued regarding mythic constructions of liberation all over the world. '[C]hapters are almost always rendered as the singular action of exceptional individuals.' In modern India's myth of finally, formally confronting its brutal history of caste, Bhimrao Ambedkar is that exceptional individual. But every Great Man story is also a story of circumstance. Had India not been devastated by Partition, the formidable lawyer and scholar who led the untouchables might not have become the founding father most meaningful to ordinary Indians today.

It's almost unsayable, even among historians, that Partition was a boon to India's Dalits and other oppressed minorities. But I've long suspected it was so. India's largely upper-caste nationalist elite had patently failed to convince most of the subcontinent's Muslims to trust their future to an independent India. To prevent what they saw as a further stab in the back of national unity, they needed to convince lower castes and outcastes that *their* interests would be protected. The Constituent Assembly to write a Constitution for a free India began meeting late in 1946. Its debates are usually presented as a triumphal coda to the coming of freedom, but all through them you can hear a backbeat of regret and anxiety among privileged and soon-to-be-powerful men. Just after being empowered to make laws, they learned how hideously Indians could treat one another.

For Ambedkar, this time of elite self-doubt presented a moment he had been training for all his life. Born Bhimrao Ambavadekar, born incisive, born, in his own description, difficult, he grew up to become one of the most educated men in the India of his time. For two decades preceding Independence, he stood with his followers well outside the nationalist movement, condemning the Congress party as 'fools and knaves'. He found Gandhi's condescension towards untouchables, and his claim to speak for them, a manipulative strategy to keep them fighting on behalf of their upper-caste oppressors.

The equal rights of a minority shouldn't be a paternalistic gift from the upper castes, Ambedkar believed. This conviction led him to see much force in Jinnah's first hints, in 1940, that some form of partition was the way to protect the interests of Indian Muslims (see **39 Jinnah**). It also led him briefly to contemplate a territorial homeland for India's Dalits, and even a Dravidistan for the Tamil lower castes – an idea he discussed, in 1944, with **Periyar (34)**. But he moved away from territorial solutions as a way to protect the interests of minorities, and came to believe it might be possible to achieve this within the shared constitutional order of a united India. By the time talks between the Congress and the Muslim League finally broke down, in 1946, he angled to be one of 296 people elected from across the country to serve in the Assembly that would draft the Constitution.

At the time, he was just one of thirty untouchables elected to the Congress-dominated Assembly; he had only a small party behind him, and few real supporters among the Congress (not surprisingly: that 'fools and knaves' line was Ambedkar being polite). But as Partition made the protection of minorities one of new India's most important legislative issues, he wielded his superior policy and legal education to accrue power.

In his youth, Ambedkar had burned a copy of the Laws of Manu, the legendary Brahminic law-giver whose ancient decree was said to have created the caste order. Now he wasn't about to waste the chance to subvert that order by pressing into the Constitution the most sweeping system of affirmative action anywhere in the world.

What Ambedkar helped realize, in this fertile historical moment, has made him omnipresent in contemporary India: bestatued and bespectacled in a three-piece blue suit, Constitution in his left hand, right finger pointing upwards. In tens of millions of Dalit or Shudra homes, you'll find his face on a poster, painting or coloured tile – a protective household man-god. If to Indian schoolchildren he is the man who wrote the Constitution, to India's politicians he is a public emblem both of how far we've come in addressing the blight of caste, and how central the state and politics are to that rectification.

These readings simultaneously exaggerate and ghettoize Ambedkar's contribution. He was a sophisticated, long-sighted constitutional collaborator whose interests extended beyond caste to the very structure and psychology of Indian democracy. In a way, he was India's Tocqueville: not in aristocratic background, of course, but as a critic of the *ancien régime*, realistic enough to know that even a serious assault upon that regime (the introduction of democracy, the creation of a new legal order) would still leave alive the insidious limbs of past history, ready to nudge political action and policy away from their intended goals.

Ambedkar's unprecedented story of moving from untouchability to shaper of modern India has inspired a succession of 'firsts': first Dalit president, first woman Dalit leader, first Dalit millionaire, first Dalit billionaire, first Dalit woman wrestler. It's as if the very fact of those achievements changes the status of the average Dalit and scrubs away history. Instead, the gold plating around such 'firsts' makes it hard to recover such people as individuals. This was something Ambedkar thought about himself even at the height of his renown. 'If you want to write what I tell you about my private life in your biography I have no objection,' he informed his biographer with characteristic insouciance. 'I am also not worried whether people look at me in a bad way because of that.' As a scholar, he was at ease with complexity and attentive to particularity; and he might have chuckled at the popular sermon-book version of his life as a dutiful struggle from the very bottom of the pile.

Ambavadekar's Maharashtrian family was one of a small outcaste elect created by the preferences of the British. In addition to favouring elites such as the Parsis for government contracts, the Raj had pet service communities. Among these were the Mahars, a group who comprised two thirds of all the untouchables in western India. Historically, the Mahars' work was to clear street carrion and collect food scraps. The British found in their diligence and loyalty the ideal human material for military service.

Both of Ambavadekar's parents were of this military line, and both were educated, since the British afforded westernized schooling to the offspring of those who served the Crown. Bhimrao, the last of the couple's fourteen children, got this education too – an opportunity fewer than one in a hundred of his untouchable contemporaries had. His mother died when he was young, and afterwards his father, Ramji, supervised his education. The head of a military school in a garrison town in central India, Ramji would rouse his son at 2 a.m. to study for exams. Having known **Phule** (24), Ramji also taught his son to see untouchability – the label that translated in a young man's life to being barred from drinking from certain wells, eating with schoolmates, or studying Sanskrit – as an outrage to be challenged.

By his teenage years, the boy's intellectual abilities had drawn the attention of both a Brahmin teacher, who gave him the name Ambedkar, and the Maharaja of Baroda, a lower-caste Maratha eager to train gifted non-Brahmins to serve in his administration. The prince helped Ambedkar to attend Bombay's prestigious Elphinstone College and, after his 1912 graduation, to further his education at Columbia University in the United States.

Those New York years are often treated cosmetically in India, as if they primarily taught Ambedkar how to rock blue suits. But he acquired crucial analytic tools in America as well. From the historian James Harvey Robinson, he came to see history as a progressive movement, and from James T. Shotwell, an expert on labour and human rights, he saw how the expansion of rights could be the driver of that progress. From the philosopher John Dewey, he learned optimism about the capacity of democratic institutions to make more socially equal societies. More generally, from men like Booker T. Washington, he learned the value of compromise in order to secure what was most vital to free a disenfranchised people: education. So stimulated, he began an intellectual and political career that would evolve into a groundbreaking analysis of caste.

Although Ambedkar shared the British scepticism that India constituted a nation, at Columbia, seeing his homeland from a distance, he came to view India as possessing a cultural unity. But it did not lie in tolerance of diversity or accommodation of differences, as some upper-caste intellectuals liked to claim (see **28 Vivekananda** and **32 Tagore**); instead it was built on a foundation of oppression rooted far deeper than the political rule of the Raj.

He rubbished the argument that caste had a basis in the functional division of labour. Nor did he see caste as based on racial difference – as, for instance, in Phule's history of Aryan Brahmin invasions of Dravida lands. To Ambedkar, the caste system was generated by the exclusionary social and kinship rules of the Brahmins, and it spread because other groups, especially those lowest down the order, aped the Brahmins' precepts. They did so believing spiritual, social or economic benefits might come to them too.

This analysis would lead to a crucial insight: that the caste hierarchy was able to enforce itself with minimal physical coercion. It operated largely by voluntary submission, based on what Ambedkar described brilliantly as 'an ascending scale of reverence and a descending scale of contempt'. This kept at bay any concerted challenge to the system:

> All have a grievance against the highest and would like to bring about their downfall. But they will not combine. The higher is anxious to get rid of the highest but does not wish to combine with the high ... The low ... would not make a common cause with the lower ... Each class being privileged, every class is interested in maintaining the system.

Ambedkar's expansion of these ideas, in books, pamphlets and speeches, became not just a critique of untouchability, but one of the most consequential pieces of polemical scholarship of his times. In their combination of subtle analysis and raw, angry political expression, many passages remind me of the Italian Marxist Antonio Gramsci. But Ambedkar's political ideas, unlike Gramsci's, would survive him in the code of law.

By the time Ambedkar returned to India in 1923, in his early thirties, to call him the first untouchable to receive a Ph.D. would have done him down. He had also passed the Bar exams and was on his way to receiving a second Ph.D., from the London School of Economics (this time with the support of another lower-caste ruler, the Maharaja of Kolhapur). But if his economic, social science, policy and legal training outmatched the elites he was about to contend with (what American minorities refer to as the requirement that they be 'twice as good to get half as much'), Indian life was doing its part to keep his anger fresh. As he later wrote, humiliated, he had had to quit a coveted position as Military Secretary in the Maharaja of Baroda's administration when he could not find a place to live. No landlord was willing to rent to an untouchable.

Unlike the **Buddha** (1) or **Mahavira** (2), or even Periyar, who were taking on the caste just a notch or two above, Ambedkar now wanted to take on the whole edifice – from the bottom. In caste Hindu quarters, that made him a despised figure, which in turn made him more impatient and defiant. He would learn only after failure to take the long view.

A crucial lesson came in 1927, when, as founder of a group advocating for untouchables and lower castes, he led a march for water access in a caste-ridden Maharashtra town. After he drank from the local tank and claimed victory, upper-caste Hindus attacked the participants, who were later further ostracized for their activism. The experience convinced him that fighting in the streets was less likely to bring success than fighting through the law.

The realization was probably fortunate for modern India, since mass organization was never Ambedkar's strength. Over the next decades, he started a sequence of associations, federations, political parties, pressure groups and campaigns, while considering alliances with communists, Sikhs, socialists and the Raj, among others. Some of his campaigns worked. In the hope of eliminating his followers' self-image as polluting persons, he popularized the term 'Dalit' – the Marathi for 'broken' – which he used to refer to those usually called 'untouchables' but whom he called in English 'Broken Men'. But he wasn't as charismatic before large groups as he was charming and convincing to small ones. Like Periyar, he seemed poised to be a merely local leader – until the unexpected intervention of the Raj.

In 1930, as part of the British plan to gradually give India more self-government, leaders of different communities were invited to a round-table to discuss a future constitution for India under dominion status. Jinnah was plucked to represent Muslims, and Ambedkar to represent untouchables, nationwide – a significant social promotion for a man little known outside his region. His bell-clear argumentative skills got him invited back to the next year's round-table, where he began an intellectual battle with **Gandhi** (38) that would last until the end of the Mahatma's life.

To Gandhi, the 'sin' or 'stain' of untouchability could be removed by altering personal attitudes – by requiring everyone at his ashram, for instance, to clean toilets. But Ambedkar bridled at the notion that untouchability was an excrescence on a caste system that was, on the whole, functional. He considered Gandhi a caste orthodox in a democratic reformer's clothing, and later claimed he had seen past the disguise to 'the bare man in him' – that he had seen Gandhi's 'fangs'.

In fact, it was an argument with Ambedkar – not the British – that occasioned Gandhi's most famous hunger strike in 1932. Underlying the immediate dispute, about separate electorates for untouchables, was a more fundamental clash: should Indians first unite to fight for freedom against the British (as Gandhi believed), or should they first render justice to one another, before asking for it from the British (as Ambedkar insisted)? It was also, as fundamentally, an argument about who could profess to represent the diverse interests of the Indian people. The year before, Gandhi had famously said, 'I claim myself in my own person to represent the vast mass of the Untouchables'. It was an imperious view that left no room for self-representation. At first, Ambedkar had seemed to accept Gandhi's view that touchables and untouchables had to come together through love, not through electoral arrangements or law, but he now came to feel co-opted and used.

Ambedkar turned sharply against Gandhi and the Congress, convinced that untouchables would have to fight their own fight. Unable to float a movement that could compete with the Congress, he decided to pursue his cause with British help, taking up a post in the

Viceroy's government. But by the mid-1940s, the British were fed up
with him too. For all his demands for concessions, he lacked the
representational base some other untouchable leaders had, and so
they marginalized him as a policy-making adviser. This might have
irked Ambedkar more were it not fast becoming clear that the over-
whelming power to establish equality for low-caste and out-caste
people would soon belong to the Congress. He sought out Muslim
support. He made speeches backing proposed Congress policies. He
signalled that an allegiance might be up for grabs. And when the
Constituent Assembly was called, in December 1946, he had a seat at
the table.

All modern Constitutions enact a structural separation of government powers and establish individual rights. In India, the former,
pressured by executive and judicial imperatives, has often proved
fragile. In contrast, among the more robust and transformative elements of the Indian Constitution are those articles that grant
fundamental rights to citizens defined primarily as members of communities rather than as individuals. This range of community rights
remains, in its scope, quite unique to India. Rights against discrimination (including, quite specifically, caste discrimination), give the
state positive powers to eliminate it. A right to equality of opportunity in public employment has also been affirmed. Ambedkar did
more than anyone to embed these principles in the Constitution. But
out of them grew a politics of reservations, or affirmative action,
that was paradoxical in its effects.

Initially, the principles were supposed to sanction, for a finite
period, the reservation of places, in government employment and
educational institutions, for Dalits, tribal groups and others defined
as 'economically backward'. (A ten-year jumpstart was the initial
hope.) But the power to determine eligibility for reservations was
given to India's state legislatures, and a constitutional principle
thereby became an electoral expedient. Politicians can promise, in
the name of equality, to expand the number of reserved places, and
to extend them to include newly defined 'backward classes'. Caste
groups, even successful ones, compete and sometimes campaign

violently to be deemed as backward in order to benefit from reservations, which today apply to just under half of all positions in India's national government institutions. In one state, the figure approaches 70 per cent. Down is the new up, in terms of social mobility. It's one of the profound ironies of India's democracy: reservations, designed to erode caste identities and fortify individual citizens, have invigorated caste categories now defined by the state.

As a result of his role in creating these rights, all India's political parties, including those whose views he opposed, claim Ambedkar today. He's become a necessary electoral magnet for any politician who wants the votes of the dispossessed. Prime Minister Narendra Modi, the low-caste leader of the Hindu-nationalist Bharatiya Janata Party (BJP), recently celebrated Ambedkar's 125th anniversary by applying a *tika* on the forehead of a statue of the man who spent his entire life fighting Hinduism.

How did such a latecomer to nationalism, and opponent of Gandhi, come to have so central a role in modern India? Nehru never fully trusted Ambedkar, and the feeling was mutual. But Ambedkar, vexing as he was to some, had intellectual skills Nehru and the senior Congress leadership required in the blood-dark wake of Partition. Ambedkar wasn't only a Dalit representing a vulnerable community: he showed himself able to think across a range of issues, and to ask about the consequences, intended and otherwise, that various laws might have for the society as a whole. After the disaster of Partition – a disaster of political judgement as well as policy – avoiding further short-sighted decisions on minorities could not have mattered more.

Hence, in 1947, after plans for Partition nullified Ambedkar's seat in the Constituent Assembly (he was elected from, of all places, eastern Bengal), Nehru and Rajendra Prasad, the leader of the Assembly and later India's first president, scrambled to keep him involved. 'Apart from any other consideration we have found Dr. Ambedkar's work both in the Constituent Assembly and the various committees to which he was appointed to be of such an order as to require that we should not be deprived of his services,' wrote a worried Prasad as he manoeuvred to rig up another electoral post for Ambedkar. By August, Ambedkar had been given the Drafting Committee chairmanship.

In the end, he would lose battles for many specific provisions to aid minorities. It's strange, in contemporaneous letters, to find a man with revolutionary impulses regularly credited for negotiating compromises. But what those compromises amounted to was an uncommonly progressive document: both a synopsis of India's deep historical conflicts and an extravagant promissory note for their future reconciliation in a pluralist, federal structure. In addition to enshrining affirmative action, the Constitution formally abolished untouchability. And, against the Gandhian ideal of decentralizing power, it created – with Ambedkar's constant prodding – a state strong enough not to be captured by powerful caste groups in the future. It recognized both individuals and communities as bearers of fundamental rights – an original vision which would leave plenty of opportunity for future conflict and contradiction.

Like the reunion achieved by the American Civil War, the Constitution Ambedkar helped to draft marked not the end of a story, but the beginning of a history – involving the pursuit of a still out of reach democratic equality. In May 2015, a young man visiting a small town in Maharashtra was beaten to death on receiving a call on his mobile. Other villagers set upon him when they heard his ringtone: a song praising Ambedkar. Thousands of stories of such violence fill the decades between 1950 and the present.

It's worth taking the comparison with America a bit further. In the United States, slavery was a 300-year-old institution. After abolition, it took another century of struggle for equality to secure full civil rights for black Americans. A half-century later, the struggle is hardly over. In India, caste has, over several millennia, woven itself into the fabric of society, infused itself as a climate of mind. Was it ever conceivable that one remarkable individual, a bracing, brave Constitution, and a few dozen free elections would blow it away?

Ambedkar lived only six years beyond the promulgation of the Constitution in January 1950. He was under no illusion that Indian equality was closing in. He took no great satisfaction in having helped to forge the Constitution or in its final form. It had to be worked by men, through politics, in a society shaped by power. His own experience of that kept him restless. Nehru had made him the Minister of Law in India's first cabinet – an 'empty soapbox', he said. In 1951, he resigned in protest at the failure of a bill, in his view the 'greatest social reform measure ever undertaken by the legislature of the country', to reform Hindu marriage laws to give women rights, including those of inheritance and divorce. It was defeated by conservative Hindus. He said in parting, 'To leave inequality between class and class, between sex and sex, which is the soul of society, untouched, and to go on passing legislation relating to economic problems is to make a farce of our constitution and to build a palace on a dung heap.'

In his final year, he created another political party – the Republican Party – and converted to Buddhism with his followers, in a last effort to conceive of individuals apart from caste. But it wouldn't have escaped his sense of irony that reservations, and the politics around it, have entrenched the very thing that he wanted to annihilate. 'We are going to enter into a life of contradictions,' Ambedkar famously said, closing the debates of the Constituent Assembly in December 1949: 'How can people divided into several thousands of castes be a nation?' Alone of all India's founders, he recognized the importance of fraternity, the ability to treat each other with dignity, as fundamental to the creation of a political community. Without fraternity, Ambedkar reminded his fellow Indians, 'equality and liberty will be no deeper than coats of paint'.

42
Raj Kapoor

The Politics of Love
1924–1988

In a scene I like from the film *Boot Polish*, a 1954 Raj Kapoor production about growing up in the Bombay slums, a brother and sister are begging on a train, pretending to be disabled, when a shock sighting makes the boy forget his job of being blind. Isn't that shabby man dozing in a corner, like any other spent commuter, the legendary Raj Kapoor? His younger sister scoffs. 'Everyone looks like Raj Kapoor these days,' she says as they scoot on.

In life, Raj Kapoor was a compulsive seducer, a habit that made him a scene-stealer as an actor and effective as a director, persuading cast and crew to do his bidding. But as the wink of a cameo in *Boot Polish* hints, he was keenly aware of the distance between his celebrated Everyman persona and his actual, everyday self. 'Raj Kapoor was just an image,' he would say in his seventies, 'a carcass of flesh and bones.' He'd been acting since early childhood, and the duty of rising to screen-hero dimensions must, by then, have felt something of a chore.

But the brass tacks of making movies never did. Chasing the next, better idea for a film was a singular obsession in a directorial career that extended from the late 1940s to the mid-1980s. One of his sons, the actor Rishi Kapoor, recalls that growing up, 'from morning to night, his only conversation, whatever you spoke to him about, was cinema. You talked to him about food – he had great passion for good food – it goes down to cinema when he starts to talk. Any topic led to cinema. And only his own cinema.' Kapoor's command over the art that enthralled him produced some of the most watched films, anywhere, in the history of the medium.

Hindi cinema is so popular these days that we forget it once

345

wasn't. Raj Kapoor didn't just make films: he made the mainstream Indian film audience, before the term 'Bollywood' was even a glint in a marketer's eye. Which is not to say he didn't also make flops: two of his favourite films tanked – though he loved them a little more, he knew, because audiences loved them less. But when he hit, he hit big, by bringing romance, sexuality, song and soul to Indian socialism in its heyday.

The world of Hindi film, **Satyajit Ray (47)** once wrote, was 'a synthetic, non-existent society [where] one can speak of credibility only within the norms of this make-believe world'. But as both left- and right-leaning artists understood, Hindi film was also a means of education and exposure in a country where the literacy rate at Independence was 18 per cent. Many village schools were bad, if they existed at all; unread pamphlets became paper airplanes. So an important vehicle of education – religious, cultural and political – was an actual vehicle: a truck juddering from village to village with a projector and a rolled-up film screen, to be erected on a maidan or in a field.

Kapoor's own family were landowners in Punjab from a merchant caste, the Khatris. Not least because of him, Khatris came to dominate Bombay's film industry and made Punjabi song and dance a stand-in for all-India entertainment. But the vision Kapoor staged and sang was not provincial; it was recognizably Nehru's India, featuring an urbanizing, modernizing milieu. Behind his yearning, moist-eyed heroines and sometimes slapstick comedy was often a cheerful nagging that promises made to the poor in advance of Independence be recouped.

Kapoor had a keen eye for tiny deprivations that dash the spirits of the unprivileged. In another moment from *Boot Polish*, the camera pans down a long line of people waiting for rations. It's a glimpse of a country's have-nots, united in need. Suddenly, though, the rain starts, and the class of need divides again: there are those who pull out umbrellas, and those who get thoroughly drenched. The humiliation of the poorest makes you cringe. But this being a Raj Kapoor film, it also makes you laugh, and soon enough there's a really good song.

Kapoor's was an ideology, if one can call it that, of emotionalism and entertainment. He sugared his social concerns with sauciness and music and melodrama; the solutions he posited to a collective, post-Independence let-down had little to do with politics, and a lot to do with love. As much as that tendency would frustrate his more political collaborators, it would introduce Indian cinema to the world and lay the groundwork for Bollywood, India's greatest cultural ambassador after Gandhi – a considerable achievement, if an ambivalent one. How did he pull it off? Raj Kapoor didn't just have uncanny comic timing – he had historic timing, too, which would bring him, in socialist and communist countries, followings bigger than those of his fan, Jawaharlal Nehru.

Although Kapoor typically played poor, often in Chaplinesque style, he was born to spanking artistic advantage. His father, Prithviraj, was a renowned stage actor who starred in India's first talkie, *Alam Ara*, in 1913. Today, we're often dismissive of the sixteen years of Indian cinema stretching from that groundbreaking film to Independence – as if it consisted only of village romances, 'mythologicals' about gods, or swashbuckling Douglas Fairbanks-style fare. As if the cinema of a new India needed itself to be bracingly new. In fact, many Indian film-makers and actors of the 1930s, Prithviraj included, were devoted to social concerns, including the criticism of untouchability. There was even a woman director, now forgotten: Jaddanbai, the mother of the legendary Nargis, who would become Raj Kapoor's most famous co-star.

Prithviraj and his wife were living in Peshawar when Raj was born, but his childhood was spent between Calcutta and Bombay, where Prithviraj acted and in the 1940s helped found the Indian People's Theatre Association (IPTA). The collective sought to use theatre for progressive political aims, from addressing famine to supporting the nationalist Quit India movement. It took inspiration from a wide range of sources, including Soviet silent cinema, Italian neorealism and Charlie Chaplin. Prithviraj's eldest son drank it all in, often in greasepaint, treading the boards.

His father permitted him his first stage role when he was five. 'It was then that the whole thing just entered me,' he recalled, 'and I could not think of anything except belonging to the world of show business.' His first film role came five years later. His looks were Pathan – pale skin and striking blue eyes – but cuddly rather than chiselled. The screen effect, a slightly unplaceable comeliness, later underwrote his international appeal. A precocious teacher's pet and self-described 'pampered brat', he was also widely admired for his singing and dancing. But in adolescence, cherubic plumpness turned to fat. Bullied despite or because of his prettiness, he was initiated into the hard childhood truth that more tearful protests only bring on more brutal beatings. 'So instead I put on the mask of a joker by reacting as though I thoroughly enjoyed being made the butt of practical jokes,' he later said. 'Indeed, I even took this a step further by inventing jokes on myself, which would make my colleagues laugh.' This defence mechanism would serve him well.

He had a feel for the moods of his audience, even in high school. Seeing people grow bored in the front row, he'd try something unscripted to rouse them. Getting and giving love was an addiction from early on. After failing high school (Latin and maths were his undoing), he persuaded his father to help him enter the film line, first as a production assistant, then, effortfully slimmed down, as a star. He was handsome enough now to have become the Indian Errol Flynn. Instead, in 1948, at the age of twenty-three, he became the youngest film director of his time anywhere in the world, with a 'studio' in an old car: R. K. Films.

Kapoor's 1948 directorial debut, *Aag* ('Fire'), was about a young man who wanted to be a stage actor, disappointing parents who had hoped for a lawyer. Young Indians' desire for self-realization in modern India, and the resulting conflicts with their parents' expectations and traditions, would become a theme in his work (and then in much of Hindi cinema), but it was only one of several ways in which *Aag* announced its modern idiom. In addition to employing a more naturalistic acting style than was typical in Hindi film, and more humour, he was taking risks with a new means of waking up the dozers in the front row – eroticism.

Kapoor considered eroticism central to the Indian tradition, from the sculptures of Konarak and Khajuraho to temple dance. (He dated his own interest in eroticism to bathing as a child with his beautiful mother.) This put him at odds with industry mores, which held that showing men slapping women was fine, but caressing them was outrageous. Shortly after Kapoor started making films, Nehru – himself a bit of a *pas devant les enfants* liberal – created a national board of film censors, to centralize existing regional ones. Keeping a thousand lips closed during kisses was a function of the market as well. Going to the pictures was a family affair, and too much hotness hurt sales. The risk of offending religious groups and social conservatives was high even in the city: in the mid-1950s, Nehru received a petition about cinema corrupting the young signed by 13,000 women residents of Delhi.

In his first film, Kapoor managed a fine balance been realism and propriety, redefining the cinematic portrayal of love. In one scene, the hero he plays tries to rebuff a beautiful actress whom his best friend wants to marry. What is it that I have that my friend doesn't? he asks her. As she makes an ardent list, beginning with his eyes and hair, her lust is unabashed, and a cinema convention of the woman as passive love-object is toppled.

The actress was Nargis, and she and Kapoor would go on to become one of the legendary pairings of Indian cinema, in large part because of their sexual chemistry. (In a later film, she would be – again, unconventionally – the innocent hero's ardent pursuer.) Nargis was already a star when she signed up with the first-time director, and became more than his muse and mistress. She was an intellectual and practical partner in the films. Nargis was Muslim, and the actress she plays in *Aag* was a Partition refugee – one of the first mentions of the tragedy in Indian cinema. As Bollywood expert Nasreen Munni Kabir points out, even a glancing mention of the communal bloodshed, only months after the fact, took courage; it was a time when many elites feared that discussing the subject would incite new violence. *Aag*'s attempts to evoke both sex and politics signalled what an R. K. film would come to stand for: work that, for all its escapism, inhabited the same world as its audience.

*

In *Awara* (1951), Kapoor's third film and one of the most successful of all time, Nargis plays not just the love object but a practising lawyer. Kapoor plays a thief and vagabond – an *'awara'* – who adores her. As in many of Kapoor's films, the faults of the poor spring from the wrongs of the rich. In one exchange, Kapoor's character describes the miracle of modern society: 'Capitalists, black marketers, profiteers and money lenders: Who are they? All thieves like me.'

By now Kapoor had assembled a trusted team of collaborators, among them the Marxist novelist, political columnist and neorealist scriptwriter Khwaja Ahmad Abbas, who, like Kapoor's father, had belonged to the IPTA group. Abbas had modelled himself on the muckraking American novelist Upton Sinclair. Shailendra, a poet and author of many of Kapoor's most famous songs, was only slightly less left-wing. *Awara* spoke to the mass unemployment following Independence, as well as corruption in the criminal justice system. Kapoor's next film, the enduringly popular *Shree 420* (1955) was an even sharper critique of upper-class corruption, and conveyed a deep appreciation of the difficulty of behaving ethically in a world intricately rigged against the poor – even for honest souls with college degrees, like its protagonist. The title comes from section 420 of the Indian Penal Code, on fraudsters. The rich in the film seem to be born dishonest; the dishonesty of the poor is India-made. It was a theme that packed in the film-goers.

But even in such populist films Kapoor's primary interest was fun. He knew how to honour Shailendra's work by the clever integration of lyrics and dance into the scripts. By the time Kapoor made *Bobby*, in the 1970s, Abbas was complaining about his pointed dialogue getting cut to cram in songs – though he also joked that if he'd made the films according to his own vision, they'd have flopped.

As Kapoor's career continued, a crucial aspect of the lives of the poor – discrimination based on caste – remained largely implicit. Paradoxically, he had strong feelings on the subject, dating back to a childhood visit to his grandfather's home in Punjab. Having joined some other children to pick cotton, he fell asleep in the field and woke up alone. An untouchable worker on the estate discovered him and carried him home. Upon delivery, the worker apologized to the family for having soiled the child with his touch, and Raj wasn't allowed inside until he had bathed. 'I didn't know the implications of all this then,' he later recalled, 'but I knew that what was being done was wrong.'

However, like Nehru, and a whole post-Independence generation, Kapoor seems to have internalized the constitutional fiat that caste no longer existed. The dream of the 1950s – soon fading – was that if one didn't speak of the old social divisions still oppressing hundreds of millions of people, they might go away. In fact, nation-building actively required it to disappear. So the gradations of inequality captured gracefully when the umbrellas came out in *Boot Polish*, among countless other moments, would not be explored through the biggest source of inequality in Indian life.

The acuity of Kapoor's class analysis reached an apex with his production of the relatively unsung *Jagte Raho* (1956), in which a rumour of a thief loose in a middle-class community prompts the people to organize their impoverished neighbours into armed goon squads: poor men eager to beat off the 'thief', who is really a destitute peasant, recently migrated, in search only of a drink of water. This absurdist comedy of middle-class snobbery and petty perfidy demonstrates a canny handle on how the lower classes are used as tools to undermine those with whom they might find common cause. But as is typical in Kapoor's films, the conflict is ultimately mollified by kindness. As hard as the world gets, there's usually a loving Nargis on the way, ready to slake thirst with a small gift of water.

It was, as Nasreen Kabir puts it, a Marxist analysis of problems that proposed no Marxist solution. A 'professional emotionalist', Kapoor seemed to be suggesting that you could love your way towards equality and dignity, or at least love your way around the structural problems of your society. In *Shree 420*, Raj and Nargis walk in the middle of an empty road during a monsoon shower, singing 'Pyar Hua Ikrar Hua', the most famous love song in the Kapoor repertoire. The couple is in a bubble of romance, apart from the world, and they know the road ahead is hard, despite a future in central government 'people's housing'. But as Nargis makes clear with a gesture and a flash of her eyes, babies will figure in the couple's non-centralized five-year plan. If the promise of Indian Independence was not to be realized imminently, Kapoor seems to hint, perhaps the second generation of young, spirited Indians would have better luck.

Kapoor's last film, *Ram Teri Ganga Maili* (1985), is known today mainly for a scene in which the heroine's thin white sari is drenched under a waterfall: a moment of such transparent eroticism that nobody but Kapoor could have got away with it. By 1985, says Rachel Dwyer, Professor at the School of Oriental and African Studies, he 'was such an establishment figure that he could set the norm'.

There's political commentary as well as titillation, of course: for instance, a secret plot between an industrialist and a politician to build a factory whose effluent will contaminate Calcutta's Hooghly river, a channel of the holy Ganga. While the corrupt are duly vanquished in the end, to watch that final film is to be reminded that, as associated as Kapoor came to be, retrospectively, with Nehru's project, none of his work demonstrated faith in politicians.

Perhaps the best expression of Kapoor's political scepticism comes in *Shree 420*, when the tramp-hero comes to a Bombay maidan to hawk sand he hopes to pass off as toothpaste. Crowds have gathered to hear a politician promise his listeners the world. Kapoor's seller convinces the crowd that the politician is also a salesman, but with a product of lesser value. Toothpaste, he argues charmingly, will change your life more than hot air. As ever, Kapoor's sentimental hope lies in individuals, not institutions. That his heroes weren't bureaucrats deciding how many tractors to make helped give the film-maker a worldwide reach he'd never imagined.

Awara opened in the USSR in 1954, the year after Stalin's death. Under the so-called Khrushchev thaw, there was suddenly new freedom in the media and the arts. In that year alone, a stunning 64 million people – mainly young people – are estimated to have bought tickets to *Awara*. 'Kapoor-mania', as it was called in the USSR, became even more frantic with *Shree 420* the next year. Soviets didn't require Marxist solutions in their films; there was plenty of that on the state-run radio. They celebrated the songs, which became ubiquitous on the airwaves, and bought postcards with Raj's image (cult collectors' items to this day). They made the young hero who pursued his desires against social traditions their own.

On Nehru's first prime ministerial visit to Russia, in 1955, the crowds who turned out to see him shouted out to the Indian leader: 'Awara hoon!' – 'I am a vagabond!' There would soon be many more enthusiastic young vagabonds, in East Africa, Romania, Egypt, Afghanistan, Iran, the Middle East and China – despite the fact that Chairman Mao was a Raj Kapoor fan too. In Turkey, where Awara was made into a popular television show, the 'Awara hoon' song still matters enough that there's a hip-hop version.

But the legacy of Kapoor is strongest in India, and literal: he created a dynasty. Both of his brothers became actors, as did all three of his sons, two successfully. His granddaughters Karishma and Kareena became major screen heroines, and his grandson Ranbir Kapoor, a celebrity star, acted in *Yeh Jawani Hai Dewani* ('This Youth is Crazy') (2013), one of the highest-grossing Bollywood films of all time. It's a silly film, but stands out from the action pics and science fiction dominating the top-ten list because what doesn't feel silly is the love story. Politics may have leached out of the Kapoor bloodline – at least as seen on the screen – but the deft command of romance endures.

43
Sheikh Abdullah

Chains of Gold
1905–1982

Should you ever get it into your head to publish, in India, a map of the country's external boundaries that includes its northernmost state – the vast mountainous territory of Jammu and Kashmir, wedged between China and Pakistan – you'd better prepare to suspend disbelief. Approval will require, in addition to a 'scrutiny fee' of Rs 2450, ratification by the Survey of India's Boundary Verification Wing, a branch of the Indian government that specializes in geographical fantasy. It only approves maps that show India in possession of the whole of Jammu and Kashmir – something that, since the state's accession to India in October 1947, has never been true. At that time, large parts of Jammu and Kashmir came under the forcible control of Pakistan, which continues to hold them. China, too, controls a substantial chunk, which it captured in its 1962 war with India. That leaves India with less than half of what the official maps claim. It's an almost comical delusion, but one that bears witness to a contested history and to the fragilities of India's self-image as a democratic nation.

That embattled history took a crucial turn in the waning years of British India, when a powerful Muslim movement emerged to challenge the despotic Hindu dynasty, the Dogras, that ruled British India's biggest princely state. Leading the campaign was an idealistic forty-year-old from a family of shawl-makers who, as a boy, had been given darning tools instead of a pen. He had fought his family to get to a school, then he fought his teachers to get to a better one, eventually securing a university degree in science. Then, in 1946, he

SHEIKH ABDULLAH

launched the largest popular agitation ever seen in his part of the world.

'We Kashmiris want to inscribe our own destiny,' Mohammad Abdullah said, as tens of thousands of people from the kingdom's Muslim majority took to the streets of the capital, Srinagar. They called on both the Dogra maharaja and his British advisers to 'Quit Kashmir'.

The maharaja did what he usually did to his challengers – and locked them up. But Abdullah took consolation in the knowledge that a powerful friend in Delhi might come to his aid. Jawaharlal Nehru was at that moment negotiating delicately with both the British and Muhammad Ali **Jinnah** (39) over India's future, but on learning of Abdullah's imprisonment, he rushed north to defend him – only to be detained by Dogra forces himself. It was the first act of a political drama about two freedom fighters that is still in search of its ending.

By the following year, princes across India had come to realize that summary incarcerations of their subjects were of no use. As the Raj was dismantled, the rulers of all the princely states were forced to fold their tents and join one of the new post-Partition countries. In Kashmir, where the religion of the ruler and most of his subjects differed, that choice was not straightforward. The Dogra maharaja havered over whether to join India or Pakistan, or to declare his own independence. Abdullah emerged from prison with a somewhat clearer view: though he believed the poor Kashmiri Muslims he represented should rule themselves, he thought it best to trust, temporarily, in Nehru's promise to build a democratic state in a multi-religious nation. Once Kashmiris had an elected government, they could deliberate over what their future should be.

This reasoned position didn't account for the tribal fighters – an estimated 5,000 to 8,000 of them – who poured into the Kashmir Valley from the newly created West Pakistan two months after Partition, intent on capturing the state for Jinnah. Abdullah and the maharaja now found themselves in agreement: Kashmir needed outside military help and would have to accede to India to get it. And so began the second act. A week and a half into the invasion, Abdullah scrawled a note to Nehru, now the Indian prime minister, on a scrap of paper: 'If I am able to carry on, it is simply because of you.' Days later, Indian forces repulsed the attackers from the Kashmir valley, though Pakistan would henceforth control most of the northern half of the state.

There is a famous photo of the two friends hugging each other shortly after the invasion was over. The photo looks more sinister now than it probably felt then. To Abdullah, this moment was meant to be a reprieve that would allow those people still under his control to move towards self-determination. For Nehru, it was the moment when the ineffably beautiful Kashmir, land of his own ancestors, permanently entered the fold of independent India as its single majority-Muslim state. In the third act, characterized by betrayal, violation and recrimination, Abdullah would come to see his old friend's embrace as a stranglehold.

To some Indians today, the Kashmir conflict feels like a long-running sideshow. In truth, it goes to the core of India's foundational commitment to political liberty. Originally intended to be evidence of the country's religious pluralism, Kashmir is still part of India only because twenty of the state's twenty-two districts are essentially under martial rule. Designated as 'disturbed areas', these are districts where insurgents are claimed to be actively fighting the Indian government. In 2015, human rights activists applauded when six army men were given life sentences by a military court for the illegal killings of three Kashmiris. It was an exception that proved a rule of government impunity. According to Amnesty International, 'Not a single member of the security forces deployed in Jammu and Kashmir over the past 25 years has been tried for alleged human rights violations in a civilian court.' In short, the rulers of Kashmir today are not unlike the Dogras under whose boot Mohammad Abdullah grew up – a boot that shaped, and eventually hardened, his politics, just as the Indian government boot shapes and hardens the politics of young Kashmiris today.

Abdullah was born in Srinagar as a burden: his mother was the third and junior wife of a man who died just before she went into labour. Dispossessed of their share of family property, Abdullah and his two elder brothers were expected to make the cheap cotton shawls on which their extended, devout family depended. But the young boy discovered he had a gift for reciting the Qur'an that allowed him to get out of darning. Eventually, it would help him see more of the world than his shabby corner of Srinagar.

In the 1920s, after college in Lahore, Abdullah was admitted to the most prestigious place an Indian of his faith could go for a modern education: Aligarh Muslim University, in the United Provinces. There, hearing **Iqbal** (35), himself of Kashmiri origin, speak passionately about injustices against Muslims in Kashmir, he felt 'transported into a strange world', in earshot of the 'trumpet of Israfel'. But returning to Kashmir in 1930, he felt the oppression of the Dogras afresh.

Despite having a Master's in Chemistry, Abdullah couldn't get a government job: the Dogras had reserved most of these for Hindus. If recruits were scant in the small Pandit community in the Kashmir Valley, administrators brought in other Hindus, from the Punjab. Some educated Muslims got around that bias by sucking up, but Abdullah was repelled by the idea of ingratiating himself with his oppressors in order to secure a position for which he was already qualified. Instead, he settled on being a schoolteacher, and passed his evenings in reading clubs with other educated young Kashmiris, building a political base.

Bearded and in possession of a fine baritone voice, 'Master Abdullah' by his mid-twenties had become a popular orator, speaking on Fridays from the platform of Srinagar's wooden Jamia Masjid. Telling the history of Kashmiri Muslim dispossession and demanding rights from the Hindu princely state, he sometimes spoke so movingly that people wept and tore their clothes. But it wasn't until the Dogra slaughter of more than twenty protesters on 13 July 1931 – Martyrs' Day, as it is now known – that a mass movement to defend the rights of Muslims truly began in Kashmir. It was, Abdullah later wrote, the Kashmiris' Amritsar 1919 moment.

As the Dogras responded with martial law, Abdullah became the leader of a newly formed movement, the Muslim Conference. Soon known as the Sher-e-Kashmir, or 'Lion of Kashmir', he successfully united the Valley's many sects and factions around the call of 'Islam in Danger'.

It's a truism of power to this day that the ability to organize people around a cause is a gift others will soon seek to co-opt. Jinnah, down in the plains, was following Abdullah's resistance closely and assumed he would be a ready recruit to the growing Muslim League. But when the two men met in 1935, Jinnah's more conservative views put off Abdullah, who was not just younger and less politic, but far more socially and economically progressive. As they ended their meeting, Jinnah warned him that Hindus could not be trusted, adding ominously, 'A time will come when you will recall my words. But it will be too late then.'

Abdullah left his first encounter with Nehru, a few years later, bowled over. Nehru, then at the peak of his career as a glamorous rebel nationalist, was leading a drive to attract more Muslims to the Congress movement. The burly Kashmiri with a popular touch was Nehru's kind of Muslim: not so preoccupied with religion that he failed to be a spokesman for the social concerns of the poor. Nehru had been waiting, he told Abdullah, for someone to 'awaken the Kashmiri people from their slumber'. Despite divergent class backgrounds, they developed such a warm friendship that soon Abdullah was hosting Nehru's daughter Indira (see **46 Indira Gandhi**) on her honeymoon. Only much later would a disillusioned Abdullah note bitterly that Nehru kept the *Arthashastra*, **Kautilya**'s (**4**) ruthless guide to realpolitik, 'by his bedside'.

Nehru believed the Lion's charisma could draw others besides Kashmiri Muslims to the nationalist movement – constituencies like Kashmiri Hindus and Sikhs. So he was heartened when, in 1938, Abdullah (beard now shaved) vexed the Muslim League by announcing he would turn his own Muslim Conference into a secular party. The following year he launched the new All Jammu & Kashmir National Conference, and draped it in a notion of Kashmiri cultural and religious tolerance known as Kashmiriyat, which asserted that the Islam practised in the Valley was more syncretic than Islam elsewhere. It was a debatable construct, and the new conference remained primarily Muslim, but from it came, in 1944, a radical social and economic manifesto that would fundamentally change Kashmir.

Srinagar during the 1940s was a haven for Indian and European communists, and with their guidance the Conference called for women's rights and a redistribution of land to the tiller. It also took a page from Stalin, envisaging distinct nationalities coming together to form a union like the USSR without losing the right to secede. To Abdullah, this offered an alternative to the divisiveness of Jinnah's two-nation view and to the Congress's one-nation acquisitiveness. After 1948 – when, following Nehru's military intervention, Abdullah took on the role of Kashmir's prime minister – some of the manifesto's ideals became law.

His greatest achievement was to dismantle Kashmir's system of land ownership, which had served the interests of the Dogras until accession ended their rule. All holdings above twenty-three acres were abolished, without compensation to landlords, and land was redistributed to peasant cultivators, most of whom were poor Muslims. The reform massively expanded Abdullah's loyal following and laid the basis for the emergence of a Kashmiri middle class. In the place of the starvation, forced labour and beggary that had been common under the Dogras, Abdullah created a largely egalitarian society. As the journalist and writer Basharat Peer points out, it was a revolutionary achievement in the context not just of India, but of South Asia (one matched only by Kerala, in the south). But amidst post-Partition religious mistrust, that social transformation quickly took on communal overtones.

Around a third of the land in the Valley was once owned by Kashmiri Pandits who, in the late 1940s, formed just 5 per cent of the population. It was this Hindu community that lost the most in the land reforms. Almost immediately, Hindu nationalists in Kashmir and across India began accusing Abdullah of the sort of systematic dispossession for which Kashmiri Muslims had once blamed the Dogras. That outrage, shared by leaders in New Delhi with Hindu sympathies, eventually fastened on the special autonomy that Abdullah had secured for his people in the country's 1950 Constitution.

Nehru saw that losing India's only majority-Muslim state to Pakistan would tarnish his vision of India as a multi-religious nation. So the autonomy given to Kashmiris, under Article 370 of the Indian Constitution, was unique among Indian states. Kashmir's elected assembly would now have greater legislative powers than other state assemblies, and would be able to decide for itself on what terms it wished to associate with India. The fury over these concessions increased exponentially in 1953, when the Hindu political leader Shyama Prasad Mookerjee, founder of the precursor of today's Bharatiya Janata Party (BJP), arrived in Kashmir to protest against policies that restricted other Indians from settling in the state. Abdullah imprisoned him, and he died in his cell of a heart attack.

The treatment of Mookerjee was not a one-off. As the state's new leader, Abdullah had inherited many of the repressive powers of the Dogra rulers, and he used them to silence critics. Lacking the sort of political deal-making and negotiation experience that was part of the Congress culture in British India, he ran Kashmir as a one-party state. When elections were held in 1951 to form a Constituent Assembly for Kashmir, he permitted no opposition to his party – a pattern of anti-democratic rule Abdullah set, and that would long outlast him.

Many Kashmiris might have tolerated Abdullah's autocratic style had he been able to provide them with more of the autonomy so resented by the Hindu right. But Nehru dragged his feet on a promised plebiscite, fearing that independence or even Pakistan would be the Kashmiris' choice. Abdullah's efforts to give the people of Kashmir a say in their political future came to nothing. Meanwhile, the protagonists of the Cold War were trying to extend its theatre to the subcontinent – a circumstance that would help to seal Abdullah's fate.

In May 1953, he had three meetings with US Senator Adlai Stevenson during an American fact-finding visit to India. Later, Stevenson only acknowledged hearing an earful of charges about conspiracies and bad faith, but Abdullah hinted that he had been promised American support should he decide to declare Kashmir independent. To Nehru's intelligence officers, Abdullah was becoming seriously troublesome and 'anti-national'; before a popular uprising began, he'd have to be curbed.

Late in life, Abdullah recalled a moment during his negotiations with Nehru over Kashmir's constitutional relationship with India. Leaning over, Nehru had whispered: 'Sheikh Sahib, if you waver in embracing us, we will put gold chains in your neck [sic].' In August 1953, the chains were finally pulled tight.

Unconstitutionally, Abdullah was stripped of his position as Kashmir's prime minister and arrested; among the charges was 'establishing foreign contacts of a kind dangerous to the prosperity of the state'. His Nehru-vetted replacement was a corrupt deputy who proved to have little support apart from that of the Indian army. The 'world has not seen a more glaring rape of democracy', Abdullah later wrote to Nehru from prison.

Nehru always claimed that the arrest happened without his knowledge. But the week before, he'd written with alarm to his closest confidante about how the 'lure of American money to develop Kashmir' was encouraging Abdullah's impulse towards independence. Shortly before sending that letter, he had set out his orders with clinical precision: 'The members of Government should not speak in different voices' when it came to the policy of Kashmir's place in the Indian Union; 'it may be desirable to arrest one or two such persons, who are known to be corrupt'.

'I suppose one has to do some things for the greater good,' Nehru's daughter, Indira, wrote to him on hearing of Abdullah's arrest. She had just been to the USSR and was reminded of hearing news of the arrest of one of Stalin's henchmen, Lavrentiy Beria – not, she reassured her father, that she was making a comparison!

Abdullah was released from jail only once in the subsequent ten years, but as soon as he began rallying his people towards independence, he was returned there. Though freed again just before Nehru's death, in 1964, he was exiled from Kashmir for another decade. Only in 1977, after the Emergency (see **46 Indira Gandhi**), was Abdullah, now past seventy, permitted to stand for re-election. He then won the fairest election in the dismal history of Kashmiri democracy. But his resumption of power came at a cost: Indira Gandhi had forced him to surrender key elements of Kashmiri autonomy.

In the late 1980s, about seven years after the death of Sheikh Abdullah, an armed separatist movement began in Kashmir. Before long, tens of thousands of young men were trekking across the border to Pakistan and returning as trained fighters. Islamist militants from outside Kashmir also joined in – many of them mujahideen demobbed after the Soviet withdrawal from Afghanistan in 1989. By 2006, the Indian government was deploying some 600,000 military and paramilitary forces to control a population of around 10 million. According to the Kashmir state government, the conflict left more than 43,000 people dead between 1990 and 2011; civil society groups cite much higher figures.

The historian Chitralekha Zutshi, who is writing a biography of Sheikh Abdullah, says that many young people in Kashmir blame Abdullah for the conflict: 'They see him as the reason why Kashmir is in the position it is today. He's the reason why Kashmir allied with India in 1947. He's the reason why autonomy was chipped away.'

For many Hindu nationalists, the problem remains too much autonomy. They argue for abolishing Article 370 and giving India full sovereignty over the state. Meanwhile, some secularists think that Kashmiris should be eager to forge a stronger link to India, with its economy growing at 7 per cent, instead of turning to a dysfunctional Pakistan. But as Basharat Peer points out, Kashmiris today are well aware of the way India's current governing party, the Bharatiya Janata Party, is eroding the rights of religious minorities, particularly Muslims. In such a climate, chains, even golden ones, are as likely to inspire resistance as allegiance.

During his imprisonment, Abdullah had tried to work on Nehru's guilty conscience. Wasn't it a travesty that Kashmir was receiving harsher treatment from independent India than from the Dogra regime they had once linked arms to oppose? After Nehru's death, a weary Abdullah would try to work on the conscience of his begrudged countrymen, in ways that resonate even more today. The treatment of Kashmir was 'an open book', he said, hardly hidden to history. 'Let every Indian search his own heart.'

44

V. K. Krishna Menon

Sombre Porcupine
1896–1974

From Independence until India's 1962 military defeat by China ended his career, V. K. Krishna Menon – intellectual confidant and global troubleshooter to Prime Minister Jawaharlal Nehru – was one of the most reviled figures of the Cold War era. From the early 1950s, American administrations tried to force the 'unpleasant mischief-maker' out of office. The British detested his 'arrogant extremism' and, against all diplomatic rules, MI5 tapped his phones and read his mail while he was India's envoy in London: they thought he was in bed with the Soviets. The Soviets considered him 'a lackey of the British'. As for the Chinese, they never forgave the condescension with which he tried to school them in international affairs.

To know Menon better wasn't necessarily to like him. One of his lovers said he was a 'sombre porcupine', but 'with the potential to evolve into a human demon'. Edwina Mountbatten and Nehru spoke of him as 'our "problem child"'. The strong-featured, sharp-elbowed Menon was, in short, a full-tank drama queen – the kind of man whose finger you wouldn't want on the nuclear trigger. But the country he represented had no such trigger. Recently free from colonial rule, it had a vast poor population, a slow-growing economy and a large army whose rifles malfunctioned and jeeps failed to start.

So why should the emotionally labile representative of an undeveloped, weapons-deficient country attract such animosity among the world's great powers? Because, as the voice of India's foreign policy for some two decades – a 'dangerously persuasive' voice, in the US State Department's view – he prosecuted an agenda that deeply unsettled the superpowers but became one of independent India's most important early achievements.

In a polarized Cold War world, India refused to ally with either the US or the Soviet Union. Instead, with immodest ambition, it struck out on its own. Relying not on military weaponry but on diplomatic energy, it tried to build an international order in which weaker states like India could better resist the bullying imperatives of the superpowers. That policy acquired the name of 'non-alignment' when Menon inadvertently used the term in the course of a UN speech. This ad-lib would come to define India in the world.

Years before, Menon had speculated that if India overthrew British imperialism, it might change the planet by 'transform[ing] the power relations of other countries and cutting at the root of the causes of international rivalry'. After independence, he tried to realize this vision. Shuttling frantically and often uninvited between world capitals, snatching rest with the help of Luminal, a barbiturate that was a regular part of his otherwise meagre diet, he kept himself at the centre of virtually all the diplomatic engagements that shaped India's international identity. The Korean War, the Indochina peace talks, the 1955 Bandung Conference, the Suez and Hungary crises, nuclear disarmament, the campaign against apartheid in South Africa, the Congo crisis – Menon was there, a lambaster of colonialism and a defender of Indian interests in Asia and beyond. While insisting on India's right not to be subservient to other nations, he cared little for diplomatic niceties. In early 1962, when Henry Kissinger first encountered him in Delhi, he was surprised when Menon attacked the American ambassador at the time, J. K. Galbraith, as too pro-Indian. 'Don't embrace us', Menon bristled, characteristically. 'We pick our own friends.'

As the post-war era turned nuclear weapons into the currency of global affairs, India's leaders invested instead in words. International deliberative assemblies – the Commonwealth, gatherings of Asian and African leaders, and above all the United Nations – became their natural habitat. While the UN may have been an attempt by the great powers to legitimate and maintain their dominance after the

Second World War, Nehru and Menon took the institution seriously from its inception. They thought it might actually be used to constrict the influence of the great powers and slowly alter the international balance in favour of the poorer states then emerging from colonial subjection.

As India's most persistent voice at the UN, Menon could be a self-parodic embodiment of the country's commitment to resolving conflict and shaping public opinion through discussion. Once, during a 1957 Security Council debate on the Kashmir conflict, he delivered a speech, punctuated by fits of fainting, that lasted either seven, eight or nine hours, depending on which account you accept. The performance reflected his belief in his own persuasive capacities, a belief bearing the imprint of the Bari Memsahib, **Annie Besant (29)**. From his teenage years, Besant had groomed him to shine in an international parliament that she envisaged would one day govern and save the world.

In his wealthy, high-achieving family on Kerala's Malabar coast, Menon hadn't been considered so promising. It's a region where many family systems are matriarchal, and his mother, an accomplished Sanskritist and musician in the town of Calicut, expected her children to excel. His sister had published a book by the age of fourteen. His brother was a sports champion. The young Menon, however, was prickly and given to sulks – qualities he'd never outgrow. Afraid of evil spirits, he went to bed with the lights on (and was a chronic insomniac for the rest of his life). When his worried father sent him to Madras to train in his footsteps as a lawyer, Menon happened to hear Besant speak. Soon, he was making an alternative home on the Theosophical Society's grounds at Adyar, a wooded sanctuary for Western spiritual seekers and the promising young Indians Besant was bringing into her movement.

After law school, Menon was enthusiastically performing Theosophy-inspired social service when Besant sent him to England. He was to become an educationalist and to propagate, back in India, the teachings of her most famous protégé, Krishnamurti. But soon after arrival, Menon discovered that he wasn't an esoteric after all. Instead, he enrolled at the London School of Economics, where he became a star pupil of the political theorist and Labour politician Harold Laski. Warmly welcomed into Bloomsbury salons, he mixed with the likes of Kingsley Martin, Lytton Strachey, the Woolfs and, unknowingly, informers for British intelligence. In 1927, three years after moving to London, Scotland Yard opened its first file on potential seditionist V. K. Krishna Menon. Over the years, British intelligence and police files on him would expand to fill many boxes.

'Our work here should have the moral force of India behind it,' Menon wrote in 1930, as he converted an old-time London theosophical offshoot into the India League, which became a rousing advocate of Indian independence. Following a research tour around India, where he was appalled at the colonial authorities' repression of both nationalists and ordinary citizens, he spread his anti-colonial message in British newspapers and from Hyde Park Corner soapboxes. His arguments began to bring British left intellectuals and Labour politicians round to the cause of Indian independence. Bertrand Russell, Aldous Huxley, Stafford Cripps, Aneurin Bevan and Michael Foot lent India their public support, as did American radicals like Paul Robeson.

Menon's quickfire intelligence constantly sought places to settle, and in the second half of the 1930s, he and the editor Allen Lane helped to create one of Britain's most beloved publishing institutions, the Penguin and Pelican paperbacks. Handling the non-fiction side, he published authors such as George Bernard Shaw and H. G. Wells, until he and Lane fell out (temperamental differences). So Menon must have felt immense relief when, just out of hospital following a breakdown prompted by a failed love affair, his energies suddenly found a wider channel. Jawaharlal Nehru, another Indian who had passed through Theosophy before finding socialism and politics more compelling, was visiting London.

The relationship between Nehru and Menon is one of the curiosities of twentieth-century Indian history. Like the partnership between Nixon and Kissinger, it brought both glory and stain to their country's international reputation. But, unlike the Americans' records, Menon's vitally important papers remain in disarray and largely inaccessible to scholars. Once, thinking I was settling in with some important Menon files, I opened an archive box and found an old hairbrush of his. It seemed fitting: under-the-radar was Menon's style. In British secret files of the pre-Independence years, there's an entry, referring to a Congress decision in 1937, which describes his method in a way that holds true for many other instances in his career: 'There is also evidence that though [Menon] handed on the idea to Nehru, he was most anxious it should pass for Nehru's own in order that it might thereby carry greater weight.'

At the time, Nehru was, along with Bose, the modern, international face of the Indian freedom movement. He was also on the look-out for someone who could help convey sophisticated political opinions to the West. Almost immediately, Menon became his spokesman abroad, his back channel to international developments during his frequent imprisonments, and his friend. 'There is hardly anyone here to whom I can speak with frankness about myself,' Nehru wrote to Menon in 1939, as events in India, Europe and at home brought him close to a breakdown himself.

The view from the intelligence files in the years leading up to Independence was that Menon was working quietly with the Communist party to turn Nehru into one of its puppets. Many British officials were eager to catch this 'Extremist of the worst possible kind' in an illegal intrigue with the Soviets, and jail him. That they could never nail him probably had to do with something one of their analysts had noticed: 'Menon has no genuine Party loyalties: he is first and foremost anti-British and thereafter, only, an extreme Socialist.'

Menon was chronically incensed at the primitive image of the Indian people that the British promulgated to the world and he harboured a special animus for the promulgators, 'men who draw their incomes from India and spend the evenings of their lives in maligning her and her people'. As Independence neared, he began to sense the role he could play in changing the world's idea of Indians.

In 1946, he became the chief emissary between Nehru and the British, applying his knowledge of British political and constitutional procedure to the intricate negotiations over the transfer of power and independent India's membership, as a republic, in the British

Commonwealth. Meanwhile, he and Nehru fell into what would become a habit of their friendship: staying up half the night at Nehru's home, arguing over politics, philosophy and India's future.

Visiting New Delhi in the early 1960s, the political philosopher Isaiah Berlin met Nehru and his left-wing 'gadfly', Menon. Ever the aesthete, Berlin decided Nehru was the T. S. Eliot to Menon's Ezra Pound – 'the same beliefs at much lower tension, milder, more compatible with respectable life, but deriving from the same constellation of values; gently, firmly, tolerantly, decently anti-Western'.

It was perhaps not Nehru's safest idea to assign his Pound to a newly independent India's most important foreign mission, in London. Menon's tenure there laid bare his flaws: administrative incompetence, erratic management of staff (including affairs with their spouses), and bouts of depression and mania, during which he wrote long letters back to New Delhi threatening suicide if forced to resign. But his relentless pursuit of Indian interests made him essential to Nehru, who felt his friend generally bore his personal difficulties with admirable fortitude. Had he shared Menon's 'highly strung' nature, Nehru once wrote, he probably would have committed suicide.

In early 1951, not long after presiding over a financial scandal involving faulty jeeps procured for the Indian army, Menon staggered unkempt into a private meeting with Nehru. 'Obviously very far from well . . . ,' Nehru wrote later that night. 'He had the appearance of a person on the verge of going off his head.' It attests to the depth of his belief in Menon's abilities that, instead of retiring him, he made him India's face to the world. In 1952, Menon joined India's delegation at the UN and, soon after, became its chief representative. Almost immediately, he and Nehru embarked on a furious period of international diplomacy, much of it focused on Asia.

Menon's arrival at the UN coincided with America's first successful hydrogen bomb test, a particularly ominous event for Asia given the situation in Korea, where the two-year-old war between the US-supported South and the Soviet- and China-backed North had reached a parlous stalemate. To Menon and Nehru, the Korean crisis threatened to transplant the Cold War into Asia and to subordinate the continent to American and Soviet interests. It also threatened to extend Chinese influence. Ensuring that Asian conflicts did not spiral into atomic confrontation became a priority for the two men, and a vital test case for India's non-aligned policy.

The Korean impasse centred on the repatriation of prisoners of war, and Menon took the lead in trying to unblock it, putting forward a series of bold proposals based on giving the prisoners freedom to decide their own fates. Menon's principle offended the Chinese, his style annoyed the Americans, and his plan was rejected at first. But in June 1953 he helped to break the deadlock. Further diplomatic interventions followed, as Nehru and Menon waded into matters far above India's power grade. As Nehru put it, 'When the scales are balanced, even a little makes a difference.' Both men shared the belief that small, skilfully chosen, independent moves were a better way to secure India's interests than pursuing big alliances.

This diplomatic precept guided Menon when, in 1954, he barged into negotiations over the conflict in Indochina. For Eisenhower, Vietnam was the 'domino' whose fall would ineluctably spread communism, and in May 1954, against the background of France's defeat at the Battle of Dien Bien Phu, the four major powers – America, Russia, Britain and France – convened in Geneva, along with China, the northern Viet Minh, the Southern Vietnamese and the Laotians.

The US saw no reason for India's involvement, and Soviet Russia and China actively manoeuvred to keep India out. Turning up uninvited in Geneva anyway, Menon plunged into a hectic schedule of diplomatic speed-dating. He worked corridors and side rooms, hotel lobbies and bars, holding some 200 meetings with the assembled delegates. The conference's outcome, which he played an important role in securing, was an uneasy armistice that would nevertheless last almost a decade.

After Geneva, contemplating India's impact, he wrote with realism to Nehru, 'The influences we have exercised in the last four or five years have not been of a conventional quality and have not been amenable to formal methods. We have not the power to shift equilibriums, except by the wise and timely use of influence and the power of idea and personality and as will become increasingly evident, by the internal strength of the country in every respect . . . All else necessarily flows from it.'

Although other letters from the mid-1950s reveal a man in wrenching mental pain ('far from being a help to you or relieving you of burdens I am an embarrassment and add to your worries'), this period was the summit of his and Nehru's international success – a moment when India's standing as an international actor was acknowledged even by those who did not approve of its choices. But that achievement was soon followed by serious missteps.

In 1956, Khrushchev ordered the Soviet invasion of Hungary; Menon abstained from a UN resolution condemning the Russians and voted against a motion for free Hungarian elections. He may have feared that India would be subjected to a similar UN vote on Kashmir (see **43 Sheikh Abdullah**), where Nehru was temporizing on a promised plebiscite. The Indian government's failure to live up to its vaunted policy of non-alignment was noted around the world, and cost it the moral high ground.

A still greater error resulted after Nehru, wanting to ensure civilian authority over the army (neighbouring Pakistan was about to fall into the hands of its generals), sent the frail, resolutely civilian Menon from the UN to the Ministry of Defence. The appointment angered the top brass, while Menon for his part was appalled by the military's disarray. In an urgent private note to Nehru in 1961, he wrote, 'Although I have explained it to you several times it appears little understood that in an emergency we can meet Defence's requirements, even conservatively, only if the apparatus of Defence Production is capable of expansion ten times over.' The following year, Mao Zedong surprised India by starting a war to assert Chinese control over borders claimed by India in remote Himalayan regions and the north-east. Indian defences crumpled like tinfoil, and Menon was held responsible for the loss.

The short war cost the lives of 1,400 Indian soldiers, making it, by the twentieth century's standards, a glorified skirmish. The country's failure to predict the war seems less egregious in a wider context: all over the world, thousands of diplomats since have misread China's intentions and underestimated its willingness to play hardball. But the defeat succeeded both in asserting China's superiority over India and in disengaging India from Asia for the better part of four decades – outcomes that benefited the Chinese as they developed into one of the world's greatest powers. It also ruined Menon's political career. As so often in popular judgements of historical figures, the bad end vaporized the good that preceded it.

A large part of what had driven Menon's and Nehru's mid-century diplomatic initiatives was their wariness over China. India, they held, had to use diplomatic means to restrict China from extending its sway over Asia's weaker states, and to get it to respect the identities of the small countries that were emerging from the end of European colonialism in Asia. But the 1962 defeat cast a heavy shadow over Nehru's foreign policy, and non-alignment came to be seen in many foreign policy circles as a naive failure.

That negative assessment has been widely accepted by critics of Nehru and Menon abroad, and also in India, which is drawing increasingly close to the US. So I was struck recently to come across an unexpected admirer of non-alignment: Henry Kissinger. For decades one of the strongest opponents of India's foreign policy choices, he's come to see India's position less partially. 'However irritating to Cold War America,' he wrote in 2014, 'it was a wise course for an emerging nation. With a then-nascent military establishment and underdeveloped economy, India would have been a respected but secondary ally. As a free agent it could exercise a much wider-reaching influence.' Perhaps Menon's reputation may be ready for a similar recovery.

45
Subbulakshmi

Opening Rosebuds
1916–2004

In the summer of 1838, a small troupe of dancers, of a 'bright copper colour', captivated audiences across Europe. In Paris, they danced in the Tuileries before the court of King Louis Philippe. 'Their dances,' the *Journal des débats* wrote, 'are like nothing we have seen or that can be imagined.'

> They dance with their whole frame. Their heads dance, their arms dance – their eyes, above all, obey the movement and fury of the dance. Their feet click against the floor – the arms and hands flash in the air – the eyes sparkle – the bosom heaves – their mouths mutter – the whole body quivers . . . It is a mixture of modesty and abandonment – of gentleness and fury.

They were devadasis, 'servants of god' – temple dancers from south India. It was a brief, anticipatory moment of Indian cultural branding, but European interest in the 'Orientals' soon moved on. Back in India, the dancers returned to their unglamorous lives. It would be a century before the daughter of another devadasi mesmerized audiences around the world.

Her gift lay not in rhythmic athleticism, but in her voice. In 1926, at the age of ten, she had begun her career before an audience outside a bicycle shop in the Tamil town of Madurai. That same year, a gramophone company recorded her singing a devotional song, in the Carnatic style of the Indian South. After she finished, she cleared her throat and declared: 'I am Madurai Subbulakshmi.'

Listening to her early recordings, the Carnatic musician and critic T. M. Krishna hears a gay abandon, a flair for embellishment and nuanced phrasing, and a complete lack of diffidence, which he puts down to her upbringing in the devadasi world – a harsh world where an aura of self-possession was necessary to the work. Her singing voice, striking from the start, would ultimately range three octaves, one more than Carnatic singers usually need. As she grew into it, she excised the hand and body gestures often associated with south Indian vocal performance. 'The language of her eyes accomplished for Subbulakshmi what flying arms did for another singer,' wrote the biographer T. J. S. George. A perfectionist, she had the capacity to cross genres, but reduced her performances over the years to what another connoisseur of her music has called a 'provokingly small' repertoire. In time, the ambitions of those who loved and profited from her combined with her gift to take her from the concert stage to film to All India Radio to near-official status as an icon of independent India.

It is a moment now past: a moment in which it was possible to believe in an Indian 'national culture' and in singers and artists who could embody it. But what was required of Subbulakshmi, in moving from south Indian musical celebrity to national cultural symbol, is deeply uncomfortable when considered through the prism of contemporary values. For she publicly styled herself as a submissive, asserting her dependence on others and often acting as if her music, too, were visited upon her – as if her greatness was quite apart from her own doing. And yet, beneath the placid surface of an icon, there was striving and decisiveness. Even in a patriarchal society, an artistic woman's volition counted for something, and in many cases allowed her to perfect her art. One clear choice Subbulakshmi made was to distance her skill from the striking south Indian tradition that shaped it. The art of the devadasi would be valuable, but the devadasi herself was not.

Creating and sustaining an immaculate public image is relentless work, and around Subbulakshmi, one frustrated biographer wrote, was a fortress. It was strange, even by the paternalistic standards of mid-twentieth-century India, how often her husband and manager, Kalki Sadasivam, fielded media questions on her behalf. He lectured the questioners: 'If you ask a rosebud how it opens into a flower, can it answer?'

That she said so very little, and certainly nothing controversial, made me assume, seeing her on television or in the occasional concert growing up, that there was little in the famous singer's head. It was only later, via candid shots of her off-duty, that I made out the mischief and intelligence behind the somewhat bovine mask. In one of my favourite photos, she and her friend, the dancer Balasaraswati, are probably in their late teens. Decked out in striped pyjamas, they're raffishly feigning to smoke cigarettes – a pleasure strictly forbidden to young south Indian women. Instead of the soulful gaze that was her professional trademark, Subbulakshmi's eyes are alive with fun – *girlish* fun: a quality that might have been tough to preserve in her actual girlhood, during which her talent was turned like a machine.

M. S. Subbulakshmi, or 'MS' as her admirers called her, was born in 1916 in Madurai, far south and inland on the Indian peninsula. Her brother, her younger sister and she grew up in a small house not far from Madurai's famed temple to the goddess Meenakshi, around which ran streets humming with the town's economic and cultural life. The temple drew thousands of visitors every day, and annual festivals brought more than a million to the town: crowds to be entertained, for music was integral to the worship.

So while her brother got formal schooling, MS and her younger sister were taught music and performance. That was the tradition of the devadasis, and it upped the odds that a woman would have a roof over her head. Subbulakshmi's great grandmother was a dancer whose moment of regional celebrity came when she performed in the presence of the viceroy, in 1886. Her grandmother was a violinist (an instrument adopted early into Carnatic music), and her mother, Shanmugavadivu, played the traditional south Indian string instrument, the veena.

In this family of professional artists, there was a glaring absence: fathers. For in addition to being the custodians of local arts, devadasis were sacred concubines. Officially 'wed' to deities of the temples they served, they took patrons – often high-caste Brahmins or members of the landed class who were married to women of their own castes. When children were born from these alliances, they belonged to the mothers. Daughters, in due course, would be 'dedicated' to the temple devadasi tradition.

In Subbulakshmi's house, a separate stairway led directly from the street to her mother's parlour, for the discretion of her mother's patrons. Subbulakshmi's published biographies would identify her father as a Brahmin lawyer, though Madurai gossips fingered a local musician as the likely candidate. Whoever it was, the money that patrons gave the household appears to have been limited. Shanmugavadivu continued to earn income through her veena performances, and by introducing her daughters to the stage as soon as they were able.

Subbulakshmi's abilities were evident early on. Although she'd grown up in a house full of music, she wasn't adept on the veena, despite her mother's best efforts. However, from a young age she could listen to a song on the gramophone and effortlessly imitate it. Her mother, seeing the potential, exposed the girl to still more concerts, and to tutors. After the ten-year-old released her first record, her mother took her out of Madurai to perform elsewhere in the region, including at the Tamil royal court of Ramanathapuram.

In keeping with tradition, Shanmugavadivu was also seeking to match her girls to wealthy patrons, and a scion of Ramanathapuram's ruling dynasty was taken with Subbulakshmi. When her mother tried to settle her with him, however, the girl resisted. It couldn't have been easy to buck a multigenerational expectation. But as a celebrated southern music critic underlined after meeting MS when she was thirteen, she was 'not a fragile child but a strong silent girl' – one with 'the will of a woman of forty'.

Her sister, less skilled and perhaps less wilful, would soon be attached to a Coimbatore-based millionaire. But she died at the age of twenty-two. 'If I had stayed in Madurai I would have died long ago,' Subbulakshmi later wrote in a private letter. Publicly, she spoke only elliptically of the adult life she had averted. 'When I was small, men would only think of how to spoil me.' She recalled 'seeing it all and getting frightened by it'. She wanted to focus only on her music.

Her big break came in 1932, when she was sixteen. The renowned temple at Kumbakonam, near Madras, hosted a great festival once every twelve years. A singer meant to perform there fell ill, and a determined Shanmugavadivu persuaded the organizers to give her daughter the slot. She performed to such an ecstatic reaction that she was asked to sing again, for a larger audience, the next day. It was the beginning of MS's rise to Tamil stardom – and the beginning of the end of her relationship with her mother and the tradition into which she had been born.

In earlier centuries, devadasis were so esteemed that some kings dedicated their daughters to temples. But in colonial India, this was one of many indigenous traditions held up to a different light. The vision of a Sanskritic golden age, inspired by the work of **William Jones (21)** and other Orientalists, and the cultural revivalism associated with movements like Theosophy (see **29 Annie Besant**), produced changes in the lived and performed arts. So, too, did the arrival of technologies like the gramophone and, by the mid-1930s, the radio. By the time of Subbulakshmi's birth, the place of music among elite circles had changed.

The aim was to create a more controlled, less improvised structure of performance with good moral tone. A tradition of performing for private and usually male audiences in cloistered spaces, for long hours reaching into the dawn, gave way to the evening concert, with specified timings and access by ticket. The devadasi tradition, with its intimate etiquette of connoisseurship, went from being a subject of admiration to an object of shame. By the turn of the twentieth century, a female member of the Madras legislature could remark: 'the appellation of the devadasi as every one of us here knows, whatever the original meaning may have been, stands for prostitute'. Local temple bans were soon followed by stricter laws, supposed both to protect the devadasis and to regulate licentiousness. Their art, tamed, was appropriated by male singers, including great masters whose music Subbulakshmi studied as she developed.

By the time Subbulakshmi started singing in the mid-1920s, the maharani of the neighbouring princely state of Travancore officially 'abolished' the devadasi system in her domains, after which the census report noted the district had no more prostitutes, the recent abolition having 'contributed to this happy circumstance'. In such a climate, Subbulakshmi had to proceed with care. An association with prostitution would repel the audiences her singing was drawing in. She and her mother had set up household in Madras as she continued to expand her fan base and, in 1936, she received a request for an interview from a popular feature magazine. The interviewer was the magazine's co-founder, Sadasivam.

A Brahmin born in Madras, Sadasivam had been an anti-British radical in his youth, and was jailed for it. For a while he was a follower of Subramania Sivam, the revolutionary comrade-in-arms of **Chidambaram Pillai** (30). Now he became a disciple of the Tamil Congress leader C. Rajagopalachari, agitating for independence as he ran the magazine. MS was nineteen. Sadasivam was thirty-three, hot-tempered, and decidedly married. His subsequent pursuit of her was so dogged that, before long, her panicked mother rushed her home to Madurai and arranged a marriage to a businessman. But instead of going to the businessman's house, where she was expected, MS fled back to Madras, and to Sadasivam, whose wife was away having their second child. It was the beginning of several years of vicious behind-the-scenes fights; meanwhile, Subbulakshmi kept singing serenely.

Her mother charged Sadasivam with using her famous daughter as a meal ticket. Sadasivam charged the mother with the same. As the two of them scuffled, rumours of elaborate schemes to kidnap MS and return her to Madurai enlivened Madras parties. Subbulakshmi compounded the drama by falling in love with another great Carnatic singer and actor, G. N. Balasubramaniam. There was no musician she admired more. Her biography includes excerpts of love letters she dispatched to him, chiding him, in erratic grammar, for his inattentions and proclaiming him the love of her life: 'Henceforth even for a moment I will not be separated from you.' (The letters also confirmed her lack of trust in her mother and brother.)

Around the same time, in 1940, Sadasivam's wife died after a prolonged depression. Rumours of suicide persisted. And while it wasn't quite funeral meats furnishing marriage tables, in a matter of months he quietly married Subbulakshmi.

Though her love for him was flagging, and if the immediate circumstances created a scandal, Sadasivam ultimately offered her more respectability than marriage to another entertainer could. Since the dance of the devadasi had become less seductive (turning into a Brahminically inflected style that now became the classical form, *Bharatanatyam*) and as Carnatic music became tame enough for upper-caste housewives to perform, it made marketing sense for Subbulakshmi to look like an upper-caste housewife. In Madras, away from the evidence of her heritage, Sadasivam had already been arranging what T. J. S. George, the biographer, called 'an all-out putsch' to broaden her fame and link it with the interests of nationalism.

By the mid-1950s, when Jawaharlal Nehru described MS as 'the queen of music', her name had become synonymous with the Carnatic tradition. She commanded reverence even among those who only vaguely knew of classical music. Her spiritual image was as Sadasivam had constructed it: 'She is a simple woman, and naive', he told reporters. Her supposed innocence left her well situated for roles in religious or socially instructive films, which he had begun arranging for her almost immediately after she'd fled her mother.

As she played historical or mythological figures, or embodied progressive concerns like the plight of dowry-less young girls forced to marry old men, Subbulakshmi was ill at ease delivering her lines, even after much instruction. But the Tamil films were full of songs, and her musical talents transferred beautifully to the new medium. So much so that, after a few years, her success brought her husband into rare agreement with her mother: this film thing was something to get out of.

Just as Subbulakshmi felt ashamed of her mother, her mother was embarrassed that her daughter had abandoned classical music to become a popular singing starlet. For Sadasivam's part, he appreciated the money his wife was making, but not the adulation she was receiving, especially from charismatic male film stars. At the same time, his friends in the national movement thought that Subbulakshmi's representation of classical music could be the soundtrack of a new India.

With this in mind, he decided to produce a final film for MS on the life of the iconic bhakti singer **Mirabai** (15). Released initially in Tamil as *Meera* (1945), a Hindi version followed, part of Sadasivam's plan to make his wife a star – or saint – of India's emerging national culture. As the poet and nationalist Sarojini Naidu said, 'The story of Mira is the story of India, the story of Indian faith and devotion and ecstasy. Subbulakshmi's performance [shows] that she is not an interpreter of Mira but Mira herself.'

The final film achieved its purpose. Henceforth Subbulakshmi had a faithfully devoted, all-India bandwagon. Not yet thirty when the film was first released, she would to the end of her life sustain her persona as a new-age bhakti saint: an artist who sang only for God, and for whom God was the only inspiration. MS herself reinforced this image: 'At a time when so much is said about the liberation of women the world over,' she once wrote, 'it is good to think of a woman whose soul wanted to liberate itself and merge with the Lord.'

There is a tone of idiot-savant in this that might make a contemporary feminist cringe, but Subbulakshmi was complicit in nurturing it. As she told an interviewer late in her life: 'I have never gone out alone. I have never been educated. I have been brought up listening to elders . . . I never get angry with anyone on any issue.' However, such rare and tedious press statements don't account for a life that included running away, across the state, from a marriage her mother had arranged, or living with one man while in love with another.

While MS played placid and apolitical, Sadasivam worked to turn her musical success into cultural conquest. He used his political connections to present her in the highest circles of the national leadership and then the Indian government. She sang before Gandhi and Nehru, and for the common folk. She sang at the United Nations and across the United States – the world stage being Sadasivam's greatest ambition. Above all, she sang to raise money for hospitals, schools, orphanages, TB clinics and Hindu temples. Her husband worked her for causes as hard as her mother had worked her. And that choice, too, helped her go down in history not merely as a musician, but as the ideal of the cultured, virtuous, selfless Indian woman.

As with many Indian women who have been elevated to canonical status, Subbulakshmi's human reality got drained away and replaced by idealizing myth. It's worth noting that her love letters, saved by the recipient, are among the few documents of her candid thoughts. The rest of the record was under her husband's control. But the words so often used for her – 'tranquil', 'content', 'beatific'– fit awkwardly with the choices she made when it counted. As in so many other stories of exceptional, hard-working women, their own ambition is denied a role in their achievement.

In 1998, Subbulakshmi was the first musician to receive the Bharat Ratna, India's highest honour. Sadavisam had died the year before, after which she never gave a public performance again.

46
Indira Gandhi

The Centre of Everything
1917–1984

Before senior Congress party leaders orchestrated Indira Gandhi's ascent to the young nation's prime ministerial office, a *chhokari* or *gungi godiya* – a 'chit of a girl' or a 'dumb doll' – was how some politicians described her. All the easier, the old Congressmen thought, to make her a cat's paw. But they soon grasped their misjudgement. From the mid-1960s to the mid-1980s, India's first – and so far only – woman prime minister would subvert the political establishment and dominate India's public life. After Margaret Thatcher, she was the most powerful woman of the twentieth century.

While her brusque manner and ability to elicit the sycophancy of her colleagues are sometimes compared to Thatcher's, a better mirror might be her American contemporary, Richard Nixon – a man who found it so distasteful to negotiate with a woman leader as prickly as himself that he termed Mrs Gandhi a 'witch' and a 'bitch'. Although ideologically incompatible, both politicians harboured paranoid and anti-democratic tendencies, and both were deeply insecure. ('I was so sure I had nothing in me to be admired,' Mrs Gandhi confided to a close friend days before her death in 1984.) Both were also acclaimed for international achievements while sabotaging their reputations at home.

The comparison starts to falter thereafter. The choices Indira Gandhi made between 1975 and 1977 – a time known as the Emergency – make Nixon's corruption and cover-up during Watergate look like fudging a line call in badminton. She suspended democratic liberties, amended the Constitution, imprisoned political rivals (in total, some hundred thousand are reckoned to have been rounded up), censored the press, and effectively coerced a mass sterilization of the poor. In short, she demonstrated just how fragile a young democracy can be.

To the intelligentsia, there is no political figure in independent India more loathed. She's seen as malevolent, megalomaniacal and responsible – to use Salman Rushdie's line about her betrayal of India's founding ideals – for 'the smashing, the pulverizing, the irreversible discombobulation of the children of midnight'.

Yet Indira Gandhi is a polarizing figure in Indian life, not a pariah like Nixon. If you shrink-wrap her story to the contours of a cautionary parable, and see the Emergency as an aberration in the history of Indian democracy, you miss something crucial. During years of severe economic crisis, for the poor Indian majority and for many minority citizens, she was their best hope for some prosperity and protection. Three years after being ousted from office in early 1977, she was voted back in; even today, she's rated in polls as one of India's most popular prime ministers.

It's one of many paradoxes about the Indira Gandhi era. She made India, officially, a socialist state while loosening trade policy and fostering crony capitalism. She ruthlessly controlled senior politicians, but was herself dominated, to the country's great detriment, by her difficult younger son. And while she created the greatest threat to democracy in independent India's history, weakening constitutional regularities established by her father, the enduring effect of her rule was to open the state to a deeper and more accessible democracy. Despite herself, she made democracy ordinary for Indians – not pretty, just ordinary. It was an achievement of stupendous proportions.

'Politics is the centre of everything.' When she told the *New York Times* this, in 1966, Indira Gandhi could have been articulating a family motto. Born in 1917, Jawaharlal and Kamala Nehru's only child was raised at their Allahabad home, which had been established by Jawaharlal's father, Motilal, a prominent and ambitious lawyer of Kashmiri ancestry. When Indira was a toddler, Motilal threw his lot in with Mohandas Gandhi; through the house whirled a pageant of twentieth-century India's political and intellectual life.

Politics also exposed Indira, early on, to loss. Through the 1920s and 1930s, her parents, aunts, relatives and family friends were all in and out of prison, at the pleasure of the Raj. Her father's incarcerations were so frequent that their relationship became largely epistolary. Nehru's first book, a survey of world history in which he tried to adopt a non-European perspective, was written as a series of letters to his daughter from prison – an anti-colonial nationalist's version of the Victorian father's advice book. The Nehrus were not a typical Hindu 'joint family'. In Motilal's household, deliberation and personal choice were encouraged – within limits – and women were educated. Indira, though never an enthusiastic pupil, studied in India, in Geneva, with **Tagore** (32) in Shantiniketan, at an English boarding school and at Oxford, after which it was expected that she would slip into a professional life.

Her mother, only seventeen years older, wasn't a role model for the life she would come to lead. Kamala's family were unanglicized Kashmiris of modest means, and the strain of becoming a Nehru cracked her confidence and took its toll on her health. She died of tuberculosis at the age of thirty-six. (Indira, who was not yet nineteen at the time, never quite forgave her hale, preening father and his two younger sisters for belittling her mother and her ailments.) Afterwards, defying her father, Indira took up with and married Feroze Gandhy, a young Parsi nationalist who had cared for Kamala during her illness (the Parsi spelling of his family name was later altered to blur his origins).

The unpublished correspondence between father and daughter from these years is charged with accusation and guilt, as well as an intense emotional interdependence. Indira was herself frequently ill in her youth, and she wrote to her father with the clarity of someone trying to set the historical record straight about his neglect – the Nehru household not being deficient in a sense of its own historical significance. When she ultimately married Feroze, in 1942, after years of her father's resistance, she seemed to be trying, pointedly, *not* to be a Nehru.

Four years later, though, she and two young sons were back with her father. Feroze had proved unfaithful, and erratic as an earner.

There was little time to mourn the rupture. Within months, the country would be independent, her father its first prime minister, and she among the leading female faces new India was presenting to the world.

At first, Indira was content with entertaining world leaders and managing the family's new home, in the grand former residence of the British commander-in-chief. But her interests deepened as she accompanied her father overseas two dozen times between 1949 and 1959, including to the famous Bandung conference of 'non-aligned nations' in 1955. She'd dabbled in politics and economics at Oxford, but only now did the political animal in her genetic make-up begin to stir.

Although Nehru's letters make clear he initially saw his daughter as more of a calming influence than an adviser, she was soon taking over internal Congress matters for which he had little stomach, and moving up the hierarchy of the party. She also began to offer unsolicited advice to her father about appointments and acted as an earpiece for political gossip, sometimes put up to it by Nehru's manipulative private secretary, M. O. Mathai, and sometimes on her own.

One scholarly biography, by Katherine Frank, suggests that the new confidence reflected a sudden improvement in her health. She had secretly been battling TB for more than fifteen years and had spent nearly a year at a Swiss sanatorium. After the discovery of new antibiotic treatments for the illness, she was cured. She became stronger, and her appearance changed. She campaigned strenuously on behalf of the Congress in the general elections of 1957, and in 1959 became the party president.

Some Congress members were frustrated by the nepotism. Today, more than half a century later, the influence held by successive generations of Nehrus and other prominent political families has weakened the proclaimed openness of Indian democracy. Certainly, once Mrs Gandhi had acquired power, she would do everything to see it remained in the possession of her family. But rumours that Nehru schemed to have his daughter become party leader and, later, prime minister, find little support in the historical record. Nor did

Indira initially have designs on the job; by the 1960s, she was writing to close friends that she'd had enough of public life – a feeling she acted upon when she stepped down from her Congress post instead of serving a second term. It would take a series of deaths to create the conditions – political and personal – that brought her to power.

In 1962, India went to war with China and lost, an experience that broke Nehru mentally and physically. By May 1964, at the age of seventy-four, he was dead. His successor, as he'd hoped, was Lal Bahadur Shastri, a politico loyal to Nehru's wishes. Shastri offered Indira Gandhi the portfolio of Information and Broadcasting, a minor Cabinet position. She took it partly from a desire for financial security. Her estranged husband had died, leaving her no property. Her only income was the royalties from Nehru's books. The family mansion had been donated to the nation as a museum, and she could no longer live in the prime minister's residence.

When Shastri suddenly died two years later, five senior Congress leaders chose the not quite fifty-year-old Mrs Gandhi (as she was now known, despite the absence of a Mr Gandhi) to replace him. They were compelled by the combination of name recognition and her lack of a power-base in the party or country. Given her gender and vague ideological vision, they expected her to defer to their ideas. What the men hadn't properly factored in was the home tuition on power-consolidation she had received as her father's confidante. If there is such a thing as political osmosis, Mrs Gandhi was its exemplar. Before long, she would become a master of the art of political undermining. But first, she had trials to face.

India was in economic distress when the inexperienced Mrs Gandhi took up her post. The costly war with China had been followed by one with Pakistan, and a series of monsoon failures had led to famine. After several months in office, she went to the US and, building on negotiations begun by Shastri, secured from President Lyndon B. Johnson a promise of $900 million in aid and IMF support. One of the conditions, however, was a near 60 per cent devaluation of the Indian currency relative to the dollar. Returning from what had seemed a triumphant visit, she was burned by a firestorm at home: nationalist fears about India's vulnerability to international pressures had flared up.

Unlike most of her political peers, Mrs Gandhi hadn't before been subject to such heated criticism. Wounded as well by electoral setbacks to the Congress party, she attempted to win back support by altering her economic approach. Enacting protectionist measures, nationalizing banks and other industries, and engaging in populist politics by, for example, divesting India's former maharajas of stipends that had been constitutionally promised, she worked to build a direct line to the Indian voters and improved her public speaking to sustain it. Her political growth in these years obliquely undercut the Congress party and its leaders, but a more direct blow was struck in 1969. Faced with opposition from the right, she split the party, moving it leftwards while sidelining regional leaders – a self-preserving move that foreshadowed what later became an even more concerted drive to centralize and control.

Following Congress tradition, her father had given regional bosses a fairly long leash. Those leaders hustled money from supporters and used it for electioneering in their own patches, in return for benefits negotiated from the centre. But now Mrs Gandhi changed the rules. Cash from the regions' business houses would henceforth be delivered to her private secretaries (their offices famously two-doored, so no visitor was aware of who had preceded him), with the distribution of election expenses controlled directly from her office. The rupees came first in briefcases, then in suitcases: money that created a material chain of fidelity between her chosen party men and herself. She was now able to make or break the political careers of Congressmen across the country – a power no Congress leader had ever held before.

Mrs Gandhi's march on mass adulation reached its apex in 1971, when she called a snap election and launched a cult-of-personality campaign. Appealing directly to the poorest and lowest in the social order – Dalits, Muslims and women – she projected herself as a unique scourge of Indian poverty, through socialist policy. As she explained to a journalist, the language of socialism was what the people wanted to hear. Her policies over the next years of economic turmoil would position her well to the right of her rhetoric, but the rhetoric served: she won the 1971 election handily. She was poised, unwittingly, to become an international humanitarian superstar.

While she was campaigning across India to 'Remove Poverty', the military leadership of West Pakistan had been pursuing a genocidal policy against the Bengalis of East Pakistan. Millions of refugees were flowing into India, and international condemnation was generally sharp – except from the Nixon administration, which sided with Pakistan, in part because Nixon and Kissinger hoped that Pakistani officials would help them facilitate secret detente talks with China.

Gandhi thought military action against Pakistan was inevitable, and she was given the pretext she sought when the trigger-happy General Yahya Khan, the Pakistani leader, launched an attack on India in December 1971. The war was short, and resulted in India's first major military victory – a decisive one for Mrs Gandhi. The 'dumb doll' was now, according to a Gallup poll, the world's most admired woman.

International opinion was more mixed three years later, when, after years of research and development, India conducted its first successful nuclear test. Mrs Gandhi was now one of very few non-Western leaders accorded respect – and a certain amount of apprehension – in world capitals. Perhaps this is why, in domestic politics, her sense of her own capability was creeping towards narcissism.

Between 1973 and 1975, the Indian economy, still absorbing the cost of the upheaval in Bangladesh, was given a further knock by the global oil crisis. Year-on-year inflation surged over twenty points, to as much as 33 per cent. Worried by public opinion turning against her, she closely tracked prices across the country, annotating weekly reports by hand. Her efforts to keep opinion on-side perhaps revealed her to be less of a natural dictator than she would have liked to be. But when parliamentary politics impeded the implementation of her plans for economic stabilization, she began to think she could do without facing obstreperous and misguided parliamentarians. Confident of her legitimacy after her electoral success, and convinced of the urgent need for more state control in other arenas of life, she began to embrace a Jacobin – or what the historian Patrick Clibbens has called an 'authoritarian republican' – conception of political power, in which acclaim at the polls was thought to absolve leaders from the other forms of accountability.

A *Washington Post* reporter covering dissent about the Emergency gets kicked out of the country, his notebooks confiscated as he goes. The notebooks are mysteriously returned to him several months later, the names of his government sources underlined in red. Many of the sources had been picked up and taken to prison.

That is just one story of thousands from the start of the Emergency in the summer of 1975 – the season when a daughter separated from her father in childhood by the British use of prison as a political muffler began taking political prisoners of her own. Over the course of a few days, jails filled up with her critics. Journalists and editors were detained alongside the political opposition, as she had also ordered a news blackout. Under the provisions of the Emergency, those arrested could be held without trial and judicial review for as long as the Emergency lasted. To justify it, she talked over the heads of the elites to the people, as was her wont. They needed her to save the economy, to protect them from black-marketeers and other enemies.

The trouble had started with a court judgement that overturned Mrs Gandhi's 1971 election to Parliament – and therefore her eligibility to be prime minister – on the basis of a minor technicality concerning campaign conduct. She became convinced that there was a large-scale conspiracy, possibly international, to overthrow her; she told her ambassador in Moscow to let Brezhnev know that the CIA was 'aiming at killing her'. The idea wasn't totally crackpot: Chile's Salvador Allende had been deposed not long before, and Sheikh Mujibur Rahman of Bangladesh was assassinated not long after, both with the involvement of the CIA. Gandhi didn't trust anyone else to lead in these days of economic instability. She decided that instead of resigning, she would rule by decree, drawing upon state emergency powers inherited from the Raj.

As shocking as the Emergency was to international opinion, it was the police-state version of what she'd been doing for years: draining away power from India's regional governments and channelling it towards New Delhi and herself. With the opposition locked away, her party could act with legislative abandon, and indeed brought some stability to the economy through measures to control prices and to increase productivity. But a 1976 programme to reduce the birth rate by incentivizing sterilization quotas was a major misjudgement.

Officials who oversaw large numbers of sterilizations were rewarded (in some cases, with Ambassador cars). Those who failed to meet quotas saw their salaries held up. Thus, in communities across India, poor people were coerced by government workers to exchange their fertility for housing, access to water or medical care. Deeply involved in running this sterilization effort was Mrs Gandhi's younger son Sanjay, an unsuccessful apprentice engineer who commandeered a wing of the party, the Youth Congress, and directed its thuggish methods. The sterilization programme was a physical and psychological violation of some of Mrs Gandhi's most passionate supporters. And ironically, it barely moved the population-control needle. Instead, as she confided to one of her officials in 1976, it made parents afraid to bring their children for routine TB and smallpox vaccinations.

In 1977, after almost twenty-one months, Mrs Gandhi ended the Emergency and called for an election. Her policies, particularly on the economy, had supporters (J. R. D. Tata, then chairman of the Tata business empire, found them 'refreshingly pragmatic and result-oriented'). And she believed that ordinary citizens, too, would trust that her actions were in their long-term interest. But being deprived of their rights sensitized many citizens to just how valuable those rights really were. Voters in north India in particular roundly rejected her and the Congress, and, for the first time since Independence, the party was out of office in New Delhi.

Mrs Gandhi's countermand of democratic principles instilled something important in independent India's public life: it deepened a spirit of dissent, and of civic and legal activism. 'For the first time,' says the Delhi social scientist D. L. Sheth, recalling the spontaneous protests, 'you felt that democratic culture had been imbibed in Indian life.' Congress's stranglehold on power ended and, among other things, a Hindu nationalist party was revived in a new mould – the

Bharatiya Janata Party, or BJP, which is now in government. The memory of Mrs Gandhi's transformation during the 1960s and 1970s into democratic India's most powerful leader has helped create a polity in which it has been difficult for any subsequent leader to accumulate the power she did. Being able to vote so dominant a leader out of office in 1977 gave voters a sense of the power they now held – and in subsequent decades, Indians participated in elections and politics at higher rates than ever before.

Another way to understand the Emergency, I think, is as a critical episode in the history of the conflict between the two ideas that have defined modern India – the idea of the state and the idea of democracy. The Emergency was a parodic version of the desire to retain the Indian state in the hands of a do-good elite. And it came at the very time when, as a result of Indira Gandhi's own electoral style, the democratic idea was achieving an unprecedented diffusion across Indian society. In effect, she was stepping on the brake and the accelerator at the same time – a move that, in the end, politicized India more profoundly than ever before.

The coda to her story – that she came back to power in 1980 – was less a result of her mollification and the people's forgiveness than of infighting among the opposition. But now she had to face the political blowback provoked by her centralizing urges and by the breakdown of federal structures that might have moderated rising challenges to New Delhi's authority. As she mourned the death of Sanjay in a plane accident, she was also wrangling with the escalating demands and actions of regionalist parties and factions across the county – Assam to the east, Punjab to the west and Kashmir to the north. Some pressed for secession, and were prepared to use violence. Her botched efforts to take control in Punjab resulted in the 1984 assault on the Sikhs' Golden Temple (see 13 **Guru Nanak**), which in turn led to her own assassination by her Sikh bodyguards a few months later.

'As a child I wanted to be like Joan of Arc,' Mrs Gandhi told a close adviser early in her premiership: 'I may yet be burnt at the stake.' She ended up achieving a certain kind of political martyrdom. But the broader political legacy of the era she dominated was to imprint on the political imagination of Indians the vital necessity of democracy.

47
Satyajit Ray

India without Elephants
1921–1992

One of the most iconic scenes in the career of the Bengali film-maker Satyajit Ray was shot during his very first week of making movies. The camera follows a young village boy, himself tracking his mischievous older sister as she goes deep into a field of kash. Unnerved by her rashness and fearful of getting lost, he begins to panic when the blooming reeds, taller than his head, obscure his sister's zigzagging path. The panic grows when the reeds start to tremble and a faraway sound becomes a roar. But his adventuresome sister has lured him here for a loving reason. A black locomotive – the first he's ever seen – chuffs by.

Ray had been planning the minutest aspects of this film, *Pather Panchali* (1955), in his head for years. But he became nervous with equipment in his hand, so he asked an experienced photographer to be his cameraman. At a moment of particularly exquisite light, the cameraman suggested a close-up of the girl. The shot was lovely – a loveliness that, Ray saw afterwards, had nothing to do with the meaning of the scene or the film. As if justifying what the Japanese director Akira Kurosawa would later say of him – 'There is nothing irrelevant or haphazard in his cinematographic technique' – he decided to reshoot. But having a day job, he had to wait until the next weekend. By then, cattle had wrecked the continuity of his shot by eating the tops of the reeds. He wouldn't have the money to re-shoot the scene until two years later, the reeds once again in bloom.

The lesson Ray took from this costly mistake – to trust his own vision, even against expert advice – helps explain the arc of a career spanning some three dozen films. Some film-makers start by doing everything themselves, then make enough dosh to delegate. Ray started out doing plenty – directing, casting, costuming, roving all over Calcutta picking up props – and eventually did more. He wrote music for his films, did most of the lighting, illustrated the screen credits and served as primary cameraman. He loosened his control only with his best actors, which is why they returned to him again and again. He liked 'hiding' behind the camera, he used to say, so that the actors couldn't tell if they had his approval. They relaxed, became more real.

The result was a body of work of which Kurosawa would remark, 'Not to have seen the cinema of Ray means existing in the world without seeing the sun or the moon.' You can see Ray's influence in many contemporary film-makers, among them Wes Anderson and Martin Scorsese. In Ray's films, Scorsese has said, 'the line between poetry and cinema dissolved'.

But not all Westerners have seen the point. 'I don't want to see a movie of peasants eating with their hands,' François Truffaut shrugged, while the legendary American critic Dwight Macdonald thought Ray should stick to homely village tales – cities and their themes being too difficult for him to handle. When I read that one, I had to laugh, for as we can deduce from his failure to factor roaming cattle into the kash scene, village life was where he was winging it. Urbane Calcutta was his home.

Ray's father, who died so young that Satyajit barely knew him, had been a brilliant illustrator and inventor of Bengali nonsense verse, writing lilting gibberish that delights Indian children to this day. Ray's grandfather, uncles and cousins were intellectuals deeply involved in the Brahmo Samaj founded by **Rammohun Roy (22)**. They drew, took photographs, argued philosophy, made music, and invented fantastical stories. A printing press and a photographic developing room were among the furniture of Ray family life and, for children, making art was as expected as going to school. In 1947, after taking a practical degree in economics at Presidency College, Calcutta, Ray started the Calcutta Film Society, gathering his friends to watch foreign films, including ones directed by Frank Capra and John Ford.

'What is wrong with Indian films?' Ray wrote in an article the next year. 'The raw material of cinema is life itself. It is incredible that a country that has inspired so much painting and music and poetry should fail to move the film-maker. He has only to keep his eyes open, and his ears. Let him do so.' Later, after his employer, an ad agency, sent him to London – where he was introduced to the work of the Italian neorealist director Vittorio De Sica – 'Let him do so' became 'Let *me* do so'. 'It just gored me,' Ray said later of De Sica's *Bicycle Thieves* (1948), claiming he left the movie theatre determined to make his own films.

In the history of Indian cinema, there is a Before Ray, and an After. He's the first truly modern film-maker we have, though his career in India might not have continued past its first few films had he not been celebrated in the West. I first saw one of his films, *The Chess Players* (1977), at an art-house cinema just as I began university in England, and I'm hardly the only one of his Indian fans who first encountered him outside the country.

In Bengal, several of his films were popular. More were disliked, and in today's thriving Bengali film culture, he's often held at arm's length: the guy who served it up for the West, and served it up a little sweet. Indeed, Ray looks almost as sentimental as **Raj Kapoor** (42) in comparison to the harsh, brilliant, but lesser known Bengali film-maker Ritwik Ghatak.

Representing the mainstream Indian critique of Ray was the screen legend Nargis, who in later life became something of a politician. She was one of many who felt he had done the country a disservice by making poverty and India synonymous in the minds of the West. Films like *Pather Panchali* were popular abroad '[b]ecause people there want to see India in an abject condition,' she argued, adding, 'What I want is that if Mr. Ray projects Indian poverty abroad, he should also show "Modern India".'

But Ray had no interest in doing a report card on Indian modernity, just as he had no interest in doing a report card on Indian poverty (the latter could be left to Louis Malle). Nor was he especially original when it came to themes. The Apu Trilogy (the three films he made about the little boy in the reeds, growing to manhood) explores the conflict a young man feels between tradition and modernity, the village and the city – already, by the early 1960s, a global cinematic cliché from Ozu to Visconti. But his films made ideas hanging in the air feel fresh, for Ray brought to them an unusually large wodge of small gifts: psychological and sensory acuity, humour, humanism, a deep appreciation of family relationships, an ability to withhold judgement, an ear equally adept at dialogue and sound, and the visual imagination of a third-generation illustrator and photographer. These were sufficient to allow him, time and again, to achieve a realism few in Indian cinema wanted to confront. 'It's the truth in a situation that attracts me,' he told his actors. 'And if I've been able to show it, that's enough for me.'

'Our mind has faculties which are universal,' Rabindranath **Tagore** (32) once wrote, 'but its habits are insular.' The medium of film in India, Ray felt in the late 1940s, was too bound by that insularity. Indian directors, preoccupied with song-and-dance diversions, had failed to develop a cinematic vocabulary to articulate the fine grades of emotion and humour in Indian life. These habits had to be broken, so that Indian film-makers and their audiences could fully join a more universal conversation. But it would be a mistake to think that Ray, as he studied films from the 'developed' world, felt himself to be an outsider looking in. High Bengali culture – and sophisticated, upper-caste Brahmo Samaj culture particularly – had long seen itself in cultural and intellectual dialogue with the West. Ray was himself a product of Tagore's incubator of universal humanism, the school and university at Shantiniketan.

Not long after his young man's outburst against Indian films, Ray met the French director Jean Renoir, who had come to India to make *The River* (1951), a meditative film about an English girl's adolescence in Bengal that Hollywood studios had declined to finance. 'In every case the response was the same – India without elephants and tiger-hunts was just not India,' Renoir said later.

Ray, who considered Renoir's earlier film *The Southerner* (1945) a narrative breakthrough, pinioned the older man at a hotel and told him his idea for *Pather Panchali*. Renoir didn't run screaming. Instead, sensing Ray's intelligence and eye, he took off with the twenty-eight-year-old to scout locations for *The River*. Ray's job prevented him visiting Renoir's shoots regularly, though. Instead, nightly, he would go through the script and grill a friend who was working on set about how each scene had been filmed. Through the friend, he also passed on the occasional thought about how a scene might be done. He was moved when he heard that Renoir had taken his advice.

It's interesting to speculate to what extent the long-distance tutorials that Ray received from Renoir shaped his film-making. Like Renoir, he would come to value multiple viewpoints, even though he figured that deviating from the Bengali film norm of a single perspective hurt him at the box office. But Ray wasn't particularly impressionable, and he didn't spend enough time watching Renoir's work to be overly influenced by the director who showed him kindness. I think he was just a formidably confident Bengali. Later, several young film-makers would point to him as the sterling example of the ability to internalize influences and then break free of them. 'He didn't follow anyone,' the director Shyam Benegal said. 'He showed us you had to make your own way.'

In a Calcutta tenement, a bored young bride fans her husband as he eats his dinner – your quintessential patriarchal set-up. The camera pulls close to the fan, moving rhythmically back and forth. When it pulls back, we find the man, equally bored, fanning his wife.

This delightful, expectation-subverting move in the final part of the Apu trilogy, which tells so much about a young marriage, is one of many moments in early Ray films that we might put down to crack editing. But much of Ray's early film work was, as the phrase goes, 'cut in the camera'. Lacking editing skills, or the money to hire someone with them, he had to get it exactly right on set. Sharmila Tagore's first role, at the age of thirteen, was that young bride; she would become one of Ray's most famous heroines. She recalls the tall, softly spoken director on that first set smoking constantly, chewing nervously on a handkerchief, wolfing down his lunch, telling her how to hold her shoulders just so, and seeming to concentrate like mad on hundreds of things at once.

'We all had to come prepared, because he didn't have the money to do 3 or 4 takes,' she says. 'And even the studios had potholes, making simple trolley shots almost impossible.' There were also frequent power cuts. 'Imagine if your film is in the lab then. You lose the negatives.' But even with these kinds of obstacles, Ray still thought he could do something new and start that creative dialogue with the best directors in the world. In 1961, he was amused to read an article in *American Cinematographer* that credited Ingmar Bergman's *Through a Glass Darkly* (1961) with inventing a technique simulating shadowless, diffused sky light; Ray's cinematographer Subrata Mitra had been using it since 1954, to circumvent the difficulties of shooting in Indian glare.

The scene of the newlyweds and the fan represents another trademark of Ray's films: the implicit argument that cinema can get by on fewer words. A sitar riff by Ravi Shankar is the only thing that speaks. Finding the dialogue of most Hindi films inane and incessant, Ray strove for lyrical but realistic speech, with pauses. Better still was replacing words altogether, and letting a knot tied in a dupatta or the reed-trills of a shennai elicit the emotion of the viewer. (If you're a Ray aficionado, you'll know just the moments I mean.) *Charulata* (1964), based on the Tagore story 'The Broken Nest', opens with the excruciating ennui of the bright, neglected wife of a wealthy editor (a woman soon to fall in love with her visiting cousin-in-law). In five minutes, virtually wordless apart from a call for tea, sounds alone convey an irresolute anxiety that make the viewer want to climb the walls too. Book pages flip. A clock strikes four. Birdwings flap. A beggar drums. Window slats clack open and closed. Ray's choices, psychologically astute, are the polar opposite of what's known in the American film industry as 'sound by the pound'. They also overturn the convention of loud background music that had featured in Indian film since the first talkies. To Ray, everyday noise – radio static, a thunderstorm, a drip from a tap, voices in a tenement building – was not just a potential score. It was another way of storytelling. In *Charulata*, the sounds themselves hint at how all the tension might break.

Ray was equally sparing with words when running the set. 'He was *so* brief,' Sharmila Tagore recalls. 'He never over-instructed. He just read it out, and we understood what he wanted. His praise was equally brief. "Excellent. Next shot." It was enough.'

Making an inconstant wife like the eponymous Charulata a heroine was also typical Ray. Though he's probably most associated with male characters, such as Apu, his filmography includes an array of contemporary female possibilities – free-spirited thief, journalist, vacuum cleaner saleswoman, student, restless wife. Ray's sense that women could have multiple identities perhaps goes back to his own widowed mother, who had a career. His women are never seen exclusively through the eyes of men; nor are they exemplars of Womanhood. Like his male characters, they are too complex and particular to serve as social message boards.

None of these innovations – the subtlety and silence, the everyday scores, the refusal to make his female characters pure and his male ones anything but ordinary – helped convince theatres in Bengal to show his films. So in 1957, when *Aparajito* (1956), the second film of the Apu Trilogy, unexpectedly won the Golden Lion at the Venice Film Festival, it served as a bailout for what was beginning to look like a minor career. That the trilogy went on to critical acclaim in America, connecting Ray to famous directors and cool young fans, made him still more frustrated with Indian cinema-goers. 'One realizes what the Indian film-maker is up against – a colossal ignorance and only a moderate inquisitiveness,' he groused to a Sri Lankan director friend after being lionized in New York. 'The East is still as far away from the West as it has ever been.'

By the 1960s, however, young people in the East and West had something to share: a sense of political alienation. In India, faith in Nehru's project had begun to fade, and issues of economic and political discontent started making their way into Ray's films. He wasn't signing up to the politics of the streets, like his contemporary the *radicalisant* director Mrinal Sen, and others. Instead, Sharmila Tagore recalls him sitting by his television, in a room surrounded by paintbrushes and books, studying 'not politics per se but the effects of politics on ethical and moral values'.

In *Days and Nights in the Forest* (1969), Ray wittily explored those effects through four willing victims of cultural imperialism: young men raised in Calcutta to be more English than the English (the type of Bengalis Tagore would have called '*ingabangas*'). During a weekend in the jungle, the young men find out that they can only appreciate an Indian sunset through the lens of a Burt Lancaster western. When they meet the Santal tribals who live in the forest, they regard them as a different species. Almost half a century old, in its mordant humour the film feels entirely contemporary with those made by the Jim Jarmusch generation.

Perhaps Ray was thinking about his own distance from fellow Bengalis, which he had begun to bridge, just before *Days and Nights*, by using yet another of his great small gifts. Like his father and grandfather, he had always written and illustrated fantastical children's books on the side; in fact, he postponed his films from time to time to see them through. Now, thinking of his own children, he made a delightfully loopy adventure film, *Goopy Gyne Bagha Byne* (*The Adventures of Goopy and Bagha*) (1968). It's the story of a poor grocer's son who dreams of being a singer, despite a froggy voice, and through magic and cleverness achieves the near-impossible: a Ray film without a moody ending! *Goopy* and its sequel, still unknown in the West – your loss, little people – rightfully became classics and are beloved by children across Bengal today.

Another Ray work, sci-fi this time, is uncomfortably related to a film beloved by American children. In the late 1960s, Ray authored 'The Alien', a script based on his own short story, but he lacked the technical resources to turn it into a film. Hollywood types jumped in with flattery and promise. Columbia Pictures would produce; Peter '*Pink Panther*' Sellers and Marlon Brando wanted in. But then, in what Ray sardonically referred to as his Kafka period, an unstable partner copyrighted his script and pocketed his advance, after which Sellers dumped him by sending a rhyme. Ray tried to view the experience philosophically, until he saw Steven Spielberg's *E. T.* in 1982. To biographer Andrew Robinson, Ray made the careful allegation that the film, one of the highest grossing of all time, 'would not have been possible without my script of "The Alien" being available throughout America in mimeographed copies'. Sci-fi legend Arthur C. Clarke perceived a similar influence. But Spielberg denied it, and Ray was outmatched.

It's a mark of a great director not always to be acknowledged, and Ray knew enough film history to accept that. But a lingering sense that he'd been exploited by Hollywood caused him to steer clear of that world until shortly before his death, when, with the support of Scorsese and other prominent directors, he became the first Indian, then or since, to receive an Academy Award for lifetime achievement.

Looking back at Ray's career, I find him an unusual modernist: Bauhaus in the light-handedness and clarity of his technique; Bengali and Shantiniketan in that what he did and loved best always had the quality, even flourish, of the handmade. As young Indian directors become more literary in approach and more economical in style, and as they study Western directors who themselves have absorbed traces of Ray's influence, I keep waiting for those of his films more adult than *Goopy* to move from the Indian art-house to the multiplex mainstream. You never know: one day, India's most internationally respected film-maker might become one whom ordinary Indians actually like to watch.

48
Charan Singh

A Common Cause
1902–1987

How wealthy does a developing country have to become before it has a distinct class known as the poor? When, in popular imagination, are 'the impoverished' no longer synonymous with 'the people'? For India, that moment came first in the cities, where a professional elite emerged under the British and manufacturing produced, in addition to textiles and trinkets, a politically significant lower-middle class. But semi-feudal rural India appeared to these Indian elites, even at Independence, as a vast, undifferentiated mass of abjectness. In the West, the image was of ribs sticking out, begging bowls and desperation – a mental picture upon which chubby Western children were commanded to eat every last bite of their dinners.

But rural India had hierarchies as intricate as they were rigid; you just had to get closer to see them. Charan Singh, the bright, methodical child of better-off-than-average Meerut peasants, saw. He came from an oppressed cultivating caste, the Jats, and grew up to be a lawyer, then a politician, in the United Provinces (later Uttar Pradesh). He melded a generations-old knowledge of rural life with an analytical study of land reforms and agricultural subsidies around the world to do something in north India that doesn't happen much in the country: he redistributed power and altered the social structure – without violence.

'India's villages are the colonies of the city,' Singh often complained about Nehruvian India. Today, he's remembered as a nemesis of the Nehrus: the politician who took on Indira Gandhi in the Congress party's heartland, ending its stranglehold on the national government and becoming prime minister. That his term swiftly unravelled through infighting and political treachery, and that his personality was short of panache, tends to obscure what he achieved before failing when he reached the top. Step by step, reform by reform, he became the first national public figure in India's long history to plausibly claim to represent the rural landed peasant. That's especially striking given the vast numbers of Indians involved in agriculture – probably more than in any other country. Charan Singh's life is a window onto that world.

Against the driving Nehru-era concerns of urbanization, industrialism and making India a world power, Singh prosecuted a slimmer agenda: making the rural farmer as productive and prosperous as possible. From that, he argued, all else would follow. 'Agriculture is the first condition,' he once said. 'Our people live in the villages; 72 per cent of our workers are now engaged in agriculture. So unless agricultural production goes up – unless there is purchasing power with the people – non-agricultural employments will not come up. Industry will not develop. Commerce will not develop. Transport will not develop. Unless these develop, there will be no improvement in the living standard of our people.'

The British had allowed Indian agriculture to stagnate before Independence; from 1911 to 1941, per capita access to grains decreased by a third. After Independence, there was truth in the novelist Vikram Seth's crack in *A Suitable Boy* that north India's entrenched, upper-caste landlords weren't pulling their weight in the fledgling nation: 'For most of the landlords the primary question of management was not indeed how to increase their income but how to spend it.' Roughly 20,000 such landlords owned 60 per cent of land in the United Provinces. Singh's legislative drives played a major role in changing that. Over the course of the 1950s, after centuries of dominance, those landlords were forced to share turf and political influence with some of the people who ploughed and sowed. This and other successful political campaigns on behalf of farmers would in time help give north India a rural middle class.

Although his vision of rural development was not nearly as inclusive as he claimed, and was only partially realized, Singh would, over a political career that spanned six decades, change the fortunes of millions and millions of villagers. And yet the full bill for that achievement – from caste tension to increased rural inequality to near-catastrophic water depletion – is still being paid to this day.

> *And in the winter nights we would wrap rice stalks in old discarded clothes, and then hide under that. What did we know what a quilt was? We didn't even know what shoes were!*
>
> United Provinces sharecropper Ram Dass

To study old photographs from UP villages like the one where Ram Dass lived is to be reminded of how rural history writes upon the body. Mughal governments from the time of **Akbar** (16) had empowered large landholders, known as *zamindars*, to collect rents and taxes from the peasants, and to serve as moneylenders. The British, who considered the zamindars natural leaders, yeomen of the subcontinent, entrenched that tradition. So by the twentieth century, many of this elect were pale and smooth from generations of living in palatial homes that protected them from sun and rain; they were tall and broad from generations of being amply fed; they were loose-limbed from generations of being spared the daily, aching stoop to sow. At first glance, they might appear to be a different race from the manual workers whose labour funded their lifestyles, a race whose muslin and silken robes could house two or three farmers within them.

The power of the zamindars, who were mainly Brahmin or Rajput, was challenged in a series of peasant movements between 1919 and 1921, when Charan Singh was in his late teens. A young Nehru had experienced rural India for the first time when he came out to support the peasants, who wanted to organize and become part of the Congress. But the agitation was put down by local power and tepid support from a Congress reluctant to alienate the rich landowners whose backing they needed. The British weakened the zamindars' power a little, beginning in the 1930s, but you can get a glimpse of how potent the system remained from an essay about the peasantry written by a landlord and politician in 1935:

> [The villager] is a willing tool in the hands of any self-seeking, intelligent man . . . His political life is blank. He is completely ignorant

of his rights and privileges. Any man with a little knowledge or power can lord it over him.

While the zamindars were essentially middlemen for the government, Singh's people, the Jats – a caste whose men and women actually worked the fields – didn't see them that way. The people to whom the Jats directly paid what they considered exploitative rents on their land seemed larger in their minds than the regional politicians and Brahmin bureaucrats with whom they rarely dealt. The zamindars were unwavering objects of Jat resentment, and became the target of Singh's first successful legislative campaign.

From early on, Singh had conceived of himself as not just a representative, but a rescuer, of his people. This was in part because he had advantages many of them lacked. He was uncommonly tall and handsome, and though he'd grown up 'under a thatched roof supported by *kachcha* mud walls', as he often put it, his father had worked his way from tenant farming to ownership of more acres than the average peasant farmed. This allowed Singh a crucial bounce off the socioeconomic springboard: he was able to study science and history at Agra College, after which he was called to the Bar. His practice lasted barely a few years: his long-term objective had been politics all along.

After joining Gandhi's civil disobedience movement, in 1930, and doing jail time for it, Singh rapidly ascended the Congress hierarchy. In 1937, at the age of thirty-four, he was one of the Congressmen elected to the new Legislative Assembly of the United Provinces. A protégé of the powerful conservative provincial operative Gobind Ballabh Pant, he was by the 1950s respected in his own right, at high political levels, for the size of his following of farmers. The peasant's son had risen from district-level politics to state politics by pulling off something that many earlier Indian social reformers had longed to do: convince peasants to make common cause with each other as a class, *across* their caste affiliation. This was a significant practical as well as a conceptual advance, for Jats on their own made up a paltry 1.2 per cent of the UP population – hardly a numerical force sufficient to confront centuries-old power structures.

In pre-Independence campaigns for debt relief for rural workers, and against rapacious traders, one of Singh's recurring themes was that farmers were habitually betrayed both by rural elites and by the urban dwellers who dominated nationalist politics and were often as unconcerned about farming as the British. To Singh, farmers were not just a majority; they were an intellectual resource, possessing under-utilized knowledge of how to expand the food economy and address poverty, including their own. But instead of being heard, they had become the nation's beasts of burden – a problem for state policy, rather than makers of it.

When you read speeches Charan Singh made to his followers, his populist riffs and habit of referring to himself in the third person seem almost demagogic. But to *hear* Charan Singh address a crowd was to be in the presence not of some Indian Fidel Castro but of anti-charisma. The social scientist and politician Yogendra Yadav recalls going as a teenager to hear Singh speak in his small Haryana town: 'There was no attempt to please the masses. He asked people to either sit down or leave, then went on to give a one-hour-long, school-teacher-like lecture on the political economy of Indian agriculture. This is the last thing you expect from a major politician who's out there to woo the public, but it quite characterized who he was – plain, straight, no-nonsense and to the point.'

Singh was probably more naturally suited to writing, and his many books and pamphlets on rural policy are exhaustively argued. While Russia produced more than a dozen agrarian intellectuals, and China produced a few, Singh may have been independent India's one and only. But that's part of what's affecting about the size of his following: it wasn't necessary for him to deliver stem-winders at the stump, because millions of peasants understood that he, one of their own, was in a better position to fight for their interests than anyone had ever been before.

Unlike Nehru, Singh was deeply sceptical of policies to create agricultural cooperatives, pointing to the unimpressive productivity rates that followed Russian collectivization. (Nehru would, after several such policy failures of his own, come to agree.) Instead, Singh thought that undermining the zamindari system and strengthening access to land at the 'base of the pyramid' would help India avoid not only class conflict, but also food shortages and famine.

Immediately upon Independence, after at least six years of study, Singh issued a manifesto to that end. Five years later, in 1952, legislation he had designed – the historic UP Zamindari Abolition and Land Reforms Act – became law. The Act gave some tenant farmers secure claim to their land, allowed their children to inherit it, and eliminated the role of zamindars in collecting revenue from them. The Act didn't wholly dispossess the zamindars, however: they kept land historically under their personal cultivation (an unfortunately expandable category) and received government payment for land they had to divest – compromises the Congress was obliged to make to keep the support of the rural rich. While the effects of the legislation were further softened by corruption in its implementation, something significant had doubtless been achieved. Zamindari ceased across 60.2 million of the states' 72.6 million acres. The peasant's son had created a new class of landowners in the United Provinces.

The thought that land had become the peasant's and his children's property 'in perpetuity', Singh wrote in 1959, 'lightens and cheers his labour and expands his horizon'. He went on, 'The feeling that he is his own master, subject to no outside control, and has free, exclusive and untrammelled use of his land drives him to greater and greater effort.'

Who were these happy, productive beneficiaries of UP's land reform? A reliable way to wind up Singh, later in life, was to accuse him of having created an Indian version of the Russian kulaks – that rich, entitled peasant class that Lenin described as 'profiteers, who fatten on famine'.

Singh had set a high cap (30 acres) on the land an individual farmer could own, against helping a greater number of peasants; and favouritism in the implementation of the new law further excluded weaker farmers. Soon after, another of Singh's legislative achievements – consolidating fragmented land holdings to help farmers increase their efficiency – gave further advantages to already somewhat advantaged peasants. Not coincidentally, many of them were Jats from Singh's home region, in western UP.

In any country, land reforms addressing immense disparities between landowners and tenant farmers create finer grades of inequality. But I wonder if Singh might have been more thoughtful about diminishing this risk had his view of the economic behaviour of village farmers not been so rosy. The peasant, Singh contended, wasn't a normal capitalist actor. Rather, his traditional values and staunch character rendered him less money-obsessed and more virtuous than, say, a factory worker. Even when employing others to help tend his fields, he claimed, the farmer didn't exploit them.

It was probably good for the statistical incidence of apoplectic stroke in India that landless UP peasants – mainly Dalits who worked for cultivators like the Jats – had been systematically denied the leisure and education to read the collected pamphletry of Charan Singh. The lot of the landless had been touched by land reform in only one important way: a larger and more diverse group of people were now able to work them like animals and pay them little, when they got around to it. And because Singh fought to keep farmers, even very rich ones, exempt from meaningful taxation – something true to this day in UP and all across rural India – there was little wealth for a state in the agrarian heartland to redistribute.

Even now, landless Dalits view the Jats with as much distrust as the Jats had once viewed the zamindars. Though that animosity of course predated Singh, he intensified it. Through a long career in which he rhetorically positioned himself as an advocate of the masses, he initiated very little for his most needy constituents. Meanwhile, by the late 1960s, it was becoming hard to argue that his sustained largesse to cultivators had trickled down and created a better-fed populace. When modern India's first famine threatened, it was in eastern UP – not because there was not enough grain, but because the poorest lacked the cash to buy it.

At a time when Indian poverty required urgent political action, Singh's view – that preferences and subsidies given to his base of farmers would transform the wider economy – placed him at odds with the

Congress, which had to appease constituencies other than farmers. So, in 1967, Singh quit the party, announcing he was fed up with its corruption and incompetence. The Congress instantly felt the effects of losing his support. Within three weeks, the state government fell. Singh, at the head of a coalition of opposition parties, became UP's first non-Congress chief minister – a historic achievement in the heartland of Congress politics. It was a lesson he would apply nationally in the 1970s, to take on Indira Gandhi.

'The farmers are forgotten by this government,' Singh lectured on his seventy-sixth birthday to an audience massed on the broad avenue leading from India Gate up to Parliament House in Delhi. It was 1978. After imprisonment during the Emergency, he had achieved a sweet revenge, forming a joint opposition party that brought down Indira Gandhi's government. Now he wanted to be India's first peasant prime minister. The audience he addressed was unprecedented in the capital: nearly a million farmers in dhotis and turbans, many of whom, said a *New York Times* report, were still dusty from their work in the fields.

Some in the foreign press saw the crowds as threatening and abject, but that got their relative position in Indian life quite wrong. Indira Gandhi had in the previous ten years averted famine and drastically reduced the country's dependency on foreign food aid, which had once allowed Lyndon Johnson's agriculture secretary to gloat, 'We had them over a barrel and squeezed them.' India's so-called Green Revolution – one of the final economic policy initiatives of Indira Gandhi's father – had entered its second decade, and high-yield seed varieties, tube wells and fertilizers were increasing food stores, if depleting the environment. So Singh and the farmers who gathered weren't merely begging for help; they were demanding that their vast newfound political power be rewarded. Many of the subsidies and tax breaks farmers (including fabulously wealthy ones) receive today for water, electricity, fertilizer and machinery can be found in the budget demands Singh made after his followers' strength was impressed upon Delhi. By the next year, 1979, those farmers had helped him gain the prime ministership.

That's the happy moment on which the children's-book version of the story ought rightly to end, because the denouement was fast and ugly. Members of his coalition quickly turned against one another, and Singh was gone from the highest office in a trice (just twenty-four days in power, though he remained a caretaker prime minister for several months), replaced by a returning Indira Gandhi. Decades later, we are yet to see another genuine member of the peasant class rise to become a serious contender for prime minister.

As the political economist Terence Byres says, Singh was in the vanguard of Indian 'capitalism from below', but today his popular legacy is oddly diminished. He's thought of mainly as the leader of his own caste, the Jats. In Yogendra Yadav's assessment, Singh's 'inability to speak for different classes of Indian farmers, especially his inability or unwillingness to speak about the landless farmers, has proved to be a very severe limitation of his legacy'.

Though the Jats prospered during Charan Singh's lifetime, in more recent years some of the state subsidies and favourable pricing mechanisms that enabled them to do so have shrunk, leaving them more exposed to the market. Many have invested their profits in small businesses – furniture and metal workshops, real estate – and are seeking ways out of agriculture. A caste that has not traditionally valued education, Jats are now pressing to be recognized as one of the less privileged caste communities, known as the Other Backward Classes, eligible for reservations or affirmative action in educational places and government jobs. I wonder what Charan Singh would have made of the fact that the people whose farming skills he celebrated and defended are themselves giving up on the land.

49
M. F. Husain

'Hindustan is Free'
1917–2011

'Hindustan has for a thousand years been enslaved. For 700 years it was ruled by Muslims, then by the English, and works made during these periods gave false stories about Indian art, culture and history,' Ashok Deendayal Sharma, a large man in a neatly pressed safari suit, explained recently as he settled himself under a tree in the city of Ahmedabad. 'But now Hindustan is free, and anyone who abuses or attacks the gods of the majority Hindus will not be tolerated by the majority community.'

Sharma, the founder of a small right-wing organization, the Hindu Samrajya Sena, belongs today to the regional Hindu party, the Shiv Sena. While unspooling his version of Indian history, he gazed evenly at the modern art gallery just across the concourse from where we sat. In the two decades since the art gallery's opening, he and his ideological allies have attacked it three times. The gallery, whose series of low white domes become, from the inside, a modernist interpretation of the meandering caves of Ellora, was inspired and houses murals by one of the bogeys of Hindu extremism: the puckishly exuberant Muslim artist Maqbool Fida Husain.

Husain, who is recognized in other quarters as *the* face of modern art in independent India, learned to paint boldly and quickly in the 1930s while making ends meet by working on billboards for films. In the course of a long life, he racked up some 10,000 works – created on walls, chairs, hoardings, plates, toys and film as well as canvases. Some of those works were exhilarating commentaries on the emergence of a new nation. Some were the market-driven confections of a whimsical playboy. Had a fraction of the works not been of Hindu goddesses and Indian female icons in the nude, I suspect his legacy in India would be roughly as polarizing as that of Andy Warhol in America today – a matter of *vernissage* dispute, not an occasion for mob rampage. But modern Indian cultural debates have never been known for their proportionality.

In addition to the assaults on the Ahmedabad gallery, Sharma and his comrades have successfully intimidated other Ahmedabad and Mumbai galleries that planned to show the late modernist painter's work. So when Sharma speaks of Husain, who was approaching eighty when he became a cultural lightning rod, it is with the relaxed mock-sympathy of a man who's won more battles than he has lost. 'It was Husain's mental disease that caused him to inflict this,' Sharma says. 'To do it in front of the whole world – he was a man who was trying to glorify his own name in the world market . . . But the moment we stood up and showed him our strength, he had to stop doing such work.'

The threats didn't stop Husain, actually. What they did, after nearly a decade of pressure, was to drive a consummately Indian painter into exile. There, refusing either to apologize for his controversial works or to excoriate those who attacked him, he kept painting, in accordance with his own vision of India, until his death.

Many liberals of the time were distressed to see a free-spirited popular artist become, late in life, a butterfly on the wheel of Hindu nationalism. But now that he's gone, to view him only as what he came to represent in that controversy – as an emblem either of free expression or of religious insult – shunts aside one of his original contributions to Indian culture. From the 1950s, long before he became a political shuttlecock, Husain was a democratizer of Indian modern art.

Many twentieth-century artists, in India and elsewhere, came from culturally sophisticated elites and produced work substantially for people like themselves to appreciate. M. F. Husain's own wanderings from childhood through a variety of villages, towns, cultures, and later countries, inspired him to build, over the course of his career, a bigger tent: an artistic public space that had room for popular audiences as well as privileged ones. There was no other modern art-ist whose name the average Bombay rickshaw-wallah was likely to know, not least for the many paintings he made of India's greatest film diva of the 1990s, Madhuri Dixit (who also starred in a feature film he directed).

Despite the breadth of his later popularity, Husain was not origi-nally part of any mainstream. His roots were Gujarati, and further back Yemeni, but he was born, probably in 1917, in the temple-town of Pandharpur, in what is now Maharashtra. His working-class fam-ily were Suleimanis, a sub-sect of the Shia community of Bohras. Being from a tiny minority, the artist who later became hated in part because of his religion recalled in the 1990s that, 'until recently, we never disclosed our religion. We did not even build mosques.' This sense of being outside the fold also described his relationship to his family.

His founding wound, in his own telling, was the death of his mother before he was two – a loss he connected to his later obsession with female forms, including those of Hindu goddesses. His father, who moved the family to Indore and took a job as a millworker, paid him only sporadic attention; when he remarried, young Maqbool lived for a time with his grandfather. But he considered himself, from a very young age, to be on his own.

Later, Husain made his enforced independence sound more like a lark than a hardship. Naturally sociable and obsessed with playing football, he assembled an alternative family from people he met on the maidans and streets. But his uncertainty about his real family's support also made him view the world through a practical lens; he realized that as much as he'd like to kick a ball around all day, another of his skills – drawing – could be more readily converted into income. Nor did he mind the attention he received in middle school, when his patriotic headmaster selected him to draw a portrait of Gandhi on the great man's birthday. 'I don't need any degree because of this brush in my hand,' he recalled telling his family upon finish-ing high school. 'If nothing happens, I'll whitewash the walls.' He later described that decision as his 'great liberation, one of the great-est events of my life – that I got the freedom to work'.

He didn't have to whitewash much. Instead, he began his career as a professional artist in Bombay, where he painted garish Bollywood film hoardings for a pittance. Typically working outdoors, sometimes between monsoon downpours, he mastered with confident strokes a scale and sense of proportion that other artists working on large canvases would have required detailed sketches and grids to pull off. Years later, when extremist vandals ransacked his home, destroying paintings worth millions on the market, he accepted it with equanimity: 'I know how it is to work so hard on a hoarding that is put up for only a couple of weeks, and then destroyed. Isn't it funny?'

I've always been moved by Husain's account of how, new to the city and uncertain how to be an artist, he caught a showing of an American melodrama starring Charles Laughton as Rembrandt. The fictional Rembrandt's anguish at his inability to be true to his art while earning enough to eat disquieted Husain, but the faces in the portraits on-screen fired him up. He started cutting photos of ordinary Indians out of newspapers and painting them. I still feel slightly cheated that his Bollywood hoardings were lost to history. I bet the faces, never to be seen up close, were very good, and maybe even a little Dutch.

Rembrandt, in film and in life, died poor; the pragmatic Husain simply acquired more marketable skills. Seeking a steadier income after he married in 1941, he learned to be a miniaturist, decorating nursery furniture for posh children. It was Jack and Jill and Little Bo Beeps by the dozen. In his spare time, he started to design furniture he considered cooler than the stuff on which he was painting – productions that helped him think about shape and form. This subsistence work benefited his private art, which he continued on the side. As Independence loomed, he began playing with Indian artistic traditions, painting the fisherfolk and labourers in his neighbourhood, and preparing for the first time to show a few pieces in an exhibition put on by the Bombay Art Society.

To four artists on the cutting edge of the city's art world, among them the iconoclastic Francis Newton Souza and the Tantric-abstractionist painter S. H. Raza, the Society's exhibitions were a provocation: proof that conservative critics couldn't judge what was and wasn't good in modern art. In 1947, the frustrated four founded the Bombay Progressive Artists' Group. Rejecting the academic manner imported by British institutions from the West, as well as the historicism and quaint stylistics of the nationalist Bengal School, they sought, as they wrote in a manifesto, to bridge 'the widening gulf between the artists and the life of the people'. They nevertheless attended some of the despised exhibitions; at one, Souza encountered Husain's painting *Kumhar* ('Potters') and invited him to join the progressive ranks.

Krishen Khanna, a surviving member of the group, recalls with astonishment how little Husain or the other supposedly political artists discussed the fact that India had just been split into two nations. 'He never had a political philosophy or anything,' Khanna remembers. 'He had a general philosophy, which was a very good philosophy, but this country couldn't take it. He said that this is a multicultural subcontinent – all sorts of people live here, which is actually an enrichment, and we get along all right.' A striking aspect of Husain's early work was that the religions of many figures remained ambiguous.

Around this time he began to take an interest in Pahari School paintings from Basohli (see 20 **Nainsukh**) and Jain miniatures, and travelled with Souza to see an exhibition of sculptures from the temples of Mathura. The influence of those red sandstone forms, particularly of yakshis (female spirits and divinities, often shown nude or semi-nude), would be lasting, and would emerge in one of his finest paintings, the monumental *Man* of 1950. Cubist vocabulary engages with Indian forms, motifs, colours and images in a composition that could connect equally to Partition or to universal existential struggle. A formidable, nude black figure broods, chin on hand, astride a low stool, as a mêlée of torsos and limbs whorls around him, including the distinct, fateful hand of a female deity.

The year Husain painted *Man*, Souza was leaving for London and Raza for Paris, where they'd each find stimulation and fame in the wider international avant-garde. But Husain, who lacked the others' resources and exposure to Western art, stayed put with his wife and young children, and by comparison developed less. Later, he recalled that abstract art and pure cubism were so unloved in India that when, after *Man*, he made five figureless paintings, he couldn't sell them for even five rupees. Instead he would evolve, to great profit and mixed reviews, the modern-folk amalgam that came to define him.

Against the backdrop of a makeshift village theatre – a deep-red stretch of cloth – a tribal woman, stunningly hieratic in head and form, dangles a giant spider on a thread. Flanking her are a peasant woman in a white sari, a lamp balanced on her head, and an adolescent girl, her naked body gilded with turmeric paste. 'It could have been conceived and executed nowhere else but on location in India,' the critic and art historian Geeta Kapur wrote about Husain's best-known painting, *Between the Spider and the Lamp* (1956). It's a testament to Husain's mainstream popularity from the mid-1950s to the mid-1980s that this enigmatic, beautifully composed and slyly erotic painting was featured, in 1982, on an Indian postage stamp.

Husain wanted his art to reach Indians who, like him, grew up outside big cities, in places like his own Pandharpur and Indore. Eschewing a studio, he typically made his art while travelling – later in life, famously, barefoot. The religious and cultural influences he encountered and drew on were motley. Growing up, he'd been enchanted by the white stallions in Muslims' Muharram processions, and horses became a recurring motif in his work. But he'd also acted as the Hindu god Hanuman in skits he'd put on with his friends, and eagerly awaited the appearance of the god in annual Ramlila performances. These, too, became an obsession in his art.

When urban critics failed to understand Husain's abstract or symbolic work, his usual riposte was that the non-urban public did. 'I had done paintings of Ramayana, about eighty paintings over eight years,' he once said. 'We took them to villages near Hyderabad on a bullock cart. The paintings were spread out, and the people saw them, and there was not one question. In the city, people would have asked: Where is the eye? How can you say this is Ram? and so on. In the villages, colour and form have seeped into the blood. You put an orange spot on a stone and the people will say it is Hanuman. They would never ask where the eye was and so on. This is living art.'

He later said he had done his best work in the 1950s. But in 1971, the former hoardings artist was asked to exhibit in São Paulo alongside Picasso, an artist whose work, when he first saw it, left him cold, but whom he slowly came to appreciate. He decided to paint his own response to *Guernica*: a series of large canvases based on India's version of a war epic, the Mahabharata. Once the art world's spotlight was turned on him, the charismatic sociability he'd developed in boyhood kept it there.

'He is fond of the media glare,' his son once admitted. 'He won't say no even if he's asked to wear leather and pose on a motor bike.' This fascination with glamour and fame extended to legendary women, from Mother Teresa to Indira Gandhi, whom he began to turn into subjects of his art. Of the three films he made, the most talked about was the one starring his great obsession, Madhuri Dixit. In his nineties, Husain still grinned at the thought of her hip-bucking backsteps before she burst into one of the film's songs, '*Didi tera devar diwana*'. With a lesser dancer, he thought the moves might have been vulgar. But in Madhuri's dance he said he found the sanctity of Indian womanhood, the ineffable ideal of the mother he had never known.

By the 1990s, the flamboyant bohemian had more rich patrons than he knew what to do with, and was basically living up to an old jest of Souza's: that the secret of his success was '40% your beard, 30% your personality, 20% your friends, and 10% maybe your talent!' He was an easy person to caricature by the time he came into focus in the viewfinder of the Hindu right.

The upsurge of Hindu nationalism in the 1990s was articulated in the language of victimhood that Ashok Sharma still uses today: of injuries by Muslims, Europeans and India's post-Independence constitutional state. In 1992, the grievances funnelled into rage about a historic sixteenth-century mosque in the Uttar Pradesh town of Ayodhya. Many Hindus believed the mosque was erected on the birthplace of the god Ram, so it was destroyed in order to make way for a temple. In the ensuing riots, Muslims and religious minorities were targeted. Years of threats, terrorizing attacks and uncertainty for minorities across the country followed.

In 1996, amid multi-pronged Hindu nationalist efforts to redefine India, a Hindi weekly magazine printed a line drawing of the goddess Saraswati that Husain had made around 1970. 'M. F. Husain: A Painter or a Butcher?' was the headline. To look at the drawing today is to see a sinuous and elegant trifle: the goddess faceless, with a river flowing over her arm, her small breasts bare and a veena covering her privates. Female Hindu deities were often shown nude, in far more erotic positions, in temple sculpture as well as in folk and miniature painting; Husain was toying quite innocently with cultural tradition. But what enraged right-wing Hindus was that a Muslim artist had done the toying. And so began the harassment that would drive Husain from his homeland.

If he had been less popular beforehand, he probably would have been less hated – which is to say, his popularization of modern art helped create the very conditions of the subsequent fury. Controversy-averse, Husain tried to downplay the uproar. The *tamasha*, or commotion, was 'a small thing', he said, in a country that remained otherwise free. But a decade later, when another nude, *Bharat Mata* ('Mother India') was printed as the cover of a catalogue, the antagonism was too great for an artist in his nineties to dismiss. One extremist group announced a reward of about $11 million for the painter's head; macabrely, money and gold were specifically offered for his hands and his eyes.

'Had I been forty, I would have fought them tooth and nail,' he said in an interview. Instead, he left for Qatar and London – never to return, but consistently, fundamentally optimistic. 'This is about a few people who have not understood the language of Modern Art,' he commented while in exile. 'Art is always ahead of time. Tomorrow they will understand it.'

A liberal tolerance of a different point of view causes no damage. It means only a greater self restraint. Diversity in expression of views whether in writings, paintings or visual media encourages debate. A debate should never be shut out. 'I am right' does not necessarily imply 'You are wrong'. Our culture breeds tolerance – both in thought and in actions. I have penned down this judgement with this fervent hope that it is a prologue to a broader thinking and greater tolerance for the creative field. A painter at 90 deserves to be in his home – painting his canvas.

In perhaps the clearest judgement we yet have on the freedom of art in India, in 2008 the Delhi High Court quashed legal charges against Husain in relation to *Bharat Mata* – charges that ranged from obscenity to violating religious sentiments to promoting enmity between religious groups. That Husain did not return to India after this decision left some of his staunchest defenders feeling let down. They wanted him to fight harder, at home, for the liberal space that had championed him, and for the idea of a diverse, mix-and-match Indian culture that seemed to be fast disappearing.

But I think they were demanding too deeply political a response from an artist with a fairly apolitical nature, whose genial superficiality about contemporary conflicts allowed him, over the decades, to keep seeing India at her best. The real betrayal lies in the separation of Husain from the audience he once reached, and should reach in the future. Today, some of the Indians who buy his paintings, for one million dollars or more, keep them abroad, out of fear. The only big exhibition of Husain's work since the controversy, and his death in 2011, was in London.

Bitterness simply wasn't one of the entries in Husain's encyclopedia of emotional traits. In life as in art, he worked with what he had, accepted the inevitability of loss and change, and typically made the best of each new situation. But the fact that most of his work is now sequestered in the homes of the rich, while Indian museums quake to display it in spaces accessible to those of lesser means, feels bitter to me. It's one of the sad, unexpected ironies in the afterlife of one of our most important modern Indian painters.

Across the world in the twentieth century, the greatest threat to cultural freedom and expression was often the state. In twenty-first-century India, the threat comes also from within civil society, from groups and individuals who claim to defend the majority against insult, and who know that governments in Delhi and across India's states are often ready tacitly to collude. It's gutting to consider that, by present standards, exile may have been a lucky fate for Husain. Today, India's writers and intellectuals are being murdered for their beliefs.

Just before Ashok Sharma and I left the grounds of the gallery Husain helped make for his work, he mentioned that, when Husain died, his friends and defenders attempted to bring his body home to be buried. 'We were successful in stopping that too,' he said, his voice hardening a little. 'Whoever has insulted Bharat Mata, who has shown her naked – we will never allow him even six feet of her soil.'

50
Dhirubhai Ambani

Fins
1932–2002

Whenever I pass what may be the world's largest private home, Mukesh Ambani's twenty-seven-storey Antilia in Mumbai, a boast made by his father, the founder of the Reliance Industries fortune, flashes through my mind: 'I'm a bigger shark.' Although poor workers often linger at Antilia's massive wooden gates, gazing up at the tower in reverent silence, this monument to money-making probably wouldn't exist had Dhirubhai Ambani been an entirely virtuous man. His wealth was, though, entirely self-created, which makes him an icon of economic possibility.

Dhirubhai Ambani's first home in Mumbai was nearly as humble as the ones the gawking labourers inhabit: a pigeonhole chawl four kilometres from Antilia, in the pushcart-clogged trading neighbourhood of Bhuleshwar. The goods wheeling through Bhuleshwar's narrow byways this season – candy-coloured flip-flops, dreadlocked wigs styled after a Sri Lankan cricket hero – bear little resemblance to the fashion items sold here in 1960. But the energy of the place is much the same as it was when a restless young trader of spice and sugar heard a yarn trader in his chawl mention the killing he was making from a government anti-smuggling initiative. Ambani would spin this tip into dominance of the polyester market, and then into the most powerful business empire in the developing world. Today, 15 per cent of all Indian exports go out under his company name.

How did the son of a penurious schoolteacher pull it off? Ambani himself credited an 'almost animal instinct' for trading. Add to that a steel-trap memory, an appetite for audacious risk, an elastic view of ethics and an ability to charm a wide range of people, including fellow traders, retailers, bureaucrats and football stadia full of stock-holders. But one of his most underrated talents, I think, was a gift for maximizing and monetizing inequality.

Some of us may view great inequalities (say, billion-dollar, twenty-seven-storey homes overlooking ones made of scrap metal and wood) with apprehension. But Ambani turned inequalities – primarily of information and access – into power tools. This strategy first occurred to him after leaving a Gujarat village in 1950, aged seventeen, to become an economic migrant in the rough port of Aden, then a British Protectorate.

A peon and ship-refueller for a trading company, he was shocked one day when a superior spent a princely sum, equivalent to 5,000 rupees, to secure, via overseas telegram, information his competitors didn't have. Through trial and error, during lunch hours in the Aden souk, Ambani began to test his own ability to capitalize on gossip and stray bits of information about commodities and global economic trends. He was soon known as one of the souk's canniest traders and as a man so personally fearless that he liked to relax after a long week of work by taking a swim in Aden's shark-infested port. The nature of his majestic swimming companions would be incorporated into his persona: it was useful, in a competitive business, to be known as fast-moving and dangerous should anyone get between him and his prey.

Reliance, now run by Mukesh, is the country's most profitable private-sector undertaking, with interests in everything from refining and transporting petroleum to grocery stores and that crucial contemporary resource, wireless spectrum. Lately, it's been expanding to Africa, South East Asia, the US and Latin America; where it isn't already, it may be coming soon. Reliance has also spawned a second business superpower, run by Dhirubhai's other son, Anil, whose interests range from telecoms to infrastructure to Hollywood film production. And despite the sons' tendency to feud – clashes volatile enough to rattle the whole Indian economy – they've both honoured their father in one way: by sustaining the dominance of bigger-shark values in twenty-first-century Indian life.

*

The first tiny Reliance office, in Bombay's Masjid Bunder neighbour-hood, overlooked a fountain built by an earlier trader-made-good. Observing it, as well as the city's grand Flora Fountain, Dhirubhai Ambani found another metaphor for his bifurcated style: let the splendour of the jet be marvelled at; keep the ugly mechanics hidden underground. After his own corporate fountains began pumping cash, he and his sons and associates did their best to control what would get unearthed.

'Coincidentally with disputes with Reliance,' the investigative journalist Hamish McDonald has slyly written, Ambani rivals were hit by government inspections, tax problems, bad press, deportation orders, assaults and a career-damaging forgery caper. (In the late 1990s, the Indian publisher of McDonald's biography of Dhirubhai Ambani was served with a legal notice not to distribute it; more than a decade would pass before an Indian edition was released, by a dif-ferent publisher.)

Still, it's hard not to be moved by the image of the teenage Dhirub-hai (born Dhirajlal) hungering for success when he was on his own, far from home, in Aden. As a small-town schoolboy he'd been active in local socialist politics and anti-British campaigns. Once thrown into the world of business, he saw that he wouldn't get ahead unless he could teach himself the language of the colonizers. So he began poring over two books that happened to be on hand, Nehru's *Glimpses of World History* and *The Discovery of India*. He turned them into a self-development course for the aspiring tycoon. From accounts of ancient sages, kings and freedom fighters, he derived two related lessons: that what he described as a 'delicate, sensitive, under-standing human touch' helped you get ahead; and that building something big required not just cash, but influence and power.

When Ambani entered the synthetics business, it was an opaque, high-risk, high-margin field that suddenly became even more attrac-tive when screen heroines began dressing diaphanously on film. To stop rampant smuggling of yarn for hot saris – a must for every dowry – the government decided to let firms import fixed quanti-ties of nylon. Ambani, who'd developed global trading contacts in Aden, realized he could use them to exploit the scheme in a handsome way; soon he was a monopoly importer, mainly from Japan, of 50,000 pounds of the shiny new material. As his wife later wrote, he 'struck gold', making a small fortune before India's stately old textile families and other producers figured out how to enter the game. Then they all got shafted when India's 1962 war with China caused the price of many commodities, yarn included, to crash.

It wasn't the first time Ambani had taken full advantage of a passing windfall moment. In Aden, to the authorities' dismay, he'd started melting down Yemen's silver riyal coins and selling them to London bullion dealers after he realized they were worth more as ingots than at face value. In polyester as in bullion: by the time others caught on to the profit potential, or the scheme itself went bust, he would already have his hand in something new.

According to his wife, Dhirubhai cut deals so fast – 'The faster the deal, the sooner the goods could be delivered, and the quicker the investments could be realized'– that the business partner with whom he had founded Reliance got queasy and left. Dhirubhai henceforth surrounded himself with more like-minded people. 'I needed gutsy, street-smart guys with a lot of common sense and bazaar skills for the sort of business I was doing,' he would say, 'not young men in clean shirts.'

'Manage the environment you're in,' Ambani liked to tell the people around him. This instruction would have been less arduous to follow had he been working in the US, where the tax regime and the spirit of capitalism had long encouraged entrepreneurs to make money. But Ambani was operating in Indira Gandhi's looking-glass socialist society, where personal income tax rates approached 99 per cent at the upper end, and corporate taxes were also punitive. Like most of his fellow businessmen, he had to break rules to succeed. But he went further, managing the environment by convincing the babus of the Licence Raj that it was in their interests to benefit him. The sensitive, human touch worked wonders.

'Ambani used the government better than absolutely any other businessman that we've ever had,' the journalist Mihir Sharma says. 'He was the kind of entrepreneur that you get only in countries that have very, very closely controlled economies. He was someone who, rather than coming up with a brilliant idea, came up with a brilliant business method – which was talking to the right bureaucrats and the right politicians.'

In 1966, the Gujarat government provided Ambani with 125 acres of land, at a giveaway price, on which he opened a textile mill to spin his synthetic yarn into cloth. He gave the fabric the brand name Vimal, which means 'spotless' or 'pure'. Not long after, gorgeous French chiffon saris he'd brought home to his wife disappeared from her wardrobe. Their designs were being copied at the Gujarat factory, on their way to becoming so commonplace that she would be embarrassed to wear the originals. To Ambani, they were just another kind of information to be parlayed into money.

By 1975, the World Bank had declared the arriviste's textile concern the only one in India on a par with international standards. Naturally, the old textile families detested him. Two years later, when rivals' complaints convinced the government to ban the import of polyester yarn because of 'profiteering', Ambani's connections got the ban repealed in twenty-four hours. Around the same time, he secured a licence to manufacture another valuable kind of polyester yarn – 'an opportune move', his wife recalled, for the government soon after withdrew all export incentives. This put him ahead of the field to supply the domestic market. By now, he manifestly possessed the influence he'd craved since studying Nehru's books.

As Vimal grew from a fabric brand to a large network of retail stores, Ambani's ear for strategic information also helped him build foreign markets, which compensated for his occasional expensive local mistake. Early on, sitting on a great quantity of texturized fabric that the Indian market didn't care for, he got wind of a Polish delegation visiting Delhi. He took them to his mill, applied his charm, and the Poles bought half a million metres of the stuff – a figure so beyond not only his excess stock but also his mill's capacity that he had to fly in machines from Germany to meet the order.

Later, inspectors complained he had secretly developed far more capacity than he was licensed to have, evading a staggering amount of tax in the process. But for every government representative who protested against his tactics, there were several aiding his growth: first, low-level bureaucrats involved in textile regulation, then up the chain – until he was sitting on a stage with **Indira Gandhi (46)** when she celebrated her return to the prime ministership in 1980. Over the next ten years, as private players were ushered into new sections of the economy, Reliance racked up licences like business awards, including ones for chemicals, petroleum and oil refining, which allowed it to become India's first vertically integrated company.

How powerful was Ambani? After a tip from an underworld don led to a police raid in the 1990s, Reliance senior executives were accused of violating the Official Secrets Act by possessing sensitive Cabinet documents, including a draft national budget. A joke quickly did the rounds in Delhi: the budget wasn't leaked to Reliance; Reliance had leaked the budget to the ministry.

As Ambani's lavish spending on advertising – often featuring film stars, cricketers and models – wove the slogan 'Only Vimal' through the minds of middle-class Indians, he proved adept at managing the media, too. If a small newspaper criticized the company, he could cripple it by pulling his advertisements. Some papers learned to attack Reliance in order to court its rupee, becoming promoters of the company when an ad spend was agreed. Occasionally, Ambani cut out the middleman, buying publications outright. His sons have followed suit: Anil's company has a significant stake in one of the leading business TV channels, while Mukesh's Reliance Industries group has a controlling interest in a media conglomerate that operates more than a dozen cable news channels.

As his fountain grew splashier, Dhirubhai Ambani became the country's first business celebrity: his oval, smiling face, capped by receding slicked-back hair, was as recognizable to the middle classes as a film star's. He had grown too big in stature for the Chevy Impala he'd dreamt of when first in Bombay. He traded up to a Cadillac: white, with fins.

By the late 1970s, Ambani's image was seductive enough to start changing the culture itself. Just as Indira Gandhi democratized Indian politics, Ambani helped to popularize a more cavalier capitalism. To become rich like me, be daring like me: that was the gist of Ambani's sales pitch to his employees; then to shopkeepers whom he convinced to cut out the wholesalers and get their Vimal directly from him; then, after he went public in 1977, to his shareholders. 'In their prosperity, our prosperity. For we are a family' was a line he maintained even when maximizing inequality of information at their expense.

In 1985, 12,000 Reliance shareholders gathered on Bombay's Cooperage Football Ground to approve the previous year's financial results for the twenty-year-old polyester manufacturing company, in what was then the biggest Annual General Meeting in history. It's now seen as a foundational moment in the creation of India's first cult of equity. But shortly after the Cooperage meeting, a setback forced Ambani to raise capital at high speed through a debt and equity sale. Prospectuses and broker subscription forms were hawked like carnival tickets from loudspeakers strapped to auto-rickshaws, and dropped like wartime propaganda from helicopters over Ahmedabad. Along with tens of thousands of Indians, a huge battery of overseas companies also subscribed. Many of these, it turned out, were 'shelf companies' with connections to Reliance – insider buys that inflated the value of the stock. The profusion of on-paper firms was so great that a raft of names was taken from a portion of the Mahabharata called the *Vishnu Sahasranama*, 'the thousand names of Vishnu'. It's a joke Dhirubhai would have appreciated, even if he hadn't authored it.

Within months, this and other instances of jugglery began to surface in a series of exposés by the *Indian Express* newspaper. The investigations, which alleged tax evasion and other corporate wrongdoing, also brought to light Reliance's financial consideration for one of its biggest backers, the editor of the *Times of India*. The government confirmed some of the *Express*'s findings, and Reliance later had to repay evaded excise duty.

Ambani suffered a stroke as the exposés began, and it took him a hard year to recover. As for the *Express*, by 1988, according to the biographer McDonald, it faced over 230 prosecutions by agencies in charge of company law, customs, income tax, foreign exchange and import quotas. Notably, it was the *Express*'s lead investigator, not anyone from Reliance, who saw the inside of a jail. For in addition to the obvious boons Indian politicians grant favourite corporate houses – preferential policies, government contracts, tax-free special economic zones – there's also the perk of encouraging judicial delays in determining serious charges. One famous case, involving a senior Reliance official charged with conspiracy to murder a rival textile industrialist, has been dragged out for twenty-five years, and still shows no signs of resolution.

'Reliance is a triumph of trust,' Dhirubhai Ambani asserted in 2000, a year and a half before his death. If the trust was debatable, the triumph was not. Legal cases had slipped off his back, and following the economic liberalization of 1991, corporations like his were more free than ever from government regulation and control. Some people even credited Ambani as a leading economic unshackler. In the account of the journalist and former minister in charge of privatization Arun Shourie, people like Ambani, in boldly flouting the rules of India's centralized economy, 'created the case for scrapping those regulations. They made a case for reforms.' It's an argument so stirring we nearly forget the more prosaic reality: that India was compelled to change not by reasoned policy arguments but by an acute balance of payments crisis, and by the International Monetary Fund.

Mihir Sharma gets closer to the significance of Ambani's legacy when he argues that it freed ordinary Indians from caring about whether the money their icons made was clean or dirty. 'Once you've made your money, you are a hero of the republic,' he says. 'And Dhirubhai Ambani is sainted now, up there with many of the founders of modern India.'

Ambani was the first to make that sort of sainthood possible in India. In that sense, he marks the end of an epoch, and the beginning of another.

As a teenage socialist and activist, Ambani was shaken deeply on the winter's day that Mahatma Gandhi was assassinated. But individuals' values change, as do countries'. In the decades after Gandhi's death, Indians came to hunger less for equality than for growth, and found Gandhi's critique of industrialization and warnings about thoughtless consumption about as useful as they found his home-spun khadi. I've long suspected that Ambani was casting shade on the skinny man with the stick and the glasses when he once advised an audience, 'A society which condemns creators of wealth will always remain poor and miserable.' One reason we no longer have much suspicion of excess and inequality, or those who facilitate it, is because, when compared to men like Gandhi or Ambedkar, Dhirubhai Ambani was just as he'd claimed to be – the bigger shark.

References

NOTE ON SOURCES AND REFERENCES

In many of the essays, cross-references to other individuals are signalled by names and chapter numbers in bold font. The wealth of cross-references is a sign of the rich historical interconnections between these figures. Sources for all direct quotes which I have taken from written or recorded archive material will be found in the references that follow. Direct quotes that are not referenced are taken from interviews recorded for the radio series and book (the interviewees are all named in the text). In addition to these sources, *Incarnations* draws upon a vast body of scholarship, and for those interested in delving deeper, a bibliography of the sources I have used to research and write the book will be available online, at the website of the King's India Institute.

The radio version of *Incarnations* is available free online, as a series of podcasts, from iTunes and at the BBC Radio 4 website: *Incarnations: India in 50 Lives.*

I THE BUDDHA: WAKING INDIA UP

p. 4   'My body became extremely lean . . .': *Majjhima Nikaya*, in Edward J. Thomas, *The Life of the Buddha as Legend and History* (New York, 1927; 3rd edn, 1949, repr. 2000), p. 65.

p. 4   'without sensual desires . . .': *Majjhima Nikaya*, in Thomas, *The Life of the Buddha as Legend and History*, p. 66.

p. 6   'deserted and in ruins . . .': Xuanzang, *Si-Yu-Ki. Buddhist Records of the Western World*, trans. Samuel Beal (London, 1884), p. 98.

p. 7   'I renounce the Hindu religion . . .': B. R. Ambedkar, *Dr Babasaheb Ambedkar Writings and Speeches*, ed. Vasant Moon (Bombay, 1979), cited in Gail Omvedt, *Buddhism in India* (New Delhi, 2003), p. 262.

2 MAHAVIRA: SOLDIER OF NON-VIOLENCE

p. 8 'right from their respective . . .': Mohandas K. Gandhi, 'Three Vital Questions', *Young India*, 21 January 1926, in *Collected Works of Mahatma Gandhi*, vol. xxix (Ahmedabad, 1994), p. 411.

p. 9 ' "soldier" of non-violence': Mohandas K. Gandhi, 'On Ahimsa: Reply to Lala Lajpat Rai', *The Modern Review*, October 1916, in *Collected Works of Mahatma Gandhi*, vol. xiii (Ahmedabad, 1990), p. 297.

p. 11 'After fasting two and a half days . . .': *Kalpa Sutra*, in Hermann Jacobi (trans.), *Gaina Sûtras, Part I* (Oxford, 1884), p. 259.

p. 13 'Jainism's consistent historical stance . . .': Paul Dundas, *The Jains*, 2nd edn (London, 2002), p. 233.

p. 13 'a strange but perfect aloofness . . .': Heinrich Zimmer, *Philosophies of India*, ed. Joseph Campbell (London, 1951), p. 214.

p. 15 'Only they saw deeper . . .': Gandhi, 'Three Vital Questions', *Young India*, 21 January 1926, in *Collected Works of Mahatma Gandhi*, vol. xxix, p. 411.

3 PANINI: CATCHING THE OCEAN IN A COW'S HOOFPRINT

p. 18 'Take this sutra . . .': *Ashtadhyayi* sutra 6.1.74, example adapted from Saroja Bhate and Subhash Kak, 'Panini's Grammar and Computer Science', *Annals of the Bhandarkar Oriental Research Institute*, vol. 72 (1993), pp. 79–94.

p. 20 'and therefore undergone the influence . . .': Johannes Bronkhorst, 'Panini and Euclid: Reflections on Indian Geometry', *Journal of Indian Philosophy*, vol. 29 (2001), p. 45.

4 KAUTILYA: THE RING OF POWER

p. 25 'Three Cheers for Togo': Jawaharlal Nehru to Brajlal Nehru, cited in B. K. Nehru, *Nice Guys Finish Second* (New Delhi, 1997), p. 7.

p. 27 'An arrow unleashed . . .': *Arthashastra* 10.6.51, in Patrick Olivelle (trans. and ed.), *King, Governance, and Law in Ancient India: Kautilya's Arthasastra* (Oxford, 2013), p. 387.

p. 27 ' . . . made *The Prince* look "harmless" ': Max Weber, 'Politik als Beruf' (Politics as a Vocation), in H. H. Gerth and C. Wright Mills (trans. and eds), *From Max Weber: Essays in Sociology* (New York, 1946), p. 124.

p. 29 'Just as it is impossible to know . . .': *Arthashastra* 2.9.33, in Olivelle (trans. and ed.), *King, Governance, and Law in Ancient India*, p. 118.

p. 29 'Nine strokes with a cane . . .': *Arthashastra* 4.8.22, in R. P. Kangle (trans. and ed.), *The Kautilīya Arthasastra: An English Translation with Critical and Explanatory Notes*, 2nd edn (Bombay, 1972), Part II, p. 276; cf. Olivelle (trans. and ed.), *Kingdom, Governance, and Law in Ancient India*, pp. 240–41.

p. 30 'Even if it is possible . . .': *Arthashastra* 2.9.34, in Olivelle (trans. and ed.), *King, Governance, and Law in Ancient India*, p. 118.

p. 30 'more into line with the mainstream . . .': 'Introduction', Olivelle (trans. and ed.), *King, Governance, and Law in Ancient India*, p. 8.

5 ASHOKA: POWER AS PERSUASION

p. 33 'Wherever there are stone pillars . . .': Seventh Pillar Edict, trans. Venerable Shravasti Dhammika, in Charles Allen, *Ashoka: The Search for India's Lost Emperor* (London, 2012), p. 425; cf. N. A. Nikam and Richard McKeon (trans. and eds), *The Edicts of Asoka* (Chicago, 1958), pp. 35–6.

p. 34 'I have made the following arrangement . . .': Sixth Rock Edict, in. D. C. Sircar (trans. and ed.), *Inscriptions of Asoka* (New Delhi, 1957), p. 44.

p. 34 'The king, who is called Priyadarsin . . .': trans. Henry Falk, 'The Preamble at Panguraria', in P. Kieffer-Pulz and J. Hartmann (eds), *Bauddhavidyasudhakarah* (Swisttal-Odendorf, 1997).

p. 35 'One hundred and fifty thousand persons . . .': Thirteenth Rock Edict, in Nikam and McKeon (trans. and eds), *The Edicts of Asoka*, p. 27; cf. Jules Bloch (trans. and ed.), *Les Inscriptions d'Asoka* (Paris, 1950), p. 125.

p. 37 'tendencies like jealousy . . .': First Kalinga Edict, in Alf Hiltebeitel, *Dharma: Its Early History in Law, Religion, and Narrative* (Oxford, 2011), p. 48; cf. Bloch (trans. and ed.), *Les Inscriptions d'Asoka*, p. 138; Nikam and McKeon (trans. and eds), *The Edicts of Asoka*, p. 62.

p. 38 'Promulgation of dhamma . . .': Fourth Rock Edict, translated by Alf Hiltebeitel in Vishwa Adluri and Joydeep Bagchee (eds), *Reading the*

Fifth Veda: Studies on the Mahābhārata – Essays by Alf Hiltebeitel, vol. I (Leiden, 2011), p. 83.

p. 38 'restraint in speech . . .': Twelfth Rock Edict, translated by the Venerable Shravasti Dhammika, in Allen, *Ashoka: The Search for India's Lost Emperor*, pp. 412–13; cf. Nikam and McKeon (trans. and eds), *The Edicts of Asoka*, p. 52; and Sircar (trans. and ed.), *Inscriptions of Asoka*, pp. 50–51.

p. 38 'Beloved-of-the-gods, King Piyadassi . . .': Seventh Pillar Edict, trans. Venerable Shravasti Dhammika, in Allen, *Ashoka: The Search for India's Lost Emperor*, p. 424; cf. Nikam and McKeon (trans. and eds), *The Edicts of Asoka*, pp. 33–4; and Sircar (trans. and ed.), *Inscriptions of Asoka*, p. 76.

p. 39 'monster of piety': Romila Thapar, *Ashoka and the Decline of the Mauryas*, 3rd edn (New Delhi, 2012), p. 3.

p. 40 'I am exceedingly happy . . .': Jawaharlal Nehru, Speech in the Constituent Assembly, 22 July 1947, in *Constituent Assembly Debates: Official Report*, vol. IV, no. 7 (New Delhi, 1947), p. 765; available online at http://parliamentofindia.nic.in/ls/debates/vol4p7.htm.

6 CHARAKA: ON NOT VIOLATING GOOD JUDGEMENT

p. 43 'violations of good judgement': in Dominik Wujastyk (trans. and ed.), *The Roots of Ayurveda* (London, 2003), p. 20.

p. 44 'not represent a completely unique ayurvedic point of view': Dagmar Wujastyk, *Well-Mannered Medicine: Medical Ethics and Etiquette in Classical Ayurveda* (Oxford, 2012), p. 147.

p. 45 'To produce a son . . .': Mitchell G. Weiss, '*Caraka Samhita* and the Doctrine of Rebirth', in Wendy Doniger O'Flaherty (ed.), *Karma and Rebirth in Classical Indian Traditions* (Berkeley, CA, 1980), p. 97.

p. 46 'Doctors have almost unhinged . . .': Mohandas K. Gandhi, '*Hind Swaraj*', in Anthony J. Parel (ed.), *Gandhi:'Hind Swaraj' and Other Writings* (Cambridge, 1997), p. 63.

7 ARYABHATA: THE BOAT OF INTELLECT

p. 48 'By the grace of Brahma . . .': adapted from W. E. Clark (trans. and ed.), *The Aryabhatia of Aryabhata* (Chicago, 1930), p. 81.

p. 49 'When sixty times sixty . . .': adapted from Clark (trans. and ed.), *The Aryabhatia of Aryabhata*, p. 54.

p. 51 'for only thus can it be stable . . .': Johannes Bronkhorst, 'Panini and Euclid: Reflections on Indian Geometry', *Journal of Indian Philosophy*, vol. 29 (2001), p. 55.

p. 51 'Classical Indian geometry . . .': Bronkhorst, 'Panini and Euclid: Reflections on Indian Geometry', p. 59.

8 ADI SHANKARA: A GOD WITHOUT QUALITIES

p. 55 'all-knowing and virtuous . . .': Madhava-Vidyaranya, *Sankara-dig-vijaya: The Traditional Life of Sri Sankaracharya*, translated by Swami Tapasyananda (Madras, 1978), p. 14.

p. 57 'merciless refutation of all hostile creeds . . .': Madhava-Vidyaranya, *Sankara-dig-vijaya: The Traditional Life of Sri Sankaracharya*, p. 136.

p. 59 'I am neither earth nor water . . .': Adi Shankara, 'Dasa Sloki', trans. *Paramartha Tattvam* newsletter, vol. 6, issue 1–2, pp. 3–4, verses 1 and 5; available online at http://svbf.org/newsletters/wp-content/uploads/paramartha-tattvam-articles/Issue-1-21.pdf

p. 59 'hidden Buddhism': see Upinder Singh, *A History of Ancient and Early Medieval India: From the Stone Age to the 12th Century* (New Delhi, 2009), p. 610; Natalia Isayeva, *Shankara and Indian Philosophy* (Albany, 1993), pp. 12–16; Govind Chandra Pande, *Life and Thought of Sankaracarya* (New Delhi, 1994), ch. 9.

p. 60 'ultimately unreal generally siphons off . . .': Wendy Doniger, *On Hinduism* (Oxford, 2014), p. 131.

p. 60 'the way out of colossal error': Jonardon Ganeri, *The Concealed Art of the Soul: Theories of Self and Practices of Truth in Indian Ethics and Epistemology* (Oxford, 2007), pp. 3–4.

9 RAJARAJA CHOLA: COSMOS, TEMPLE AND TERRITORY

p. 63 'rhapsody to size': David D. Shulman, *The King and the Clown in South Indian Myth and Poetry* (Princeton, 1985), p. 401.

p. 68 'Like blood sucking yakkhas . . .': *Culavamsa* 55.16–22, cited in George Spencer, 'The Politics of Plunder: The Cholas in Eleventh-century Ceylon', *Journal of Asian Studies*, vol. xxxv, no. 3 (May 1976), p. 412.

p. 70 'Can a mortal . . .': 'Posters seeking Jayalalithaa's release unravel a new facet in T. N. politics', *The Hindu*, 5 October 2014; available at http://www.thehindu.com/news/national/tamil-nadu/posters-seeking-jayalalithaas-release-unravel-a-new-facet-in-tn-politics/article6471917.ece.

10 BASAVA: A VOICE IN THE AIR

p. 71 'Make of my body . . .': A. K. Ramanujan (trans. and ed.), *Speaking of Siva* (New Delhi, 1993), p. 65.

p. 71 'a voice in the air': Ted Hughes, 'The Art of Poetry No. 71' (interview with Drue Heinz), *The Paris Review*, no. 134 (Spring 1995), p. 11.

p. 72 'I don't know anything . . .': Ramanujan (trans. and ed.), *Speaking of Siva*, p. 64.

p. 73 'Like a monkey on a tree': Ramanujan (trans. and ed.), *Speaking of Siva*, p. 50.

p. 74 'a dagger of "crystal" ': D. R. Nagaraj, 'Critical Tensions in the History of Kannada Literary Culture', in Sheldon Pollock (ed.), *Literary Cultures in History: Reconstructions from South Asia* (Berkeley, 2003), p. 353.

p. 74 'You are a blacksmith . . .': in Sadashiva Wodeyar, 'Humanism of Basava', *Basava Journal*, vol. 9, no. 3 (March 1985), p. 31; cited in S. A. Palekar, *Concept of Equality and Ideal Society: Basaveshwara's Model* (Jaipur, 1997), p. 70.

p. 75 'The crookedness of the serpent': Ramanujan (trans. and ed.), *Speaking of Siva*, p. 59.

p. 76 'Don't you take on': Ramanujan (trans. and ed.), *Speaking of Siva*, p. 61.

p. 77 'The rich / Will make temples . . .': Ramanujan (trans. and ed.), *Speaking of Siva*, p. 70.

11 AMIR KHUSRAU: THE PARROT OF INDIA

p. 80 'There is a prosperous . . .': Ghazal 1772, in Paul E. Losensky and Sunil Sharma (trans.), *In the Bazaar of Love: The Selected Poetry of Amir Khusrau* (New Delhi, 2013), p. 75.

p. 81 'The Muslim martyrs . . .': in Mohammad Habib, *Hazrat Amir Khusrau of Delhi* (Aligarh, 1927), p. 16.

p. 82 'O Delhi and its artless idols . . .': from 'The Fine Lads of Delhi', in Losensky and Sharma (trans.), *In the Bazaar of Love: The Selected Poetry of Amir Khusrau*, pp. 93–4; and see Sunil Sharma, *Amir Khusraw: The Poet of Sultans and Sufis* (Oxford, 2005), pp. 23–4.

p. 83 'Composing panegyric kills . . .': in Sharma, *Amir Khusraw: The Poet of Sultans and Sufis*, p. 18.

p. 84 'I am an Indian Turk . . .': cited in Muzaffar Alam, 'The Culture and Politics of Persian in Precolonial Hindustan', in Pollock (ed.), *Literary Cultures in History: Reconstructions from South Asia*, p. 144.

p. 84 'I have become you . . .': in Sharma, *Amir Khusraw: The Poet of Sultans and Sufis*, p. 47.

p. 85 'When shall we see . . .': Mohandas K. Gandhi, 'Speech on Music, Ahmedabad', 21 March 1926, printed in *Young India*, 15 April 1926, in *Collected Works of Mahatma Gandhi*, vol. xxx, p. 160.

p. 86 'If a Khurasani . . .': in Sharma, *Amir Khusraw: The Poet of Sultans and Sufis*, p. 88.

12 KABIR: 'HEY, YOU!'

p. 87 'Strutting about . . .': in Arvind Krishna Mehrotra (trans.), *Songs of Kabir* (New York, 2011), p. 82.

p. 89 'A weaver's son . . .': in Mehrotra (trans.), *Songs of Kabir*, p. 59.

p. 00 'If you say you're a Brahmin . . .': in Mehrotra (trans.), *Songs of Kabir*, p. 28.

p. 90 'I'm Rama's slave . . .': in Mehrotra (trans.), *Songs of Kabir*, p. 54.

p. 92 ' "Me shogun." . . .': in Mehrotra (trans.), *Songs of Kabir*, p. 67.

p. 93 'I've squandered my whole life . . .': from 'Banaras & Magahar', in Vinay Dharwadker (trans. and ed.), *The Weaver's Songs* (London, 2003), p. 139.

13 GURU NANAK: THE DISCIPLINE OF DEEDS

p. 96 'As a team of oxen . . .': cited in Khushwant Singh, *A History of the Sikhs, Vol. I: 1469–1838* (New Delhi, 2004), p. 44.

p. 97 'The Qazi tells untruths . . .': from 'Raga Dhanasari Q', in Navtej Sarna, *The Book of Nanak* (New Delhi, 2003), p. 25.

p. 98 'There is but one God . . .': in Sarna, *The Book of Nanak*, p. 133.

p. 99 'Those who abjure meat . . .': in Sarna, *The Book of Nanak*, p. 58.

p. 101 'When all has been tried . . .': Guru Gobind Singh, *Zafarnama*, verse 22, translated by Navtej Sarna (New Delhi, 2011), p. 23.

14 KRISHNADEVARAYA: 'KINGSHIP IS STRANGE'

p. 103 'with eyes like blue sapphires': Allasani Peddana, *The Story of Manu*, translated by Velcheru Narayana Rao and David Shulman (Cambridge, MA, 2015), p. 13.

p. 104 'Oh! What is this glorious empire?': Krishnadevaraya, *Amuktamalyada* II.78, in Srinivas Reddy (trans.), *Giver of the Worn Garland: Krishnadevaraya's Amuktamalyada* (New Delhi, 2010), p. 45.

p. 105 'In this city . . .': Domingo Paes, 'Narrative of Domingo Paes', translated by Robert Sewell, in his *A Forgotten Empire (Vijayanagara): A Contribution to the History of India* (London, 1900), p. 256.

p. 107 'Seated enthroned in the hall . . .': Peddana, *The Story of Manu*, pp. 13–14.

p. 108 'If you ask "Why Telugu?" ': Krishnadevaraya, *Amuktamalyada* I.15, in Reddy (trans.), *Giver of the Worn Garland: Krishnadevaraya's Amuktamalyada*, p. 5.

p. 108 'If a neighbouring kingdom . . .': Krishnadevaraya, *Amuktamalyada* IV.266, translated by Velcheru Narayana Rao, David Shulman and Sanjay Subrahmanyam, in 'A New Imperial Idiom in the Sixteenth Century: Krishnadevaraya and His Political Theory of Vijayanagara', in Sheldon Pollock (ed.), *Forms of Knowledge in Early Modern Asia: Explorations in the Intellectual History of India and Tibet, 1500–1800* (Durham, NC, 2011), pp. 102–3.

p. 109 'The king is non-violent . . .': Krishnadevaraya, *Amuktamalyada* IV.278, trans. Rao, Shulman and Subrahmanyam, in 'A New Imperial Idiom in the Sixteenth Century', in Pollock (ed.), *Forms of Knowledge in Early Modern Asia*, p. 105.

15 MIRABAI: I GO THE OTHER WAY

p. 111 'Mira sang because . . .': M. K. Gandhi, interview with the musicologist Dilip Kumar Roy, 2 February 1924, cited in *Among the Great* (Bombay, 1947), p. 83.

p. 111 'She became Mira . . .': in T. J. S. George, *MS: A Life in Music* (New Delhi, 2004), p. 186.

p. 111 'How will the night pass? . . .': in A. J. Alston (trans.), *The Devotional Poems of Mirabai* (New Delhi, 2005), p. 66.

p. 112 'Some praise me . . .': in S. M. Pandey, 'Mirabai and Her Contributions to the Bhakti Movement', *History of Religions*, vol. 5, no. 1 (Summer 1965), p. 57.

p. 113 'How can anyone touch me? . . .': in Alston (trans.), *The Devotional Poems of Mirabai*, p. 43.

p. 113 'Your slanders are sweet . . .': in Pandey, 'Mirabai and Her Contributions to the Bhakti Movement', p. 57.

p. 114 'On your lips . . .': in S. M. Pandey and Norman H. Zide (trans.), *Poems from Mirabai* (Chicago, 1964), p. 2.

p. 115 'Approve of me or disapprove . . .': 'Why Mira Can't Come Back to Her Old House', in Robert Bly and Jane Hirshfield (trans), *Mirabai: Ecstatic Poems* (Boston, 2004), p. 21; translation adapted.

16 AKBAR: THE WORLD AND THE BRIDGE

p. 118 'His expression is tranquil . . .': J. S. Hoyland (trans.) and S. N. Banerjee (ed.), *The Commentary of Father Monserrate, S. J.: On His Journey to the Court of Akbar* (London, 1922), p. 197.

p. 118 'He can give his opinion . . .': in Hoyland (trans.) and Banerjee (ed.), *The Commentary of Father Monserrate, S.J*, p. 201.

p. 119 'his eyes and eyebrows . . .': in Alexander Rogers (trans.) and Henry Beveridge (ed.), *The Tuzuk-i-Jahangiri: Or, Memoirs of Jahangir* (London, 1909–14), pp. 33–4.

p. 121 'Thou hast come to . . .': in Muzaffar Alam, *The Languages of Political Islam in India: c. 1200–1800* (Chicago, 2004), p. 136.

p. 123 'With the help of reason . . .': in Ali Anooshahr, 'Dialogism and Territoriality in a Mughal History of the Islamic Millennium', *Journal of the Economic and Social History of the Orient*, vol. 55 (2012), p. 228.

p. 123 'Knowest thou at all . . .': in H. Beveridge (trans.), *The Akbarnama of Abu-l-Fazl* (Calcutta, 1907), vol. I, pp. 16–17.

p. 124 'the great advantage . . .': Fr Daniel Bartoli SJ, *Missione al gran Mogor del p. Ridolfo Aquaviva della Compagnia de Gesú* (Rome, 1663), cited in Vincent Arthur Smith, *Akbar: The Great Mogul, 1542–1605* (Oxford, 1917), p. 212.

17 MALIK AMBAR: THE DARK-FATED ONE

p. 129 'a cruel Roman face . . .': translated from Pieter van den Broecke, 'Travels of Pieter van den Broecke', in W. Ph. Coolhass (ed.), *Pieter van den Broecke in Azië*, vol. I (The Hague, 1962), pp. 147–8.

p. 130 'the ill-starred Ambar': in Rogers (trans.) and Beveridge (ed.), *The Tuzuk-i-Jahangiri: Or, Memoirs of Jahangir, passim*.

18 DARA SHIKOH: THE MEETING-PLACE OF THE TWO OCEANS

p. 132 'This was not one of the majestic . . .': François Bernier, *Travels in the Mogul Empire, A. D. 1656–1668*, 2nd edn, translated by Archibald Constable, edited and revised by Vincent A. Smith (London, 1916), p. 98.

p. 134 'Since [this book] is the meeting-place . . .': Dara Shikoh, *Majma al-bahrayn*, ed. Muhammad Riza Jalali Na'ini (Tehran, 1987–8), translated by C. Ernst, in his 'Muslim Studies of Hinduism? A Reconsideration of Arabic and Persian Translations from Indian Languages', *Iranian Studies*, vol. 36, no. 2 (June 2003), p. 186.

p. 135 'in a clear style . . .': cited in B. J. Hasrat, *Dara Shikuh: Life and Works* (Calcutta 1953; New Delhi, 1982), p. 266; in William Theodore de Bary (ed.), *Sources of Indian Tradition* (New York and New Delhi, 1958), pp. 446–8.

p. 136 'Over-confident in his opinion . . .': Niccolao Manucci, *Storia do Mogor: Or Mogul India 1653–1708*, vol. 1, translated and edited by William Irvine (London, 1907), pp. 221–2.

p. 136 'The fear of seeing . . .': in Manucci, *Storia do Mogor: Or Mogul India 1653–1708*, vol. 3, translated and edited by William Irvine, p. 261.

19 SHIVAJI: DREAMING BIG

p. 141 'proud-spirited and warlike . . .': in Thomas Watters, *On Yuan Chwang's Travels in India, 629–645 A. D.*, edited by T. W. Rhys Davids and Stephen W. Bushell, vol. II (London, 1906), p. 239; cf. Samuel Beale (trans.), *Si-Yu-Ki. Buddhist Records of the Western World* (London, 1884), p. 256.

p. 144 'What is the solution? . . .': *Sabhasad bakhar* (1694), as cited in Prachi Deshpande, *Creative Pasts: Historical Memory and Identity in Western India, 1700–1960* (New York, 2007), p. 27.

p. 144 'Negligence for a single moment . . .': Jadunath Sarkar, *Anecdotes of Aurangzib* (Calcutta, 1963), p. 49; cited in M. N. Pearson, 'Shivaji and the Decline of the Mughal Empire', *The Journal of Asian Studies*, vol. 35, no. 2 (February 1976), p. 230, reprinted in Meena Bhargava (ed.), *The Decline of the Mughal Empire* (New Delhi, 2014), ch. 5, p. 96.

p. 144 'exercising all the powers . . .': Bernier, *Travels in the Mogul Empire, A. D. 1656–1668*, p. 198.

p. 145 'Sevagee is making a throne . . .': Narayan Senavi, Letter to the Deputy Governor of Bombay, 4 April 1674, in *English Factory Records on Shivaji (1659–1682)* (Poona, 1931), p. 328; cited in V. S. Bendrey (ed.), *Coronation of Shivaji the Great: Or the Procedure of the Religious Ceremony performed by Gagabhatta for the Consecration of Shivaji as a Hindu King* (Bombay, 1960), p. 30.

p. 145 'on each side of the throne . . .': Henry Oxinden, 'Oxinden's Narrative', 13 May–13 June 1674, in *English Factory Records on Shivaji (1659–1682)*, p. 375; cited in Bendrey (ed.), *Coronation of Shivaji the Great*, p. 39.

p. 145 'many elephants . . .': Narayan Senavi, Letter to the Deputy Governor of Bombay, 4 April 1674, in *English Factory Records on Shivaji (1659–1682)*, p. 328; cited in Bendrey (ed.), *Coronation of Shivaji the Great*, p. 31.

p. 146 'a "peasant boy" ': James W. Laine, *Shivaji: Hindu King in Islamic India* (Oxford, 2003), p. 22.

21 WILLIAM JONES: ENLIGHTENMENT MUGHAL

p. 153 'The Laws of the Hindus . . .': in Lord Teignmouth (ed.), *Memoirs of the Life, Writings and Correspondence of Sir William Jones*, new edn (London, 1804), p. 228.

p. 153 'A far-seeing man . . .': cited in Michael J. Franklin, *Orientalist Jones: Sir William Jones, Poet, Lawyer, and Linguist, 1746–1794* (Oxford, 2011), p. 37.

p. 154 'From my earliest years . . .': William Jones, Letter to C. Reviczki (undated, probably January/February 1768), in Lord Teignmouth (ed.), *Memoirs of the Life, Writings and Correspondence of Sir*

William Jones (London, 1804), p. 44. The text breaks off at this point, with a note from the editor which reads: 'The remainder of this letter is lost; but from the context, and the answer of Reviczki, we may conclude that it contained an elaborate panegyric on Eastern poetry, expressed with all the rapture which novelty inspires, and in terms degrading to the muses of Greece and Rome.'

p. 154 'certainly not preach . . .': William Jones, Letter to Lord Ashburton, 27 April 1783, in Garland Cannon (ed.), *The Letters of Sir William Jones*, vol. 2 (Oxford, 1970), p. 616; cited in Franklin, *Orientalist Jones*, p. 4.

p. 156 'The *Sanscrit* language . . .': William Jones, 'The Third Anniversary Discourse, on the Hindus', delivered to the Asiatick Society of Bengal, 2 February 1786, in Anna Maria Jones and Lord Teignmouth (eds), *The Works of Sir William Jones. In Six Volumes*, vol. I (London, 1799), p. 26.

p. 157 'If now it be asked . . .': William Jones, First Discourse delivered to the Asiatick Society of Bengal, 24 February 1784, in J. Elmes (ed.), *Discourses Delivered Before the Asiatic Society: And Miscellaneous Papers . . . by Sir William Jones*, with an essay by Lord Teignmouth, 2nd edn, vol. 1 (London, 1824), p. 4.

p. 158 'Gentlemen, when I was . . .': William Jones, First Discourse delivered to the Asiatick Society of Bengal, 24 February 1784, in Elmes (ed.), *Discourses Delivered Before the Asiatic Society: And Miscellaneous Papers . . . by Sir William Jones*, p. 1.

p. 158 'so much like Shakespeare . . .': William Jones, in Cannon (ed.), *The Letters of Sir William Jones*, p. 806; cited in Franklin, *Orientalist Jones*, p. 262.

p. 158 'Her charms cannot be . . .': cited in Franklin, *Orientalist Jones*, pp. 265–6.

p. 158 'all is animated . . .': Friedrich von Schlegel, *Lectures on the History of Literature, Ancient and Modern*, 2nd edn, vol. 1 (Edinburgh, 1819), p. 211.

p. 159 'I never was unhappy . . .': William Jones, in Cannon (ed.), *The Letters of Sir William Jones*, p. 778; cited in Franklin, *Orientalist Jones*, p. 241.

p. 159 'Morning – One letter . . .': in Lord Teignmouth (ed.), *Memoirs of the Life, Writings and Correspondence of Sir William Jones* (London, 1804), p. 242.

p. 160 'a single shelf . . .': T. B. Macaulay, Minute on education dated 2 February 1985, in H. Sharp (ed.), *Selections from Educational Records,*

Part I (1781–1839) (Calcutta, 1920; reprinted New Delhi, 1965), pp. 107–117.

22 RAMMOHUN ROY: 'HUMANITY IN GENERAL'

p. 162 'lion of the season': Lord Bentinck, in C. H. Philips (ed.), *The Correspondence of Lord William Cavendish Bentinck, Governor General of India, 1828–1835*, vol. 1 (Oxford, 1977), pp. 658–9; cited in Lynn Zastoupil, *Rammohun Roy and the Making of Victorian Britain* (New York, 2010), p. 7.

p. 164 'peculiar delirium of pieties': Iqbal Singh, *Rammohun Roy: A Biographical Inquiry into the Making of Modern India*, vol. 1 (London, 1958), p. 23.

p. 164 'I have never ceased . . .': Rammohun Roy, *Translation of the Ishopanishad, One of the Chapters of the Yajur-Ved, According to the Commentary of the Celebrated Shankar-Acharya: Establishing the Unity and Incomprehensibility of the Supreme Being; And that His Worship Alone Can Lead to Eternal Beatitude* (Calcutta, 1816), in Kalidas Nag and Debajyoti Burman (eds), *The English Works of Raja Rammohun Roy* (Calcutta, 1995), part 2, p. 52.

p. 166 'After having bathed . . .': Fanny Parkes, *Wanderings of a Pilgrim in Search of the Picturesque*, edited by Indira Ghose and Sara Mills (Manchester, 2001), p. 80.

p. 167 'Forbid it, British Power! . . .': William Ward, *A View of the History, Literature, and Mythology of the Hindoos: Including a Minute Description of Their Manners and Customs, and Translations from their Principal Works* (Serampore, 1817); cited in Lynn Zastoupil, *Rammohun Roy and the Making of Victorian Britain*, p. 63.

p. 169 'A more remarkable man . . .': 'Death of Rammohun Roy', *The Times*, 30 September 1833, p. 3.

23 LAKSHMI BAI, RANI OF JHANSI: BAD-ASS QUEEN

p. 171 'An accumulation of adequate causes': Benjamin Disraeli, Speech to the House of Commons, 27 July 1857, reproduced in T. C. Hansard (ed.), *The Parliamentary Debates*, third series, vol. 147 (20 July 1857–28 August 1857) (London, 1857), p. 475.

p. 171 'The Indian Mutiny has produced . . .': General Hugh Rose, 23 June 1858, Rose Papers, vol. XLI. Add MSS 42812, November 1857–October 1859, Oriental and India Office Collection, British Library, cited in Joyce Lebra-Chapman, *The Rani of Jhansi: A Study in Female Heroism in India* (Honolulu, c.1986), pp. 113–14.

p. 172 'this Jezebel Ranee': Thomas Lowe, *Central India during the Rebellion of 1857 and 1858* (London, 1860), p. 261; cited in Antonia Fraser, *Boadicea's Chariot: The Warrior Queens* (London, 1988), p. 292.

p. 173 'she sometimes appeared . . .': Vishnu Bhatt, in Vishnu Bhatt Godshe Versaikar, *1857: The Real Story of the Great Uprising*, translated by Mrinal Pande (New Delhi, 2011), p. 85.

p. 173 'Does it entitle them . . .': cited in Joyce Lebra-Chapman, *The Rani of Jhansi: A Study in Female Heroism in India* (Honolulu, 1986), p. 37.

p. 174 'We fight for independence . . .': there is no historical source for this, despite it being quoted regularly by many writers.

24 JYOTIRAO PHULE: THE OPEN WELL

p. 180 'Without education, wisdom was lost . . .': Gail Omvedt, *Seeking Begumpura: The Social Vision of AntiCaste Intellectuals* (New Delhi, 2008), pp. 175–6.

p. 181 'What boldness and what loyalty . . .': Vishnushastri Chiplunkar, 'Marathi Pustake', *Nibandhamala*, 2 vols (Pune, 1993), vol. 1, p. 453; cited in Dominic Vendell, 'Jotirao Phule's *Satyasodh* and the Problem of Subaltern Consciousness', *Comparative Studies of South Asia, Africa and the Middle East*, vol. 34, no. 1 (2014), pp. 52–66 (p. 52; his translation).

p. 182 'At places one finds . . .': Jyotirao Phule, *Cultivator's Whipcord (Shetkaryacha Asud)*, 1883, in G. P. Deshpande (ed.), *Selected Writings of Jotirao Phule* (New Delhi, 2002), p. 160; cited in Ramachandra Guha (ed.), *Makers of Modern India* (Cambridge, MA, 2011), p. 84.

p. 183 'With an earnest desire . . .': Jotirao Govindrao Phule, *Collected Works of Mahatma Jotirao Phule*, vol. 1, *Slavery – In the Civilised British Government Under the Cloak of Brahmanism* (Bombay, 1991), p. xxvii.

25 DEEN DAYAL: COURTIER WITH A CAMERA

p. 185 '"imps" with "screeching clarinets"': cited in Matthias Schulz, 'Diary Rediscovered: Franz Ferdinand's Journey around the World', *Der Spiegel*, 25 February 2013; translated by Paul Cohen for Spiegel Online International, 1 March 2013; available at http://www.spiegel. de/international/zeitgeist/diary-of-archduke-franz-ferdinand-details-1892-journey-around-world-a-886196.html.

p. 188 'a form of conspicuous consumption . . .': Lewis Gann, 'Western and Japanese Colonialism', in *The Japanese Colonial Empire, 1895–1945*, edited by Ramon H. Myers and Mark R. Peattie (Princeton, NJ, 1984); cited in Stephen Kotkin, *Stalin*, vol. 1: *Paradoxes of Power, 1878–1928* (London, 2014), p. 62.

p. 190 'So pleased was his Highness . . .': *The Deccan Budget*, 6 July 1894; cited in a personal communication from Deborah Hutton.

26 BIRSA MUNDA: 'HAVE YOU BEEN TO CHALKAD?'

p. 194 'When the oppressor . . .': in 'The Kols, the Insurrection of 1862 and the Land Tenure Act of 1869', *Calcutta Review*, vol. 49 (1869), pp. 109–58; cited in K. S. Singh, *Birsa Munda and his Movement (1872–1901): A Study of a Millenarian Movement in Chotanagpur* (Calcutta, 1983; new edn, 2002), p. 4.

p. 195 'laughing and restless . . .': cited in Singh, *Birsa Munda and his Movement (1872–1901)*, p. 39.

p. 196 'Deep in the wild forest': cited in Singh, *Birsa Munda and his Movement (1872–1901)*, p. 314.

p. 196 'Deep amidst forest . . .': cited in Singh, *Birsa Munda and his Movement (1872–1901)*, p. 311.

p. 196 'The beloved son . . .': cited in Singh, *Birsa Munda and his Movement (1872–1901)*, p. 311.

p. 197 'with the one object . . .': cited in Alpa Shah, 'Religion and the Secular Left: Subaltern Studies, Birsa Munda and Maoists', *Anthropology of this century*, issue 9, January 2014; available at http://aotc press.com/articles/religion-secular-left-subaltern-studies-birsa-munda-maoists/.

p. 197 'mere act of . . .': cited in Shah, 'Religion and the Secular Left: Subaltern Studies, Birsa Munda and Maoists'.

p. 197 'Under the garb of . . .': cited in Shah, 'Religion and the Secular Left: Subaltern Studies, Birsa Munda and Maoists'.

p. 198 'About 9 p.m . . .': cited in Surendra Prasad Sinha, *Life and Times of Birsa Bhagwan* (Ranchi, Bihar Tribal Research Institute, 1964), p. 89.

27 JAMSETJI TATA: MAKING INDIA

p. 201 'You don't know what character . . .': cited in R. M. Lala, *The Creation of Wealth: The Tatas from the 19th to the 21st Century* (Bombay, 1981), p. 22.

p. 203 'I am sorry to say . . .': Calvin W. Smith, letter dated 25 April 1865, Calvin W. Smith Papers, Massachusetts Historical Society; cited in Sven Beckert, *Empire of Cotton: A Global History* (New York, 2014), p. 272.

p. 208 'What advances a nation . . .': cited in Lala, *The Creation of Wealth: The Tatas from the 19th to the 21st Century*, p. 37.

p. 208 'never looked to self-interest': Mohandas K. Gandhi, 'The Late Mr. Tata', *Indian Opinion*, 20 May 1905, translated from Gujarati in *Collected Works of Mahatma Gandhi*, vol. IV (Ahmedabad, 1960), p. 442; cited in Ramachandra Guha, *Gandhi before India* (New Delhi, 2013), p. 180.

28 VIVEKANANDA: BRING ALL TOGETHER

p. 209 'the contribution from the . . .': Narendra Modi, cited in 'Modi Cautions against commodifying Yoga', in *The Hindu*, 21 June 2015.

p. 209 'An orator by Divine right': 15 November 1894, *Letters of Swami Vivekananda* (Kolkata, 2013), p. 58.

p. 210 'a personal inspiration': Narendra Modi (@narendramodi), tweet on 12 January 2015; available at https://twitter.com/narendramodi/status/554449411065929729.

p. 210 'because it never conquered . . .': 'The Work Before Us', *The Complete Works of Swami Vivekananda*, 7th edn (Kolkata, 2013), vol. 3, p. 299.

p. 210 'only common ground . . .'12 November 1897, 'The Future of India', *Complete Works of Swami Vivekananda*, vol. 3, p. 312.

p. 211 'No religion on earth . . .': 20 August 1893, *Letters of Swami Vivekananda*, p. 41.

p. 212 'Kali and Kant': cited in C. A. Bayly, 'Afterword', *Modern Intellectual History*, vol. 4, issue 1 (April 2007), p. 166.

p. 212 'the pure monism of the Vedanta . . .': Brajendranath Seal, 'Swami Vivekananda', in *Prabuddha Bharata* (April 1907), reprinted in A. Raghuramaraju (ed.), *Debating Vivekananda: A Reader* (New Delhi, 2014), p. 5.

p. 212 ' "booby religion" ': 24 May 1894, *Complete Works of Swami Vivekananda*, vol. 7, p. 453.

p. 213 'Being driven mad with . . .': George M. Williams, *The Quest for Meaning of Swami Vivekananda: A Study of Religious Change* (Chico, CA, 1974), p. 38.

p. 214 '[W]e must travel . . .': 20 September 1892, *Letters of Swami Vivekananda*, p. 28.

p. 214 'a cigar costs eight annas . . .': 20 August 1893, *Complete Works of Swami Vivekananda*, vol. 5, p. 21.

p. 215 'Oh, how my heart ached . . .': 20 August 1893, *Complete Works of Swami Vivekananda*, vol. 5, p. 23.

p. 215 'the power of organization and combination': 1894, *Letters of Swami Vivekananda*, p. 94.

p. 215 'I give them spirituality . . .': 19 March 1894, *Letters of Swami Vivekananda*, p. 82.

p. 216 'by means of maps . . .': 19 March 1894, *Letters of Swami Vivekananda*, p. 82.

p. 217 'Bring all together': 1894, *Complete Works of Swami Vivekananda*, vol. 6, p. 287.

29 ANNIE BESANT: AN INDIAN TOMTOM

p. 218 'dazed and as in a dream': Jawaharlal Nehru, *An Autobiography* (London, 1936), p. 15.

p. 218 'I shall never forget the feeling . . .': Annie Besant, *An Autobiography* (London, 1893), p. 116.

p. 218 'a mark for ridicule': Besant, *An Autobiography*, p. 342.

p. 219 'land-stealing, piratical policy': Besant, *An Autobiography*, p. 175.

p. 219 'joyously and defiantly . . .': Besant, *An Autobiography*, p. 170.

p. 220 'We came, we saw . . .': Lata Mani, 'Multiple Mediations: Feminist Scholarship in the Age of Multinational Reception', *Feminist Review*, no. 35 (Summer 1990), p. 35.

p. 220 'pizza-effect': Agehananda Bharati, 'The Hindu Renaissance and its Apologetic Patterns', *The Journal of Asian Studies*, vol. 29, no. 2 (February 1970), pp. 273–4.

p. 222 'I felt that here was the key . . .': Nehru, *An Autobiography*, p. 15.

p. 222 'Natural law has been utilised . . .': cited in V. Geetha and S. V. Rajadurai, 'One Hundred Years of Brahminitude: Arrival of Annie Besant', *Economic and Political Weekly*, vol. XXX, no. 28 (15 July 1995), p. 1768.

p. 223 'I am an Indian tomtom . . .': cited in Sir Verney Lovett, *A History of the Indian Nationalist Movement* (London, 1921), p. 107; also cited in Daniel H. H. Ingalls, 'The Heritage of a Fallible Saint: Annie Besant's Gifts to India', *Proceedings of the American Philosophical Society*, vol. 109, no. 2 (9 April 1965), p. 87.

p. 225 'You are accustomed to authority . . .': Jiddu Krishnamurti, 'Truth is a Pathless Land', speech to the Order of the Star, 3 August 1929, in Mary Lutyens, *J. Krishnamurti: A Life* (New Delhi, 2005), pp. 278–81.

30 CHIDAMBARAM PILLAI: SWADESHI STEAM

p. 227 'Long before the World War . . .': cited in Stephen Kotkin, *Stalin*, vol. 1: *Paradoxes of Power, 1878–1928* (London, 2014), p. 87.

p. 227 'Bengal united is a power . . .': cited in Sumit Sarkar, *The Swadeshi Movement in Bengal*, 2nd edn (New Delhi, 2010), p. 15.

p. 229 'Between 1895 and 1916 . . .': David Washbrook, *The Emergence of Provincial Politics: The Madras Presidency 1880–1920* (Cambridge, 1976), p. 233.

p. 229 'made me feel that India . . .': V. O. Chidambaram Pillai, in S. V. Bapat (ed.), *Reminiscences and Anecdotes of Lokamanya Tilak*, vol. 3 (Poona, 1928), p. 158.

p. 230 'expect to be "shunned" ': Pillai, speech on 7 March 1908; reported in Criminal Investigation Department Madras, 'History of V. O. Chidambaram Pillai', G. O. no. 1502 Judicial and Secret (3 October 1911), p. 391.

p. 231 'to be held exclusively . . .': W. H. Coates, *The Old 'Country Trade' of the East Indies* (London, 1911), p. 203.

p. 231 'dissolute habits': CID Madras, 'History of V. O. Chidambaram Pillai', p. 373.

p. 232 'each company lowering its tariff . . .': from *The Hindu*, 10 December 1906; cited in R. A. Padmanabhan, *V. O. Chidambaram Pillai* (New Delhi, 1977), p. 36.

p. 233 'despicable sinners': CID Madras, 'History of V. O. Chidambaram Pillai', p. 375.

p. 233 'If you get swaraj . . .': CID Madras, 'History of V. O. Chidambaram Pillai', p. 389.

p. 233 'Union does not mean . . .': CID Madras, 'History of V. O. Chidambaram Pillai', pp. 389–90.

p. 234 'revolutions always brought good . . .': cited in Sumit Sarkar, *Modern India: 1886–1947* (Noida, 2014), p. 112.

p. 234 'if anything goes wrong . . .': CID Madras, 'History of V. O. Chidambaram Pillai', p. 391.

p. 234 'The torch is lighted . . .': Maud Boyton to Mary Ashe; cited in A. R. Venkatachalapathy, 'In Search of Ashe', *Economic and Political Weekly*, vol. XLV, no. 2 (9 January 2010), p. 41.

p. 236 'Chidambaram, who once bestowed . . .': translated by A. R. Venkatachalapathy, personal communication, 25 May 2015.

31 SRINIVASA RAMANUJAN: THE ELBOW OF GENIUS

p. 237 'Dear Sir, I beg to introduce myself . . .': S. Ramanujan, letter to G. H. Hardy, 16 January 1913; in Bruce C. Berndt and Robert A. Rankin (eds), *Ramanujan: Letters and Commentary* (Providence, RI, 1995), pp. 21–2.

p. 238 'Shiver in ecstasy': Cliff Pickover (@pickover), tweet on 14 March 2015; available at https://twitter.com/pickover/status/576760672886771713.

p. 239 'my elbow has become rough . . .': in S. R. Ranganathan, *Ramanujan: The Man and the Mathematician* (Bombay, 1967), p. 26.

p. 239 'I did not invent him . . .': G. H. Hardy, *Ramanujan*, 3rd edn (New York, 1978), p. 1; cited in Kanigel, *The Man who Knew Infinity*, p. 207.

p. 242 'an equation has no meaning . . .': reported by Prof. R. Srinivasan; cited in Ranganathan, *Ramanujan: The Man and the Mathematician*, p. 88; also cited in Ashis Nandy, *Alternative Sciences: Creativity and Authenticity in Two Indian Scientists*, 2nd edn (New Delhi, 2001), p. 137.

p. 244 'I am extremely sorry . . .': S. Ramanujan, letter to G. H. Hardy, 12 January 1920; in Berndt and Rankin (eds), *Ramanujan: Letters and Commentary*, p. 220.

32 TAGORE: UNLOCKING CAGES

p. 247 'The history of the growth of freedom . . .': Rabindranath Tagore, 'The Philosophy of Our People', in Sisir Kumar Das (ed.), *The English Writings of Rabindranath Tagore*, vol. 3: *A Miscellany* (New Delhi, 1996), pp. 559–69.

p. 248 'the voluntary submission . . .': Rabindranath Tagore, 'Nationalism in the West', *Nationalism* (London, 1917), pp. 26–7.

p. 248 'The sort of language that is admired . . .': Bertrand Russell to Nimai Chatterji, 26 April 1967; cited in Ray Monk, *Bertrand Russell: The Spirit of Solitude, 1872–1921* (New York, 1996), p. 281.

p. 249 'Oriental Croesus': Charles Dickens, 'A Curious Marriage Ceremony', *All the Year Round: A Weekly Journal*, no. 154 (5 April 1862); cited in Krishna Dutta and Andrew Robinson, *Rabindranath Tagore: The Myriad-Minded Man* (London, 1995), p.25.

p. 250 'My mother feared for this . . .': Rabindranath Tagore, 'Streer Patra', translated by Supriya Chaudhuri, in Fakrul Alam and Radha Chakravarty (eds), *The Essential Tagore* (Cambridge, MA, 2011), pp. 606.

p. 250 'a cage or "khancha" ': see, e.g., Amit Chaudhuri, *On Tagore* (New Delhi, 2012), p. 85.

p. 250 'Hindu ideal of marriage . . .': Rabindranath Tagore, 'The Indian Ideal of Marriage', *Visva-Bharati Quarterly*, vol. 3, no. 2 (July 1925); reprinted in Hermann Keyserling (ed.), *The Book of Marriage: A New Interpretation by Twenty-Four Leaders of Contemporary Thought* (New York, 1926), p. 104.

p. 250 'one of the most fruitful sources . . .': Tagore, 'The Indian Ideal of Marriage'; in Keyserling, *The Book of Marriage: A New Interpretation by Twenty-Four Leaders of Contemporary Thought*, p. 122.

p. 250 'the harsh touch of domesticity': Tagore, 'Suchana', *Chokher Bali*, reprinted in *Rabindra Rachanabali*, vol. 3 (Kolkata, 1940), p. 283; cited and translated by Supriya Chaudhuri.

p. 251 'pale stereotypes': Georg Lukács, 'Tagore's Gandhi Novel', *Die Rote Fahne* (1922), in Lukács, *Reviews and Articles from 'Die Rote Fahne'*, translated by Peter Palmer (London, 1983), p. 8.

p. 252 'Where the mind is without fear . . .': Tagore, *Gitanjali: Song Offerings*, (London, 1913), p. 27.

p. 253 'The British Government . . .': cited in Dutta and Robinson, *Rabindranath Tagore: The Myriad-Minded Man*, p. 152.

p. 253 'Those people who have got . . .': Tagore, 'Nationalism in India', *Nationalism* (London, 1917), p. 121.

p. 254 'a spirit of persecution . . .': Tagore, 'The Call of Truth', in Das (ed.), *The English Writings of Rabindranath Tagore*, vol. 3: *A Miscellany*, p. 419.

p. 254 'divine chastisement . . .': Mohandas K. Gandhi, 'Bihar and Untouchability', *Harijan*, 2 February 1934, in *Collected Works of Mahatma Gandhi*, vol. LVII (Ahmedabad, 1971), p. 87.

p. 254 'a fundamental source . . .': Rabindranath Tagore to Gandhi, published in *Harijan*, 16 February 1934; in Krishna Dutta and Andrew Robinson (eds), *Selected Letters of Rabindranath Tagore* (Cambridge, 1997), p. 537.

33 VISVESVARAYA: EXTRACTING MOONBEAMS FROM CUCUMBERS

p. 257 'promises to extract moonbeams . . .': cited in D. V. Gupta, 'A Gentleman to the Press Too', in *'M. V.': Birth Centenary Commemoration Volume* (Bangalore, 1960), p. 112.

p. 258 'Indian in blood and colour . . .': T. B. Macaulay, Minute on Education, dated 2 February 1835; in H. Sharp (ed.), *Selections from Educational Records, Part I (1781–1839)* (Calcutta, 1920; reprint New Delhi, 1965), pp. 107–17.

p. 259 'In action he was a great autocrat . . .': A. P. Srinivasa Murthy, *Sir M. Visvesvaraya: His Economic Thoughts and Achievements* (Bangalore, 1995), p. 17.

p. 262 'top to bottom . . .': cited in Chandan Gowda, ' "Advance Mysore!": The Cultural Logic of a Developmental State', *Economic and Political Weekly*, vol. XLV, no. 29 (17 July 2010), p. 94.

p. 262 'By ignoring merit and capacity . . .': M. Visvesvaraya, *Memoirs of my Working Life* (Bombay, 1951), p. 87.

p. 264 'If you feel that by giving . . .': cited in P. Rajeswar Rao, *The Great Indian Patriots*, vol. 1, 2nd revd edn (New Delhi, 1991), p. 226.

p. 265 'Take care of the pieces . . .': cited in Pandri Nath, *Mokshagundam Visvesvaraya: Life and Work* (Bombay, 1987), p. 97.

34 PERIYAR: SNIPER OF SACRED COWS

p. 267 'the "stupidity" of Sanskrit epics': A. Arulmozhi, 'Relevance of Periyar Feminism', in K. Veeramani (ed.), *Periyar Feminism* (Thanjavur, 2010), p. 26.

p. 267 'Have cats ever freed rats? . . .': Periyar, 'Why did women become enslaved?', cited in Sarah Hodges, 'Revolutionary family life and the Self Respect movement in Tamil South India, 1926–49', *Contributions to Indian Sociology*, vol. 39, no. 2 (June 2005), pp. 255–6.

p. 268 'There is no God . . .': cited in Vaasanthi, *Cut-outs, Caste and Cine Stars: The World of Tamil Politics* (New Delhi, 2006), p. 1; and in Gail Omvedt, *Dalit Visions: The Anti-caste Movement and the Construction of an Indian Identity*, revd edn (Hyderabad, 2006), p. 56.

p. 269 'If you see a snake . . .': cited in Marguerite Ross Barnett, *The Politics of Cultural Nationalism in South India* (Princeton, 1967, 2015), p. 71; see also Paula Richman, 'E. V. Ramasami's Reading of the Rāmāyaṇa', in Paula Richman (ed.), *Many Rāmāyaṇas: The Diversity of a Narrative Tradition in South Asia* (Berkeley, CA, 1991), p. 197.

p. 271 'reaping the reward . . .': Mahadev Desai, cited in Eleanor Zelliot, *From Untouchable to Dalit*, 2nd edn (New Delhi, 1996), p. 161.

p. 272 'If a son had been born . . .': cited in Vijaya Ramaswamy, 'Gender and the Writing of South Indian History', in Sabyasachi Bhattacharya (ed.), *Approaches to History: Essays in Indian Historiography* (New Delhi, 2011), p. 220.

p. 273 'no god; no religion; no Gandhi; . . .': Periyar, *Kudi Arasu*, 2 May 1925, cited in Nicholas B. Dirks, *Castes of Mind: Colonialism and the Making of Modern India* (Princeton, NJ, 2001), p. 259.

p. 273 'If a wife has to obey . . .': Periyar, *Kudi Arasu*, 7 April 1929, cited in Hodges, 'Revolutionary family life and the Self Respect movement in Tamil South India, 1926–49', p. 266.

35 IQBAL: DEATH FOR FALCONS

p. 276 'where the Arab and non-Arab . . .': Abu Bakr al-Baghdadi, 'A Message to the Mujahidin and the Muslim Ummah in the Month of Ramadan' (2014); available at http://www.gatestoneinstitute.org/documents/baghdadi-caliph.pdf.

450

p. 276 'The earth . . . is Allah's': al-Baghdadi, 'A Message to the Mujahidin and the Muslim Ummah in the Month of Ramadan'.

p. 277 'though a Brahman's son . . .': Muhammad Iqbal, 'Persian Psalms', no. 9, translated by A. J. Arberry, in *Collected Poetical Works of Iqbal* (Lahore, 2014), p. 231; available at http://www.iqbalcyberlibrary.net/pdf/848.pdf.

p. 277 'performing artist of conversation': Muhammad Daud Rahbar, 'Glimpses of the Man', in Hafeez Malik (ed.), *Iqbal: Poet-Philosopher of Pakistan* (New York, 1971), p. 44.

p. 277 'the colour of his face changed . . .': Javid Iqbal, 'Iqbal: My Father', in Malik (ed.), *Iqbal: Poet-Philosopher of Pakistan*, p. 59.

p. 277 'tremendous work . . .': cited in Q. M. Haq and M. I. Waley, *Allama Sir Muhammad Iqbal: Poet-Philosopher of the East* (London, 1977), p. 7.

p. 277 'a man in disagreement with his age': cited by R. A. Nicholson, 'Introduction', in Muhammad Iqbal, *The Secrets of the Self*, revd edn (Lahore, 1940), p. xxxi.

p. 278 'If an effective principle of cooperation . . .': Muhammad Iqbal, Presidential address to the annual session of the All-India Muslim League, 29 December 1930, in Syed Abdul Vaid (ed.), *Thoughts and Reflections of Iqbal* (Lahore, 1964), p. 168.

p. 278 'sang with impudence . . .': Rajmohan Gandhi, *Eight Lives: A Study of the Hindu-Muslim Encounter* (Albany, NY, 1986), p. 70.

p. 278 'visionary idealist . . .': Muhammad Iqbal, Presidential address to the annual session of the All-India Muslim Conference, 21 March 1932, cited in Javed Majeed, *Muhammad Iqbal: Islam, Aesthetics and Postcolonialism* (New Delhi, 2009), p. 83.

p. 279 'For a falcon . . .': Muhammad Iqbal, 'Conquest of Nature', translated by Mustansir Mir, in *A Message from the East*, in *Collected Poetical Works of Iqbal*, p. 82; available at http://www.iqbalcyberlibrary.net/pdf/702.pdf.

p. 279 'Keep desire alive . . .': Muhammad Iqbal, *The Secrets of the Self*, translated by R. A. Nicholson, revd edn (Lahore, 1940), p. 23.

p. 280 'Pleasure is the only effect . . .': Iqbal, 'The Message', translated by M. A. K. Khalil, in *The Call of the Marching Bell*, in *Collected Poetical Works of Iqbal*, p. 162; available at http://www.iqbalcyberlibrary.net/pdf/786.pdf.

p. 280 'O Western world's inhabitants . . .': Iqbal, 'Ghazals', in *The Call of the Marching Bell*, in *Collected Poetical Works of Iqbal*, p. 172.

p. 280 'the greatest danger to modern humanity': Iqbal, *Six Lectures on the Reconstruction of Religious Thought in Islam* (Lahore, 1930), p. 248.

p. 280 'declined to give absolute obedience . . .': Iqbal, 'Islam as a Moral and Political Ideal', in Vaid (ed.), *Thoughts and Reflections of Iqbal*, p. 42.

p. 280 'bifurcate the unity of man . . .': Iqbal, Presidential address to the annual session of the All-India Muslim League, 29 December 1930, in Vaid (ed.), *Thoughts and Reflections of Iqbal*, p. 163.

p. 281 'Man is a free responsible being . . .': Iqbal, 'Islam as a Moral and Political Ideal', in Vaid (ed.), *Thoughts and Reflections of Iqbal*, p. 38.

p. 281 'There is no mediator . . .': Iqbal, 'Islam as a Moral and Political Ideal', in Vaid (ed.), *Thoughts and Reflections of Iqbal*, p. 38.

p. 281 'As a human being I have a right . . .': cited in Atiya Begum, *Iqbal*, edited by Rauf Parekh (Karachi, 2011), p. 23.

p. 281 'Iqbal, as I knew him in Europe . . .': Begum, *Iqbal*, p. 46.

p. 282 'Arabian Imperialism': Iqbal, *Six Lectures on the Reconstruction of Religious Thought in Islam* (Lahore, 1930), p. 222.

p. 282 'Our essence is not bound . . .': Iqbal, *The Mysteries of Selflessness: A Philosophical Poem*, translated by A. J. Arberry (London, 1953); cited in Iqbal Singh Sevea, *The Political Philosophy of Muhammad Iqbal* (New York, 2012), p. 126.

p. 282 'Muslim political constitution': Iqbal, 'Islam as a Moral and Political Ideal', in Vaid (ed.), *Thoughts and Reflections of Iqbal*, p. 52.

p. 282 'absolute equality of all . . .': Iqbal, 'Islam as a Moral and Political Ideal', in Vaid (ed.), *Thoughts and Reflections of Iqbal*, p. 53.

p. 282 'best form of Government . . .': Iqbal, 'Islam as a Moral and Political Ideal', in Vaid (ed.), *Thoughts and Reflections of Iqbal*, p. 51.

p. 282 'one man from the brain . . .': cited in Iqbal Singh, *The Ardent Pilgrim: An Introduction to the Life and Work of Mohammed Iqbal* (London, 1951), p. 116.

p. 282 'the law of God . . .': Muhammad Iqbal, 'Islam as a Moral and Political Ideal', in Vaid (ed.), *Thoughts and Reflections of Iqbal*, p. 52.

p. 282 'how the many can become One . . .': Muhammad Iqbal, Presidential address to the annual session of the All-India Muslim Conference, 21 March 1932, cited in Sevea, *The Political Philosophy of Muhammad Iqbal*, p. 155.

p. 282 'a social structure regulated . . .': Muhammad Iqbal, Presidential address to the annual session of the All-India Muslim League, 29 December 1930, in Vaid (ed.), *Thoughts and Reflections of Iqbal*, p. 162.

p. 283 'the light of God': Iqbal, *The Mysteries of Selflessness*, cited in Majeed, *Muhammad Iqbal: Islam, Aesthetics and Postcolonialism*, p.72.

p. 283 'the freedom of Ijtihad . . .': Iqbal, *Six Lectures on the Reconstruction of Religious Thought in Islam*, pp. 219–20.

p. 283 'each generation, guided but unhampered . . .': Iqbal, *Six Lectures on the Reconstruction of Religious Thought in Islam*, p. 234.

p. 283 'Islam itself is Destiny . . .': Iqbal, Presidential address to the annual session of the All-India Muslim League, 29 December 1930, in Vaid (ed.), *Thoughts and Reflections of Iqbal*, p. 167.

p. 283 'sink their respective individualities . . .': Iqbal, *Six Lectures on the Reconstruction of Religious Thought in Islam*, pp. 240–41.

p. 284 'the thought that produced Pakistan': Aakar Patel, 'Mir, Ghalib, Iqbal, Faiz. The list isn't complete', *Mint*, 9 June 2012; available at http://www.livemint.com/Leisure/ldYJBUjDLWYWbmAuN5IuPP/Mir-Ghalib-Iqbal-Faiz-The-list-isn8217t-complete.html.

p. 284 'When I am rolling . . .': Muhammad Iqbal, *Payam-i Mashriq* (Lahore, 1954), p. 150; cited in N. P. Anikeyev, 'The Doctrine of Personality', in Malik (ed.), *Iqbal: Poet-Philosopher of Pakistan*, p. 270.

36 AMRITA SHER-GIL: THIS IS ME

p. 285 '*God please save me* . . .': Amrita Sher-Gil to Victor Egan, October 1933, cited in Yashodhara Dalmia, *Amrita Sher-Gil: A Life* (New Delhi, 2006), p. 52.

p. 285 'the queen of Indian art': M. F. Husain with Khalid Mohamed, *Where Art Thou: An Autobiography* (Mumbai, 2002), p. xvi.

p. 285 '[R]ather self-consciously arty': Malcom Muggeridge, *Like it Was: The Diaries of Malcolm Muggeridge* (London 1981), p. 128; cited in Dalmia, *Amrita Sher-Gil: A Life*, pp. 68–9.

p. 286 '[Y]ou will say that I am a self-opinionated monkey . . .': Amrita Sher-Gil to her mother, 8 February 1934, in Vivan Sundaram (ed.), *Amrita Sher-Gil: A Self-Portrait in Letters and Writings*, 2 vols, vol. 1 (New Delhi, 2010), p. 127.

p. 286 'Poor little bride . . .': Amrita Sher-Gil, diary entry 1 August 1925, in Sundaram (ed.), *Amrita Sher-Gil: A Self-Portrait in Letters and Writings*, vol. 1, p. 29.

p. 287 '"sentimentalists" lacking "passionate souls"': in Dalmia, *Amrita Sher-Gil: A Life*, p. 145.

p. 287 'Pomposity or exhibitionism': Sher-Gil to Nehru, 6 November 1937, in Jawaharlal Nehru (ed.), *A Bunch of Old Letters: Being Mostly Written to Jawaharlal Nehru and Some Written by Him*, revd edn (New Delhi, 2005), p. 257.

p. 288 '[A]ll art, not excluding religious art . . .': Amrita Sher-Gil to Karl Khandalavala, 6 March 1937, in Sundaram (ed.), *Amrita Sher-Gil, A Self-Portrait in Letters and Writings*, vol. 1, p. 347.

p. 289 'odious character': Amrita Sher-Gil to Victor Egan, 1931, cited in Dalmia, *Amrita Sher-Gil: A Life*, p. 47.

p. 289 'But little by little . . .': Amrita Sher-Gil to Victor Egan, 1931, cited in Dalmia, *Amrita Sher-Gil: A Life*, pp. 48–9.

p. 290 'I began to be haunted by an intense longing . . .': cited in N. Iqbal Singh, 'Amrita Sher-Gil', *India International Centre Quarterly*, vol. 2, no. 3 (July 1975), p. 213.

p. 290 'Modern art has led me to the comprehension . . .': Amrita Sher-Gil to her parents, September 1943, in Sundaram (ed.), *Amrita Sher-Gil: A Self-Portrait in Letters and Writings*, vol. 1, p. 165.

p. 290 'Europe belongs to Picasso . . .': cited in Dalmia, *Amrita Sher-Gil: A Life*, p. xiii; and in Vivan Sundaram (ed.), *Amrita Sher-Gil: Essays* (Bombay, 1972), p. 15.

p. 290 'I have for the first time since my return . . .': Amrita Sher-Gil to her parents, December 1936, in Sundaram (ed.), *Amrita Sher-Gil: A Self-Portrait in Letters and Writings*, vol. 1, p. 267.

p. 290 'It is slightly irritating . . .': Amrita Sher-Gil to Karl Khandalavala, 15 June 1937, in Sundaram (ed.), *Amrita Sher-Gil: A Self-Portrait in Letters and Writings*, vol. 1, p. 383.

p. 291 'cramping and crippling effect . . .': cited in Iqbal Singh, *Amrita Sher-Gil: A Biography* (Delhi, 1984), pp. 71–2.

p. 291 'the drawing perhaps the most powerful . . .': Amrita Sher-Gil to her sister, 25 January 1937, in Sundaram (ed.), *Amrita Sher-Gil: A Self-Portrait in Letters and Writings*, vol. 1, p. 307.

p. 291 'best thing so far': cited in Singh, *Amrita Sher-Gil: A Biography*, p. 102.

p. 292 'her vivid, forceful, direct . . .': Malcolm Muggeridge, *Chronicles of Wasted Time*, vol. 2: *The Infernal Grove* (London, 1973), p. 48; cited in Dalmia, *Amrita Sher-Gil: A Life*, p. 72.

p. 292 'sugary . . . that rotten paper': cited in Singh, *Amrita Sher-Gil: A Biography*, p. 103.

37 SUBHAS CHANDRA BOSE: A TOUCH OF THE ABNORMAL

p. 294 'I had in some respects . . .': in Sisir K. Bose and Sugata Bose (eds), *An Indian Pilgrim: An Unfinished Autobiography* (New Delhi, 1997), p. 35.

p. 294 'Will the condition of our country . . .': Subhas Chandra Bose to Prabhavati Devi, 1912, cited in Sugata Bose, *His Majesty's Opponent: Subhas Chandra Bose and India's Struggle against Empire* (Cambridge, MA, 2011), p. 23.

p. 294 'second to none': Mohandas K. Gandhi, 'How to Canalize Hatred', *Harijan*, 24 February 1946, in Collected Works of Mahatma Gandhi, vol. LXXXIII (Ahmedabad, 1981), p. 135.

p. 295 'The blood of the martyr . . .': Subhas Chandra Bose, 'My Political Testament', letter to H. E. the Governor of Bengal et al., 26 November 1940, in Sisir Kumar Bose and Sugata Bose (eds), *The Alternative Leadership: Speeches, Articles, Statements and Letters, June 1939–January 1941 (Netaji: Collected Works*, vol. 10) (New Delhi, 1998), p. 197.

pp. 296–7 'It was in the voice . . .': Subhas Chandra Bose, 'The Individual, the Nation and the Ideal' (1929), in Sisir Kumar Bose and Sugata Bose (eds), *The Essential Writings of Netaji Subhas Chandra Bose* (New Delhi, 1997), p. 97.

p. 297 'Nothing makes me happier . . .': Subhas Chandra Bose, letter to Hemanta Kumar Sarkar, 12 November 1919, in Bose and Bose (eds), *An Indian Pilgrim: An Unfinished Autobiography*, p. 195.

p. 297 'Life loses half its interest . . .': cited in Bose, *His Majesty's Opponent: Subhas Chandra Bose and India's Struggle against Empire*, p. 39.

p. 297 'The younger generation . . .': Bose to Kitty Kurti, 23 February 1934, in Kitty Kurti, *Subhas Chandra Bose as I Knew Him* (Calcutta, 1966), p. 59.

p. 298 'The war had shown . . .': Bose and Bose (eds), *An Indian Pilgrim: An Unfinished Autobiography*, p. 74.

p. 298 'Bose's appeal . . .': Joseph Goebbels, diary entry, 2 March 1942, cited in Romain Hayes, *Subhas Chandra Bose in Nazi Germany:*

Politics, Intelligence, and Propaganda 1941–43 (New York, 2011), p. 215n.

p. 299 'enemies of British imperialism . . .': Bose, 'The Fall of Singapore', first broadcast on Azad Hind Radio, 19 February 1942, in Sisir Kumar Bose and Sugata Bose (eds), *Azad Hind: Writings and Speeches 1941–3* (*Netaji: Collected Works*, vol. 11) (New Delhi, 2002), p. 63.

p. 299 'fascist or imperialist . . .': in Sisir K. Bose and Sugata Bose (eds), *The Alternative Leadership: Speeches, Articles, Statements and Letters, June 1939–January 1941* (*Netaji: Collected Works*, vol. 10) (New Delhi, 2004), p. 82.

p. 299 'spoilt child': Mohandas K. Gandhi to C. F. Andrews, 15 January 1940, in *Collected Works of Mahatma Gandhi*, vol. LXXI (Ahmedabad, 1978), p. 113.

p. 301 ' "do or die" effort': see esp. Mohandas K. Gandhi, Speech at A.I.C.C. Meeting, 8 August 1942, in *Collected Works of Mahatma Gandhi*, vol. LXXVI (Ahmedabad, 1979), p. 392.

p. 303 'It is a bad thing psychologically . . .': Jawaharlal Nehru, press conference 12 April 1942, in *Selected Works of Jawaharlal Nehru*, vol. 12 (New Delhi, 1979), p. 226; cited in Leonard A. Gordon, *Brothers against the Raj: A Biography of Indian Nationalists Sarat and Subhas Chandra Bose* (New York, 1990), p. 473.

38 GANDHI: 'IN THE PALM OF OUR HANDS'

p. 306 'modest downward face . . .': V. S. Srinivasa Sastri to V. S. R. Sastri, 10 January 1915, in T. N. Jagadishan (ed.), *Letters of The Right Honourable V. S. Srinivasa Sastri* (Bombay, 1963), p. 41.

p. 307 'I should have passed him by . . .': Rufus Isaacs (Lord Reading) to Montagu, 19 May 1921, British Library Oriental and India Office Collections Mss. Eur.F.238/3; cited in Claude Markovits, *The Un-Gandhian Gandhi: The Life and Afterlife of the Mahatma* (New Delhi, 2004), p. 14.

p. 308 'It is not for me to say . . .': Gandhi, *Indian Opinion*, 28 April 1906, cited in Ramachandra Guha, *Gandhi before India* (New Delhi, 2013), p. 194.

p. 308 'dressed quite like a bania': V. S. Srinivasa Sastri to V. S. R. Sastri, 10 January 1915, in Jagadishan (ed.), *Letters of The Right Honourable V. S. Srinivasa Sastri*, p. 41.

p. 310 'every known Indian anarchist': Gandhi, ' "Hind Swaraj" or the "Indian Home Rule" ', *Young India*, 26 January 1921, in *Collected Works of Mahatma Gandhi*, vol. XIX (Ahmedabad, 1966), p. 277.

p. 310 'Indian school of violence': Gandhi, ' "Hind Swaraj" or the "Indian Home Rule" ', *Young India*, 26 January 1921, in *Collected Works of Mahatma Gandhi*, vol. XIX, p. 277.

p. 310 'We will assassinate a few . . .': Gandhi, 'Hind Swaraj', in Anthony J. Parel (ed.), *'Hind Swaraj' and Other Writings* (Cambridge, 2009), p. 75.

p. 310 'As is Japan, so must India . . .': Gandhi, 'Hind Swaraj', in Parel (ed.), *'Hind Swaraj' and Other Writings*, pp. 26–7.

p. 310 'What is granted under fear . . .': Gandhi, 'Hind Swaraj', in Parel (ed.), *'Hind Swaraj' and Other Writings*, p. 76.

p. 310 'English rule without the Englishmen': Gandhi, 'Hind Swaraj', in Parel (ed.), *'Hind Swaraj' and Other Writings*, p. 27.

p. 310 'What we need to do': Gandhi, 'Hind Swaraj', in Parel (ed.), *'Hind Swaraj' and Other Writings*, p. 75.

p. 311 'The show of violence . . .': Reinhold Niebuhr, 'What Chance has Gandhi?', *The Christian Century*, 14 October 1930, p. 1275.

p. 312 'empire of opinion': see, e.g., 'Report of the General Committee for Public Instruction', *Friend of India*, 27 October 1836, cited in C. A. Bayly, *Empire and Information: Intelligence Gathering and Social Communication in India, 1780–1870* (Cambridge, 1996), p. 2.

p. 313 'in the palm of our hands': Gandhi, 'Hind Swaraj', in Parel (ed.), *'Hind Swaraj and Other Writings*, p. 71.

p. 313 'like the coil of a snake': Gandhi, 'Neither a Saint nor a Politician', *Young India*, 12 May 1920, in *Collected Works of Mahatma Gandhi*, vol. XVII (Ahmedabad, 1968), p. 406.

p. 314 'eccentricities, whimsicality, metaphysics': Nathuram Godse, statement to the court, 8 November 1948, reprinted as *Why I Assassinated Gandhi*, edited by Virender Mehra (New Delhi, 2014), para. 69, p. 59.

39 JINNAH: THE CHESS PLAYER

p. 315 'impossible to work . . .': Muhammad Ali Jinnah, 'Statement on the question of Democracy in India', 1939, in Jamil-ud-Din Ahmad (ed.), *Some Recent Speeches & Writings of Mr Jinnah*, vol. 1, 5th edn (Lahore, 1952), p. 99.

REFERENCES

p. 316 'It is a sub-continent composed . . .': Muhammad Ali Jinnah to
    Mohandas K. Gandhi, 1 January 1940, in Ahmad (ed.), *Some Recent
    Speeches & Writings of Mr Jinnah*, vol. 1, 5th edn, p. 139.

p. 316 'a good claim to be . . .': Perry Anderson, *The Indian Ideology* (London, 2013), p. 77.

p. 318 'He wanted to discover himself . . .': Fatima Jinnah, *My Brother*
    (Karachi, 1987), p. 81.

p. 320 'religious gathering celebrating the advent . . .': K. R. Munshi,
    Pilgrimage to Freedom (Bombay, 1967), p. 18; cited in A. G. Noorani, *Jinnah and Tilak: Comrades in the Freedom Struggle* (New
    Delhi, 2010), p. 53.

p. 320 'Free institutions are next to impossible . . .': John Stuart Mill, *Considerations on Representative Government* (London, 1861), p. 289.

p. 321 '[I]t is necessary to redistribute . . .': Muhammad Iqbal to Muhammad Ali Jinnah, 28 May 1937, in *Letters of Iqbal to Jinnah: Allama
    Iqbal's Views on the Political Future of Muslim India* (Lahore, 1942,
    3rd repr. 1963), p. 19.

p. 321 'federation of Muslim provinces': Iqbal to Jinnah, 21 June 1937, in
    *Letters of Iqbal to Jinnah: Allama Iqbal's Views on the Political
    Future of Muslim India*, p. 24.

p. 322 'The Mussalmans were in the greatest danger . . .': Jinnah, speech at
    Aligarh Muslim University, 5 February 1938, in Ahmad (ed.), *Some
    Recent Speeches & Writings of Mr Jinnah*, vol. 1, 5th edn, p. 43.

p. 322 'a "massacre" campaign': Jinnah, in *Star of India*, 4 January 1937;
    cited in Venkat Dhulipala, *Creating a New Medina: State Power,
    Islam, and the Quest for Pakistan in Late Colonial North India*
    (Cambridge, 2015), p. 67.

p. 323 '"atheistic socialism" of Nehru': Iqbal to Jinnah, 28 May 1937, in
    *Letters of Iqbal to Jinnah: Allama Iqbal's Views on the Political
    Future of Muslim India*, p. 18.

p. 323 'one as a numerical minority . . .': Jinnah, Presidential address to
    annual session of the All-India Muslim League, Lahore, 23 March
    1940, in Ahmad (ed.), *Some Recent Speeches & Writings of Mr Jinnah*, vol. 1, 5th edn, p. 178.

p. 324 'a kind of Muslim Never-Never Land . . .': Office of Strategic Services, Research and Analysis Branch, report 112, 'Pakistan: A
    Muslim Project for a Separate State in India', 5 February 1943,
    IOR:l/PJ/12/652; cited in Nisid Hajari, *Midnight's Furies: The
    Deadly Legacy of India's Partition* (New York, 2015), p. 42.

40 MANTO: THE UNSENTIMENTALIST

p. 326 'Loot. Fire. Stampede . . .': Saadat Hasan Manto, 'Khol Do', in *Manto: Selected Stories*, translated by Aatish Taseer (Noida, 2008), p. 51.

p. 326 'too few leaders . . .': Manto, 'Freedom', in *Manto: Selected Stories*, translated by Aatish Taseer, p. 150.

p. 326 'Don't say that a hundred thousand . . .': Manto, 'Sahai', in *Manto Rama* (Lahore, 1990), p. 20; cited in Ayesha Jalal, *The Pity of Partition: Manto's Life, Times, and Work across the India–Pakistan Divide* (Princeton, NJ, 2013), p. 20.

p. 327 'If you cannot bear my stories . . .': cited in Jisha Menon, *The Performance of Nationalism: India, Pakistan, and the Memory of Partition* (Cambridge, 2013), p. 149.

p. 327 'You have brought him to the wrong place . . .': cited in Khalid Hasan, 'A Manto Remembrance', published on the Academy of the Punjab in North America website, 16 January 2004; available at http://www.apnaorg.com/prose-content/english-articles/page-118/article-7/index.html.

p. 327 'I write because I'm addicted . . .': Manto, 'How I Write Stories', translated by Muhammad Umar Memon, *The Annual of Urdu Studies*, vol. 28 (2013), p. 367.

p. 329 'You can be happy here . . .': cited in Gyan Prakash, *Mumbai Fables* (Princeton, NJ, 2010), p. 146.

p. 329 'In the beginning . . .': Manto, *Stars from Another Sky: The Bombay Film World in the 1940s*, translated by Khalid Hasan (New Delhi, 1998), p. 2.

p. 330 'In any case, it didn't evoke . . .': Manto, 'Ten Rupees', in *Manto: Selected Stories*, translated by Aatish Taseer, p. 25.

p. 331 'as blanched and lifeless . . .': Manto, 'For Freedom's Sake', translated by Muhammad Umar Memon, in M. Asaduddin (ed.), *Black Margins* (New Delhi, 2003), p. 117.

p. 331 'very bitter': G. M. Asar, cited in Khalid Hasan, 'A Manto Remembrance'.

p. 332 'This country, which we call Pakistan . . .': Manto, 'Do Gaddhay', in Aakar Patel (trans. and ed.), *Why I Write: Essays by Saadat Hasan Manto* (Chennai, 2014), p. 134.

41 AMBEDKAR: BUILDING PALACES ON
DUNG HEAPS

p. 334 'A society, almost necessarily, begins . . .': Ta-Nehisi Coates, *Between the World and Me* (New York, 2015), p. 96.

p. 335 'fools and knaves': cited in Ramachandra Guha, *India after Gandhi: The History of the World's Largest Democracy* (London, 2007), p. 146.

p. 336 'If you want to write what I tell you . . .': in C. B. Khairmode, *Dr Bhimrao Ramji Ambedkar*; cited in S. Anand, 'Bhim Row', *Outlook*, 5 December 2005; available at http://www.outlookindia.com/article/bhim-row/229435.

p. 338 'All have a grievance . . .': B. R. Ambedkar, 'Untouchables or the Children of India's Ghetto', in Vasant Moon (ed.), *Dr Babasaheb Ambedkar: Writings and Speeches*, vol. 5 (Bombay, 1987), pp. 101–2; cited in Christophe Jaffrelot, *Dr Ambedkar and Untouchability* (New Delhi, 2005), pp. 36–7.

p. 340 'the bare man in him': Ambedkar, interview with Francis Watson, 26 February 1955, British Broadcasting Corporation Sound Archive.

p. 340 'I claim myself in my own person . . .': Gandhi, 'Speech at Minorities Committee', 13 November 1931, in *Collected Works of Mahatma Gandhi*, vol. XLVIII (Ahmedabad, 1971), p. 297.

p. 342 'Apart from any other consideration . . .': cited in Sanjay Hegde, 'A nation builder's pride of place', *The Hindu*, 14 April 2015; available at http://www.thehindu.com/opinion/lead/sanjay-hegde-on-br-ambedkar-the-hero-who-built-an-independent-india/article7099218.ece.

p. 344 'empty soapbox': Ambedkar, Cabinet resignation speech, 10 October 1951, in Moon (ed.), *Dr Babasaheb Ambedkar: Writings and Speeches*, vol. 14, p. 1318.

p. 344 'greatest social reform measure . . .': in Moon (ed.), *Dr Babasaheb Ambedkar: Writings and Speeches*, vol. 14, pp. 1325–6; cited in Gyanendra Pandey, *A History of Prejudice: Race, Caste, and Difference in India and the United States* (Cambridge, 2013), p. 68.

p. 344 'We are going to enter into a life . . .': Ambedkar, speech to the Constituent Assembly, 25 November 1949, in *Constituent Assembly Debates*, vol. xi; available at http://parliamentofindia.nic.in/ls/debates/vol11p11.htm.

42 RAJ KAPOOR: THE POLITICS OF LOVE

p. 345 'Raj Kapoor was just an image . . .': Raj Kapoor, in Simi Garewal, *Living Legend: Raj Kapoor* (Siga Arts International, 1984).

p. 346 'a synthetic, non-existent society . . .': Satyajit Ray, *Our Films, Their Films* (New York, 1994), p. 12.

pp. 347–8 'It was then . . .': Raj Kapoor, in Ritu Nanda, *Raj Kapoor Speaks* (New Delhi, 2002), p. 2.

p. 348 'pampered brat': Kapoor, in Nanda, *Raj Kapoor Speaks*, p. 4.

p. 348 'So instead I put on the mask . . .': Kapoor, in Nanda, *Raj Kapoor Speaks*, p. 5.

p. 350 'Capitalists, black marketers, . . .': in Nasreen Munni Kabir et al., *The Dialogue of Awaara: Raj Kapoor's Immortal Classic* (New Delhi, 2010), pp. 116–18.

p. 351 'I didn't know the implications . . .': Kapoor, in Nanda, *Raj Kapoor Speaks*, p. 3.

p. 351 'professional emotionalist': cited in Madhu Jain, *The Kapoors: The First Family of Indian Cinema* (New Delhi, 2005), p. 149.

43 SHEIKH ABDULLAH: CHAINS OF GOLD

p. 355 'We Kashmiris want to . . .': Sheikh Mohammad Abdullah, *Flames of the Chinar: An Autobiography*, abridged and translated by Khushwant Singh (New Delhi, 1993), p. 78.

p. 355 'Quit Kashmir': Abdullah, *Flames of the Chinar*, p. 79.

p. 356 'If I am able to carry on . . .': Abdullah to Nehru, 5 November 1947.

p. 356 'Not a single member . . .': Amnesty International, 'Denied: Failures in Accountability for Human Rights Violations by Security Force Personnel in Jammu and Kashmir' (London: 2015); available at https://www.amnesty.org.in/images/uploads/articles/Kashmir_Report_Web_version_%281%29.pdf.

p. 357 'transported into a strange world . . .': Sheikh Mohammad Abdullah, *The Blazing Chinar: An Autobiography*, translated by Mohammad Amin (Srinagar, 2013), p. 47.

p. 358 'Islam in Danger': Chitralekha Zutshi, *Languages of Belonging: Islam, Regional Identity, and the Making of Kashmir* (New Delhi: 2003), p. 228.

p. 358 'A time will come . . .': Abdullah, *The Blazing Chinar*, p. 223.

p. 358 'awaken the Kashmiri people . . .': Abdullah, *The Blazing Chinar*, p. 167.

p. 358 'by his bedside': Abdullah, *Flames of the Chinar*, p. 74.

p. 361 'Sheikh Sahib, if you waver . . .': Abdullah, *The Blazing Chinar*, p. 368.

p. 361 'world has not seen a more glaring rape . . .': Sheikh Abdullah to Nehru, from Subsidiary Jail, Kud, 15 May 1955.

p. 361 'lure of American money . . .': Nehru, 1/2 August 1952.

p. 361 'The members of Government should not speak . . .': Jawaharlal Nehru, 'A Proposal for the Future of Jammu and Kashmir', recorded by M. O. Mathai, 31 July 1953; in *Selected Works of Jawaharlal Nehru*, vol. 23 (New Delhi, 1998), pp. 303–5.

p. 361 'I suppose one has to do some things . . .': Indira Gandhi to Nehru, 10 August 1953.

p. 362 'an open book . . .': Abdullah, *Interviews and Speeches after his Release on 2 January 1968*, Series 2, edited by G. M. Shah (Delhi, 1968), pp. 12–13; cited in Suranjan Das, *Kashmir and Sindh: Nation-building, Ethnicity and Regional Politics in South Asia* (London, 2001), p. 47.

p. 362 'Let every Indian search . . .': Abdullah, *Interviews and Speeches after his Release on 2 January 1968*, Series 2, edited by G. M. Shah, p. 13; cited in Das, *Kashmir and Sindh: Nation-building, Ethnicity and Regional Politics in South Asia*, p. 47.

44 V. K. KRISHNA MENON: SOMBRE PORCUPINE

p. 363 'unpleasant mischief-maker': M. G. L. Joy, British Embassy in Washington DC, to C. T. Crowe, Far Eastern Dept, Foreign Office, 25 January 1954, National Archives, DO 35/9014, 'Top Secret' File on Krishna Menon.

p. 363 'arrogant extremism': Alan Burns, UK delegation to the United Nations, New York, to Sir Thomas Lloyd, Colonial Office, 1 March 1954, National Archives, DO 35/9014 'Top Secret' File on Krishna Menon.

p. 363 'a lackey of the British': cited in Janaki Ram, *V. K. Krishna Menon: A Personal Memoir* (New Delhi, 1997), p. 101.

p. 363 'sombre porcupine': Marie Seton, *Panditji: A Portrait of Jawaharlal Nehru* (London, 1967), p. 173.

p. 363 'dangerously persuasive': as reported by British diplomats, M. G. L. Joy, British Embassy in Washington, DC, to C. T. Crowe, Far Eastern Dept, Foreign Office, 25 January 1954.

p. 364 'transform[ing] the power relations . . .': Krishna Menon, *India, Britain and Freedom* (London, 1941); cited in T. J. S. George, *Krishna Menon: A Biography* (London, 1964), p. 124.

p. 364 'Don't embrace us . . .': Henry Kissinger, 'Conversation with Krishna Menon', 8 January 1962, 10 January 1962, and 8 February 1962, Komer Series box 418, Folder 'India 1961–63', John F. Kennedy Library.

p. 366 'Our work here should have . . .': Menon, letter to *New Madras*, January 1930; cited in George, *Krishna Menon: A Biography*, p. 59.

p. 367 'There is also evidence . . .': note on Krishna Menon, 10 June 1940, India Office Records, Indian Political Intelligence Files, L/P&J/12/323.

p. 367 'There is hardly anyone here . . .': Jawaharlal Nehru to Krishna Menon, 5 July 1939; cited in Seton, *Panditji*, p. 100.

p. 367 'Extremist of the worst possible kind': David Robertson, MP, to Leo Amery, 10 November 1942, in Indian Political Intelligence Files, L/P&J/12/323.

p. 367 'Menon has no genuine Party loyalties . . .': note on Krishna Menon, 10 June 1940, Indian Political Intelligence Files, L/P&J/12/323.

p. 367 'men who draw their incomes . . .': Krishna Menon, Letter to the Editor, *New India* (Madras), 17 January 1937; cited in George, *Krishna Menon*, p. 53.

pp. 368 'the same beliefs at much lower tension . . .': Isaiah Berlin to Sir Saville Garner and Paul Gore-Booth, 30 November 1961, National Archives, DO 196/210.

p. 368 'Obviously very far from well . . .': Nehru, 17/18 January 1951.

p. 369 'When the scales are balanced . . .': Jawaharlal Nehru, note to Deputy Minister of External Affairs, 23 June 1954, *Selected Works of Jawaharlal Nehru*, Second Series (New Delhi, 2000), vol. 26, p. 309.

p. 369 'The influences we have exercised . . .': Menon to Nehru, 22 August 1954.

p. 370 'far from being a help . . .': Menon to Nehru, 13 May 1955.

p. 370 'Although I have explained it to you . . .': Menon to Nehru, 3 October 1961.

p. 371 'However irritating to Cold War America . . .': Henry Kissinger, *World Order* (London, 2014), p. 203.

45 SUBBULAKSHMI: OPENING ROSEBUDS

p. 372 'bright copper colour': cited in Joep Bor, 'Mamia, Ammani and other Bayadères: Europe's Portrayal of India's Temple Dancers', in Martin

Clayton and Bennett Zon (eds), *Music and Orientalism in the British Empire: 1780s–1940s* (Aldershot, 2007), p. 58.

p. 372 '"Their dances", the *Journal des débats* wrote . . .': Clayton and Zon (eds), *Music and Orientalism in the British Empire: 1780s–1940s*, p. 58.

p. 372 'I am Madurai Subbulakshmi': cited in T. J. S. George, *MS: A Life in Music* (New Delhi, 2004), p. 69.

p. 373 'The language of her eyes . . .': George, *MS: A Life in Music*, p. 31.

p. 373 'provokingly small': Keshav Desiraju, 'MS Subbulakshmi', unpublished manuscript (2009), p. 8.

p. 374 'if you ask a rosebud . . .': cited in George, *MS: A Life in Music*, p. 244.

p. 375 'not a fragile child . . .': cited in George, *MS: A Life in Music*, p. 73.

p. 375 'When I was small . . .': cited in George, *MS: A Life in Music*, p. 73.

p. 376 'the appellation of the devadasi . . .': cited in Avanthi Meduri, 'Bharatha Natyam: What Are You?', in Ann Dils and Ann Cooper Albright (eds), *Moving History/Dancing Cultures: A Dance History Reader* (Middletown, CT, 2001), p. 105.

p. 377 'contributed to this happy circumstance': cited in J. Devika, *Engendering Individuals: The Language of Re-forming in Early Twentieth Century Keralam* (Hyderabad, 2007), p. 109.

p. 377 'Henceforth even for a moment . . .': cited in George, *MS: A Life in Music*, p. 281.

p. 378 'an all-out putsch': George, *MS: A Life in Music*, p. 171.

p. 378 'the queen of music': cited in George, *MS: A Life in Music*, p. 101.

p. 378 'She is a simple woman, and naive': cited in George, *MS: A Life in Music*, p. 14.

p. 379 'The story of Mira . . .': cited in George, *MS: A Life in Music*, p. 176.

p. 379 'At a time when so much is said . . .': M. Subbulakshmi, 'Foreword', *In the Dark of the Heart: Songs of Meera*, translated with an introduction by Shama Futehally (San Francisco, 1994).

p. 379 'I have never gone out alone . . .': cited in George, *MS: A Life in Music*, p. 244.

46 INDIRA GANDHI: THE CENTRE OF EVERYTHING

p. 381 '*chhokari*': Morarji Desai, cited in D. P. Mishra, *The Post-Nehru Era: Political Memoirs* (New Delhi, 1993), p. 80.

p. 381 '*gungi gudiya*': Ram Manohar Lohia, cited in Ramachandra Guha, *India after Gandhi: The History of the World's Largest Democracy* (London, 2007), p. 445.

p. 381 'I was so sure I had nothing in me . . .': cited in Pupul Jayakar, *Indira Gandhi: A Biography* (London, 1997), p. 479.

p. 382 'the smashing, the pulverizing . . .': Salman Rushdie, *Midnight's Children* (London, 1981), p. 412.

p. 382 'Politics is the centre of everything': in Anthony J. Lukas, 'She Stands Remarkably Alone', *New York Times*, 17 March 1966; cited in Jayakar, *Indira Gandhi: A Biography*, p. 183.

p. 388 'aiming at killing her': I. K. Gujral, *Matters of Discretion: An Autobiography* (New Delhi, 2011), p. 85.

p. 389 'refreshingly pragmatic . . .': J. R. D. Tata, cited in R. M. Lala, *Beyond the Last Blue Mountain: A Life of J. R. D. Tata* (New Delhi 1993), p. 277; cited in Patrick Clibbens, 'The Indian Emergency: 1975–1977', unpublished University of Cambridge PhD thesis (2014), p. 82.

p. 390 'As a child I wanted to be like Joan of Arc': Indira Gandhi to P. N. Haksar, *c.* late February 1966; cited in Srinath Raghavan, 'Indira Gandhi: India and the World in Transition', in Ramachandra Guha (ed.), *Makers of Modern Asia* (Cambridge, MA, 2014), p. 223.

47 SATYAJIT RAY: INDIA WITHOUT ELEPHANTS

p. 391 'There is nothing irrelevant or haphazard . . .': cited in Andrew Robinson, *Satyajit Ray: The Inner Eye* (London, 1989), p. 91.

p. 392 'Not to have seen the cinema of Ray . . .': cited in Robinson, *Satyajit Ray: The Inner Eye*, p. 95.

p. 392 'the line between poetry . . .': Martin Scorsese, speech at the Freer Gallery of Art, Washington, DC, 27 February 2002; cited in Chris Inqui, 'Martin Scorsese hits DC, hangs with the Hachet', *The GW Hatchet*, 4 March 2002; available at http://www.gwhatchet.com/2002/03/04/martin-scorsese-hits-dc-hangs-with-the-hachet/.

p. 392 'I don't want to see a movie of peasants . . .': cited in Geoff Andrew, 'Charulata: The Pinnacle of Satyajit Ray's Art', 20 August 2014, BFI.org; available at http://www.bfi.org.uk/news-opinion/news-bfi/features/charulata-pinnacle-satyajit-ray-art.

p. 393 'What is wrong with Indian films? . . .': Satyajit Ray, 'What is wrong with Indian films?', in Satyajit Ray, *Our Films, Their Films* (Calcutta, 1976), p. 24.

p. 393 'It just gored me': Satyajit Ray, *Sight and Sound*, summer 1970, p. 116; cited in Bert Cardullo, *Satyajit Ray: Interviews* (Jackson, MS, 2007), p. 38.

p. 393 '[b]ecause people there want to see India . . .': cited in Robinson, *Satyajit Ray: The Inner Eye*, p. 327.

p. 394 'It's the truth in a situation . . .': Satyajit Ray, cited in interview with Sharmila Tagore, 3 August 2015.

p. 394 'Our mind has faculties . . .': Rabindranath Tagore, 'East and West', *Creative Unity* (London, 1922), p. 94.

p. 394 'In every case the response . . .': Jean Renoir, *My Life and My Films*, translated by Norman Denny (London, 1974), p. 248.

p. 395 'He didn't follow anyone . . .': Shyam Benegal, interview in 'Satyajit Ray and I: Shyam Benegal', 7 September 2007, available at http://www.youtube.com/watch?v=t5XNVPNWcpA.

p. 397 'One realizes what the Indian film-maker . . .': Satyajit Ray, letter to Lester James Peries, December 1958; cited in Robinson, *Satyajit Ray: The Inner Eye*, p. 106.

p. 398 'would not have been possible without my script . . .': in Robinson, *Satyajit Ray: The Inner Eye*, p. 295.

48 CHARAN SINGH: A COMMON CAUSE

p. 400 'India's villages are the colonies . . .': cited in Ho Kwon Ping, 'Revolt of the landless peasants', *Far Eastern Economic Review*, vol. 103, no. 2 (12 January 1979), p. 53.

p. 401 'Agriculture is the first condition . . .': Charan Singh, interview on *Analysis* programme, BBC Radio 4, 9 February 1978.

p. 401 'For most of the landlords . . .': Vikram Seth, *A Suitable Boy* (London, 1993), p. 284.

p. 402 *'And in the winter nights . . .'*: Ram Dass, in Siddharth Dube, *Words Like Freedom: The Memoirs of an Impoverished Indian Family 1947–1997* (New Delhi, 1998), p. 45.

pp. 402–3 '[The villager] is a willing tool . . .': Jagdish Prasad, cited in P. D. Reeves, *Landlords and Governments in Uttar Pradesh: A Study of their relations Until Zamindari Abolition* (Bombay, 1991), p. 228.

p. 403 'under a thatched roof . . .': Charan Singh, *Land Reforms in U. P. and the Kulaks* (New Delhi, 1986), p. 1.

p. 405 'in perpetuity . . .': cited in Christophe Jaffrelot, *Religion, Caste and Politics in India* (New Delhi, 2010), p. 435.

p. 405 'profiteers, who fatten on famine': Lenin, cited in Robert Service, *Lenin: A Biography* (London, 2000), p. 365.

p. 407 'The farmers are forgotten, . . .': Charan Singh, in William Borders, 'Farmers in India: Rally to Support Rival of Premier', *New York Times*, 24 December 1978, p. 3; available at http://timesmachine.ny times.com/timesmachine/1978/12/24/112830339.html?pageNumber=3.

p. 407 'We had them over a barrel . . .': Orville Freeman, cited in S. P. Gupta, Nicholas Stern, and Athar Hussain (eds), *Development Patterns and Institutional Structures: China and India* (New Delhi, 1995), p. 78.

49 M. F. HUSAIN: 'HINDUSTAN IS FREE'

p. 411 'until recently, we never disclosed . . .': in Madhu Jain, 'M. F. Husain, B. V. Doshi juxtapose reality and dreams in their latest creation, Gufa', *India Today*, 15 February 1995.

p. 411 'I don't need any degree . . .': interview with Riz Khan, 'One on One', Al Jazeera English (TV); uploaded on 13 February 2010, available at https://www.youtube.com/watch?v=wqxUjuVPd8A.

p. 412 'I know how it is to work . . .': in Rashda Siddiqui, *In Conversation with Husain Paintings* (New Delhi, 2001), p. 53.

p. 413 'The widening gulf between . . .': Progressive Artist Group Manifesto, *c.* 1947, cited in Ratan Parimoo and Nalini Bhagwat, 'Progressive Artists Group of Bombay: An Overview', *Art Etc: News and Views* (January 2012); available at http://www.artnewsnviews.com/view-article.php?article=progressive-artists-group-of-bombay-an-overview&iid=29&articleid=800.

p. 414 'It could have been conceived . . .': Geeta Kapur, 'Modernist Myths and the Exile of Maqbool Fida Husain', in Sumathi Ramaswamy (ed.), *Barefoot Across the Nation: Maqbool Fida Husain and the Idea of India* (New Delhi, 2011), p. 30.

p. 414 'I had done paintings of Ramayana . . .': M. F. Husain, 'An Artist and a Movement', *Frontline*, vol. 14, no. 16 (9–22 August 1997); available at http://www.frontline.in/static/html/fl1416/14160820.htm.

p. 415 'He is fond of the media glare . . .': M. F. Husain with Khalid Mohamed, *Where Art Thou: An Autobiography* (Mumbai, 2002), p. xxvii.

p. 415 '40% your beard . . .': Siddiqui, *In Conversation with Husain Paintings*, p. 78.

p. 416 'M. F. Husain: A Painter or a Butcher?': cited in Sumathi Ramaswamy, 'Introduction', in Ramaswamy (ed.), *Barefoot Across the Nation*, p. 15.

p. 416 'Had I been forty . . .': interview with Barkha Dutt, NDTV, 3 March 2010; full transcript available at http://www.ndtv.com/india-news/full-transcript-of-mf-husains-interview-411979.

pp. 416–17 'A liberal tolerance . . .': S. K. Kaul, judgement in *Maqbool Fida Husain* v. *Raj Kumar Pandey*, Delhi High Court, 8 May 2008; available at http://indiankanoon.org/doc/1191397/.

50 DHIRUBHAI AMBANI: FINS

p. 419 'I'm a bigger shark': Kokilaben D. Ambani, *Dhirubhai Ambani: The Man I Knew* (Mumbai, 2007), p. 55.

p. 419 'almost animal instinct': Ambani, *Dhirubhai Ambani: The Man I Knew*, p. 54.

p. 421 'Coincidentally with disputes with Reliance': Hamish McDonald, *The Polyester Prince: The Rise of Dhirubhai Ambani* (St Leonards, New South Wales, 1998), p. 260.

p. 421 'delicate, sensitive, understanding . . .': Ambani, *Dhirubhai Ambani: The Man I Knew*, p. 50.

p. 422 'struck gold': Ambani, *Dhirubhai Ambani: The Man I Knew*, p. 71.

p. 422 'The faster the deal . . .': Ambani, *Dhirubhai Ambani: The Man I Knew*, p. 75.

p. 422 'I needed gutsy, street-smart guys . . .': cited in Ambani, *Dhirubhai Ambani: The Man I Knew*, p. 69.

p. 425 'In their prosperity, our prosperity . . .': cited in McDonald, *The Polyester Prince: The Rise of Dhirubhai Ambani*, p. 59.

p. 426 'Reliance is a triumph of trust': Dhirubhai Ambani, acceptance speech for the Chemtech Foundation 'Man of the Century' award, Mumbai, 8 November 2000; available at http://www.dhirubhai.net/dhcmshtml/Acceptance%20Speech.pdf.

p. 426 'created the case . . .': cited in Saritha Rai, 'A Giant So Big It's a Proxy for India's Economy', *New York Times*, 4 June 2004; available at www.nytimes.com/2004/06/04/business/worldbusiness/04reliance.html.

p. 427 'A society which condemns creators of wealth . . .': Ambani, *Dhirubhai Ambani: The Man I Knew*, p. 111.

Acknowledgements

In researching *Incarnations*, I was privileged to have the guidance of many of the leading contemporary intellectuals, artists, and scholars of India. I am indebted to each of them, and to scholars of other parts of the world, for their willingness to share their knowledge and insights:

Javed Akhtar, Sunil Amrith, Shankar Bajpai, Hartosh Singh Bal, the late Chris Bayly, Gwilym Beckerlegge, Shyam Benegal, Paul Brass, Allison Busch, R. Champakalakshmi, Vikram Chandra, Supriya Chaudhuri, Carla Contractor, Anna Dallapiccola, William Dalrymple, Madhav Deshpande, Faisal Devji, Venkat Dhulipala, Sylviane Diouf, Wendy Doniger, Paul Dundas, Rachel Dwyer, Richard Eaton, Munis Faruqui, Michael Franklin, Jonardon Ganeri, B. N. Goswamy, Chandan Gowda, Nile Green, Ramachandra Guha, Shilpa Gupta, Menaka Guruswamy, Charles Hallisey, Peter Heehs, Linda Hess, Howard Hodgkin, Deborah Hutton, Ayesha Jalal, Nasreen Munni Kabir, Rishi Kapoor, Girish Karnad, Sudipta Kaviraj, Krishen Khanna, Bharti Kher, Madhav Khosla, Paul Kiparsky, Ebba Koch, Stephen Kotkin, T. M. Krishna, Nayanjot Lahiri, James Laine, Neil MacGregor, Javed Majeed, Inder Malhotra, Arvind Krishna Mehrotra, Rahul Mehrotra, Pratap Bhanu Mehta, Shivshankar Menon, Elizabeth de Michelis, George Michell, Christopher Minkowski, Rudrangshu Mukherjee, Parita Mukta, Vidya Natarajan, Joachim Nettelbeck, Patrick Olivelle, Gail Omvedt, Ken Ono, Aakar Patel, Sita Pawar, Basharat Peer, Kim Plofker, Sheldon Pollock, Srinath Raghavan, Vikram Raghavan, Niranjan Rajadhyaksha, Sujatha Ramadorai, U. R. Rao, Anil and Manan Relia, Andrew Robinson, Martin Roth, Emma Rothschild, Arundhati Roy, Tirthankar Roy, Aveek Sarkar, Sumit

Sarkar, Navtej Sarna, Katherine Schofield, Amartya Sen, Alpa Shah, Mihir Sharma, David Shulman, Dayanita Singh, Harleen Singh, Kavita Singh, Tridip Suhrud, Vivan Sundaram, Deborah Swallow, Sharmila Tagore, Romila Thapar, Sankaran Valiathan, A. R. Venkatachalapathy, David Washbrook, Andrew Whitehead, Dominik Wujastyk, Yogendra Yadav and Chitralekha Zutshi.

For expert readings of some of the essays, I owe particular thanks to: Patrick Clibbens, Keshav Desiraju, Paul Dundas, Richard Eaton, Munis Faruqui, Jonardon Ganeri, Nile Green, Linda Hess, Kim Plofker, Sheldon Pollock and Dominik Wujastyk.

Incarnations **began** in a conversation with Jane Ellison, then commissioning editor at BBC Radio 4, about the need to make India's history come alive for a wider audience. The project passed into Mohit Bakaya's excellent hands, and the radio and podcast versions of *Incarnations* grew in detailed exchanges with my editors, Hugh Levinson and Martin Smith. The fifty programmes took shape not just in the studio, but over the course of thousands miles of travel across India with the producers: Mark Savage (who made twenty-five of them), Martin Williams and Jeremy Grange. Liz Jaynes handled the digital and web platforms for the series. I thank all at the BBC for their staunch commitment to what was an ambitious, and often difficult, series to make.

At Penguin Random House UK, I thank my superb editor, Simon Winder for helping me expand and deepen the project, and his team – Andrew Barker, Maria Bedford, Richard Duguid, Jane Robertson and Cecilia Stein – for turning the complicated elements of this project into a beautiful book. Special thanks to Cecilia Mackay, who researched and hunted down photographs and images.

At Penguin Random House India, I thank Meru Gokhale, and her predecessor Chiki Sarkar, for wholeheartedly embracing this book. In the US, Alex Star at Farrar, Straus & Giroux made subtle and helpful suggestions on a number of chapters. And Nandini Mehta, my editor and wise counsellor over many years, offered valuable comments on all fifty of the essays.

It was a stroke of fortune that Alex Blasdel, a former editor at *Caravan* magazine in India, joined me on the project in January 2015. Astonishingly gifted as an editor, he's been much more than that to me over the course of writing this book. Intellectual interlocutor and comrade, thoughtful shaper of meaning, always sharp-eyed, he set a high and chastening bar. I am immensely grateful for his rigour, sensitivity and judgement.

To Manu Pillai, a historian and writer in his own right, I also owe special thanks. He was involved with the project from its inception with the BBC, and proved to be a stellar researcher, producing detailed briefs and reading several of the draft essays.

I thank my agent Gill Coleridge for her patience, faith and advice over many years, and her colleague Cara Jones for managing the various strands of the project. In New York, Amanda Urban has been uncommonly generous with her advice and support.

Several young scholars provided research assistance and briefs at different stages of the project, and I thank Aditya Balasubramanian, Chinmay Borkar, Lola Guyot, Swapna Kona Nayudu, Sudhir Selvaraj, and Unnati Tripathi.

For help with photographs, my thanks to Ashish Anand and Kishore Singh at the Delhi Art Gallery, Sheetal Mallar, Raghu Rai, Dayanita Singh, and Navina and Vivan Sundaram.

My thanks to Talvin Singh, who composed the music for the radio and podcasts series and whose rhythms are still running in my head.

I thank all my colleagues and students at the King's India Institute for making it a lively, open place of intellectual inquiry. At King's College, London, thanks also to Keith Hoggart, former Vice-Principal; to former Principal Rick Trainor; and to current Principal and President, Ed Byrne, for their unstinting support. I am also grateful to Gautam Thapar for his generosity in creating my Avantha Chair at the India Institute, and for his steadfast belief in our work. One goal of the India Institute, when established in 2012, was to bring scholarship on India to a wider audience across the world – a goal I hope this book will further.

Mary Richardson Boo has watched over this project with sustaining anxiety; I hope that may now give way to some relief. My gratitude to my sisters, and particularly to Asha Sarabhai for her perceptive, always encouraging presence.

I owe one person most of all: Katherine Boo, fiercest mind and heart I will ever know.

Index

Enfield rifles 170
English language 23, 121, 131,
228, 398
Enlightenment, the 179, 241, 252
enlightenment, spiritual 1, 9,
12–13, 13, 60, 99
entrepreneurship 202–4, 263,
419–27
Erode 268, 269
Erragudi 33
Escher, M. C. 116
E.T. (film) 398–9
Euclid 20, 48, 51
Euler, Leonhard 241
Europe 27, 291, 372; colonialism
371; interwar 321; Iqbal on 281;
Sher-Gil and 289–90; World
War II 295

Fabianism 218, 220
Faizi, Atiya 279
family 180, 308, 383–4
famine 185, 191, 196, 205, 385,
405
*Famous Monuments of Central
India* (monograph) 184
Faridabad 41
Faruqui, Munis 133, 135, 137
fasting 12, 306
Fatehpur, Sikri 116, 119, 121, 124
Fermat's Last Theorem 238
Feroz Shah Kotla 34
film industry 85, 114, 171, 256,
261, 378–9, 409, 411; Bengal
391–9; Bollywood 110, 115,
345–53, 412; Bombay Talkies film
studio 331; Calcutta Film Society
392; and Dalits ('untouchables')
350–1; R.K. Films 348, 349;
women in 347, 349

'First Discourse' (Jones) 158
'five Ks' (Sikh religion) 101
Flora Fountain 421
Flynn, Errol 348
folk songs 196, 252, 272
Foot, Michael 366
Ford, John 392
foreign policy 27, 31, 303,
363–71, 384, 388
foreign trade 201, 202–3, 204,
419–27
Forest Acts 195
forests 199
France 203, 295, 369
Frank, Katherine 383
Franklin, Michael 157
Franz Ferdinand, Archduke
185–6, 242
Free Indian Legion 300

Gaddafi, Muammar 30
Gaga Bhatt 145
Galbraith, John Kenneth 364
Galileo 48
Gandharva, Kumar 91
Gandhi, Indira 102; Abdullah and
358; and Abdullah's arrest 361;
Ambani and 424–5;
democratization 424–5; Husain
and 415; leadership 381–90;
Singh and 400, 407, 408
Gandhi, Mohandas K. (Mahatma)
xii, 8, 10, 12, 14–15, 85, 179,
202, 217, 278, 304–14;
achievement 305; Ambedkar and
340–43; anti-industrialism
261–3; assassination 304, 314;
authoritarianism 253–4;
background 307; and Besant
223; and Bose 295–303;

ALLEN LANE
an imprint of
PENGUIN BOOKS

Recently Published

William D. Cohan: *Why Wall Street Matters*

David Horspool, *Oliver Cromwell: The Protector*

Daniel C. Dennett, *From Bacteria to Bach and Back: The Evolution of Minds*

Derek Thompson, *Hit Makers: How Things Become Popular*

Harriet Harman, *A Woman's Work*

Wendell Berry, *The World-Ending Fire: The Essential Wendell Berry*

Daniel Levin, *Nothing but a Circus: Misadventures among the Powerful*

Stephen Church, *Henry III: A Simple and God-Fearing King*

Pankaj Mishra, *Age of Anger: A History of the Present*

Graeme Wood, *The Way of the Strangers: Encounters with the Islamic State*

Michael Lewis, *The Undoing Project: A Friendship that Changed the World*

John Romer, *A History of Ancient Egypt, Volume 2: From the Great Pyramid to the Fall of the Middle Kingdom*

Andy King, *Edward I: A New King Arthur?*

Thomas L. Friedman, *Thank You for Being Late: An Optimist's Guide to Thriving in the Age of Accelerations*

John Edwards, *Mary I: The Daughter of Time*

Grayson Perry, *The Descent of Man*

Deyan Sudjic, *The Language of Cities*

Norman Ohler, *Blitzed: Drugs in Nazi Germany*

Carlo Rovelli, *Reality Is Not What It Seems: The Journey to Quantum Gravity*

Catherine Merridale, *Lenin on the Train*

Susan Greenfield, *A Day in the Life of the Brain: The Neuroscience of Consciousness from Dawn Till Dusk*

Christopher Given-Wilson, *Edward II: The Terrors of Kingship*

Emma Jane Kirby, *The Optician of Lampedusa*

Minoo Dinshaw, *Outlandish Knight: The Byzantine Life of Steven Runciman*

Candice Millard, *Hero of the Empire: The Making of Winston Churchill*

Christopher de Hamel, *Meetings with Remarkable Manuscripts*

Brian Cox and Jeff Forshaw, *Universal: A Guide to the Cosmos*

Ryan Avent, *The Wealth of Humans: Work and Its Absence in the Twenty-first Century*

Jodie Archer and Matthew L. Jockers, *The Bestseller Code*

Cathy O'Neil, *Weapons of Math Destruction: How Big Data Increases Inequality and Threatens Democracy*

Peter Wadhams, *A Farewell to Ice: A Report from the Arctic*

Richard J. Evans, *The Pursuit of Power: Europe, 1815-1914*

Anthony Gottlieb, *The Dream of Enlightenment: The Rise of Modern Philosophy*

Marc Morris, *William I: England's Conqueror*

Gareth Stedman Jones, *Karl Marx: Greatness and Illusion*

J.C.H. King, *Blood and Land: The Story of Native North America*

Robert Gerwarth, *The Vanquished: Why the First World War Failed to End, 1917-1923*

Joseph Stiglitz, *The Euro: And Its Threat to Europe*

John Bradshaw and Sarah Ellis, *The Trainable Cat: How to Make Life Happier for You and Your Cat*

A J Pollard, *Edward IV: The Summer King*

Erri de Luca, *The Day Before Happiness*

Diarmaid MacCulloch, *All Things Made New: Writings on the Reformation*

Daniel Beer, *The House of the Dead: Siberian Exile Under the Tsars*

Tom Holland, *Athelstan: The Making of England*

Christopher Goscha, *The Penguin History of Modern Vietnam*

Mark Singer, *Trump and Me*

Roger Scruton, *The Ring of Truth: The Wisdom of Wagner's Ring of the Nibelung*

Ruchir Sharma, *The Rise and Fall of Nations: Ten Rules of Change in the Post-Crisis World*

Jonathan Sumption, *Edward III: A Heroic Failure*

Daniel Todman, *Britain's War: Into Battle, 1937-1941*